THE EMERGENCE OF FILM CULTURE

Film Europa: German Cinema in an International Context
Series Editors: **Hans-Michael Bock** (CineGraph Hamburg);
Tim Bergfelder (University of Southampton); **Sabine Hake**
(University of Texas, Austin)

German cinema is normally seen as a distinct form, but this series
emphasizes connections, influences, and exchanges of German cinema
across national borders, as well as its links with other media and art forms.
Individual titles present traditional historical research (archival work,
industry studies) as well as new critical approaches in film and media
studies (theories of the transnational), with a special emphasis on the
continuities associated with popular traditions and local perspectives.

**The Concise Cinegraph:
Encyclopedia of German
Cinema**
General Editor: Hans-Michael Bock
Associate Editor: Tim Bergfelder

**International Adventures:
German Popular Cinema and
European Co-Productions
in the 1960s**
Tim Bergfelder

**Between Two Worlds: The Jewish
Presence in German and Austrian
Film, 1910–1933**
S.S. Prawer

**Framing the Fifties: Cinema in a
Divided Germany**
Edited by John Davidson and
Sabine Hake

**A Foreign Affair: Billy Wilder's
American Films**
Gerd Gemünden

**Destination London:
German-speaking Emigrés and
British Cinema, 1925–1950**
Edited by Tim Bergfelder and
Christian Cargnelli

**Michael Haneke's Cinema:
The Ethic of the Image**
Catherine Wheatley

Willing Seduction:
The Blue Angel, **Marlene
Dietrich, and Mass Culture**
Barbara Kosta

**Dismantling the Dream Factory:
Gender, German Cinema, and the
Postwar Quest for a New Film
Language**
Hester Baer

Belá Balázs: Early Film Theory.
Visible Man and *The Spirit of Film*
Bela Balazs, edited by Erica Carter,
translated by Rodney Livingstone

**Screening the East: Heimat,
Memory and Nostalgia in German
Film since 1989**
Nick Hodgin

**Peter Lorre: Face Maker.
Constructing Stardom and
Performance in Hollywood and
Europe**
Sarah Thomas

**Turkish German Cinema in
the New Millennium: Sites,
Sounds, and Screens**
Edited by Sabine Hake
and Barbara Mennel

**Postwall German Cinema: History,
Film History and Cinephilia**
Mattias Frey

**Homemade Men in Postwar
Austrian Cinema: Nationhood,
Genre and Masculinity**
Maria Fritsche

**The Emergence of Film Culture:
Knowledge Production, Institution
Building and the Fate of the Avant-
Garde in Europe, 1919–1945**
Edited by Malte Hagener

THE EMERGENCE OF FILM CULTURE

Knowledge Production,
Institution Building and the Fate of the
Avant-Garde in Europe, 1919–1945

Edited by Malte Hagener

berghahn
NEW YORK · OXFORD
www.berghahnbooks.com

First published in 2014 by
Berghahn Books
www.BerghahnBooks.com

Library of Congress Cataloging-in-Publication Data

The emergence of film culture: knowledge production, institution
building and the fate of the avant-garde in Europe, 1919-1945 / edited
by Malte Hagener.
    p. cm. -- (Film Europa: German cinema in an international
context)
    Includes bibliographical references and index.
    ISBN 978-1-78238-423-6 (hardback: alk. paper) -- ISBN 978-1-78238-
424-3 (ebook)
    1. Experimental films--Europe--History and criticism. 2. Motion
pictures--Europe--History--20th century. I. Hagener, Malte, 1971-
editor author.
    PN1995.9.E96E44 2014
    791.43′61109409041--dc23

                                                            2014009540

British Library Cataloguing in Publication Data
A catalogue record for this book is available
from the British Library.

Printed on acid-free paper

ISBN: 978-1-78238-423-6 (hardback)
ISBN: 978-1-78238-424-3 (ebook)

Contents

FIGURES

ACKNOWLEDGEMENTS

This book has been helped by a number of people along the way, who listened to ideas, answered questions, made suggestions and gave advice. Thanks are due to Tim Bergfelder, Peter Bloom, Peter Decherney, Christian Cargnelli, Christophe Dupin, Sabine Hake, Jan-Christopher Horak, Charles Musser, Geoffrey Nowell-Smith, Dana Polan, Julia Riedel, Jamie Sexton, Matthias Steinle and Haidee Wasson for answering to queries I had, assisting with illustrations and generously sharing their knowledge and contacts. The process of preparing the manuscript was aided at different stages by Manuel Schnabel and Bernhard Runzheimer. Most of all, though, I have to thank the authors for generously sharing their ideas, research and writing with me, and for putting up with an editor who was not as fast as he hoped in finishing this project. Their tolerance and brilliance has made putting this book together such a worthwhile endeavour. Hopefully, the transnational network visible in the collaboration will continue to grow and spur further results.

Introduction

The Emergence of Film Culture

Malte Hagener

When film became a technological reality in the late nineteenth century, its future shape and role was far from obvious. Discussions regarding the theoretical nature, the aesthetic function and the social role of cinema began as soon as commentators took note of the medium, but conceptualizations remained fluid for the first decades. It was not until the 1920s that knowledge about film and cinema was systematically, consistently and reflexively articulated, gathered and disseminated on a broader basis. Over the course of two decades, the 1920s and 1930s, institutions, practices and arguments arose which have been crucial for any serious engagement with cinema ever since. There are many aspects that can be said to have aided this 'emergence of film culture' in the interwar period: the beginnings of film festivals; the formation of canons; the point at which film became recognized as a subject of study at institutions of higher education; the consolidation of film criticism and archiving as serious occupations; and the recognition accorded to the relevance of film history and film theory. Cinema as a discursive field of its own began to emerge slowly but steadily over the course of the 1920s. In the following decade across Europe, many film-related institutions and organizations were founded and achieved stability, such as archives, festivals and film institutes. The 'emergence of film culture' implies that the medium was starting to be taken seriously as an aesthetic object and social force, and this has to be taken into account when trying to understand the political, social and aesthetic modernity that came to dominate industrialized countries before the Second World War.

While the first steps towards the institutionalization of film culture were taken within the decidedly transnational film culture of the 1920s, many activities continued in the increasingly nationalist atmosphere of the 1930s, even though these developments were often far from smooth or unidirectional. A history which is in no small part European in nature remains largely hidden and buried. This volume aims to start uncovering the outlines of this configuration. There are effectively three major strands one has to keep in mind when drawing a preliminary map of the field: the trajectory of the avant-garde, the influence of the nation state, and the role of the industry. First of all, the avant-garde developed and grew over the course of the 1920s, articulating countless ideas and arguments as to why and how cinema was making a valuable and productive contribution to the modern world. Theoretical discussions as well as practical initiatives shaped film as an aesthetic and political force to be reckoned with. Nevertheless, the avant-garde constituted a miniscule, fragmented and fragile formation that was more geared towards temporary interventions and tactical skirmishes than durability and longevity. Thus, the avant-garde provided insights and inspirations, but other entities had to turn these forays into permanence and stability.

Secondly, the nation state has a long and complex history in relation to film and media.[1] Well into the 1920s, cinema was regularly seen as transgressive, dangerous and in need of regulation, yet state officials had also begun to realize that modern mass media, such as cinema and radio, could be an effective platform for governing and controlling a mass society. Various official initiatives in Nazi Germany, Fascist Italy, and the Soviet Union under Stalin bear witness to this active engagement of national state policy with cinema, but in a different ideological configuration, this desired symbiosis of cinema and social engagement also characterized John Grierson's activities in Great Britain. While in the 1910s, the state had frequently resorted to mechanisms of suppression and censorship, subsequent developments are more in line with what Michel Foucault has termed 'governmentality', the regulation and control of large populations not through coercion or negative sanctioning, but by way of guiding the individual (or groups) towards desired behaviour and reaction.

The third factor in this configuration is the industry, both the film industry in the narrow sense, but also industry at large, represented by sectors such as manufacturing, electricity, and consumer goods.

Cinema's emergence paralleled that of Western consumer societies which quickly gained ground throughout the first decades of the twentieth century. Film became both a mirror reflecting this social transformation, and an engine that pushed it forward. Projects such as the foundation of a film school, a national film archive or a film festival required not only state support, but also the cooperation of the industry in providing financial backing and access to commissions and resources if these institutions were expected to become a productive part of the circulation of images and films in the society at large. As might be expected from the interaction of such different force fields and interests, the 'emergence of film culture' was a complex and contested process. Moreover, even where projects were undertaken in the name of the nation state, many of the protagonists involved in these initiatives had a decidedly transnational outlook, a legacy of the cosmopolitan avant-garde of the 1920s and the various initiatives towards achieving a European film. Taking these uneven and contradictory contexts into account, the chapters in this volume attempt to sketch a history of how film culture emerged, and how various strands developed into the 1930s and beyond. The overall argument of the book is that the initiatives of this period laid the groundwork on which film culture, and hence also the discipline of film studies, still rests today.

An Entangled Story of Encounters and Exchange: The Avant-Garde and its Historiography

In some respects, this book is a collaborative attempt to begin writing a *histoire croisée* (entangled history) of the avant-garde, its legacy and aftermath; it is a story of encounters and exchange, of translation and interference.[2] Traditional national history – and this holds true for most of film history that exists – sees the nation state as the key frame of reference, a container with very few contact zones to the outside world. Movements and regulations, markets and aesthetics, production and reception are all first and foremost conceived of in terms of the national. A comparative history, a step towards leaving the nation behind, establishes a singular point of view which then determines the categories of comparison. In this vein, one can compare the national characteristics of universities and armies, of social security systems and trade regulations, of film subsidy and media policy. Transnational (or entangled) history goes further as it develops ideas first broached under labels such as connected or shared history into a focus on interaction, interdependence and complexity. The implicit aim is to multiply perspectives in order to shatter any one dominant reading, and to open up historiography to the potential limitless infinity of empirical reality. It is a misunderstanding to see a transnational approach as antithetical to regional, national or global histories; instead it complements the latter by understanding the reciprocity and interaction of developments at different speeds and in different places. Harking back to earlier approaches such as the *Annales* school, and sharing many concerns with postcolonial history, *histoire croisée* is necessarily reflexive as it denies to take one single point of view from which to survey a field. In order to make this multiplication of perspectives productive, one needs to see each of them in relative terms.

Michael Werner and Bénédicte Zimmermann, two French historians who have championed this approach, describe the fundamental premises upon which entangled history rests:

> *Histoire croisée* belongs to the family of 'relational' approaches that, in the manner of comparative approaches and studies of transfers (most recently of 'connected' and 'shared history') examines the links between various historically constituted formations. But, while these approaches mainly take the perspective of 'reestablishment/rehabilitation' of buried reality, the stress laid by *histoire croisée* on a multiplicity of possible viewpoints and the divergences resulting from languages, terminologies, categorizations and conceptualizations, traditions, and disciplinary usages, adds another dimension to the inquiry. In contrast to the mere restitution of an 'already there', *histoire croisée* places emphasis on what, in a self-reflexive process, can be generative of meaning.[3]

In order to make visible the non-synchronicity of culture, the complex temporal and spatial disparities and displacements so typical of material culture circulating on a global scale such as film, one needs to constantly change perspective. One could point to any number of examples to highlight the temporal breaks and ruptures, the glitches in concepts and definitions. Let it suffice to give but two examples here, as the book offers many more. The theoretical debate about the status of cinema (as an art form and a medium), that was current in France, Germany and the Soviet Union in the 1920s, only arrived in Italy in the 1930s. By that time, the political, technological and cultural framework had shifted considerably, and therefore ideas and terms acquired a different meaning.[4] The distinctively modernist ideas about cinema resonated in 1930s Italy and, after a turn towards narration and figuration (prefigured in the films and writing of Vsevolod Pudovkin), helped to develop what would become 'neorealism' in the 1940s. Subsequently, the reception and adaptation of neorealism, first mediated through French film culture (via André Bazin and the *Nouvelle Vague* [new wave]), took a decidedly political and even militant turn towards 'Third Cinema' in the 1960s and 1970s. In these instances, we can map an entangled history of mutual influence as much as of misunderstanding and adaptation over the course of several decades, ranging across different countries and institutional regimes.[5]

A second example for the kind of *histoire croisée* that informs the approach of this book can be provided by the shifting meaning of a term such as 'montage' through the interwar period. In the late 1920s this term was employed by Sergei Eisenstein, Vsevolod Pudovkin, Dziga Vertov and other Soviet filmmakers in very specific ways to characterize their editing style and the different registers of montage. For Eisenstein, montage in 1929 was a psychotechnique with which spectators could be manipulated in a precise manner towards desired reactions. By 1939 the same term implied pathos and organicity – a wholeness derived from nature and not anymore committed to conflict and contrast. Now, this is as much a result of the political changes as transformations in the cultural landscape that also bear witness to the international dimension of intellectual transfer.[6] Both examples might illustrate how ideas, terms and concepts are never stable, but dependent on context and usage, as well as prone to change, especially if translated and transferred. The changes from the 1920s to the 1930s were indeed significant as they coincided with a number of factors, both related and unrelated: the decades (very roughly) separate silent from sound cinema, the internationalism of the 1920s gave way to increasing nationalization in the 1930s, and the onslaught of the economic crisis in the early 1930s had repercussions all through the decade, not least in the way it helped to restructure the management and production routines of the film industry.

In the standard histories of European cinema, the 1930s are somewhat uneasily sandwiched between the late blossoming of classic silent film in the 1920s and the stirrings of neorealism in the 1940s, which is often seen as the harbinger of the new waves dominating European cinema (at least in retrospect) well into the 1980s. Therefore, in terms of film history *tout court*, the 1930s seem to belong firmly to the United States where a mature oligopoly had taken hold of the film business with fixed routes for distribution and exhibition, set routines for production, and an institutionalized form of censorship.[7] The untimeliness and non-synchronicity of the European situation on the other hand is far more difficult to map, as it lacks regularity and stability. Even though this book only details limited aspects of 1920s and 1930s European cinema, it nevertheless focuses on how knowledge was produced and disseminated, how processes of institution building and stabilization took hold, how different temporal registers led to (productive) misunderstandings and adaptive behaviour, why specific initiatives proved to be successful while others vanished (almost) without a trace. The way in which this volume proposes to understand the 1930s is to see the decade as the 'incubator' of developments that became influential much later. Many of today's insights and critical methodologies in film and media studies can be traced back to ideas and arguments in 1930s Europe, and their rivalling and often mutually exclusive claims continue to shape critical debates to this very day. David Bordwell's and Kristin Thompson's neo-formalist approach, for example, combines a psychological Gestalt theory influenced by Rudolf Arnheim and others with Russian neo-formalist vocabulary and an attention to the intricacies of montage as learned from Eisenstein and Vertov. Equally, much of current media theory is unthinkable without Walter Benjamin's and Siegfried Kracauer's interventions which took shape through their encounter with 1920s alternative film culture. In particular, Kracauer's model of writing a national history of German cinema, and Benjamin's approach to the mediality of film, have provided the classical templates for numerous subsequent analyses.[8]

On a general level, this book is concerned with the migration and traffic of images, ideas and people within the institution cinema in its widest sense. This is of course a topic that is all too familiar and current, as we today partake in the global circulation of film images via digital networks. In this sense, the collection can be understood as a genealogical investigation into how certain practices, institutions and assumptions took hold in the 1930s on a transnational level. But we should not lump all instances of border crossing together under a single term, but instead differentiate between phases and usages. Dudley Andrew has, in a discussion of contemporary film culture, proposed a historical schema of how the 'vast geographical flow of images, as well as the time-lag that inevitably accompanies it' has passed through various phases since the beginnings of film in the late nineteenth century. For him an ontological slippage lies at the heart of cinema, a *'décalage ...* between "here and there" and "now and then"'[9] that distinguishes cinema from television with its incessant liveness and direct address. Whether one wants to follow Andrew in his Bazinian media ontology or not, an outline of five phases through which the cinema has passed in rough succession, but which are nevertheless not a teleological path in the sense that they necessarily follow one another, is helpful for our purposes. Andrew terms these successive stages as cosmopolitan, national, federated, world and global. The cosmopolitan is typical of early cinema up to the 1920s, when films circulated regardless of national production, and stars were not necessarily identified by their origin – at the time Asta Nielsen, Pola Negri and Louise Brooks could all become stars in Germany, while Ewald André Dupont made films in England, Carmine Gallone directed in Germany, and Carl Theodor Dreyer worked in France. A national refocusing had already taken root by the end of the First World War (Andrew sees 1918 as a watershed in this respect), but I would argue that the avant-garde as well as the Film Europe movement[10] kept the cosmopolitan spirit of early cinema alive well into the late 1920s. The national phase becomes more clearly prominent in the developments following the introduction of sound, when voices and the bodies from which they emanated became firmly tied to specific linguistic communities and therefore specific territories. While this process was far from smooth, the 1930s were nevertheless characterized by an intensification of the bonds between nation state and film. Andrew identifies the third, federated, phase, with postwar developments in film festivals and criticism, but also in other international and intergovernmental organizations beyond film (UNESCO, EC) which coincided with the heyday of European modernist art cinema. However, it is worth noting that the first steps towards a federated structure had already been taken in 1938 with the foundation of FIAF, the international federation of film archives. The last two categories, world and global, do not need to concern us here, as they hinge on later developments from the 1970s onwards.

The chapters collected in this anthology follow but also complicate the shifts between the first three phases when a transnational and cosmopolitan film culture became nationalized and tied in one way or another to the state, successively giving way to international cooperation. This cannot be conceptualized as a unilinear story of loss and decline or of triumph and victory, but rather has to be reconfigured as a complex development in which gains in one field went hand in hand with loss in another. The avant-garde of the 1920s was cosmopolitan in the way films and ideas circulated, but also in the way that national belonging did not play any significant role. Viking Eggeling was not primarily seen as a Swede or as a German at the time, but as a fascinating filmmaker who happened to be working in Berlin, just as Eisenstein, a Latvian Jew, born in Riga to a family of German-Swedish descent, fluent in many languages, educated in St Petersburg and hailing from Moscow, could become the most celebrated film artist of the late 1920s. The national paradigm of clearly separated and circumscribed spheres, of specific aesthetics and thematic preoccupation began to hold sway in the 1930s, as can be seen in the first books on film history which introduced a logic of national schools, as well as in the birth of competitive spaces such as film festivals.[11] After the introduction of sound, the separate linguistic communities with their recognizable sounds and typical actors appeared to divide the former cosmopolitan space into nationally circumscribed entities.

In this respect, Andrew's temporal argument about how time lags and delays are to be accounted for should be complemented by a spatial one, a dimension he only hints at in passing. Here it is relevant to point to the relation of centre and periphery, as these relational terms are in constant flux and transformation.[12] In the 1920s, the avant-garde (whether individuals, films or ideas) moved easily between Paris, Berlin, Moscow, Amsterdam and London, but these metropolitan centres also provided hubs for the national and regional spaces around. Whereas the 1920s saw artists move and connect relatively easy and on an informal basis, in the 1930s this was often predicated on official state visits such as Joris Ivens' trips to the Soviet Union or Iris Barry's European journey as an official mission on behalf of the Museum of Modern Art in the mid-1930s. It is the emergence of festivals as an arena for the competition of the nation that might show most clearly how institution building was predicated upon the nation state being a partner to provide stability and durability.

Film Studies: The Origins of a Discipline

In recent years, there has been an upsurge in the number of publications detailing the beginnings of film studies in the Anglo-American world, dealing with the history of relevant institutions such as journals, museums, archives and university departments, but also encompassing questions such as canon formation that helped to create a stable configuration and therefore a subject that one could study and research. Dana Polan's monograph *Scenes of Instructions* details the early efforts towards establishing film studies at institutions of higher education in the United States.[13] In her study *Museum Movies*, Haidee Wasson illustrates how the Museum of Modern Art (MoMA) in the 1930s became a central node for the appreciation and study of the cinema as a recognized aesthetic form.[14] Peter Decherney complements these insights with an examination of the collaboration between Hollywood and institutions such as universities, museums and archives, from the end of the First World War to the start of the Cold War,[15] while Lee Grieveson's and Haidee Wasson's anthology announces nothing less than the *Invention of Film Studies*.[16] Meanwhile in Britain, Terry Bolas examines the trajectory from the early attempt at film appreciation within the framework of the emergent British Film Institute in the 1930s to the high theory of 1970s *Screen*.[17] While all these studies are highly valuable and make important contributions to our understanding of the development of the discipline, their outlook is overwhelmingly and almost exclusively Anglo-American. Within the wider force fields under consideration here, investigators have also addressed the non-entertainment uses of film[18] and the intersection of the cinema with the colonial project,[19] adjacent fields where the industry, the avant-garde and the nation state intersected in specific configurations.

This volume aims to expand on the existing scholarship by widening and broadening the field, and to chart the European film culture of the interwar period, taking into account that timing, intensity and inflection were open to many influences and depended on numerous factors. While the individual chapters may cover specific national contexts, they also highlight transnational connections; they consider the circulation of material (films, texts, ideas, people) and the foundation and stabilization of institutions. The contributions to this book examine how knowledge about the cinema was produced and disseminated, how film canons were constructed and enforced, how institutions of film culture were built and maintained – but also how many of these early efforts turned out to be dead ends.

As stated previously, the avant-garde which blossomed in the 1920s played an important part in this complex history of institution building and nationalization. It took root in the 1920s as a radical movement aimed at transforming life and art by way of aesthetic, political and social interventions. It was in no small part thanks to the avant-garde that the configurations of film culture would blossom in the 1920s. Screening societies and ciné-clubs, magazines and pamphlets, exhibitions and gatherings laid the groundwork for film schools and archives, for art house cinemas and journals, and for festivals and exhibitions. Contrary to received wisdom which sees the avant-garde as a short-lived and ultimately failed attempt at establishing an alternative film aesthetics, this book considers it as a social and political force aimed at transforming the very essence on which our discipline still depends.[20]

In this respect, this anthology also demonstrates how film studies has been, from the very beginning, a transnational endeavour.

About the Book

The contributors to this volume attempt to find out how, where and why knowledge about the cinema was discursively produced, disseminated and propagated in 1920s and 1930s Europe. The chapters examine the founding of institutions and the overall transformations in the cultural landscape regarding cinema during this period. In this sense, the book is also a genealogical investigation into the history of film studies as a discipline. Of course, such a broad, multidimensional and transnational complex cannot be mapped out in a single volume, thus this book is an invitation for further research. It consciously leaves out some aspects of European film culture in the 1920s and 1930s because they have already been treated in considerable detail elsewhere. This is especially true of developments in France which undeniably boasted an active and important cinema scene throughout the 1920s and well into the 1930s, and so substantial historical research has already been undertaken.[21] Likewise, the German scene, more politically minded than the French, has been investigated quite thoroughly,[22] while the 'little journal' *Close Up*, published in Switzerland and aiming at a transnational audience, has been reprinted in its entirety and examined in a scholarly anthology.[23] Therefore, the present volume self-consciously turns the spotlight to less-well-researched examples and case studies, trying to highlight in particular those aspects that have been neglected in the past.

The volume is organized into three sections which focus on different aspects of film culture in interwar Europe, but inevitably there are temporal as well as thematic overlaps between the different parts of the book. In fact, a number of themes echo throughout the chapters: the role of film education, the impact of Soviet film, and the translation and adaptation of ideas and theories. The first part focuses on the formation of knowledge and relates to recent concerns with the history of (film) theory. This history cannot be written in isolation as an abstract history of ideas, but needs be to put into specific material frameworks and historical contexts. These contexts range from colonialism to historiography, from gender to praxeology, as they approach film as an epistemological object – something that can give us knowledge about the world we live in.

Tobias Nagl's chapter details how 'how racial and racist representations were "normalized" through regulatory responses and institutional formations of knowledge'. Nagl's contribution serves as a reminder that knowledge about cinema was not only produced and disseminated within the 'progressive' circles of the avant-garde, but could equally well be connected to reactionary, racist and imperialist notions. Race and nation as two frameworks, despite their obvious differences, were often interchangeably applied, but they could also be mobilized in specific and very different ways. The 'complicated ideological and institutional relationship between the cinema reform movement, the film industry and the German *Reichskolonialamt* (Imperial Colonial Office)' can be seen as a prototype of the configuration sketched in several other essays between avant-garde, nation state and industry that became more central in the 1930s. As Nagl argues, this configuration anticipates 'the later 20s and early 30s, [when,] motivated by the League of Nations and the founding of the International Institute for Cinematographic Education (ICE), European discussions about the intersections of racial knowledge, ethnography, film pedagogy and institutional film policies began to assume a more internationalist direction, celebrating cinema as a harbinger of "universal humanism"'. Thus, despite its focus on a specific aspect of German cinema, Nagl's chapter demonstrates how certain ideological and institutional discourses can only be properly understood when contextualized transnationally.

Whereas Nagl highlights the importance of the often neglected category of race, **Erica Carter** reminds us that feminism and gender are also categories which are too often ignored in relation to early film theory and film culture in the 1920s, which was overwhelmingly male. Carter corrects this common assumption by examining the life and work of Béla Bálazs – critic, theoretician and filmmaker – whose transnational career between Budapest, Vienna, Berlin and Moscow is seen through the prism of the feminist movement in the early decades of the twentieth century. By 'situating Balázs's film theory within the larger cultural-historical field', Carter shows how different discourses and ideas from and around the 'new woman' were generative for his film theory which proved to be highly influential in the 1920s and beyond. Given its canonic and classical status, it is surprising how little attention has been paid to 'the conditions of emergence of Balázs's early film writing'.

Ciné-club culture has been recognized as the ferment on which many of the key ideas of film culture could blossom in the first half of the twentieth century. What has been largely overlooked is how programming can be thought of and conceptualized as a mode of producing knowledge and affect about films. By examining the concrete programming practice of the Dutch Filmliga which provides perhaps the most self-contained and coherent example in this period, **Tom Gunning** argues that the construction of a film programme can be likened to theoretical activity and can be employed as didactic tools. Working with contrast and fragments are specific modes of producing knowledge about film, specific methods that archaeologically link film studies to the activities of the 1920s avant-garde. Gunning discusses the early films of Joris Ivens as examples of how films reflexively and aesthetically embody their own programme. In this respect, it is important to remember that knowledge concerning the cinema is not just to be found in academic discourse, but also in films, in programming strategies, in discussions and in many other formats.

From the mid-1920s until the early 1930s, the Soviet Union was surely the most exciting place from which cinematic innovations and discourses emerged. While the circulation of those films, ideas and central protagonists will be looked at in more detail in other sections of the book, **Natalie Ryabchikova** presents a little-known but important aspect – how film studies was invented and institutionalized in Soviet Russia. While the explosive ideas and theories of Eisenstein, Pudovkin and Vertov circulated freely among the intellectuals and activists in Europe and beyond, the situation in the Soviet Union looked markedly different from the early 1930s onwards. Ryabchikova's chapter also charts how canonization and institutionalization interacted with film production, how the narrative that was told about the emergence and development of Soviet cinema was bound up with cinema itself, and vice versa.

The second part of the book shifts attention to the circulation of material conditions and networks of exchange, which were hallmarks of the avant-garde film culture of the 1920s that contributed to many important activities of the next decade. One example of this mobility is the circulation and reception of Soviet avant-garde art in Western Europe, discussed by **Ian Christie**. The long-term results and influences of these contacts and transmissions illustrate how the term 'avant-garde' has transformed and changed meaning over time. With Ryabchikova's study of Soviet film studies, Christie shares a concern with questions of retrospection and historiography – how have terms, arguments and concepts shaped our view and understanding of a past that is always more complex than acknowledged. By tracing out three successive waves of Russian modernist avant-garde, Christie complicates the canonical story of the sudden impact that Eisenstein's montage aesthetics and revolutionary strategies allegedly had across Western Europe. One of the key questions that this volume addresses is that of influence and impact, of transmission and transference. In this respect, Christie suggests that one lesson to draw from these successive waves is 'a recurrent pattern of *formal challenge*, combining the old and the radically new, and an insistence on the essentially hybrid nature of what might be termed "modern spectacle"'.

Turning to a more 'peripheral' part of Europe, if that qualification is allowed, **Greg de Cuir**, in an overview of the situation in the Kingdom of Yugoslavia, stresses how amateurism went hand in hand with an active cinephile culture, and how this infrastructure provided the basic context on which postwar Yugoslav cinema could blossom. Inside the multi-ethnic state, various initiatives formed connections and thus could be seen as a transnational network that was not able to sustain itself for a longer time, but that could feed into the active film culture at the service of a new nation state. Despite its relative distance from the main conduits between Moscow, Berlin, Paris, Amsterdam and London, groups in Zagreb and Belgrade nevertheless explored similar ideas, styles and aesthetics. Despite local diversity and personal idiosyncrasies, there was a common ground to fall back on which was recognized in most European urban centres.

An even wider transnational network in geographical terms is sketched by **Masha Salazkina** who discusses film cultural activities in the early 1930s in Italy, especially the active exchange with the Soviet Union. As Salazkina argues in respect to activities in the field of film education: 'The history of Italian and Soviet film cultures has a strong relevance to the institutionalization of cinema studies, and their role in this process could be argued to rival that of France'. The complex interaction of Soviet and Italian film cultures demonstrates that, even with similar ideas circulating, a specific national context could nevertheless turn out very different. More importantly, this encounter was crucial for postwar film aesthetics, as neorealism emerged from this juncture and turned out to be the signal for the various new waves that would dominate the 'modern' cinema from the 1950s well into the 1980s.

In a revisionist study of Swiss film culture of the 1930s, **Yvonne Zimmermann** sets out by contrasting two events which are not normally seen in connection – the 1929 avant-garde meeting of La Sarraz and the First European Educational Film Conference in Basel in 1927. Zimmermann points out how avant-garde and educational cinema not only ran on parallel tracks for a long time, but how it makes sense to consider them as part of the same non-commercial and non-theatrical film culture. Zimmermann also reminds us that it would be short-sighted to concentrate on the avant-garde as the only alternative to mainstream cinema, proposing instead a 'polyculture' in which educational, industrial and scientific films are equally present. At the same time, her contribution also highlights how a key figure of the 1920s avant-garde, Hans Richter, made the transition into commissioned film work and educational activities.

The third and final part of the book attempts to map some of the consequences of the interwar developments. As argued above, the nation state and its various agencies began to take an active interest in the cinema in this period, which led to the foundation and institutionalization of many bodies that are still with us today. In his contribution, **Lars Gustaf Andersson** details the various Swedish initiatives of the 1920s and 1930s at taking the cinema seriously as a cultural factor. Film archiving, theory and aesthetics, as well as film production, all belong to this wider field. The Swedish context amply demonstrates that there is no overwhelming trajectory of how cinema evolved as a medium and art form in this period, that there is no preordained path on which film interacted with progressive circles and the nation state in different countries. Andersson's study also makes a case for how local context and international developments interact and intersect, while reminding us how the key ideas about the cinema and the ways to study them were in no small measure forged in the period under discussion here.

Francesco Pitassio and **Simone Venturini**'s jointly authored contribution details how the shaping of film culture was bound up with the project of (re-)constructing the nation in the 1930s; indeed, similar (yet also, in some respects, very different) attempts can be seen all across Europe, from Grierson's socially engaged documentaries, to Nazi Germany's celebration of the Aryan body, all the way to the Socialist-Realist model heroes of Soviet cinema. The chapter concentrates on Luigi Chiarini's career as an exemplary case study to illustrate the contradictory ways in which a transnationally circulating film culture was integrated into national institutions such as festivals, schools, institutes and magazines. Whereas Salazkina's chapter highlights the debt of the Italian advances to the model put forward by the Soviet activists, Pitassio and Venturini focus more on state policy. Read together, the two essays give an impression of how and why the 1930s were such a crucial period in which Italian film culture adapted and transformed ideas from the 1920s that would reach fruition after the war. In this sense, the 1930s were much less nationally confined than is often acknowledged – they continued, albeit in a different form, what had begun in the 1920s.

The remaining three essays examine important types of institution that have become an indispensable part of film culture ever since the 1930s: film schools, archives and film festivals. **Duncan Petrie** gives an overview of the first film schools, and looks at how ideas about teaching film (making) were developed, exchanged and ossified into curricula. Even though these institutions were marked by an outward nationalization – they were usually inaugurated and branded as national film schools – it becomes obvious how they influenced each other, how patterns and routines emerged that were shared across different nation states. **Malte Hagener** examines the emergence of the film festival and illustrates how the nation state was instrumental in giving stability to what was originally nothing but a supplement to an art exhibition; he also looks at the beginnings of the archival movement across Europe, showing which factors had to be in place in order for a certain type of institution to come into existence. In a detailed case study, **Rolf Aurich** provides a history of the 'Reichsfilmarchiv', which came into existence in Fascist Germany in the mid-1930s. The trajectory that leads into the 1940s demonstrates how a Nazi prestige project retained ideas from the avant-garde and was, moreover, shaped by a clear sense of transnational circulation of film culture – even this institution cannot be seen isolated from its transnational context.

In conclusion, it is fairly safe to say that this anthology will probably raise more questions and issues than it is able to provide answers. *The Emergence of Film Culture* hopes to provide a first draft of a force field that has so far not been mapped very intensely. As the biography and the nation state remain the default values in film studies, international transfers and institutions of film culture have only recently provoked interest. If the present volume acts as a catalyst and impetus towards further examinations of such configurations, then it has already achieved a lot, because the networks, exchanges and transformations in 1920s and 1930s Europe are rich and rewarding topics for further research and studies.

Notes

1. See the collections Mette Hjort and Scott McKenzie (eds). 2000. *Cinema and Nation*, London and New York: Routledge; and Alan Williams (ed.). 2002. *Film and Nationalism*, New Brunswick, NJ: Rutgers University Press.

2. See on a historiographical level Michael Werner and Bénédicte Zimmermann. 2006. 'Beyond Comparison: *Histoire croisée* and the Challenge of Reflexivity', *History and Theory* 45 (February), 30–50.

3. Werner and Zimmermann, 'Beyond Comparison', 31f.

4. See the contributions in this volume by Masha Salazkina, Simone Venturini and Francesco Pitassio for more on the Italian–Soviet exchanges.

5. See Masha Salazkina. 2011. 'Moscow – Rome – Havana: A Film-Theory Roadmap', *October* 139 (Winter), 97–116, as well as her contribution in this volume.

6. See Wolfgang Beilenhoff. 2011. 'Montage 1929 / Montage 1939', *Montage/av* 20(1): 213–22.

7. On the *locus classicus* of Hollywood as a simultaneously economic, organizational and aesthetic system, see David Bordwell, Janet Staiger and Kristin Thompson. 1986. *The Classical Hollywood Cinema: Film Style and Mode of Production to 1960.* London: Routledge & Kegan Paul.

8. See Siegfried Kracauer. 1947. *From Caligari to Hitler: A Psychological History of the German Film.* Princeton, NJ: Princeton University Press; and Walter Benjamin. (1936) 2008. *The Work of Art in the Age of Its Technological Reproducibility, and Other Writings on Media.* Cambridge, MA: Harvard University Press.

9. Dudley Andrew. 2010. 'Time Zones and Jetlag: The Flows and Phases of World Cinema', in Nataša Ďurovičová and Kathleen Newman (eds), *World Cinemas, Transnational Perspectives.* New York and London: Routledge, 59–89, here 60.

10. See Andrew Higson and Richard Maltby (eds). 1999. *'Film Europe' and 'Film America': Cinema, Commerce and Cultural Exchange, 1920–1939.* Exeter: Exeter University Press.

11. The epitome allegorizing this development in Leni Riefenstahl's OLYMPIA, a film about the competition between nations that won the main prize at the Venice Film Festival in 1938, another event at which nations would compete in a circumscribed field for a prize. For more on the history of film festivals, see Marijke de Valck. 2007. *Film Festivals: From European Geopolitics to Global Cinephilia.* Amsterdam: Amsterdam University Press.

12. For the relationship between centre and periphery in respect to the avant-garde, see the anthology Per Backstrom and Hubert van den Berg (eds). 2013. *Decentering the Avant-Garde: Towards a New Topography of the International Avant-Garde.* Amsterdam: Rodopi.

13. Dana Polan. 2007. *Scenes of Instruction: The Beginning of the US Study of Film.* Berkeley, CA: University of California Press.

14. Haidee Wasson. 2005. *Museum Movies: The Museum of Modern Art and the Birth of Art Cinema.* Berkeley, CA: University of California Press.

15. Peter Decherney. 2005. *Hollywood and the Cultural Elite: How the Movies Became American.* New York: Columbia University Press.

16. Lee Grieveson and Haidee Wasson (eds). 2008. *Inventing Film Studies: Towards a History of a Discipline.* Durham, NC: Duke University Press.

17. Terry Bolas. 2009. *Screen Education: From Film Appreciation to Media Studies.* Bristol: Intellect.

18. See Charles R. Acland and Haidee Wasson (eds). 2011. *Useful Cinema.* Durham, NC and London: Duke University Press; Vinzenz Hediger and Patrick Vonderau (eds). 2007. *Filmische Mittel, industrielle Zwecke. Das Werk des Industriefilms.* Berlin: Vorwerk 8.

19. See Lee Grieveson and Colin MacCabe (eds). 2011a. *Empire and Film.* London: Palgrave Macmillan; Lee Grieveson and Colin MacCabe (eds). 2011b. *Film and the End of Empire.* London: Palgrave Macmillan.

20. In this respect, the present anthology can be seen as complementing Malte Hagener. 2007. *Moving Forward, Looking Back: The European Avantgarde and the Invention of Film Culture*. Amsterdam: Amsterdam University Press.
21. See Richard Abel. 1988. *French Film Theory and Criticism, 1907–1939. A History/ Anthology. I: 1907–1929. II: 1929–1939* (2 vols). Princeton, NJ: Princeton University Press; and Christophe Gauthier. 1999. *La Passion du cinéma. Cinéphiles, ciné-clubs et salles spécialisées à Paris de 1920 à 1929*. Paris: Association Française de Recherche sur l'Histoire du Cinéma / Ecole des Chartes.
22. Besides the many studies available in German, the best overview of the alternative political film culture in English is still Bruce Murray. 1990. *Film and the German Left in the Weimar Republic: From Caligari to Kuhle Wampe*. Austin, TX: University of Texas Press.
23. See the reprint *Close Up* (1927–1933). Territet (CH). Complete reprint in 10 volumes Nendeln (Liechtenstein): Kraus Reprint 1969; and James Donald, Anne Friedberg and Laura Marcus (eds). 1998. *Close Up, 1927–1933: Cinema and Modernism*. London: Cassell.

PART I

FORMATIONS OF KNOWLEDGE

Chapter 1

POLICING RACE

Postcolonial Critique, Censorship and Regulatory Responses to the Cinema in Weimar Film Culture

Tobias Nagl

German cinema – particularly the internationally recognized 'art cinema' of the silent and early sound period – for a long time was assumed to be completely 'race-less'. This epistemological absence or uncritically assumed whiteness of the German screen, however, should neither be simply understood as a scholarly oversight, resulting from the scarcity of archival material that would prove otherwise, nor be seen solely as a long-lasting after-effect of the paradigms inaugurated by Siegfried Kracauer and Lotte Eisner, who interpreted German cinema of the 1920s either as a 'retreat from reality' and the demonic foreboding of the things to come after the Nazi seizure of power or as the national expression of deeply rooted, but irrational, aesthetic sensibilities that can be traced back to German romanticism. Written in the wake of the Holocaust, such teleological and essentialist accounts have not only downplayed the role of popular genres (e.g. the German musical, or *Musikfilm*, with its occasional – implicit or explicit – references to African American idioms such as Jazz) and non-theatrical exhibition practices (e.g. the educational and ethnographic film, or colonial propaganda) in our understanding of Weimar cinema, but they also unwittingly obfuscated the role that Jewish themes, film-makers and aesthetic sensibilities actually occupied in German 'main-stream' cinema of the 1920s and early 1930s.[1] A far more important cultural and political reason for this lack, however, is the category 'race' itself, which in post-Second World War Germany, as result of the

Holocaust and the collective feeling of shame it triggered, was tabooed to a degree unknown in most other European countries. Invoking the category of 'race', even as a historically unstable, malleable and political category, was considered 'racist', resulting in a German version of the liberal Anglo-American 'colour blindness' of the 1950s, which contributed to a certain cultural and ideological provincialism in regard to the definition of German culture. This postwar censoring of the topic of 'race' effectively foreclosed any critical consideration of the changing ethnic make-up of the nation, the unequal power relations in the transnational regimes of labour migration, or the continuities between racialization practices in the German colonial empire, the Nazi period and the 'guest worker' era of the 1960s and 1970s. In this perspective, 'racism' as term could only be applied to what in North America is described as 'hate crimes', relegating the issue politically and analytically to the margins of democratic society, and equating it solely with socio-pathological forms of 'prejudice'. Although this narrow understanding of race and racism is slowly changing thanks to the grassroots activism of Germans of colour and migrant organizations, the relationship between cinema, race and representation in German media studies (and even more so in public discourse) is nevertheless largely still considered unproblematic, and conceived of in terms of 'intentionalist' top–down/sender–receiver models that focus on the question of negative/positive images. Although the critique of racial stereotyping remains politically crucial in a country where blackface performances on the stage and screen are still vehemently defended by the cultural establishment in the name of 'artistic freedom',[2] it seems productive to shift the discussion to reflect Homi Bhabha's insightful probing of the unstable and potentially excessive nature of the stereotype, which he defines not only as a form of 'identification that vacillates between what is always "in place", already known, and something that must be anxiously repeated', but also, and more importantly in the context of this chapter, as 'a form of *knowledge*'.[3]

In this chapter, I demonstrate not only that race matters as an analytical category in German film history and historiography, but also that among Weimar contemporaries race already figured as a troublesome and multiply over-determined signifier that was as much spoken about as its forms of representation were questioned. In such contemporary discourse, precisely because of its unstable nature, race was a site of disciplinary control where divergent and conflicting forms of knowledge about the cinema and its representational, affective and social functions were created. In this attempt to trace the intersections between racial knowledge and knowledge about the cinema, I aim to move beyond textual analyses of stereotyping, seeking to inaugurate a dialogue between postcolonial critiques of racist representation and film historical discourses on regulation, censorship and the constitution of 'cinema' as an epistemological object in the silent period. By invoking the term 'racial knowledge', I follow Edward Said who in his seminal *Orientalism* (1978) described representations of the 'other' in the age of imperialism as a systemic form of discourse or *dispositif* which regulates what can be said and what cannot be said, but always grants the (white) Westerner a 'positional superiority'.[4] In a more narrow sense, I follow Mark Terkessidis who defines racism as the 'conjunction of a social practice with the simultaneous creation of knowledge',[5] and who, like Philomena Essed, points out that racial or racist knowledge must always be read against the knowledge *about* racism created by its victims.[6] By reading racism as a form of knowledge, I also refer to David Theo Goldberg, who emphasizes that 'racist culture', like all culture, 'consists in knowing and doing'.[7] Racial knowledge, according to Goldberg, helps modern subjects to make sense of the world they inhabit and to mediate modernity's claim for universalism and the inequalities they encounter in the social realm. Racial knowledge, writes Goldberg, 'acquires its apparent authority by parasitically mapping its modes of expression according to the formal authority of the scientific discipline it mirrors. It can do this – and this is its second constitutive feature – because it has been historically integral to the emergence of these authoritative fields. Race has been a basic categorical object, in some cases a founding focus, of scientific analysis'.[8]

Although cinema in the first decades of the twentieth century was time and again used to generate and disseminate racial knowledge in the sense described above, regulatory and institutional responses to the cinema during this time period indicate that cinema precisely lacked the 'formal authority' that characterized scientific discourse proper. The cinema, perhaps like the category of race itself, remained a permeable and contested site of cultural discourse. During the Weimar period, school reformists, moral reformists and censorship boards aimed to 'study' the cinema anew, drawing set parameters for exhibition and viewing practices.[9] Drawing on Annette Kuhn's Foucauldian understanding of film censorship not as an 'imposition of rules on a pre-constituted entity' but as 'ongoing and always provisional process of constituting objects from and for its own purposes',[10] Lee Grieveson in his seminal study *Policing Cinema* writes about the relations between modernity, governance and cinema:

Cinema was inscribed ... into a broad 'regulatory space' focused on governing a mass public in the context of large-scale transformations associated with full-fledged industrial capitalism, urbanization, and modernization. ... Linked closely to anxieties about social dislocation and the governance of populations, the regulatory response to cinema had considerable effects on the shaping of the medium. This response was partly about the regulation of 'immoral' or 'obscene' content. Equally, it is clear that regulatory responses had effects on the form of moving pictures, shaping narrative paradigms and linking these to moral discourse. Even more substantively, though, regulatory discourses, practices, and institutions in this period were linked to fundamental debates about the *social functioning* of cinema – debates about how cinema should function in society, about the uses to which it might be put, and thus, effectively, about what it could or would be. Here debates revolved principally around conceptions of the cultural functions and relative weighting of 'entertainment' and 'education', played out frequently through discussions about narrative and film form yet also about the merits of fiction, non-fiction, indexicality, and 'realism'.[11]

In what follows, I will look at the debates sparked in German film culture of the 1920s with the release of Joe May's exotic action serial DIE HERRIN DER WELT (The Mistress of the World, 1919/1920). These debates centred on race in the cinema, stimulating new regulatory responses and in turn shaping new contemporary discourses *about* the cinema.

Although racialized images and 'views from the colonies' were already an essential part of late nineteenth-century magic lantern 'edutainment', as pre-cinema scholar Janelle Blankenship points out in relation to German cinema pioneer Max Skladanowsky,[12] race in early German cinema often figured not only in terms of the prevalent imperialist and white supremacist ideologies of the day, but also as a site to reflect on the 'merits' of indexicality and realism, turning the colonies into a testing ground for the potential of cinematic technology (or even, as Hannah Arendt would have it, into a 'laboratory of modernity' itself). Early cinema, as Fatimah Tobing Rony explains, was inextricably linked to 'discourses of race'[13] because the scientific, evidence-collecting function of the camera could best be demonstrated through the natives' 'unawareness' of its mechanisms, rendering the racialized body the ultimate signifier of cinematic 'authenticity'. Reflecting on his ethnographic studies in the German colony of New Guinea in 1904–1906 and on the use of the cinematograph he made on his trip, the Austrian scientist Rudolf Pöch wrote: 'Dances are the most grateful and simplest subject for cinematographic recordings and the best means of practising, because they allow us to find out what

appears most visual and effective when projected'.[14] Like Karl Weule,
Pöch considered ethnographic filmmaking to be a form of 'salvage
ethnography', hoping that the 'new tool' of the cinematograph would
allow 'to preserve living documents of human levels of culture, since
these cultures are quickly disappearing and the ensuing ages will not
be able to see them anymore'.[15] According to Fatimah Tobing Rony,
Assenka Oksiloff and Wolfgang Fuhrmann, German anthropology
was marked by two methodological tendencies that fostered the use
of cinematography in Imperial Germany more than in other national
traditions: a strong archival impulse, which is linked to what Renato
Rosaldo calls 'imperialist nostalgia'[16] and to nineteenth-century discourses on 'dying races' (as in the work of Adolf Bastian), and the doctrine of diffusionism (*Kulturkreislehre*) as developed by Leo Frobenius,
which emphasized the comparative study of native cultures across
time and space. These methodologies called for the use of the cinematograph both as a tool of inscription and as a didactic medium –
the latter being a concern that German ethnography shared with the
burgeoning cinema reform movement after 1907.[17] Although research
on early German non-fiction film is severely hampered by a relative
lack of archival prints and materials pointing to the actual reception
of scientific film, it is important to point out that the educational function and interpretation of racialized images constantly had to be con-
trolled and stabilized by the voice-overs of lecturers or the presence
of the anthropologists in the frame, because science and spectacle,
education and entertainment, were always already intertwined: racial
knowledge in the cinema was easily criss-crossed by desire and the
dangerous affective dimensions of cinematic spectatorship, turning the
non-white body (and its promise of 'authenticity') into an object both
of instruction and of concern. Apart from moments of cruelty, it was
often the nudity of native performers that propelled censors to intervene. In 1915, Munich censors for instance complained about images of
an African woman breastfeeding her baby in AFRIKA, DER SCHWARZE
KONTINENT [Africa, the Black Continent] (P: Expreβ-Film, 1915), pointing to a scene in which the breasts of native women 'conspicuously
protruded'.[18] The actual reception of ethnographic nudity by a popular
audience (and the riotous response it provoked among presumably
lower-class males) is described in a review of the hybrid ethnographic
feature film PORI (Adolf von Dungern, 1929) a decade later: 'Natives
are also shown, on the warpath and while performing dances. The
figures of some negresses provoke admiration from the parquet [cheap
seats]'.[19] As Wolfgang Fuhrmann in his unpublished landmark study of

early German colonial cinematography perceptively notes, there was a complicated ideological and institutional relationship between the cinema reform movement, the film industry and the Reichskolonialamt (Imperial Colonial Office) with respect to ethnographic nudity and the ever-present possibility of 'alternative' readings in the cinema: 'While the film industry emphasized their patriotic service to the viewer and most likely pleased cinema reformers in their efforts to create an educational cinema, correspondence between the RKA (Reichskolonialamt) and film companies shows that colonial officials had a rather ambivalent attitude towards the production of colonial films and often remained skeptical about such projects'.[20] For these and other, more technical, reasons, the German colonial 'movement' seems to have preferred slide-show lectures even into the 1920s as a visual propaganda tool.

With her defeat in the First World War, the loss of her overseas empire and some Eastern territories, the humiliating conditions of the Versailles peace treaty and the occupation of the Rhineland by French colonial soldiers, Germany entered a postcolonial situation which was unique among European nations: instead of playing a part in the imperialist concerto of 'civilized' nations, many Germans now saw their own country reduced to the status of a colony of the Western powers. This constellation also seriously affected racial representations and the discourse on racial knowledge in the cinema. While the residual impact of the Wilhelmine cinema reform with its emphasis on the educational and national function of cinema continued, the popular, entertainment-oriented German film industry had been strengthened by the war effort and had gained a new self-consciousness. At the same time, the tradition of ethnographic filmmaking had been radically interrupted, since the victorious colonial powers until the mid-1920s denied German filmmakers access to all overseas territories: if German colonial revisionist filmmakers attempted to shoot films on location in Africa, they had to film clandestinely. As a result of the revolution in 1918, censorship was abandoned from 1918 to 1920, and German screens were 'flooded' by a cycle of 'sex exploitation films', while several hundred former German colonial subjects, who had migrated to metropolises like Berlin in the pre-war years, under the regime of racialized German citizenship laws, now found themselves in a situation of statelessness (as German-speaking 'natives', they were also banned by the French and British from returning to their home countries) and could often only find employment in the entertainment industry.[21] In addition, the relative political isolation of Germany and the boycotts against German films abroad resulted in a new geopolitics, linking international film policy and concerns about global market shares. All these changes did not effect a complete epistemological break in the formation of racial knowledge and the production of knowledge about the cinema, but they radically reconfigured the terms of the discussion. This became nowhere as apparent as in the censorship battles surrounding THE MISTRESS OF THE WORLD by director Joe May. Such censorship debates circulated around questions of realism, indexicality, ethnographic authenticity, affect and racial stereotyping, and involved several academic authorities who were officially commissioned to 'scientifically' study the film after Chinese students had launched what was perhaps the first anti-racist media campaign in German film history.

THE MISTRESS OF THE WORLD was one production in an entire cycle (or 'local' genre) of multi-part exotic adventure films that flourished in the immediate postwar period. Unlike the American Pearl White-style serials of the pre-war years, they usually consisted of two to eight feature-length parts; one of their main attractions was their lavish exotic sets that were artificially recreated on Berlin or Munich studio lots, and which allowed audiences (who through the hardships of the war and the ensuing 'culture of defeat' had been economically, culturally and geographically isolated) to at least embark on virtual travels across the globe. With a budget of 5.9 million marks, twelve hours of screen time and thirty thousand extras, the series certainly fulfilled all requirements of screen spectacle, and set new standards for what Karen Pehla has called 'Kinoerlebnis' (cinema experience).[22] Inspired by *The Count of Monte Cristo* and Henry Rider Haggard's *She*, the film combined aspects of the Danish 'white slavery' genre of the 1910s with a convoluted revenge plot, melodrama, espionage, popular archaeology and sci-fi elements – four of the eight instalments were set in China and Africa. The shooting of the film in the large 'film city' of Berlin-Woltersdorf was supported by a gigantic multi-media publicity campaign, which stressed the ethnographic 'authenticity' of the sets and extras. Journalists, among them former colonial officers, were invited to visit Woltersdorf and attest to the realism of the illusion (which had been created by using several wagon loads of ethnographic objects from Hamburg exotica trader Johannes Umlauff), while the scriptwriter and popular novelist Karl Figdor in his extensive and richly illustrated programme notes often directly referred to or quoted from the scholarly sources he had consulted when writing the scenario, ranging from Carl Peters' archaeological studies on the supposedly non-African origins of the stone monuments in Zimbabwe, to books about Jewish diasporic communities in ancient China. The non-white extras consisted either of colonial migrants from Germany's former African colonies, or were Russian POVs with 'Asiatic' features and Chinese peddlers brought to Berlin from all across Europe. It probably does not come as a surprise that May's exotic epic The Mistress of the World with its Chinese white slave traders, yellow peril references and child-like African tribesmen contains strong racist undertones (despite its proto-feminist title character and philosemitic elements that can be credited to the Jewish background of May and Figdor). In many ways, this film prepared the ground for Germany's 'imaginary' colonialism of the Weimar and Nazi period. However, the notion of cinematic authenticity had undergone a few interesting changes when moving from early scientific film to popular genre cinema, from realism to spectacle. The racialized body during the Weimar period did not testify so much to the mimetic power and inscriptive function of the cinematic recording apparatus, but to the commercial power of the German film industry. Films like The Mistress of the World were hailed by German critics for artificially conjuring up an 'ethnographic situation' under radically new, 'de-colonial' conditions, which led writers close to the fading cinema reform movement to ascribe to these films an 'educational value' despite their inheritance to the sensationalist 'smut' films of the 1910s. For other critics, The Mistress of the World and the films made in its wake seemed to prove that exotic travelogues did not require location filmmaking (or colonies), and proved that the German film industry could create an internationally competitive product which, due to its high technical and representational standards, would finally even be able to 'invade' movie theatres in Paris, London or New York in the incipient 'film wars' of the period. As Sabine Hake writes, such techno-nationalist fantasies often 'compensated for the traumatic war experience, the collapse of the Reich, and the humiliating conditions of the Versailles peace treaty'.[23]

A key term in the discourse on The Mistress of the World was 'Echtheit' (authenticity or genuineness), which was not just applied to the sets but also to the non-white extras; early *Kulturfilm* theorists such as Gustav Benkwitz and Oskar Kalbus applauded May for having made the attempt to even create 'Rassenechtheit' (racial authenticity) by employing 'real' Chinese and Blacks.[24] Such statements are only intelligible when read on the backdrop of Germany's specific colonial and postcolonial history. Since the scale of Germany's non-white population was so small, racial representations in commercial cinema often relied on blackface and 'ethnic drag' performances, turning the presence of 'real' people of colour in the cinema into almost a dead

Figure 1.1 Ambiguous positionalities: Chinese-German actor Henry Sze and Mia May in the lost THE MISTRESS OF THE WORLD episode, *Der Rabbi von Kuan-Fu* (1919/20). [Deutsche Kinemathek]

pledge on Germany's colonial and geopolitical restitution in the future. At the same time, the notion of Rassenechtheit must be understood in relation to the growing importance of physiognomic knowledge in 1920s film theory and popular science.[25] Inspired by Hans F.K. Günther's *Rassenkunde des deutschen Volkes* (1922), Hans Spielhofer in the *Süddeutsche Filmzeitung* in a programmatic 1924 essay on 'Rasse und Film' [Race and Film] explained: 'The word race does not play a minor role in the conversations of film experts and audiences. Everybody agrees that race is among the things that filmic representation cannot have enough of'.[26] Spielhofer argued that race should be understood in the first place as the 'translucency of the soul through the body', although in artistic practice race and acting did not, unfortunately, always coalesce. In a more precise sense, which was equally impor-tant to the cinema, Spielhofer claimed that race should be understood as a 'key term of modern racial science': as the 'sum of very specific, to some extent measurable physical traits, which correspond to a spe-cific mental type and which allow inferences to be made from one to the other'. A film director trained in racial science would thus be able to 'assign individual roles due to their mental face to the one or the other race' and could find for 'every role the corresponding racial types'. What the author pointed to in discussing corresponding racial types, however, are only the different 'races' within the European – and German –'landscape'. The article makes the programmatic statement that film schools all over Germany should 'breed' or train 'Nordic', 'westisch' (Mediterranean), 'ostisch' (Alpine) or 'Dinaric' racial types, but the same would also apply to 'exotic' races.

THE MISTRESS OF THE WORLD's discourse on race, realism and authenticity was seriously challenged when members of the Chinese Student Association in Berlin saw the film upon its premiere during the 1919 Christmas season – a few months before new film censorship legislation was introduced.[27] Their frustration with the racial stereotyping in the film became a political issue and went down in the official records when the 'Commissioner for Export Questions', located in the Foreign Ministry, heard that Chinese students and journalists living in Berlin had filed a complaint against the film, and in mid-January he preliminarily interdicted the export of the film to avoid diplomatic problems. Their initial complaint (of which there is no written record) was based on the film's association of China with the white slave trade, cruel methods of punishment and widespread anti-Western xenophobia, the sensationalist depiction of Chinese bordellos, and the fact that one of the main Chinese characters (played by Henry Sze, one of the few Asian 'stars' in early Weimar cinema) in the end turns out to be a liar. In their defence to the commissioner, the film's distributor Ufa claimed that this critique was without substance 'since bordellos existed all over the globe'. Ufa officials also claimed that the Henry Sze character, despite his final treason, had noble traits throughout the film, but also interestingly quipped that the company had relied on scientific 'experts who knew East Asia from their own experience'.[28] The Chinese protests were immediately seconded by the 'Film Liga', a reform organization which sported such notable members as Paul Wegener and fought for 'clean' films that would also be acceptable to 'educated spectators'. The wider public learned about the controversy through an article by the Lübeck doctor, art collector and General Secretary of the Verband für den Fernen Osten (Alliance for East Asia), Max Linde, who repeated the charges, stressing that the protesters perceived the 'participation of one of their compatriots as a treason against his people'.[29] In the context of the ongoing attempts to create a national censorship law, the 'dangers of modern film' had been extensively discussed, but the 'connection between film and foreign policy', as Linde pointed out, had only been superficially touched upon. Since the Chinese were one of the few peoples who still held sympathies with Germany, the stereotyping in THE MISTRESS OF THE WORLD would finally and foremost hurt Germany as a nation itself. The conflict gained steam in the following weeks. While the Foreign Ministry instructed the German embassy in Vienna to take measures against a planned screening of THE MISTRESS OF THE WORLD in Austria, Ufa's legal department speculated that the Chinese protests might have been initiated by commercial competitors, and threatened the Foreign Ministry that they would hire a dozen journalists to publically critique its policy. Finally, Ufa hosted two closed screenings of the Chinese episodes on 24 February and 1 May which were attended by members of the Foreign Ministry, academic and political East Asia 'experts' and over twenty Chinese citizens, all of whom had been invited to 'study' the film scientifically.

As a result of these screenings, several participants were asked to send scientific opinions on THE MISTRESS OF THE WORLD to the Foreign Ministry in the ensuing weeks. One of the most interesting expert opinions was written by the renowned sinologist Alfred Forke (1867–1944) who had authored several classic accounts of Chinese history and taught at the Berlin Seminar for Oriental Languages. In his report, Forke praised the technical quality of the production, but he also believed that THE MISTRESS OF THE WORLD devised an 'annoying caricature' of China. On the racial politics of the film, he wrote: 'Racial conflicts in the manner how they exist between Americans and Japanese, but not between Europeans and Mongols, are artificially aroused. One has simply translated the strong racial antipathies between whites and blacks in the United States onto the relationship between Europeans and Chinese'.[30] It is interesting to note that Forke's analysis locates the origins of the film's racism in the United States. Forke had worked in the German embassies in Beijing and Shanghai before pursuing an academic career, and in many instances he turned out to be a liberal critic of German colonialism: he felt that Westerners could learn from Chinese culture, opposed the occupation of Kiautschou and the aggressive German naval and missionary politics, and also explicitly critiqued the humiliating treatment of Chinese diplomats in the West. What is also striking about his report is that he encouraged his readers in the Foreign Ministry to envision how the members of the Chinese Student Association must have felt when watching THE MISTRESS OF THE WORLD by imagining a Chinese film scenario that depicted Germany in a similarly ignorant and racist manner. In Forke's reversal, a Chinese man travels to Germany, witnesses the brutal treatment of rebellious soldiers (an allusion to the abatement of the 1918 revolution), is robbed of his belongings and becomes the victim of a financial scheme. Finally, he is saved and sent back home by his Chinese friends, but also receives help from a noble Japanese man who constantly stresses that the two old 'nations of culture' (*Kulturnationen*) of the Far East should close ranks, because they had witnessed the outcome of shallow European culture. Forke clearly believed that THE MISTRESS OF THE WORLD could not be saved by making changes to the plot or inter-titles.

Consul Walter, another diplomat who had been brought in by the Foreign Ministry to study the film and write a scientific report, argued in a similar fashion. In his eyes, the film propagated 'racial hate between the white and yellow race due to unbridgeable racial differences'. In his report, Walter reiterated Forke's and Linde's critique of the film's 'Yellow Peril' tropes and the fact that 'only people who are wearing Western garments are allowed to display nobleness' in the film. Hence, it would not make sense and would be dishonest simply to move the film's location into another country, Walter stated, fearing that THE MISTRESS OF THE WORLD could be exploited by the former Allies for Anti-German propaganda purposes. In a moralistic inversion of the discourse on racial authenticity, Walter now even considered it very 'unfortunate that the film was made not only with the support of Chinese citizens but also with the help of the Chinese embassy'.[31]

With the export of the film being blocked, Ufa partly gave in and indicated to the Foreign Ministry that they would be willing to change some of the inter-titles. As the press referent of the new democratic German government noted in a memo, it was of utmost importance to signal to foreign powers that Germany did not intend to 'hurt the feelings of other nations'.[32] At about the same time, the general assembly of the Chinese Student Association in Berlin unanimously passed a long resolution condemning the film, asking the German government not only to ban international sales of the film but also block its distribution in Germany. What seems striking about the Chinese Student Association's contribution to the 'scientific' discourse on the film instigated by the Foreign Ministry is not only that it represents what is probably the first anti-racist critique of German cinema written by people of colour – in a rather generous gesture they refer the reader back to Max Linde's article for more detail about what is wrong with the film's racial stereotyping – but also how they mobilized cinema reform arguments and inscribed their own intervention in the 'educated' political, journalistic and academic debates on cinema, ethnographic authenticity and the creation of a national film censorship board before May 1920. In their essay entitled 'How the Chinese Think about Karl Fidor's Film The Mistress of the World', the students frame their critique in the following manner:

> The film industry without any doubt is one the most significant achievements of science and technology during the last decades. Movie theatres offer entertainment to the young and old, rich and poor, in their leisure time. However, they cannot only present entertainment, but also education! … At the same time, film can greatly contribute to the understanding of the morals and habits of other peoples. All this creates the opportunity that peoples, who had been strangers, get to know each other. Thus, film inaugurates a lot of good! But there are also its dark sides. It certainly must be considered an abuse when film is used for fomenting propaganda or sexual 'enlightenment', just to mention a few examples … Among the moving pictures that require a censorship law is the monumental film (consisting of eight parts!) The Mistress of the World, which was screened in Germany during the last months. We cannot go into the details of this 'marvel' which show the inhuman cruelty, the exceptional immorality, the deeply engrained xenophobia and the folksy dishonesty of the Chinese … In addition to all these flaws, there is also the false representation of streets, houses and female fashion, which as a sign of our good will and with respect to the lack of knowledge about Asian life and to the technical possibilities of the film company we do not want to emphasize … Germany should strive to conduct its reconstruction everywhere in an energetic manner. This applies in the first place also to its foreign relations … In our eyes, the new German government does not have any reason to turn a foreign people into its enemy. This pertains especially to the Chinese people.[33]

The Chinese arguments gained further punch when the Foreign Ministry learned that *The Times* had reported negatively on the representation of China in The Mistress of the World, while a new film had been released in the U.K. which had 'exactly the opposite tendency of the German film and presented the Chinese in an extremely favourable light as cultural people [*Kulturmenschen*]'.[34] What in light of the British premiere of D.W. Griffith's Broken Blossoms (US 1919) in January 1920 seemed especially problematic now in the eyes of the Foreign Ministry was what a few months before had been praised as one of the films unique selling points: its ethnographic knowledge. Ufa and May-Film, in the eyes of the ministry, had failed both to seek expert knowledge and to consult Chinese experts through the Chinese embassy. Even worse, they had lied to the embassy when asking them for the addresses of unemployed Chinese, pretending the film would depict a 'harmless travelogue about a Chinese doctor and his European girlfriend'.[35]

After further consultation with members of the Verband für den fernen Osten, the Film-Liga, the Commissioner for Export Questions, and the Chinese critics (and after receiving an additional, equally negative analysis of the film by art historian Karl With as 'pulp' [*kolportagehaft*] and 'completely un-Chinese'), May-Film and Ufa presented a 'new' version of the film to the experts. To appease foreign policy experts, the location of the Chinese episodes had been changed from Canton to the fictional city 'Lön-San' on the equally fictional archipelago 'Ku-da-ra'. Also, some of the most offensive racial markers had been changed in the inter-titles: the 'yellow inhabitants of Canton' had become the 'long-established inhabitants of Lön-San' and they did not 'dwell' (*hausen*) anymore, but now 'lived' (*wohnen*) in the city. To 'explain' the civilized habits of the Westernized Henry Sze character, he now appeared in the inter-titles as a bi-racial individual with a European mother. In a similarly superficial fashion, May-Film and Ufa tried to deal with stereotypes of cruelty, xenophobia and white slavery through a change of inter-titles. It probably does not come as a surprise that this first version neither convinced the Foreign Ministry nor the Chinese, who complained about the still perceivable 'emphasis put on a racial antagonism between white and yellow'. Important in the context of contemporary institutional responses to the cinema (and its narrative properties), the Foreign Ministry realized that Ufa had failed to live up to its overblown promises that 'through titles anything can be achieved'.[36] Only when Ufa as the distributor of the film retreated from the negotiations, and director Joe May came in personally and agreed to work on changes, did a compromise emerge. Mediated by the cinema reformers of the Film-Liga, members of the Verband für den Fernen Osten (Association for the Far East), an Ufa representative, and the Chinese critics, Joe May began to script changes which would take the political critiques and 'scientific' analyses seriously. These involved changes to the plot and inter-titles, cuts, and the reshooting of a few scenes. Through the addition of new dialogue, the kidnapping of the heroine into a Chinese bordello in this version was now instigated by a corrupt Danish bank clerk in Canton who had to put considerable pressure on his Chinese partners to play their part in the abduction. Scenes that showed extremely cruel forms of 'Chinese' punishment (such as the bleeding to death of criminals) were shortened, and associations of the Chinese officials with organized crime were completely changed through the addition of new inter-titles. In response to the Chinese film criticism, May also shot three completely new scenes and added them to the film. As a rebuttal of the accusations that Chinese were only shown in a negative light, May added a new character, a noble old man who waits anxiously for the Western heroine to arrive and work as an au pair girl with his cute daughters. This would allow, as Joe May explained, China to be presented 'from a different, more sympathetic angle'. Later, Henry Sze's character is shown going to a temple with his father and wearing traditional garments, thus attempting to counteract the implicit connection between 'civilized' behaviour and Westernization in the film. The third new scene consisted of Henry Sze and heroine Mia May visiting the noble old Chinese gentleman at his house, resulting in a brief symbolic moment of international understanding. In August 1920, three months after the new film censorship law had been passed, the Foreign Ministry finally lifted the ban on the export of THE MISTRESS OF THE WORLD. All the surviving archival prints of the film contain the alterations that were made in response to the Chinese criticism and the analyses of academic and political 'experts', thus making the film not only a 'compromise formation between commercial and regulatory discourses and practices'[37] but also a contradictory transnational palimpsest of different knowledge paradigms about race and racism. THE MISTRESS OF THE WORLD also raises important questions about authorship, in so far as the film, as we know it, is not only the work of Joe May and Karl Figdor, but is also marked by and structured around subaltern inscriptions that are the direct result of a repressed postcolonial presence within Weimar cinema and society. The impact of the Chinese intervention and the expert discourse on racial representation, authenticity and foreign policy in the cinema exceeds THE MISTRESS OF THE WORLD. The addition of a passage to the National Film Censorship Law of May 1920 on 'endangering Germany's relations to foreign countries' as legal cause to ban a film can at least be partially accounted for as an institutional codification of the knowledge gained from the perspectives and debates on THE MISTRESS OF THE WORLD.

The conflict about THE MISTRESS OF THE WORLD remained an important reference point in the regulatory discourses of the early 1920s, indicating, as Annette Kuhn eloquently writes, how 'relations of power may operate ... in the service of producing the "truth", especially as "truth" governs the constitution of particular forms of knowledge'.[38] When Joe May was already reshooting scenes and changing inter-titles in August 1920, the Foreign Ministry discovered that Aero-Film was working on a film with the title ASIATISCHE TÜCKE [Asian Malice] and asked to see the treatment: the film was supposed to deal with the adventures of a Western businessman based in China who is duped by Chinese smugglers and then wrongly arrested by Chinese officials.

Only when a Western engineer independently tracks down the Chinese criminals is the businessman's honour restored. In an internal memo, the Foreign Ministry objected to the title as perpetuating 'a tendentious and misguided preconception in a generalized form' and thereby running the risk of endangering foreign trade and political relations with China which, through great efforts, had only just been resumed.[39] It would also make sense in this context, the ministry reasoned, to place a note in the film trade journals to stop the habit of always portraying the Chinese 'as sneaky villains'. Referring to the difficult process of rebuilding trade relations with East Asia and to the new film censorship law, the ministry asked Aero-Film to rewrite the script and offered to put them into contact with 'thorough East Asia experts'. In the face of so much institutional trouble, the small production company instead preferred to give up the exotic setting completely and simply relocated the plot to Europe.[40] Film journalists also used the scientific and political debate on THE MISTRESS OF THE WORLD as a matrix for discussing anti-Asian stereotyping in the cinema. In a review of DAS HAUS DER QUALEN [The House of Torment] (D: Carl Wilhelm, 1921), a crime film featuring Fritz Kortner and the Asian actors Nien Sön Ling and Nien Tso Ling, which was set in the exotic underworld of North American opium dens, a critic wrote: 'The fact that the old Chinese man is presented as a cold-hearted, but always smiling scoundrel might be taken as an offence by the Chinese – like in the case of THE MISTRESS OF THE WORLD'.[41]

One of the most remarkable responses to the regulatory discourse regarding Chinese representations in THE MISTRESS OF THE WORLD was the film DIE SONNE ASIENS [The Asian Sun] (D: Edmund Heuberger, 1921), for it makes apparent what Foucaudian analyses of cinema as an institution would describe as the 'productive' function of power in censorship practices. With Wilhelm Röllinghof as 'artistic director', the production company had hired one of THE MISTRESS OF THE WORLD's script writers; the main Asian role was also played by Henry Sze who in THE MISTRESS OF THE WORLD has appeared as 'Dr Kien-Lung' and now appeared as a character named 'Kuen-Li'. The film, mixing politics, melodrama and science fiction, dealt in a rather explicit manner with the popular topic of a world historical 'race war'. Sze played a Chinese chemist who is married to a Western woman and is secretly working on the invention of artificial gold, which would reverse global power relations and the imperialist world order. After a series of sensationalist and melodramatic plot twists, Kuen-Li, commander of a group of Chinese rebels, and his Western father-in-law, who is the leader of the Western colonial troops, confront each other in a dramatic shoot-out. It is only in the last minute that Kuen-Li's wife Ethel appears as a *deux ex machine* and throws herself between the two combatants, finally forcing them to reconcile. Ethel begs her father to forgive her husband, exclaiming: 'What he has done, he has done for his fatherland! Shake hands with him, for he is a courageous man!' DIE SONNE ASIENS not only attempted to develop 'positive' Chinese images by constantly stressing Kuen-Li's modernity and righteousness, but also time and again reinterpreted the Chinese 'xenophobic' actions as a form of 'patriotism' which can be compared to – and hence understood as analogous to – the more 'legitimate' forms of Western nationalism.

In the following decade, Chinese groups in Germany continued with their protests against screen racism. As Ruth Vasey points out, such protests had a strong international dimension and were supported by the Chinese government, arguing that China's 'cultivation of diplomatic channels of protest' had a 'significant impact on the industry'.[42] In several cases, however, these protests were not articulated on German soil directly, but were voiced to the German embassy in China, strategically by-passing the constraints that Chinese diplomats faced in the West. After debates over the global exhibition of films such as WELCOME DANGER (US 1929, Clyde Bruckman and Malcolm St Clair), MR WU (US 1927, William Nigh), EAST IS WEST (US 1930, Montana Bell) and SHANGHAI EXPRESS (US 1932, Josef von Sternberg), U.S. studios, as Vasey notes, developed a knowledge which corresponded with and enabled the type of normalizing strategies that THE MISTRESS OF THE WORLD had probed a few years earlier in the German context: studios tried to abstain from defining villains in terms of a precise nationality; at the same time, they sought to counterbalance Asian villains with 'positive' Asian heroes. Vasey's argument concerning Hollywood, and the institutional debates on THE MISTRESS OF THE WORLD reconstructed above, allow important insights into the materiality of (post-)colonial power/knowledge relations, giving historical substance to Homi Bhabha's and Stuart Hall's more psychoanalytic analyses of the 'fetishistic' splitting operations involved in the process of racial stereotyping. Despite the normalizing of racial representations and knowledge, Chinese critics in Germany continued to voice their concerns. According to the *Lichtbild-Bühne*, in spring 1921 the films LI-HANG DER GRAUSAME [Li-Hang the Cruel] (DE 1920, Eduard-Emile Biolet) and DAS ENDE DES STROMS [The End of the River] (DE 1921) triggered diplomatic student interventions and hence 'shared the fate of THE MISTRESS OF THE WORLD'.[43] One of the most illuminating protests in the wake of May's film concerned Willi Wolff's spectacular four-part action-adventure travelogue DER FLUG UM DEN ERDBALL [The Flight Around the Globe] (DE 1925), which, unlike THE MISTRESS OF THE WORLD, was partly shot on location. Wolff's film reinterpreted and modernized Jules Verne's *Around the World in 80 Days*, with flapper Ellen Richter as a modern female sports pilot in the main role.

From a Chinese perspective, DER FLUG UM DEN ERDBALL hit the screen at possibly the worst moment. Earlier, in April 1925, the 34-year-old Chinese merchant Cho-Ku-Sin and several of his friends had been robbed and almost killed by a group of armed men in the Kleine Markusstrasse, the centre of Berlin's tiny 'Chinatown'. Confronted with physical violence, Chinese critics began to draw direct connections between their knowledge of everyday racism and the Orientalist knowledge perpetuated by German media, now protesting not only against their treatment on the streets of Berlin, but also against their stereotyped portrayal in Hans Bachwitz's florid and sexually charged 1925 stage production *Yoshiwara – Das Haus der Laster* [Yoshiwara – House of Vice], a racially aggressive pastiche of fin-de-siècle exoticism, *Madame Butterfly* tropes and the nineteenth-century fascination with Tokyo's red-light district of the same name. By targeting the play, which was not 'explicitly' anti-Chinese, but was built around a rather vague sense of Asian decadence, it becomes apparent that what was at stake for the Chinese critics in the last instance could not be completely absorbed into the strictly nationalist framework of the German institutional and regulatory responses. At least in regard to the play, what was at stake was race, not nation.

The protest of the Chinese ambassador in Germany against DER FLUG UM DEN ERDBALL was triggered by three aspects of the film: the depiction of an attempted rape by a Malayian sailor, images of a Chinese opium den, and the physical punishment of a 'lazy' Chinese rickshaw boy (played by German comedian Hans Brausewetter) by Richter's opponent (played by Reinhold Schünzel). In the course of the debate between the Chinese embassy and the Foreign Ministry, director Willi Wolff was also asked to give his view, and in his written response he replayed several of the tropes that had been employed in the discourse on May's film. Wolff pointed out that some of the Asian sequences had been shot on German studio lots with Chinese actors and extras who had known exactly what scenes they were playing. Since they had taken no offence, Wolff argued, he assumed that these representations were legitimate. Wolff also recoded the critique of Western racial knowledge by Asian protesters in strictly national and foreign policy terms, arguing that the rapist, although played by a Chinese actor, was clearly marked in the inter-titles as 'Malayan' and not as a Chinese national. Adding insult to injury, Wolff defended his representational choices by pointing out that physiognomically 'Europeans are not usually able to tell the difference between Chinese and Siamese or between Koreans and Malayans'.[44] In respect to the physical punishment of the rickshaw boy, Wolff argued that the actor could clearly be recognized as the German comedian Brausewetter since he wore his hair in a ponytail whereas all the other Chinese did not, thus indicating that the scene was not indented to represent Chinese customs but to create a comic effect. In the opium den, Wolff argued, one could also spot 'Europeans and Negroes' and not just Chinese; in addition, Wolff emphasized, there was also an extremely helpful Chinese child who embodied 'all the good character traits'. Nevertheless, Wolff declared that he was willing to change some of the inter-titles in a way that would deflect the blame from the Chinese (e.g. the line 'Master, great danger! This man a lot of friends, very powerful and dangerous, will take revenge!' would read 'Master! Man is no Chinese! Stranger is Mongol! Chinese good like Charley!'). It is interesting to note that the Foreign Ministry, in what one might deem to be a surprising defence of popular culture, confidently supported Wolff's twisted argumentation, now lamenting that the Chinese critics were obviously not aware of the 'superficial and entertaining character' of this 'shallow botch'.[45] Questions of authenticity or concerns about the educational value of cinema had disappeared entirely from the discourse, while the perceived connection between 'harmless' entertainment and racist violence remained repressed. Nevertheless, the German Foreign Ministry promised to use even stricter guidelines in regard to representations of the Chinese in the future. In a concluding letter, the German ambassador in Beijing reported to the Chinese Foreign Ministry that all the offensive passages in YOSHIWARA and DER FLUG UM DEN ERDBALL had been removed, the merchant and his friends were recovering and the perpetrators had been arrested. Yet, the German ambassador also felt that 'he could not keep quiet about' the fact that in recent times there was a growing number of 'unpleasant Chinese elements' who lived in the 'queasy and disreputable neighbourhoods' of cities like Hamburg and Berlin, and a small number of 'cocky Chinese students' who incited the German people by means of their communist propaganda.[46]

Two years later, the American production MR WU (US 1927, William Nigh), starring Lon Chaney as a Chinese father who kills his daughter because she had engaged in premarital sex, was released in Germany and, again, became the target of protesting Chinese students, provoking a similar protest and censorship scenario. According to the censorship protocol, the Asian expert and member of the German Foreign Ministry, Basler, had filed a complaint against the film, because 'young scholars' had approached him and explained that they felt humiliated by the way the Chinese were always depicted in movies as being 'uncultivated, scoundrels or opium smokers'. At the meeting of the *Filmprüfstelle* (film censorship board) in Berlin, Basler read a letter from the Chinese Embassy which pointed out that they saw a 'system in exhibiting films of this kind' and asked the board to make changes. As a result, the film was initially banned, since the board felt that it could harm Germany's relations with China. After an objection by the distributor, Ufa, the *Filmoberprüfstelle* (the higher instance of the film censorship board) met and the film was then approved, but with changes. All inter-titles which explained Chaney's despotic actions as an expression of Chinese family laws had to be altered so that his deeds appeared motivated by his character, not by his culture, and a new ending was created through an additional inter-title which indicated that the Chaney character had to pay for his evil-doings with his life.[47] German film journals viewed the MR WU ruling as a landmark decision by the film censorship board, and it indeed clearly illustrates how racial and racist representations were 'normalized' through regulatory responses and institutional formations of knowledge in the wake of THE MISTRESS OF THE WORLD. The *Film-Kurier* commented that the first paragraph of the 1920 film censorship law (dealing with the endangerment of Germany's relations to other nations) could now only be applied if a 'foreign nation *as such*' was '*purposely* depicted in a hurtful or humiliating manner so that the spectator will be led to show less respect for this nation and its members than he would have without the inducement by this moving picture'. According to the *Film-Kurier*, Wolff's trifling changes demonstrated that no harm was meant: 'no Chinese with *normal* feelings' could legitimately take offence after the changes had been made. Hence, the goal of the film censorship law had been achieved, and it was neither the duty of the board nor the intention of the law to 'to consider the *exaggerated* sentiments of foreign nations'.[48]

The debates around screen racism in the wake of THE MISTRESS OF THE WORLD indicate to what extent racial representations after the First World War were not simply expressions of a deep-seated, white-supremacist cultural sensibility, but were rather deeply marked by moments of resistance, institutional apparatuses of knowledge production about race and the cinema, regulatory practices, commercial imperatives and foreign policy considerations. As a result of Weimar Germany's political weakness in regard to foreign affairs and its attempts at rebuilding the film export trade, critiques of racial representations by diasporic groups in Germany (such as Chinese students) were read (and probably could only be read) institutionally through the knowledge of foreign policy agencies as national and diplomatic conflicts, not as a problem 'internal' to German society. This link between race and nationhood, and the colonial power structures behind it, explains to a large extent why the critiques of the Chinese could be heard while the stateless voices of African colonial migrants were silenced, and why Asians and blacks were confronted with different forms of screen racism. In the course of these debates certain problem-solving and normalizing techniques emerged which avoided dealing with the systemic character of screen racism that people of colour in Germany pointed to. Instead, such institutional responses and normalizing techniques rested on a double strategy: first, since race was recoded as nationality, racial stereotypes were seen as legitimate as long as they were not linked to a specific nationality; second, negative stereotypes had to be counterbalanced by 'positive' images. The key site for these regulatory debates and censorship practices were the inter-titles used in silent cinema, indicating to what extent 'educated' bourgeois responses to the cinema in the period were still shaped by the traditions of literary culture: cinema indeed was 'read', not 'viewed' as a visual medium. Where questions of visuality were raised, concerns focused on the 'authenticity' of sets, costumes and actors. Such arguments were often shaped by the larger issue of the educational and ethnographic value of cinema, a concern that was historically linked to the pre-war cinema reform movement, whose impact (and class basis) was slowly fading in the course of the 1920s when political institutions began to come to terms with cinema's entertainment qualities. Yet if we look ahead to the later 1920s and early 1930s, motivated by the League of Nations and the founding of the International Educational Cinematographic Institute (IECI), European discussions about the intersections of racial knowledge, ethnography, film pedagogy and institutional film policies increasingly began to move in a more internationalist direction, celebrating cinema as a harbinger of 'universal humanism'. This perhaps found one of its boldest expressions in the French IECI delegate Henri Focillon's protest against the term 'backward races' for Europe's subjected colonial populations in Africa and Asia.[49] Although many of the films discussed in this chapter are now orphaned or lost, we are reminded that it is ultimately the task of the film historian, as Dan Streible argues, to create a 'usable past' by placing films in their original reception context, revealing 'the ways in which cultural artifacts were constructed, exhibited, interpreted, fought over, celebrated, condemned, suppressed, revived, and repurposed ... [T]hey offer us a model of how society, culture, media, and power worked at particular points in history. That history becomes usable as an alternative vision, instructive because it is so different from, at times even alien to, contemporary experience'.[50] What might be most 'useful' in the contemporary context of media practices in Germany today, however, might not be the 'difference' (or even 'alien-ness') of these past debates, but the acknowledgement that the archive of racial knowledge and screen racism was always challenged by the 'alternative vision' and knowledge production of migrants and 'other Germans', whose subterranean presence has left transformative traces on Germany's celluloid past.

Notes

1. See S.S. Prawer. 2005. *Between Two Worlds: The Jewish Presence in German and Austrian Film, 1910–1933*. New York and Oxford: Berghahn Books.
2. See Nele Obermueller. 2012. 'Does German Theatre Have a Race Problem', *Exberliner*, 30 May, retrieved 19 August 2013 from http://www.exberliner.com/articles/does-german-theatre-have-a-race-problem; Henning Hoff. 2009. 'Blackface Filmmaker Sparks a Race Debate in Germany', *Time*, 18 November, retrieved 19 August 2013 from http://www.time.com/time/world/article/0,8599,1940290,00.html
3. Homi Bhabha. 1994. *The Location of Culture*. London: Routledge, 66 (emphasis added).
4. Edward Said. 2003. *Orientalism*. London: Penguin, 7.
5. Mark Terkessidis. 2004. *Banalität des Rassismus. Migranten zweiter Generation entwickeln eine neue Perspektive*. Bielefeld: transcript, 92.
6. See Philomena Essed. 1991. *Understanding Everyday Racism: An Interdisciplinary Theory*. London: Sage.
7. David Theo Goldberg. 1993. *Racist Culture: Philosophy and the Politics of Meaning*. Chichester: Wiley-Blackwell, 8.
8. David Theo Goldberg. 1997. *Racial Subjects: Writing on Race in America*. New York: Routledge, 28.
9. See Oskar Kalbus. 1922. *Der Deutsche Lehrfilm in Wissenschaft und Unterricht*. Berlin: Heymann; and Armin Degenhard. 2001. *'Bedenken, die zu überwinden sind ...' Das neue Medium Film im Spannungsfeld reformpädagogischer Erziehungsziele, von der Kinoreformbewegung bis zur handlungsorientierten Filmarbeit Adolf Reichweins*. Munich: KoPäd. On the role of film in 'modernizing' science instruction, see Heinrich Schüen. 1927. *Geographischer Lehrfilm und moderne Geographie: eine methodisch-kritische Untersuchung*. Greifswald: Hartmann.

10. Annette Kuhn. 1988. *Cinema, Censorship, and Sexuality, 1909–25*. New York: Routledge, 7.

11. Lee Grieveson. 2004. *Policing Cinema: Movies and Censorship in Early-Twentieth-Century America*. Berkeley and Los Angeles: University of California Press, 4.

12. Janelle Blankenship. 2006. 'Leuchte der Kultur: Imperialism, Imaginary Travel, and the Skladanowsky Welt-Theater', in Martin Loiperdinger (ed.), *KINtop: Jahrbuch zur Erforschung des frühen Films: Sources and Perspectives on Early Cinema*, 14–15, 150–70.

13. Fatimah Tobing Rony. 1996. *The Third Eye: Race, Cinema, and Ethnographic Spectacle*. Durham, NC: Duke University Press, 11.

14. Rudolf Pöch. 1907. 'Reisen in Neu-Guinea in den Jahren 1905–1906', in *Zeitschrift für Ethnologie* 39, 383–400 (here: 398). Together with Karl Weule, Pöch was one of the pioneers of ethnographic filmmaking in German-speaking countries. He also became a member of the Race Hygiene Society in 1909, joining the ranks of German anthropologists Ranke, Felix von Luschan and Hans Virchow. See Assenka Oksiloff. 2001. *Picturing the Primitive: Visual Culture, Ethnography, and Early German Cinema*. New York: Palgrave, 52.

15. Pöch, 'Reisen in Neu-Guinea', 400.

16. Renato Rosaldo. 1989. 'Imperialist Nostalgia', in *Representations* 26 (Special Issue: Memory and Counter-Memory), Spring, 107–22.

17. On the 'cinema reform' movement in Germany, see, among others, Scott Curtis. 1994. 'The Taste of a Nation: Training the Senses and Sensibility of Cinema Audiences in Imperial Germany', in *Film History* 6(4), 445–69.

18. Gesellschaft der Freunde des vaterländischen Schul- und Erziehungswesens zu Hamburg (ed.). 1907. *Bericht der Kommission für 'Lebende Photographie' erstattet am 17. April und im Auftrag des Vorstandes bearbeitet von C.H. Dannmeyer*. Hamburg, Reprint: Hamburg 1980, 541, quoted in Wolfgang Fuhrmann. 2003. 'Propaganda, Science, and Entertainment. German Colonial Cinematography: A Case Study in the History of Early Nonfiction Cinema'. Unpublished dissertation, Utrecht University, 190.

19. Georg Herzberg. 1929. 'Pori', in *Film-Kurier*, 13 March. Ethnographic nudity, and its function as a publically tolerated form of Ersatz pornography, remained a constant source of dispute between film distributors and film censorship boards. A few months after the premiere of Pori, lobby cards for Gari Gari (Hugo Adolph Bernatzik, 1929) had to be taken down because they displayed the naked breasts of young African women (see Anon. 1929. 'Verbotene Negerphotos', in *Film-Kurier*, 29 June).

20. Fuhrmann, 'Propaganda, Science, and Entertainment', 190.

21. On the links between colonial migration and work in the film industry, see Tobias Nagl. 2009a. *Die unheimliche Maschine. Rasse und Repräsentation im Weimarer Kino*. Munich: edition text + kritik, 521–56.

22. Karen Pehla. 1991. 'Joe May und seine Detektive', in Hans-Michael Bock and Claudia Lenssen (eds), *Joe May: Regisseur und Produzent*. Munich: edition text + kritik, 61–72.

23. Sabine Hake. 1992. *Passions and Deceptions: The Early Films of Ernst Lubitsch*. Princeton, NJ: Princeton University Press, 120f.

24. Gustav Benkwitz. 1921. 'Der Beirat für Geschichte', in *Der Kinematograph*, 5 June; and Kalbus, *Der Deutsche Lehrfilm*, 162.

25. See also Tobias Nagl. 2009b. 'The Aesthetics of Race in European Film Theory' in Trifonova Temenuga (ed.), *European Film Theory*. London and New York: Routledge, 17–31.

26. Hans Spielhofer. 1924. 'Film und Rasse', in *Süddeutsche Filmzeitung* 24, 4.
27. On film censorship in Germany after the First World War, see Ursula von Keitz. 2000. 'Films before the Court: The Theory and Practice of Film Assessment in Germany from 1920 to 1938', in Leonardo Quaresima, Alessandra Raengo and Laura Vichi (eds). *I limiti della rappresentazione. Censura, visibile, modi di rappresentazione nel cinema* [The bounds of representation: Censorship, the visible, modes of representation in film]. Udine: Forum, 381–402.
28. Ufa Publicity Office to Foreign Ministry, 19 January 1920, Bundesarchiv Berlin R 901/72197, 2.
29. Dr Max Linde. 1920. 'Film und auswärtige Politik', in *Der Sonntag*, 1 February. Also published under the same title in *Ostasiatische Rundschau* 1/2, 15 February 1920, 18–19.
30. Alfred Forke to Consul Borch, Foreign Ministry, 2 March 1920, Bundesarchiv berlin R 901/72197, 52p.
31. Note by Consul Walter, 2 March 1920, Bundesarchiv Berlin R 901/72197, 5. With his last statement, Walter is referring to the fact that the Chinese embassy had supplied May-Film/Ufa with the names of Chinese citizens living in Germany for their recruiting of extras. Although hardly anything is known about the biography of Henry Sze, some sources indicate that he might have come to Europe as a diplomat before turning towards an acting career.
32. Memo Volz, Press Bureau of Imperial Government, Ref. F Film Propaganda, 5 March 1920, Bundesarchiv Berlin R 901/72197, 6.
33. 'Wie die Chinesen über Karl von Figdor's Film *Die Herrin der Welt* denken', Bundesarchiv Berlin R 901/72197, 51–52.
34. Note by Walter, Bundesarchiv Berlin R 901/72197, 44.
35. Ibid.
36. Note by Volz, Press Office of the Federal Government, 31 March 1920, Bundesarchiv Berlin R 901/72197, 81p.
37. Grieveson, *Policing Cinema*, 6.
38. Kuhn, *Cinema, Censorship, and Sexuality*, 4.
39. Press Office of the Foreign Ministry, 'Note', 4 August 1920, Bundesarchiv Berlin R 901/72190, 58.
40. Aero-Film to Foreign Ministry, 28 August 1920, Bundesarchiv Berlin R 901/72190, 103.
41. C.S. 1920. 'Das Haus der Qualen', in *Film und Presse* 5–6, 40.
42. Ruth Vasey. 1997. *The World According to Hollywood, 1918–1939*. Madison, WI: University of Wisconsin Press, 154f.
43. 'Ein chinesischer Protest', in *Lichtbild-Bühne*, 1 May 1921, 74.
44. Verbal Note, Foreign Ministry to Chinese Embassy (includes Willi Wolff's statement). 1 May 1925, Politisches Archiv/Auswärtiges Amt Akten der Deutschen Gesandtschaft in Peking: Chinesen in Deutschland, Kult 10-3a.
45. Ibid.
46. German Embassy in Beijing to Chinese Ministry of Foreign Affairs, 6 May 1925, Politisches Archiv/Auswärtiges Amt Akten der Deutschen Gesandtschaft in Peking: Chinesen in Deutschland, Kult 10-3a.
47. See the censorship record of Mʀ Wu by the Filmprüfstelle Berlin, Nr. 16060, 11 July 1927, and by the Film-Oberprüfstelle, Nr. 658, 15 July 1927, DIF/Frankfurt, retrieved 19 August 2013 from http://www.difarchiv.deutsches-filminstitut.de/filme/f035337.htm

48. 'Vorsicht bei der Filmdarstellung fremder Völker. Eine wichtige Entscheidung', in *Film-Kurier*, 22 July 1920 (emphasis added).
49. Peter Bloom. 2008. *French Colonial Cinema: Mythologies of Humanitarianism*. Minneapolis: University of Minnesota Press, 177.
50. Dan Streible. 2008. *Fight Pictures: A History of Boxing and Early Cinema*. Berkeley: University of California Press, 290.

Chapter 2

THE VISIBLE WOMAN IN AND AGAINST BÉLA BALÁZS

Erica Carter

In July 2011, U.K. radio audiences gained a rare insight into the life of a famously undemonstrative political dissident when the Burmese opposition leader, Aang San SuuKyi, delivered two BBC Reith Lectures on the subject of 'Liberty'.[1] Although she cited Max Weber as one source of her conviction that political opposition is driven above all by personal passion, Aang San SuuKyi began on a more intimate note. 'The first autobiography I ever read', she confided, 'was … perhaps prophetically … *Seven Years' Solitary* … [the autobiography] of a Hungarian woman [caught up in] the Communist Party purges of the early 1950s'.

Students of film theory might have pricked up their ears at this point. Published in 1957, *Seven Years Solitary* is an autobiographical account of the illegal imprisonment of one Edith Bone, née Hajós, the Hungarian émigré translator, writer and socialist activist who secured a place in the pantheon of twentieth-century film theory with her 1953 translation of Béla Balázs's *Theory of the Film*.[2] As Balázs's first wife, Hajós had in 1915 been a founder member and co-host, with Balázs and the woman who was later to become his second wife, Anna Hamvassy, of the Budapest intellectual salon, the Sunday Circle, a grouping whose members also included the cultural sociologists Arnold Hauser and Károly (Karl) Mannheim, the psychologist Julia Láng, the philosopher Béla Fogarasi, and Balázs's close confidant György (Georg) Lukács. Having moved to the Soviet Union, Hajós had later facilitated contacts there for Balázs prior to his own departure to Moscow exile in 1932. In a new home in

Britain in the early 1930s, she joined the British Communist Party, later dropped out of party activities over her disgust at their policy on the 1939 Hitler–Stalin pact, but remained active on the political left, including in Spain, where she is credited with involvement in founding the Unified Socialist Party of Catalonia (PSUC) in 1936.[3]

Though trained as a medical doctor, Hajós supported herself after her arrival in Britain with activities as a journalist for the party organ, the *Daily Worker*, and as a translator working to render into English writings by figures from the Soviet and Hungarian cultural left, including Maxim Gorki, Alexei Tolstoy, Wanda Wasilewska and, of course, Balázs.[4]

Correspondence in the Balázs archive shows Hajós re-establishing contact with her former husband after the war; she appears to have begun work on the translation of his *Filmkultúra* at around this point, and certainly maintained sufficiently close connections with Balázs to attend his funeral in Budapest in May 1949.[5] The visit was to prove fateful. On 1 October, Hajós was arrested, imprisoned on trumped-up charges of espionage, and spent seven years in solitary confinement before escaping during the turmoil of the 1956 uprising.

In a broadcast interview for Pathé News after her return to Britain, Hajós commented on her experience of Stalinist state socialism: 'I don't believe that a government which is merely the agent of a foreign invader … can rule a country against the will of 98 per cent of its population … I have seen [Communism] bring advantages to a small section, but not to the vast majority of those whom [it] claims to serve, that is to say, the working population'.[6] Hajós's experience of the perversion of Communist utopias under authoritarian rule lends particular force to her voicing of the political disillusion felt after 1956 by many of her generation of Western Marxists. But this was by no means the first time that her life experiences had intersected so closely with larger Central European political histories. Trained as a medical doctor, Hajós opted out of the profession early on to pursue her greater passion for a social emancipation that she saw as realized not only in revolutionary politics, but also in a libertarian sexuality that was actualized in her toleration of a ménage à trois with Anna Hamvassy.[7] It is, moreover, this early sexual–political embrace of free love in the Balázs/Hamvassy/Hajós love triangle, as well as her political engagement, her writing, her extraordinary courage in the face of persecution, imprisonment, and seven years of mental and physical abuse, that make her a fitting figure to open this chapter; for all these features locate her, I will be suggesting, as a symbolic figure for what Rita Felski has termed that most 'resonant' icon of early twentieth-century emancipation, the New Woman.[8]

Balázs, the New Woman and Feminism

The New Woman, as Felski shows, is an altogether ambivalent feminine figure who on the one hand emerges in the *fin de siècle* as a potent mythic fantasm or symbol that condenses the anxieties as well as the utopian fantasies surrounding gender emancipation in the modern age. On the other hand, the New Woman is the concrete subject of historical changes, including expanded women's employment, especially in white-collar sectors; political engagement, including in European and North American suffrage campaigns; extended educational opportunities and other forms of social and sexual emancipation – the latter being evident in turn-of-the-century experiments in free love, for instance, and later, in birth control and abortion rights campaigns; and new female leisure practices across the expanding consumer industries of fashion, the popular press, and entertainment forms. We know that the New Woman was a pan-European, indeed by the 1920s a global phenomenon, albeit a highly differentiated one whose contours shifted in different political territories and social milieux.[9] We know that she emerged at the *fin de siècle* as a middle-class icon and object of cross-class identification for women. We know also that her aspirations intersected, but were not coextensive with, those of feminism; and from feminist film history, we know finally of the particular significance of popular film and cinema-going in shaping the cultural experiences and the identity of the new woman.

The 'New Woman' embodied among numerous others by Edith Hajós is best understood, in other words, as a capacious socio-symbolic category that captures women both as historical actors and as mythic figures for 'the dangers and the promises of the modern age'.[10] It is in both capacities, moreover, that the new woman becomes relevant for Béla Balázs.

Balázs and the New Woman

There has, in recent years, been a revival of critical interest in Balázs. Since the collapse of communism, Hungarian film historians have sought to retrieve this altogether maverick thinker from the obscurity he suffered under an orthodox Marxist regime.[11] New German, English, French and Italian editions of his early writings have contributed to a recognition of his centrality in the development of early film aesthetics.[12] Cultural and intellectual histories have located his early writings as crystallizing philosophical and film-critical currents of their time, while contemporary cinema studies has turned to Balázs's work on the ontology of the image, on cinematic perception, and on film as a universal language as points of reference for twenty-first-century discussions of indexicality, medium specificity, and popular and transnational film.[13]

There surfaces in these accounts a standard biographical narrative of Balázs. Born in 1884, as Herbert Bauer, to German-speaking Jewish parents, Balázs changed his name at the age of sixteen when he published his first poem. The name change was an act of homage to a national artistic renaissance which Balázs himself came to embody when he emerged, after his move to Budapest in 1902, as a major poet of early twentieth-century Hungarian vernacular modernism. His associations in Budapest with the composers Zoltan Kodály and Béla Bartók, his intimate friendship with Georg Lukács, his intellectual formation under the influence of such figures as Georg Simmel and Henri Bergson: these gave to Balázs's writings, it is suggested, their peculiar character as lightning rods for such heterogeneous intellectual and artistic currents as Central European folk modernism, Bergsonian vitalism and, later, the Marxism that Balázs learned in dialogue with Lukács, and that would be an enduring commitment until his death in 1949.

A parallel story often told of Balázs sits uneasily, however, with this tale of a genius figure formed in dialogue with the great (male) thinkers of his time.[14] From his autobiographical novel *Die Jugend eines Träumers* (Dreaming Youth), as well as from the diary that he kept throughout his life, we know of tortured relationships with women that began with his adolescent witnessing of a rape by a household servant, and continued throughout two marriages and multiple erotic liaisons.[15] Many of Balázs's relationships with women seem to have taken the form of sexual or emotional predations whose dominant mood shifted bewilderingly from adoration, to aloof, if not sadistic, distance.[16] At the same time, and contradictorily, Balázs's Romantic enthusiasm for passionate friendship as the foundation of intellectual life made him an advocate for, and at times a participant in, egalitarian artistic and intellectual relationships with women. A significant instance to which we will return at the end of this chapter is Balázs's friendship with the illustrator and fairy-tale author Anna Lesznai. We know from Balázs's diary and correspondence, as well as from the modernist fairy tales that were central to his literary career, how significant was the artistic and philosophical debt that Balázs owed to Lesznai.[17] Others among Balázs's female friends who took up the position of intellectual sparring partner and muse occupied by Lesznai during their years together, first in Budapest and later in Viennese exile, included Edith Hajós. In the pre-First World War years of Balázs's friendship with Lukács, Hajós played a role alongside Balázs, Lukács and Lukács's lover, the artist Irma Seidler, in a complex double sexual and intellectual pairing that, for Lukács and Balázs at least, helped them to articulate their shared resistance to bourgeois mores and social norms.[18] That the two women foundered – Hajós suffered years of depression, Seidler killed herself after a brief affair with Balázs – is tragic indeed; but it is also emblematic of larger contradictions surrounding the New Women. Hajós and Seidler's function, in their relationship with Balázs and Lukács, as instruments mobilized to cement a powerful homosocial bond, mirrors a larger social reality in which women bidding for personal autonomy found their way blocked by expectations of feminine subservience, including in the liberal-bohemian circles to which Lukács and Balázs belonged.

His own complicity in reinforcing the double-bind facing his female peers did not, admittedly, deter Balázs from speaking publicly on women's political role, or from (often tempestuous) collaborations throughout his career with prominent women artists and intellectuals.[19] The writer Emma Ritoók was recruited early on to the Sunday Circle, alongside Lesznai, Hajós and Hamvassy; Balázs's breakthrough fairy-tale collection in German, *Der Mantel der Träume* (The Cloak of Dreams), was commissioned as a companion piece to illustrations by the Austrian-Greek feminist surrealist Mariette Lydis; and his collaboration with Leni Riefenstahl as screenwriter for THE BLUE LIGHT (1930), is well known.[20]

Tracing these and other instances of female influence does not, however, take us far in situating Balázs's film theory within the larger field of gender history. In what follows, I want therefore to explore the relation between Balázs and the New Woman through an archaeology of his film theory that takes us back to *fin de siècle* Hungary. My focus will be on Balázs's two early works of film theory, *Der sichtbare Mensch* (Visible Man, 1924) and *Der Geist des Films* (The Spirit of Film, 1930).[21] The former, the first full-length work of film theory in the German language, was received by peers as a 'foundational' work, and as necessary

Figure 2.1 Béla Balázs with Georg Lukács and Edith Hajós in Balázs's flat, 1915/16. [Georg Lukacs archive]

reading for 'all those who hold dear the medium of film'.[22] The latter was Balázs's reckoning with contemporary critics, foremost amongst them Rudolf Arnheim, who proclaimed the death of film art with the coming of sound.[23] Grounded theoretically, moreover, in a phenomenology of perception deriving from precursors including Goethe, Simmel and Bergson, both works were understood by the Marxist Balázs as contributions to a materialist history of the human subject in an early twentieth-century cinematic age.

I hope to show below, however, that this history exhibited a gendered dimension which, although occluded in Balázs's universalist account (he was, famously, one of numerous contemporary proponents of notions of film as an emancipatory universal language), surfaces both in the early history of his intellectual and political formation in pre-First World War Hungary, and in figurings of the New Woman in his writings on film. My starting point, then, is that Balázs's interwar writings can best be understood as emerging from a longer Central European intellectual, social and political history in which gender emancipation played a significant role.[24] His early film theory was thus a body of work formed, among other sources, in and through a dialogic relation to the early twentieth-century New Woman. The New Woman of the twentieth century's first two decades, I suggest below, was generative in three senses for Balázs's early film theory: as social and political agent within the pluralist intellectual-political milieu of early twentieth-century Hungary; as image and muse (my example here is Balázs's writing on Asta Nielsen, which I conceive in terms of a bringing-into-being of film theory through ekphrasis, that is to say, through poetic writing on the female image on film); and as intellectual peer and collaborator – and here I follow Hanno Loewy in focusing on Anna Lesznai, in particular her writing on fairy-tale time.

Conditions of Emergence: *fin de siècle* Hungary

For anyone involved in a twenty-first-century academic context in teaching film studies, feminist film theory necessarily features as a staple course element alongside, say, psychoanalysis, film philosophy, or film studies approaches to auteurs, genres and stars. The same cannot be said of teaching or writing on early film theory. Though there is now extensive scholarship on female audiences and the film experience, and on women writing on film from within literary modernism and the Western avant-garde, there is still work to be done on an early twentieth-century dialogue in which movements for women's emancipation gave impetus to critical engagement with film.

In this context, the case of Balázs is instructive. In both *Visible Man* and *The Spirit of Film*, Balázs envisaged a film medium that would place itself in the service of human liberation by teaching its audiences to see and know the world through different eyes. The transformation of the human perceptual faculties that Balázs saw as achieved by film represented for him, then, a chance for the medium to participate in the formation of new historical subjects. Hence his claim in *The Spirit of Film* that 'the subject of [the film medium's] development is the subject, the human subject, man in his social being'.[25]

After his turn to Marxism towards the end of the First World War, Balázs's primary commitment was to the working class, as that 'subject … in his social being' which was destined to become the collective agent of historical change. Yet Balázs's own life trajectory suggests an awareness of the political awakening of a second collective historical protagonist. The twelve heady years that Balázs spent in

Budapest, Paris and Berlin in the run-up to the First World War saw him pursuing an eclectic engagement with, among other tendencies, German Romanticism, oriental mysticism, Bergsonian philosophy, and Marxism – but also with movements for women's emancipation. This period thus not only laid the foundations for Balázs's characteristically esoteric and mystical version of Marxist politics. His involvement with women artists and intellectuals – the likes of Anna Lesznai, Emma Ritoók, Anna Hamvassy, Edith Hajós and others – also brought him into contact with what Katalin Fábián has termed turn-of-the-century Hungary's emerging 'female and feminist public sphere'.[26]

By the time Balázs moved to Budapest, the women intellectuals whose company he sought – grammar school or university-educated writers, artists and female professionals – stood already as emblems of long-standing feminist campaigns for public education. By the early 1880s, Hungarian feminist calls for educational equality had been answered with girls' schools, teacher-training colleges and, from 1895, with access for women to university education in medicine and the arts.[27] Balázs's early years in Budapest coincided with a turn to women's suffrage as a second focus of both local and international feminist mobilization. Campaigns for the right to vote were orchestrated in part through the Hungarian Association of Feminists (Magyar Feministák Egyesülete), formed in December 1904 as an umbrella organization for the approximately eight hundred associations that are estimated to have been involved in that period in campaigns on or support for women's issues.[28]

Yet the movement's signal feature was not its centralization in a single body, but its dispersal across multiple associations and informal networks. There may have been 'fierce contestations' among the highly educated bourgeois feminists of the feminist association, the socialist feminists who clustered around such bodies as the Association of Women Clerks (Magyar Nőtisztviselők Egyesület), and the non-aligned feminists – professional women of the upper bourgeoisie, among them Lesznai, Hajós and Hamvassy, who remained aloof from associational politics, but found a 'nurturing environment' for feminist ideals in progressive intellectual circles.[29] But conventional divisions between bourgeois, socialist and liberal or non-aligned feminists broke down in the context of a heterogeneous political subculture that operated at a tangent to a moribund mainstream politics. Key forums in this informal political milieu included the debating societies, the workers' educational initiatives, the open universities (including the Sunday Circle's Free School of Humanistic Sciences), the Freemasons'

Lodges, and the informal salons and cafes in which feminist activists rubbed shoulders with writers, artists and cultural intellectuals of the likes of Balázs.[30] Balázs's collaborations in the Sunday Circle thus brought him into contact with that group of often aristocratic or high-bourgeois women intellectuals whose feminist commitment was articulated not centrally in political activism, but in forms of cultural production including poetry and journalism, the literary and visual arts, and modern design.

One significant instance is Anna Lesznai's collecting of textiles from rural women, whose designs she reworked in a modernist visual idiom that echoed Béla Bartók's musical refiguring of folk rhythm and melody; or indeed Balázs's own modernist rewritings in his fairy tales of folk or popular myth. Lesznai's fairy tales also bespeak a proto-feminist commitment in their satirical treatment of popular fantasies of domesticity and Western heterosexual romance.[31] But the intersection between early feminism and the Marxist politics of Balázs was to find its most explicitly political manifestation in revolutionary activity during the Budapest Commune by a broad-based alliance that forged extensive links between the feminist movement and a multi-faceted coalition of socialists and liberal leftists, 'free-floating intellectuals'

Figure 2.2 Postcard from the Sunday Circle (photo by Olga Mate), from left: Karl Mannheim, Béla Fogarosi, Erno Lorsy, unknown, Elza Stephani, Anna Hamvassy, Edith Hajós, Béla Balázs; c.1916. [Petofi Iroldami Museum F.1745]

and others.[32] Feminists of multiple political hues were prominent in the revolution, as well as in the short-lived Soviet administration under Béla Kun. Prominent bourgeois feminists took up ministerial office in the Hungarian Soviet Republic, including Rózsa Bédy-Schwimmer and Vilma Glücklich, both senior figures in the Association of Feminists as well as the Women's International League for Peace and Freedom (WILPF) – Bédy-Schwimmer as 'ambassador extraordinary and plenipotentiary minister' to Switzerland, Glücklich as one of two female members on a committee for the municipal administration of Budapest.[33] They served as functionaries of the socialist administration alongside Balázs, who was nominated by Lukács to a post as Head of the Literature Department; but they were also joined in ministerial office by Anna Lesznai, whom Balázs appointed as a deputy minister with responsibility for fairy tales.

This shared participation of feminist intellectuals with prominent figures in institutionalized feminism, as well as with Communist Party members, and figures from a non-aligned radical or liberal left, reinforces a further argument from Szapor, which is that both Hungarian feminist organizing and socialist politics of this period took place within and contributed to a 'common political culture', one characterized by 'political and cultural pluralism' under the sign of a common 'democratic ideal'.[34] Within this shared political framework, the feminism of Bédy-Schwimmer, Glücklich and others intersected in (at least) three ways with the cultural Marxism of Balázs. Balázs's writings – as his extensive correspondence with key figures of the Marxist left including Lukács, Karl Mannheim, Ernst Bloch and others attests – first grew out of intense dialogues with kindred figures within the informal networks of a pan-European left intelligentsia. That Hungarian feminism similarly emerged both out of myriad conversations across extensive local networks, and energetic engagement with international feminism, is evidenced by the staging in Budapest of the 1913 VIIth Conference of the International Women Suffrage Alliance (IWSA). Hungary – the first country outside North West Europe to host the conference – was chosen by the Alliance, according to Katalin Fábián, in recognition of 'Hungarian women's extensive organizing and lobbying for voting rights reforms'.[35] But it surely also resulted from the intense networking activities of such as Bédy-Schwimmer and Glücklich. Both women were active in the IWSA sister organization, the International Council of Women (ICW), and both nurtured extensive informal contacts with feminist activists across Western Europe – especially, for Bédy-Schwimmer, in the Netherlands, as well as in the United States, where she lectured extensively during a 1914–15 nationwide tour.[36]

This feminist emphasis on organization through local, national and transnational networks was complemented, secondly, by a modernist commitment that similarly echoes that of Balázs. If Hungarian feminism from the early 1800s onwards participated in a larger drive towards social and political modernization – a drive focused variously on Hungarian claims for national independence, on education, and on constitutional reform – so too Balázs saw his early work as a poet, journalist and fabulist as contributing to a modernist cultural renaissance that would transform the larger socio-political domain. Hence his work with Lesznai during the Commune on public fairy-tale readings for children, staged as part of a utopian drive for social transformation through the cultural liberation of youthful minds. His later exile writings on film echo that popular modernist commitment in their embrace of the new medium as '*the popular art* of our century': an art form that 'inspires' and 'gives shape' to 'the imagination and the emotional life of the people', rendering it 'impossible in future to write a cultural history or a national psychology without devoting a large chapter to film'.[37]

And there is a third connection – one that leads us now to a discussion of the gendered substance of Balázs's writing on film. Early twentieth-century feminism was rooted politically in earlier movements for women's emancipation; but it also drew succour from those socio-economic developments identified above as underpinning the historical emergence of the New Woman. Emerging in the wake of late nineteenth-century educational reforms, the new female, urban, white-collar workforce provided the 'breeding ground' for turn-of-the-century grass-roots women's organizations.[38] But this new gender and class formation, composed in Hungary, as across the Western world, of teachers, clerks, stenographers, typists and shopgirls, also fed on and in turn generated a whole new field of popular representation that circulated around the figure of the newly emancipated New Woman. Balázs's early writings are thus peppered with references to the popular female stars – Lilian Gish, Pola Negri, Suzanne Desprès and, most famously, Asta Nielsen – who embodied the emancipatory ideals, as well as the frustrated desires, of the New Woman.

Balázs ends his *Visible Man* with an ecstatic encomium to Asta Nielsen; and it is to this and related passages that we now turn for a discussion of Balázs's film theory, and of the ekphrastic relation in which it stands to the New Woman as image, cinema icon and myth.

Asta Nielsen

There are numerous aspects of Asta Nielsen that place her in the camp of the New Woman. As the most successful female star in European box offices of the 1910s, she increasingly asserted her artistic autonomy as a star auteur with her finger on the button of the industry. Recent research on Nielsen has focused on her astute grasp of the international film business, displayed first in the distribution company that she and husband, Urban Gad, established with Paul Davidson. The company has been credited with revolutionizing early film exhibition by triggering a shift to monopoly distribution and the long-run exclusive.[39] But Nielsen's determined independence went further than this. When she founded her own production company in 1921, and included among its founding projects a transvestite version of HAMLET (1921) in which she herself stars, Nielsen confirmed her reputation as a star who played knowingly with the gendered and sexual meanings of her persona and image.

We know, moreover, from contemporary as well as more recent audience research, how powerfully that image resonated with European audiences – in particular, female audiences.[40] Nielsen has been rightly recognized, then, by feminist film history as a key figure in early twentieth-century cinema's articulation of a modern, fluid, heterogeneous and autonomous femininity. Balázs's acknowledged debt to her, however, goes further than this. *Visible Man* ends with a tribute to Nielsen, whom he places alongside Chaplin as early silent cinema's companion emblematic star. Each is presented as exemplifying in their performance and star persona what are, for Balázs, the specific aesthetic properties of the film medium. Their juxtaposition is revealing of the gendered vision on which his film theory rests. Reiterating his plea in the book's introduction that film be recognized as the quintessential modern art form, Balázs writes of Chaplin that his is a 'popular art in the best sense': a form of 'modern American folk poetry' whose stories redeem a 'reified, mechanized society' by recasting it within a 'poetry of ordinary life, the inarticulate life of ordinary things'.[41]

Chaplin's silent performances of the 'little guy' in the American city thus embody for Balázs a collective poetics: the mute visual poetry of everyday life in the modern urban mass. Nielsen's function is quite different. Richard Dyer has long since identified as a key feature of stardom its ambivalent fusion in a single personality of the ordinary and the extraordinary. Stars, according to Dyer, project an image that is 'special' and 'spectacular', but they are also known, through their screen roles as well as celebrity chatter, as emblems of the familiar everyday.[42] Balázs's *Visible Man* epilogue does not, however, reproduce the conjunction between the ordinary and the extraordinary that Dyer identifies within individual stars. Instead, it divides those qualities along gender lines, operating with a distinction that places Chaplin on the side of the ordinary – he is, as we have seen, a poet of 'ordinary life … ordinary things' – and Nielsen in the elevated realms of what Dyer calls the extraordinary, but which we might also term the modern sublime. Balázs's ecstatic prose certainly recalls Romantic adorations of the sublime when, for instance, he declaims:

> Just as we are tempted to despair that film can ever be capable of becoming a genuine form of art on its own, an art worthy of being represented by a tenth Muse on Mount Olympus; just as we are on the verge of accepting that film can never be more than a lame version of theatre … Asta Nielsen … restor[es] our faith and our conviction … [L]ower the flags in her honour, she is incomparable and without peer.[43]

The rhapsodic tone persists as Balázs moves on from this opening laudation to specify three features of Nielsen that locate her as the embodiment of an Olympian tenth muse. *Visible Man*, as is well known, presents silent cinema as the site of articulation of a new language of the body. Silent film in general, asserts Balázs, has rescued popular representation from the rationalist abstraction of a modern 'dematerialized, abstract and over-intellectualized' print culture; and screen performance in particular creates a 'language of gestures' that effects a bodily recovery from the alienation of the printed word.[44]

Nielsen's first claim to Olympian status derives thus from her command of this new 'gesturology': her performances are, for Balázs, 'stupefying' in their 'diversity', their 'wealth of mimed expressions' and their rooting in the vast 'thesaurus of gestures' on which she alone can draw.[45] Her second triumph resides in an 'erotic charisma' that makes manifest the film medium's status as the early twentieth century's emblematic secular art. As Dyer further reminds us, the prestige of the cinema star derives from historical processes of cultural modernization that have unseated ancient gods, replacing them with secular deities including the idols of the silver screen.[46] That what is involved therefore in film spectatorship is a secular version of a sacred quest is confirmed when Balázs notes of Nielsen's performances that they establish the erotic as 'film's very own theme, its essence'.[47] Here, then, the search for a blissful union with the godhead is replaced by erotic desires for the body of a desired other on screen.

But the 'mute understanding' that arises in this desired act of erotic union derives for Balázs, thirdly and finally, from a play of expressions that is exemplified not only by Nielsen's expressive body, but by her face. Studies of Balázs regularly return to the face, both as a key figure in his analyses of screen performance, and a founding metaphor in a Balázsian phenomenology attentive to the 'physiognomy of things'.[48] Equally familiar to film scholars is Balázs's celebration of the facial close-up as the 'poetry of the cinema': a 'mute pointing' that expresses within the duration of a single shot an 'entire view of life'.[49] That Nielsen's performance represents once again for Balázs the quintessence of this cinematic poetry is confirmed when he celebrates her ability to do 'what children do', which is to wear 'not only her own expression but, barely noticeably (although we always sense it), the expression of her interlocutor, which is reflected as in a mirror ... She carries the entire dialogue in her features and fuses it into a synthesis of understanding and experiencing'.[50]

Ekphrasis and Film Theory

Nielsen's screen image functions in *Visible Man*, then, as both visual foil and affective trigger for a gendered film-critical account that locates the female body on screen as the source of a quintessentially cinematic erotic power. Balázs's reflections are couched moreover not in the rationalist abstraction of, say, a new film grammar (though he would attempt just such a project in his later *Spirit of Film*) but in an ekphrastic poetics that both acknowledges and disavows the feminine autonomy for which Nielsen's image stands.

Ekphrasis – a term deriving from classical rhetoric, and defined as an 'elaborate digressive disruption [in] rhetorical discourse' – has recently attracted the attention of literary scholars seeking critical concepts adequate to the literary arts in an image-saturated modern age.[51] Stephen Cheeke, for instance, suggests that the contemporary 'immersion of poets in the "image world"' has produced a 'corresponding struggle to render or control the image verbally': a struggle he explores in an illuminating study of ekphrastic poetry from the Renaissance to the present day.[52] But Cheeke's final chapter, an essay on 'prose ekphrasis', suggests that the term – which, for him, has purchase on art history and criticism from Winckelmann, Goethe and Lessing, to Walter Benjamin – may also help to illuminate the relation between the moving image and its re-rendering in the effusive critical prose of Balázs.

Balázs's *Visible Man* was written well in advance of any fully institutionalized film theory or criticism. Drawing substantially on reviews
for the Vienna daily *Der Tag* – the first Austrian newspaper to employ,
in the person of Balázs, a fully fledged film critic – the text (the first
full-length German-language work of film theory) shares with cognate
works in other national contexts – Jean Epstein's *Bonjour, cinema* (1921),
or Ricciotto Canudo's *The Birth of the Sixth Art* (1911) – an experimental
prose style that owes more to contemporary modernisms, than to the
realist epistemology of, say, linguistic or semiotic modes of film interpretation and critique. Although Balázs cites comparative linguistics
as a possible model for a 'gesturology' of screen performance, his own
writing will only begin to emulate that discipline's realist idiom in the
formal grammar that he attempts in his 1930 *Spirit of Film*.[53] *Visible Man*,
by contrast, is notable among other features for stylistic borrowings
from expressionism, including second-person address (the 'May we
come in?' of the prologue), and a mood or voice that is typically declarative, exclamatory, interrogative or even imperative, as in the 'I have to
tell you … you must' of his opening demand to aestheticians that film
be accorded 'a chapter … in the great aesthetic systems'.[54]

In his influential theorization of the relation between film criticism
or theory and the screen image, Christian Metz notes 'the broadly pro-
jective character of the relation the cinema writer often maintains to his
[*sic*] object'. Recognizing the generative function of film criticism – its
productive capacity in relation to cinematic meaning and affect – Metz
famously dubs film writing 'the cinema's third machine': an engine of
textual production, then, that is fuelled by the desire of the critic to
maintain a 'good object relation' with the medium of film.[55]

In Metz's Lacanian account, the cinema figures as a 'technique of the
imaginary … the definitive imprint of a stage before the Oedipus complex
[and of] the exclusive relation to the mother'.[56] What he calls cinematic
writing is based therefore in an initial move on 'idealization': the critic
falls in love with the film, and produces writing that, in its crudest forms,
subsists in discourse only as fantasy, 'an uninterpreted dream'.[57] However,
the move into film theory proper, he continues, demands an Oedipal dis-
tancing and separation from this maternal imaginary; thus the film writer
must follow the Law of the Father by 'break[ing] the beneficial image', and
striving after that 'necessarily sadistic' distance from its object which is
the prerequisite for a fully elaborated theory of the film.[58]

Although Metz never advocates a cinema writing that abjures the
critic's early love of cinema and film (we must, he writes, not lose
sight of the cinephile, even while we strive 'no longer [to] be invaded

by him'[59]) he certainly repudiates those forms of early cinema theory that maintain film 'in the imaginary enclosure of a pure love'.[60] His rebuke surely extends to Balázs, whose stylistic excess in his early writings is evocative as much of their author's cinematic passions (viz. his comments on Nielsen's eroticism), as of any objectified reality of the moving image in film. But work by Cheeke and others on ekphrasis suggests a possible recasting of Metz. Ekphrastic poetry or prose, as Cheeke points out, certainly recognizes that same otherness of the pictorial object which, for Metz, fuels film-critical desire. But it strives to overcome this through a poetic emulation that is in psychic terms more akin to mimesis – a mode of embodied identification that blurs self–other distinctions – than to the objectifying symbolizations of Metz's account.[61] Ekphrasis, to put this another way, borrows from its visual object those aesthetic features that are also the signal characteristics of poetry, adopting a tone, rhythm, imagery and lyrical voice that performs an imaginary mirroring of the moving image on film.

One instance from Balázs is his account of associational montage, whose rhythmic qualities he mimics when he describes it as flowing 'smoothly and in a broad stream, like the hexameter in a classical epic, or else like a ballad, flaring up breathlessly and then … rising inexorably towards a climax, or tingling capriciously'.[62] This is just one of numerous examples of ekphrasis in Balázs that reproduce the poetic textures of their critical object – here, associational montage, elsewhere, camera and the close-up, screen performance, colour, or sound. This film-critical mimesis differs in important ways from the 'third machine' of Metz's account. Mimesis is distinguished in psychic terms from object relations in the Lacanian symbolic by the reciprocity of the relationship it establishes between self and other – or in the present context, between critic and image on screen. Ekphrasis as a rhetorical practice is mimetic, therefore, not just by virtue of its stylistic impersonation of the image. As W.J.T. Mitchell observes, the sensuous dance that ekphrasis performs with its object also suggests an understanding of the image as 'a thing that is always already addressing us … a subject with a life that has to be seen as "its own" in order for our descriptions to engage the picture's life as well as our own lives as beholders'.[63]

Mitchell's account is persuasive in the case of Balázs, whose phenomenological understanding of film as a material embodiment of modern experience leads him indeed to recognize the medium as 'a subject with a life'; hence, for instance, his exaltation of fluid montage as film's 'living breath', or of the moving image as a vital expression of the 'physiognomy of things'.[64] Balázs's condemnation of those forms of

Soviet montage that, for him, reduce film art to 'ideograms' is further evidence of a film aesthetic that privileges embodiment over intellect, and favours films therefore that, by their own agency, '*give shape* to and *provoke* thoughts'.[65] That the 'thoughts' arising in film theory should be similarly generated by an intersubjective sensual relation between screen image, audience and critic is made plain when Balázs insists to his readers that the 'greater enjoyment' his writing will bring derives not from its pedagogical function ('the cinema, thank God', he writes, 'is no educational establishment!') but from its capacity to 'stimulate your senses and nerves'.[66]

Balázs here gives expression to the Marxist Utopia of a film medium whose embodied qualities – not just its images of the human body, but the aesthetic intensities of filmic rhythm, movement, tempo, spatial transformation and temporal flow – might contribute to an overcoming of an alienated capitalist culture of the printed word. Reading Balázs through his commentary on Asta Nielsen allows us to see how that Utopia rests, in part at least, on an embrace in Balázs's own writing of precisely that feminized imaginary whose repudiation, for Metz, is the prerequisite for a theory of film. Balázs's *Visible Man*, to put this another way, can be understood as an ekphrastic mimesis in which feminine performance becomes generative of an aesthetic theory of film.

And yet, a film-critical practice deriving in the first instance from sensuous engagement produces, ultimately, its own ambivalence. If one feature of ekphrasis is its attempted reproduction in poetry of the sensual qualities of the image, then a second is its function in defending the writer against the image's overwhelming power. We might cite here Cheeke's final contention that, since word and image are ultimately incommensurable, writing for art both 'exists under the knowledge of failure', and involves therefore 'a struggle to … control the image verbally'.[67] But revealingly, it is Balázs who most eloquently evokes this drive to mastery. 'Creating meaning' through film theory, is, he avers, 'our way of defending ourselves against chaos. If an elemental force becomes so powerful that we can neither withstand it nor change it, then we make haste to discover a meaning in it lest we be engulfed by it. Theoretical knowledge is the cork that keeps us afloat'.[68]

Nielsen and Lesznai: Talking Back

Balázs's plea for film theory as a defence against 'engulfing' returns us finally to his early panegyric to Asta Nielsen. If little of the history of

Nielsen as an independent producer and distributor figures in Balázs, then this results, it seems, not only from his general disinterest, in his film theory at least, in the institutions and industrial structures of early film. There is enough in Nielsen's screen performance that might have triggered the same reflection on the intellectual, economic or socio-political motivation driving her art that he accords, for instance, to Eisenstein, his sparring partner in debates on montage, or to avant-garde contemporaries, including Hans Richter and Viking Eggeling, whom he similarly engages in his film writing as intellectual peers, even while berating them for what he considers the empty formalism of the absolute film.

In the absence of a similarly judicious engagement with Nielsen, Balázs's lavish *Visible Man* tribute invites a reading as an instance of fet-ishistic disavowal, a hypostasis that confines her image to the realm of erotic myth, obscuring her (powerful) agency in the industrial produc-tion and dissemination of her star image. For the history of film theory that this present volume attempts, the implications of this historical bracketing out are significant. If we content ourselves with Balázs's reading of Nielsen as a 'spiritual' figure who 'restor[es] our faith and our conviction' in the power of film art, then we risk perpetuating a gender division that places masculinity on the side of film-historical agency – including in the early production of film theory – and femininity on the side of ahistorical myth.[69]

An understanding of the workings of ekphrasis can once again help us here. If ekphrasis mimics the aesthetic qualities of its object, then it does so in part through its re-rendering of that object's organization of space and time. We have seen this process at work in my brief examples above of Balázs's rhythmic prose. Rhythm is deployed in *Visible Man* as a mode of film-theoretical poiesis: a poetic bringing forth or (re)making of the film image that eschews linear argument, emphasizing instead its own sensuous presence in fractured space and non-linear time. Hence the aphoristic and spatially disjunctive structuring of *Visible Man*, a text whose meaning often accrues through metaphor and associative montage, and knowledge is produced not in the linear time of reason, but in the simultaneous temporality of poetic illumination and affect.

Conceiving Balázs's writing as a poetic mimesis of a specifically cin-ematic orchestration of space and time may help us, finally, to rescue Nielsen, alongside other female stars, from the frozen temporality of a male fantasy of eroticism on screen. Indeed Balázs himself begins that work of recuperation when he takes up, first in *Visible Man*, later in *The Spirit of Film*, the issue of female performance and film time.

Let us, then, enlist for one last time the services of Anna Lesznai for a re-reading of Balázs – specifically, of his writing on the female body and cinematic time.

Writing on the close-up, Balázs observes the capacity of virtuoso performers such as Nielsen and Lilian Gish to break the teleology of narrative progression, evoking instead, through the myriad shifts in facial expression that pass across their faces in close-up, a multiplicitous time in which 'past and future expressions merge into one another and display not just the individual states of the soul but also the mysterious process of development itself'. The point is driven home when Balázs moves on to liken to a musical arrangement a performance by Pola Negri in Ernst Lubitsch's CARMEN (1918). In a flirtation with her lover José, Negri's face, Balázs suggests, displays at one and the same time 'joy and submissiveness', 'superiority' and melancholy, the pleasure of an erotic encounter, and the sadistic enjoyment of her dominant role. Those complex emotions, he continues, become visible all at once through Negri's 'polyphonic' organization of multiple facial expressions; thus her face displays 'the most varied emotions *simultaneously*, like a chord, and the relationships between these different emotions is what creates the rich amalgam of harmonies and modulations'.[70]

Although Balázs's tendency elsewhere in his early film theory is to locate in aspects of the cinematic apparatus – most notably, in the close-up and montage – the source of a specifically cinematic temporality, he recognizes in this and other passages on female performance that the female body too, in its interaction with the camera, can become the site of production of a uniquely cinematic, simultaneous and multiplicitous time. It is here, moreover, that his film theory intersects in a final sense with the history of the early twentieth-century New Woman. Rita Felski suggests that the New Woman, as cultural icon, functioned symbolically as a point of intersection between the conflicting temporalities of a contested modernity. Located within teleological narratives of social emancipation, as a 'symbol of modernity at the forefront of social change', the New Woman in her manifestation as iconic image occupied the more ambiguous time of social fantasy.[71] Fatefully, she might embody in fantasy the archaic temporality of the female archetype: the New Woman as sexual threat, for instance, as in G.W. Pabst's PANDORA'S BOX (1929), or the robot Maria in Fritz Lang's METROPOLIS (1927). But as Balázs also reminds us, she might alternatively occupy a poetic and heterotopic time of infinite possibility, a time that escapes teleology and inhabits instead a perpetual present of multiplicitous visual rhythms and 'polyphonic' emotional states.

Certainly, this is a temporal experience evoked by Nielsen, who characteristically used the long takes of early cinema to compress narrative time – volumes of narrative business are often expedited in a single shot – while at the same time evoking a heterogeneous poetic time in performances that exploit to the full the expressive possibilities of visual rhythm and pace, gestural repetition and counterpoint, or stylistic shifts from fluidity, through stasis, to resurgent flow. In AFGRUNDEN (The Abyss), the film that launched Nielsen to stardom in 1913, the story of the fall from grace of a bourgeois piano teacher is acted out by Nielsen through a progressive dynamization of her body that culminates in a famously sexually explicit exotic dance with her circus-artiste lover. Elsewhere, Nielsen uses her capacity for a multiplication of meanings in a single shot to comment knowingly on her own status as star. THE FILM PRIMADONNA (1913) features Nielsen in the role of the film actress Ruth Breton, an international star who makes her own choice of script, negotiates with producers and directors over casting and crew, reviews the rushes with the director, and demands changes when the day's footage fails to please. In an early passage, we see her bamboozling her producer into accepting her lover, Walter, as scriptwriter and actor on her current film. The sequence is notable for its display of what Balázs calls 'polyphony': hence, for instance, Nielsen's adroit manipulation of three forms of textual address: two intra-diegetic – she sustains a conversation with the producer, even while signalling the next move to her lover through surreptitious nudges and winks – alongside an extra-diegetic interaction initiated through frontal performance, and prompting a delicious complicity with the audience in her deception of her boss. Meanwhile, her characteristically nuanced stage business – a quick smoothing of her skirt, a preening of her hands, adjusting her shoulder strap, standing, perching, sitting, standing again – establishes a rhythm that undermines the stasis of the long take, and locates Nielsen as the embodiment of that fluid temporality which Balázs associates with the female body on film.

The contemporary of Balázs who most explicitly recognized the potentially emancipatory sexual politics of this simultaneous and multiplicitous time was Anna Lesznai. Lesznai's autobiography contains references Balázs's many visits to her garden, and to conversations there and elsewhere on temporality in his modernist fairy tales. But it is Lesznai's own tales, not Balázs's, that reveal her understanding of the gender trouble that is potentially fomented by simultaneous time. Her autobiography presents the fairy tale as the original form of an epic tradition that draws on feminine experience to play imaginatively with narrative time.[72] Her stories, similarly, depict female protagonists who are removed from narrative teleology, for instance by thwarted happy ends, and made to occupy instead the suspended time of enchanted spaces, mythic forests or exotic lands. In a 1918 article on the psychology of the fairy tale, Lesznai, moreover, prefigures Balázs's observations on simultaneous time in film with similar comments on the 'contiguous' nature of events in the fairy tale. Basing her remarks on the fairy tale's disruption of linear time schemes through events that erupt into a continuous present – the vision of past times in enchanted mirrors, the resurgence of past voices in present time – Lesznai notes that the fairy tale's 'transcendence of the boundaries of the ego' is linked to the fact that 'things exist in the fairy tale contiguously, on a single level'.[73]

There is a clear similarity between this passage and Balázs's comments on the simultaneous time of the close-up. But note also Lesznai's insistence here on the subjective transformation – a 'transcendence of the boundaries of the ego' – that is made possible by an imaginative move into fairy-tale time. As for Balázs, it seems, Lesznai's ultimate interest in popular cultural form – for her, the fairy tale, for Balázs, the film – is its transformation of (to return to my opening quote from Balázs) 'the subject, the human subject in his social being'.

That this transformation was to be effected not least through a re-imagining of the New Woman is evident in Lesznai, not only from her writings on the utopian possibilities of fairy-tale time, or even the wicked lampooning of gender conventions that is a feature of her fairy tales. It is visible also in the life she herself lived as an engaged intellectual who moved within, and helped to shape, the intellectual and artistic movements: first, of the pre-First World War Budapest avant-garde; later, of the short-lived Hungarian Socialist Commune; and later still, of exile communities in Vienna and her ultimate exile destination, New York. Repositioning, in a closer relation to Lesznai, Balázs's writings on cinematic time, the body and the close-up, allows us then to understand not only the significance of gender for his conceptualization of the modernist temporalities of the moving image. It also allows us to consider the conditions of emergence of Balázs's early film writing. His was, I have argued, a body of work in which the New Woman played a part both as mythic figure or muse, and crucially, as a historical agent in forms of intellectual and artistic production, including Lesznai's fairy tales and theoretical writing; Asta Nielsen's acting, as well as her entrepreneurial activities; and Edith Hajós's translations of the text to which anglophone readers owe their first acquaintance with Balázs, his *Theory of the Film*.

Acknowledgements

Thanks to Annemone Ligensa and Izabella Füzi for helpful comments on early drafts.

Notes

1. The Reith Lectures are the BBC's annual public lecture series, staged to contribute to public debate on significant issues of contemporary interest.
2. Béla Balázs. 1953. *Theory of the Film: Character and Growth of a New Art*, trans. Edith Bone, London: Dobson.
3. Tom Buchanan. 2007. *The Impact of the Spanish Civil War on Britain: War, Loss And Memory*, Eastbourne: Sussex Academy Press, 218.
4. See, for instance, Alexei Tolstoy. 1935. *Darkness and Dawn*, trans. Edith Bone and Emile Burns, London: Victor Gollancz; Wanda Wasilewska. 1945. *Just Love*, trans. Edith Bone, London: Hutchinson International Authors Ltd; Maksim Gorky. 1946. *Literature and Life: A selection from the Writings of Maxim Gorki*, intr. V.V. Mikhailovski, trans. Edith Bone, London and New York: Hutchinson International Authors Ltd; Balázs, *Theory of the Film*.
5. Hajós was briefly married to Gerald Martin following her move to the U.K. in 1933/34. She wrote to Balázs as 'Edith Martin' on 30 September 1945: see MTA Ms 5021/286: P. Although Hajós's autobiography does not mention her attendance at Balázs's funeral – she was already visiting Budapest to arrange details of a new translation, and to write on Hungary for the *Daily Worker* – her presence is attested by film footage of her alongside Anna Hamvassy at Balázs's graveside; see Claudia Lenssen and Réka Gyulás (dir.), *Béla Balázs – der sichtbare Mensch – L'homme visible. 1884–1949*. ZDF 1999. See also Edith Bone. 1957. *Seven Years Solitary*, London: H. Hamilton, 36–58.
6. Pathe News. 19 November 1956. Retrieved 16 October 2012 from http://backup.britishpathe.com/record.php?id=32456
7. A ministerial decree of December 1895 had opened university medical and arts faculties for the first time to women; see Judith Szapor. 2004. 'Sisters or Foes: The Shifting Front Lines of the Hungarian Women's Movements, 1896–1918', in Sylvia Palatschek and Bianka Pietrow-Ennker (eds), *Women's Emancipation Movements in the Nineteenth Century: A European Perspective*, Stanford, CA: Stanford University Press, 194. Hajós entered the medical faculty at Budapest University in 1908 at the age of 19, but found conditions at the medical school 'intolerable', and moved first to Berlin, later to France, and later still to Switzerland. When war broke out in 1914, she returned to Budapest, where she worked in a military hospital while studying for her final examinations. See Bone, *Seven Years Solitary*, 9–13.
8. Rita Felski. 1995. *The Gender of Modernity*, Cambridge, MA: Harvard University Press, 14.
9. Comparative studies of the *fin de siècle* New Woman as a precursor to the 'modern girl' of the interwar period are briefly offered in The Modern Girl Around the World Research Group, A.E. Weinbaum. 2008. *The Modern Girl around the World: Consumption, Modernity and Globalization*, Durham, NC and London: Duke University Press. See especially ch. 4, Mary Louise Roberts, 'Making the Modern Girl French: From New Woman to *Éclaireuse*'.

10. Felski, *The Gender of Modernity*, 3.
11. See, for instance, Izabella Füzi. 2009. 'Arc, hang, tekintet: szemiotikai, esztétikai és politikai összefüggések Balázs Béla filmesztétikájában' (Face, sound, gaze: semiotic, aesthetic and political relations of Béla Balázs' film aesthetics), *apertúra. Film-Vizualitás-Elmélet*. Retrieved 21 October 2012 from http://apertura.hu/2009/osz/fuzi
12. New editions of Balázs's German-language original texts, Béla Balázs. 1924. *Der sichtbare Mensch oder die Kultur des Films*, Vienna and Leipzig: Deutsch-Österreichischer Verlag; and Béla Balázs. 1930. *Der Geist des Films*, Halle: W. Knapp appeared with Suhrkamp Verlag in 2001, with editorial afterwords by Helmut Diederichs and Hanno Loewy respectively: Béla Balázs. 2001. *Der sichtbare Mensch oder die Kultur des Films*, Frankfurt/Main: Suhrkamp; and Béla Balázs. 2001. *Der Geist des Films*, Frankfurt/Main: Suhrkamp. Translations have included Leonardo Quaresima. 2008. *L'uomo visibile*, Turin: Lindau; Claude Maillart. 2010. *L'homme Visible et l'Esprit du Cinéma*, Belval: Circé; and Béla Balázs. 2010. *Béla Balázs: Early Film Theory. Visible Man and The Spirit of Film*, ed. Erica Carter, trans. Rodney Livingstone, Oxford: Berghahn Books.
13. Key cultural and intellectual histories are Sabine Hake's chapter on Balázs in Sabine Hake. 1993. *The Cinema's Third Machine: Writing on Film in Germany 1907–1933*, Lincoln: University of Nebraska Press; Hanno Loewy. 2003. *Béla Balázs. Märchen, Ritual, Film*, Berlin: Vorwerk 8. Franceso Casetti discusses Balázs's significance for discussions of medium specificity and cinematic perception in Francesco Casetti. 2008. *Eye of the Century: Film, Experience, Modernity*, New York: Columbia University Press. See also Mattias Frey, 'Cultural Problems of Classical Film Theory: Béla Balázs, "Universal Language" and the Birth of National Cinema', *Screen* 51(4), 324–40.
14. Joseph Zsuffa's biography of Balázs is a treasure trove for researchers, but is also part of the critical edifice that constructs him as a genius figure (Joseph Zsuffa. 1987. *Béla Balázs, the Man and the Artist*, Berkeley: University of California Press); see also Tibor Frank. 2007. 'The Social Construction of Hungarian Genius (1867–1930)', Von Neumann Memorial Lecture, Princeton.
15. Béla Balázs. 2001. *Die Jugend eines Träumers. Autobiografischer Roman*, Berlin: Das Arsenal.
16. Balázs's correspondence with his Russian translator Nadja Fridland following his move to the Soviet Union in 1932 offers one unusually detailed example of what Fridland terms the 'bitterness' left behind by his erratic shifts from ecstatic friendship, to verbal or other abuse: MTA Ms 5021/211–19, 1937–1939. As for Balázs's sexual liaisons, these will, as Jack Zipes has observed, 'never be wholly unravelled', though they do find allegorical representation in artistic works – Zipes examples are fairy tales including Balázs's Bluebeard libretto for Bartók – that depict 'love as rapture and ecstasy' and the 'constant motif' of women associated with 'orgiastic death'. Jack Zipes. 2010. 'Béla Balázs, the Homeless Wanderer, or, The Man who Sought to Become One with the World', in Béla Balázs, *The Cloak of Dreams: Chinese Fairy Tales*, trans. and intr. Jack Zipes, Princeton, CA: Princeton University Press, 15.
17. Hanno Loewy discusses Balázs's relationship with Lesznai at length, situating it among other contexts in the Sunday Circle, of which Lesznai was a founder member. The complementary but subordinate role in the Circle allotted by Balázs to women, including Lesznai, is starkly evidenced by a diary entry of 28 December 1915: 'Woman is stupid … her original instinct is, in contrast to the rootless intellect of men, stubborn and limited, generating nothing but trouble'. Béla Balázs. 1982.

Napló 1914–1922, Budapest: Magvető, 102. Quoted in Loewy, *Béla Balázs. Märchen, Ritual, Film*, 228.

18. Ibid., 84–100.
19. I am grateful to Izabella Füzi for pointing me in this context towards Balázs's undated lecture on women in politics, dating probably from the mid-1940s, which addressed women's political maturity (*érettség*) in the aftermath of the Second World War: 'Előadás', MTA MS 5014/34.
20. Béla Balázs. 1922. *Der Mantel der Träume*, Munich: Verlagsanstalt D. & R. Bischoff, available in English translation in Balázs, *The Cloak of Dreams: Chinese Fairy Tales*.
21. Balázs, *Early Film Theory*.
22. Andor Kraszna-Krausz. 1926. 'Béla Balázs: Der sichtbare Mensch. Eine Filmdramaturgie', *Filmtechnik* 21, 16; reprinted in Béla Balázs. 2001. *Der sichtbare Mensch*, Helmut Diederichs (ed.), Frankfurt/Main: Suhrkamp, 169.
23. Although he had written extensively on his reservations about sound film well before the publication of this volume, Arnheim's best-known work on the subject is Rudolf Arnheim. 2008. *Film als Kunst*, Frankfurt/Main: Suhrkamp.
24. I derive this insight into the intellectually and philosophically formative nature of Balázs's early years in Budapest from Hanno Loewy's magisterial intellectual biography *Béla Balázs. Märchen, Ritual, Film*.
25. Balázs, *Early Film Theory*, 96. The original German term in this quote is '*Mensch*', but here as elsewhere in the translation on which I collaborated with Rodney Livingstone, the generic 'man' is used in English to signal the assumption of a masculine norm that underpins Balázs's writings on the cinematic subject.
26. Katalin Fábián. 2007. 'Making an Appearance: The Formation of Women's Groups in Hungary', *Aspasia* 1, 110–13.
27. Szapor, 'Sisters or Foes', 194.
28. Fábián, 'Making an Appearance', 111.
29. Szapor, 'Sisters or Foes', 102.
30. Ibid., 200.
31. Lesznai's fairy tales are collected in German in Anna Lesznai. 2008. *Wahre Märchen aus den Garten Eden*, ed. György Fehéri, trans. András Hecker and Ilka Russy, Berlin: Das Arsenal.
32. Given Karl Mannheim's early association with Balázs in the Sunday Circle, it seems appropriate to use his term for a 'free-floating' intelligentsia here. Elaborated most famously in Mannheim's *Ideologie und Utopie* (Frankfurt am Main, 1985, orig. 1929), the term can arguably be seen as rooted in the experience of a pluralist Hungarian political culture in which, until the defeat the Commune, intellectuals could express a leftist (or other) political engagement without formally linking themselves to party politics.
33. Franziska de Haan, Krasimira Daskalova and Anna Loutfi (eds). 2006. *Biographical Dictionary of Women's Movements and Feminisms in Central, Eastern, and South Eastern Europe*, Budapest: CEU Press, 487, 163.
34. Szapor, 'Sisters or Foes', 190, 199.
35. Fábián, 'Making an Appearance', 111.
36. Ibid. See also de Haan, Daskalova and Loutfi, *Biographical Dictionary*, 483–87.
37. Balázs, 'Visible Man' in *Early Film Theory*, 4–5.
38. Szapor's examples are the Association of Women Clerks, and the Mária-Dorothea Schoolteachers' Association (Mária-Dorothea Egyesület), both founded in 1897; Szapor, 'Sisters or Foes', 194.

39. Martin Loiperdinger. 2012. 'Afgrunden in Germany: Monopolfilm, Cinemagoing and the Emergence of the Female Star Asta Nielsen, 1910–11', in Daniel Biltereyst, Richard Maltby and Philippe Meers (eds), *Cinema, Audiences and Modernity: New Perspectives on European Cinema History*, London and New York: Routledge, 142–53.

40. Ibid. See also Emilie Altenloh. 1914. *Zur Soziologie des Kino. Die Kino-Unternehmung und die sozialen Schichten ihrer Besucher*, Jena: Diederichs (extract translated as 'A Sociology of the Cinema and its Audience', *Screen* 42(3) (2001), 249–93; Heide Schlüpmann. 2010. *The Uncanny Gaze: The Drama of Early German Cinema*, transl. Inga Pollmann, Urbana and Chicago: University of Illinois Press, 110ff; Andrea Haller. 2012. 'Diagnosis: "Flimmeritis". Female Cinemagoing in Imperial Germany, 1911–18', in Biltereyst, Maltby and Meers, *Cinema, Audiences and Modernity*, 130–41; Annemone Ligensa. 2013. 'Asta Nielsen in Germany – A Reception-oriented Approach', in Martin Loiperdinger and Uli Jung (eds), *Importing Asta Nielsen: The International Film Star in the Making (1910–1914). KINtop. Studies in Early Cinema* 2, New Barnet: John Libbey, 342–52.

41. Balázs, 'Visible Man' in *Early Film Theory*, 85–86.

42. Richard Dyer. 1998. *Stars*, 2nd revised edn, London: BFI Publishing, 35.

43. Balázs, 'Visible Man' in *Early Film Theory*, 87–88.

44. Ibid., 11.

45. Ibid., 87.

46. Dyer, *Stars*.

47. Balázs, 'Visible Man' in *Early Film Theory*, 87.

48. Ibid., 46. See also Gertrud Koch. 1987. 'Béla Balázs: The Physiognomy of Things', *New German Critique* 40, Special Issue on Weimar Film Theory, 167–77.

49. Balázs, 'Visible Man' in *Early Film Theory*, 41 and 39.

50. Ibid., 88.

51. Stephen Cheeke. 2008. *Writing for Art: The Aesthetics of Ekphrasis*, Manchester and New York: Manchester University Press, 19.

52. Ibid., 2.

53. Even here, Balázs wavers between poetic and realist approaches to film: viz. his introductory comment that, 'I wish now to outline a kind of grammar of this language. A stylistics and a poetics, perhaps'. Balázs, 'The Spirit of Film', in *Early Film Theory*, 97.

54. Balázs, 'Visible Man', in *Early Film Theory*, 3.

55. Christian Metz. 1986. *The Imaginary Signifier: Psychoanalysis and the Cinema*, trans. Celia Britton and Annwyl Williams, Bloomington: Indiana University Press, 4–5. Sabine Hake historicizes Metz's psychoanalytic account in her *The Cinema's Third Machine*.

56. Ibid., 4.

57. Ibid., 14.

58. Ibid., 3 and 80.

59. Ibid., 15.

60. Ibid., 13.

61. On mimesis, see Jan Campbell. 2005. *Film and Cinema Spectatorship: Melodrama and Mimesis*, Cambridge: Polity, 54–55.

62. Balázs, 'Visible Man' in *Early Film Theory*, 67. Rodney Livingstone's translation is exemplary here in its nuanced attention to the rhythmic qualities of the German original.

63. W.J.T. Mitchell. 2005. *What do Pictures Want? The Lives and Loves of Images,* Chicago: University of Chicago Press, 49; cited in Cheeke, *Writing for Art,* 14.

64. Balázs, 'Visible Man' in *Early Film Theory,* 67 and 46.

65. Ibid., 128.

66. Ibid., 7.

67. Cheeke, *Writing for Art,* 2.

68. Balázs, 'The Spirit of Film' in *Early Film Theory,* 97.

69. Balázs, 'Visible Man' in *Early Film Theory,* 87.

70. Ibid., 34.

71. Felski, *The Gender of Modernity,* 158.

72. Hanno Loewy makes this point in his reading of a passage in which Lesznai claims the first epic poet to have been a woman who comforts her war-wounded lover by spinning tales of the heroic exploits that may have brought him to his wounded state. For Lesznai, the scene of that idyllic moment of epic creation is a garden in which 'the past does not dissipate. I know I only have to open a door …'. This presentation of the garden as a utopian site that opens doors to multiple temporalities is a recurrent trope in Lesznai's writing. It is also, for Loewy, an example of the spatialization of time that is a feature both of the fairy tale, and, in Balázs's later film theory, of the close-up: Loewy, *Märchen, Ritual, Film,* 134. See also, Anna Lesznai. 1965. *Spätherbst in Eden,* Karlsruhe: Stahlberg; and Fiona Stewart. 2011. *In the Beginning was the Garden: Anna Lesznai and Hungarian Modernism 1906–1919,* Ph.D. Dissertation, York University. Retrieved 16 October 2012 from http://udini.proquest.com/view/in-the-beginning-was-the-garden-pqid:2409600781/

73. A. Lesznai. 1918. 'Babonásészrevételek a meseés a tragédialélektanához' (Superstitious remarks on the psychology of the fairy tale and of tragedy), *Nyugat* 13. Retrieved 16 October 2012 from http://epa.oszk.hu/00000/00022/nyugat.htm

Chapter 3

ENCOUNTERS IN DARKENED ROOMS

Alternative Programming of the Dutch Filmliga, 1927–31

Tom Gunning

Encounters in Darkened Rooms

At the end of the 1920s, in a number of countries, diverse energies seem to coalesce in a novel and polemic task: the definition
of film as an art form. The most obvious forms this definition
takes are theory (a number of essays and books, the first classics
of what we would now call 'film theory') and practice (a body of
films produced in the late silent cinema by an international avant-
garde that provided models for a radical form of filmmaking – the
work of Sergei Eisenstein, Dziga Vertov, Jean Epstein, Hans Richter,
Germaine Dulac, Walter Ruttmann, Joris Ivens and others). But if
these works of theorists and filmmakers (often the same figures:
Eisenstein, Vertov, Epstein, and Dulac produced important works in
both categories) have provided the written and filmic texts that
now define for us the canon of late silent cinema, as historians our
understanding of this period remains incomplete if it restricts itself
to textual analysis. A host of other practices, harder to embody
in texts and by nature more elusive, mediated between films and
writings and a public: institutions and programmes of screenings,
systems of distribution, publication and discussion. The ciné-club or
film society movement of the late 1920s served as seedbed for late
silent film culture, providing contexts not only in which films were
shown, but in which they were digested, picked apart and argued

over, and from which new ideals of spectatorship and film criticism were developed. Beyond its immediate, rather narrow scope of a handful of devoted members, the network of international film societies offered the first widely circulated definitions of film art, the first canon of masterpieces and the terms of initial debates on film culture.

When we look back to the Filmliga, a Dutch film society active from 1927 to 1933, particularly from the viewpoint of the New Film History, we find not simply a bedrock of foundation but a welter of contentions, debates and discussions triggered by the screening of a series of film programmes. To re-encounter and re-imagine the nature of that energy we must focus not only on the images of light projected on the screen, and the statements printed in the journal *Filmliga*, but on the experience of viewers gathered in the darkness decades ago.

An emphasis on film audiences, on what we could call the reverse angle of film studies – those watching the screen rather than what is on it, the viewers rather than the viewed – has become a key issue in the New Film History, but also a vexed one. How can one ever attempt to recreate, or even describe, the way films were received? By its very nature such experience does not embody itself in easily analysed texts. But this problem involves more than a contingent lack of documents. The audience is not only the reverse angle of film history, but also its vanishing point. In fact, the search for an audience's experience uncovers one of the basic aporias of film history: no experience can be analysed unless it has in some way left its trace. Whether examining today's film viewers or historical audiences from the past, we cannot assume an objectified 'experience' somehow lurking fully immanent in the consciousness of viewers, which a historian can reconstruct or a contemporary researcher simply extract. Seeking such private mental entities involves us in a miasma of speculation at best, and an outright falsification at worst. We do not seek the private 'black box' of an interior personal experience in our attempt to write a history of film viewing. We are, rather, seeking the traces of film viewing as a social practice, one shared and communicated among audience members, even if not recorded in official reviews or criticism.

Of course, an investigation of the audience's experiences and reception of films can never ignore more traditional textual analysis of films and of written statements (manifestos, criticism, etc.). The films themselves must be probed, not as individual works of brilliant auteurs, but as components of specific programmes and as part of a broad class of films by which Filmliga defined film art. Getting at what the *range* of films offered the membership of Filmliga, rather than analysing individual masterpieces, must be our approach. Analysis of the films as a corpus, and of the way they were presented, will raise questions about the discussions these films prompted and the way viewers processed them. The history of film exhibition, in any country or period, demands a reconstruction of film-going as social practice, and of the audience as a space of social interaction – not an accumulation of isolated ideal spectators. The architecture of film theatres (exteriors, lobbies and auditoriums), the protocols of film viewing, the nature of film programmes, the presentation of music, lectures or other performative events, as well as the treatment of the screen itself, all provide evidence that allows us to reconstruct the social experience of film viewing. All of these elements interact, of course, with the images projected on the screen, rather than super-sede them. In fact, such elements serve as mediators between images and viewers, shapers of reception.

These elements of film exhibition are important in all periods of film history, although their nature varies greatly. In the Filmliga, for instance, the decorative functions of the theatre would seem to be minimized in contrast to the contemporary commercial cinema from which it wished to dissociate itself (e.g. the elaborate decorations of the picture palaces exemplified by the Tuschinski in Amsterdam, in contrast to the rather plain interiors of both the Centraal Theater and later the Uitkijk, where the Filmliga held their screenings), while other aspects of presentation (such as programming order) take on a primary importance. Further, the journal *Filmliga* not only recorded many of the discussions about the programmes but cued its members to the importance of discussion and reflection in their viewing experience. The whole set up of the Filmliga informed its audience that these screenings were not ephemeral viewings serving to pass time; they were important and unique events, scheduled once a month like a cultural event, in contrast to the consumer-friendly continual showings of commercial theatres. Likewise, the audiences' identity as dues-paying, enrolled members in an organization with a manifesto and a purpose contrasted sharply with the contingent and aleatory crowd one could find in commercial theatres. A greater sense of uniformity and, most importantly, a purposeful and serious attitude towards the films therefore characterized a Liga audience. No one there was simply dropping in. This film-going was a cultural event, similar to traditional theatre or to concert-going, and attendance indicated an audi-ence member's identification with the Filmliga project. But what was that project?

Defining Film: The Logic of Theory versus the Mess of History

In his philosophical examination of film theory, philosopher and film scholar Noël Carroll has defined what he calls the 'aesthetics of silent film', typified for him by the work of Rudolf Arnheim. For Carroll the aesthetics of silent film undertook the challenge of defining film as a unique art form and tried to distinguish it from related art forms, such as photography or theatre. Carroll understands that this task was undertaken by practice as well as theory: 'Silent film theory, then, can be seen as a reflection and a codification of the principles underlying the ambitious and aspiring society of filmmakers who were seeking to turn their medium into an art on the terms set by the culture and the art world of their day'.[1] Applying Carroll's description to the Filmliga, we could simply substitute Menno ter Braak (and other writers in Filmliga) for Arnheim, and it seems to fit. The Filmliga played a dynamic role in this reflection on film art, not only expressing and publicizing the ideas of a theorist like ter Braak, but creating a place where film screenings, lectures by filmmakers, and public discussion stimulated a dynamic interchange between film theory and practice. A perceptive theorist like Carroll realizes such an interchange must have taken place to move from filmmaking to written theory. A historical investigation of Filmliga could reveal this process and interchange at work. However, history always uncovers something of a mess compared to the clarity of theory: the contested wrestling over categories rather than their logical construction. Silent film theory and practice of the late 1920s forged a conception of the specific essence of film as the definition of film as an art form. However, as Yuri Tsivian has pointed out in his groundbreaking discussion of film style during 'the teens',

> notions like 'cinematic', 'nature' or 'medium' are merely cultural and aesthetic configurations which, for all the power they may have over critics and filmmakers, live and die together with their epoch ... [O]ur notion of what is and what is not part of the 'nature' of cinema is somewhat different from the ideas held by filmmakers of the teens.[2]

In fact, film practice (and even theory) during the silent era often vacillated about which of the arts it wanted to declare itself independent from. As Tsivian makes clear, film stylistics in the teens primarily wanted to separate itself from theatre. But it did this partly by borrowing compositional techniques from painting and drawing. Likewise, an essentialist like Vertov strenuously denied cinema's relation to theatre or to the novel, but forged a strong link between film and the 'new photography' of Alexander Rodchenko and the futurist poetry of Vladimir Mayakovsky. In other words, definitions of the essence of film never proceed through a logical exclusion of 'non-cinematic elements'; instead they create a system of oppositions as well as affiliations by which the nature of the cinematic is fashioned rather than deduced.

The Filmliga fashioned its own definition of what film was, or should be. By examining the Liga's programming, we capture this defining 'as a process', rather than simply a theoretical argument. Although the essential terms of this definition were laid out in manifestos and statements by the Liga organizers, its actual negotiation took place in the film programmes that Filmliga put together, the series of experiences offered to their membership. We must balance theoretical and critical statements with an examination of what the Liga audiences were seeing, and – as much as we can reconstruct it – how they were seeing it.

Definitions take place as creative acts, rather than logical deductions. One defines something by tearing a semantic space away from something else, an act of differentiation that in an avant-garde context always retains a degree of violence, however sublimated that violence may appear. The evening that engendered the Filmliga, the famous screening of MATJ [Mother] (SU 1925, Vsevolod Pudovkin) outside of a commercial theatre – at De Kring, an artists' club – acts out redefinition in spatial and social terms. Blocked from their regular outlet for film viewing, a group of audience members refused to take what was on offer to them through regular channels (or to accept that something can be denied) and set up their own alternative space. The excitement of this showing led directly to the decision to create a new space for film viewing, thus initiating a process by which alternative films could be made available, and forging a concept of a dedicated, purpose-driven audience organizing itself self-consciously. It is on this level that we see the ideology of the Filmliga at work, as definitions spring from actions.

While a theoretical definition of film as an art form may primarily set film against other art forms, the Filmliga primarily distinguished itself from other film experiences. The semantic space of the Filmliga drew its first borders *within* the film world, offering a different idea of film exhibition and programming as well as a different idea of film. Their opening manifesto makes this clear: 'Once in a hundred times, we see: the film. For the rest, we see: cinema' [Eens op de honderd keer zien wij: de film. Voor de rest zien wij: bioscoop]. It is less a distinction between film and theatre or literature that must be made first, than a distinction between *film* as the good object and *cinema* as the abject, the thing to be scorned and discarded. The cinema is defined primarily in social terms – its association with commerce, with the common herd, with America – and identified as kitsch, the opposite of art. In contrast, film is defined primarily in aesthetic terms, with purity and autonomy marking the art of the future by isolating it from the commercial demands and low tastes of *bioscoop* (cinema) audiences.

The cultural conservatism at the core of this radical manifesto articulates a tension between radical aspirations for an 'art of the future' and disdain for its commercial embodiment. Will the purity of the artistic film be recognized by 'its difference from the other traditional arts' (the logical theoretical position of a theory of an autonomous film and at least one definition of a 'pure' film)? Or will an artistic film be marked by 'its difference from the *bioscoop* and its mass audience', in effect affirming its similarity to the traditional arts (its autonomy in contrast to the demands of the commercial market, and its purity coming from traditional artistic motivations and methods of work)? We must recognize that the tension between these two positions worked itself deeply into not only this organization but nearly all conceptions of alternative cinema of the period (and, I would claim, succeeding periods), with varying degrees of emphasis on one side or the other, but never achieving a complete and ultimate resolution.

Dichotomy or Dialectic? Antinomies of an Avant-Garde

Here the mess that lurks behind the theoretical distinctions of the silent film era, and the film society movement, swims into view. The Filmliga (and the film society movement in general) provided the battleground on which these contradictions were put in play, rather than a realm in which they were definitively sorted out. Coming to terms with film as a mass medium was not a simple thing for the Filmliga (nor, I should add, is it a simple issue for scholars, filmmakers or critics today). Let us imagine two extreme and opposing positions, ideal poles within 1920s avant-garde film culture.

The first position defines film as a radical force shaking the very categories of the traditional arts through its lack of concern with aesthetics or making art. Through its roots in popular culture, film provided an energy and anarchy typified by grotesque slapstick comedies or early trick films. Through its mechanical nature, film launched a challenge not only to traditional aesthetic forms (everything in motion, avoiding the traditional aesthetic value of repose, showing little concern for pictorial values) and dramaturgy (its absurdist plots, or total lack of narrative structure), but even to common experience of space and time – as in Theo van Doesburg's description of a Sennett slapstick comedy as the 'end of time and space! The destruction of gravity! The secret of fourth dimensional motion'.[3]

The opposing position identified the mass nature of the cinema with commercial compromise and the realm of cliché. Film could only become an art if a filmmaker consciously, and usually with great difficulty, asserted independence from the market and the forms of kitsch. Such filmmakers would draw on artistic sources (most likely modern ones, such as expressionism or cubism) to produce films which were likely to be incomprehensible to a mass audience.

Certainly the Filmliga manifesto and its programming, both strongly influenced by ter Braak, seems to tilt more towards the second viewpoint. But the Filmliga showed tendencies in both directions: a grave suspicion of cinema's role as a mass medium, as well as a celebration of the possibilities of a new popular form. The Filmliga founding manifesto cites King Vidor's THE BIG PARADE (US 1925) and mentions Chaplin when it gives examples of film (as opposed to cinema), which would indicate some appreciation for film as a mass art. In other words, while these two positions oppose each other in fundamental ways, they did not, in practice, exclude each other. Instead, we must see the attempt to create an alternative film culture as oscillating between these two positions, this tension and ambiguity creating a rich semiotic space of encounters, debates and discussion, profiting from a certain equivocal quality in the nature of film as an art form of the future.

Film historians usually divide 1920s avant-garde film into a series of movements and genres: the impressionist school, the expressionist movement, the Soviet montage film, the absolute abstract film, the Dadaist film, the surrealist film, and the city symphonies. Although these terms make it possible to sort individual films into categories, the programmes of the Filmliga included all these categories, frequently in promiscuous proximity. Liga programmes served a varied cinematic menu in which films often contrasted sharply with each other. Yet all these films were understood as relating to the Liga project of defining film art. We must try to understand what they had in common, not by boiling them down to the lowest common denominator, but by reconstructing the film programmes as an experience in which diverse film practices could jostle each other. Examining film history from the point of view of an exhibition practice, like the Filmliga's, reveals an avant-garde smorgasbord, quite different from the demarcated categories of traditional stylistic histories.

This conflicted field on which the avant-garde forged a new sense of film art could be charted by what I call the antinomies of 1920s avant-garde cinema – a series of oppositions within the writings and practices of alternative cinema. I describe these, not to accuse the movement of absurdity or of using contradictory terminology, but rather to chart tensions within the movement, which were often vital and dynamic rather than self-defeating.

Commercial/Non-commercial or Money is the Root of What?

In 1929 the Congrès international du cinéma indépendent, whose avowed purpose was the support of films 'conceived and realized outside of all commercial influences and considerations in order to support the development of cinema's means of expression and develop its human significance', was held at La Sarraz, Switzerland. This seminal event gathered together critics, filmmakers, and executives of film societies (including Mannus Franken as the representative of the Filmliga). The undisputed star of the event was Sergei Eisenstein, who arrived on the second day. His ebullient personality persuaded the congress participants to put aside their agenda and rush outdoors to improvise a collaborative film (often described as co-directed by Hans Richter and Sergei Eisenstein). The film presented a tongue-in-cheek allegory of the congress's *parti pris*. Sporting a large banner inscribed 'Independent Film' (as well as some piquantly arranged film reels), the patron of the conference, Madame de Mandrot, was held prisoner jointly by 'Commerce' and 'Industry', and ultimately rescued by Eisenstein and Richter. The parodically melodramatic nature of this lost film (some scholars doubt if, in fact, the cameras were loaded), underscores the ironic act of representing non-commercial cinema by Hélène de Mandrot, a woman of enormous wealth. The economic model for a non-commercial cinema remained under-defined. Would it be state supported, or dependent on the beneficence of wealthy patrons? Would delivery from commerce automatically result in the flourishing of film art?

Likewise, the role commerce plays in destroying film art remained under-theorized. Is it simply the rule of money that degrades the pure art of cinema? In some sense, the creation of the film society movement affirms this, creating a space for cinema not regulated by profit motives. The film society movement of the 1920s set up alternative

systems of exhibition (such as the Filmliga), and encouraged the production of low-budget experimental films, often providing not only
venues where they could be shown, but studio space, as in the Théâtre
du Vieux Colombier's attic being used to shoot Jean Renoir's LA PETITE
MARCHANDE D'ALLUMETTES [The Little Matchgirl] (FR 1928).

But was direct contact with money and the corporations of advanced
capitalism necessarily a hex on film creativity? Many of the films produced as outstanding examples of pure or abstract cinema by Ruttmann,
Richter, Pinschewer and Fischinger were literally commercials – films
financed by corporations to advertise their goods and make them
attractive to mass consumers. Filmliga showed an enormous number
of this sort of 'commercial film', and the Dutch Philips radio company
became a leading source of commercially sponsored films, including
Ivens' PHILIPS RADIO (NL 1931) and Richter's EUROPA-RADIO (NL 1933),
two Liga films. The aesthetic of the abstract film, its explorations of
visual rhythms, and experiments in editing all seemed to thrive rather
than decay under the sponsorship of high commerce. It seems to me,
then, that when Filmliga attacks 'the commercial regime', it is not the
power of money that corrupts, but other aspects of the commercial film
industry – its need for a mass audience, for instance.

Autonomous/Tendentious Films or the Purity of Music and Politics

The claim that a liberated cinema must be freed from the trammels,
not only of commerce and industry, but from the outmoded traditions
of the other arts was, as we have seen, riddled with exceptions and
contradictions. Only certain arts or styles (theatre most often, literature next) were excoriated, while others (poetry, music) were at least
tacitly considered appropriate sources of inspiration. If film was to be
autonomous, what would it look like?

One answer lay in the abstract films of Ruttmann, Fischinger,
Eggeling and early Richter. These films staked out a territory at
antipodes from the basic Hollywood product: the feature-length narrative film. The play of pure form made up of shadow and light (and
occasionally colour), and the rhythmic metamorphosis of shapes in
rhythm: these devices seemed to define the bedrock of an autonomous
film form. Representation gave way to a purely 'musical' articulation
of visual form in time. Such abstract, rhythmic films seemed to follow
Walter Pater's dictum that all art forms aspired to the condition of
music. The analogy to musical form provided a foundational metaphor for the autonomous art of the cinema within the international

avant-garde film of the 1920s generally, having the status that Tsivian claims pictorial representation had in the 1910s. The absolute film also drew on the abstract forms found in contemporary painting. However, these sources of analogy and inspiration did not reduce abstract films to passive reproduction of other arts. Abstract films radically transformed its progenitors. The musical analogy remained a mere analogy. A fundamental switch from hearing to sight had taken place. This switch often claimed effects of synesthesia – music that was seen rather than heard, as the absolute film was described as 'visual music'. While the films of Richter, Eggeling, Ruttmann or Fischinger recalled abstract styles of painting (Kandinsky or Delaunay or De Stijl – although few of such similarities are very literal), cinematic motion and temporal rhythm transformed these visual influences (Richter and others spoke of the abstract film as a culmination and solution to the problems of abstract painting). Growing out of other arts, but radically transforming or sublimating them, the abstract film became one of the greatest achievements of the alternative cinema of the 1920s, a touchstone for claims of an autonomous cinema.

But the musical analogy pervades not only the abstract film. We could plot a continuous progression for these 'musically conceived' films, arching from entirely abstract animated films through films which use photographic techniques to abstract objects such as Dulac's Étude Cinégraphieque sur une Arabesque (FR 1929) and Disque 957 (FR 1928), which use soft focus, multifaceted lenses, superimpositions, stop-motion, reflections and split screen; through films which photograph objects more or less recognizably but submit them to rigorous rhythms of editing and camera movement such as Léger and Murphy's Ballet Mécanique (FR 1924) or Charles Dekeukeleire's Impatience (BE 1928); taking in a spate of early sound films which include music on the soundtrack and portrayed music making, with rhythmic editing and careful composition designed to produce lyrical images that are presumably the visual equivalent of the music we hear such as Alexandrov, Tissé, and Eisenstein's Romance Sentimental (FR 1929) or Ruttmann's In der Nacht [In the Night] (DE 1931). From these it is a short distance to the sequences in Soviet films in which musical performances are portrayed through similar means – the sequences, say, of balalaika playing in Matj, or the tavern band in Kain i Artem [Cain and Artem] (SU 1930, Pavel Petrov-Bytov). Ultimately we could include the most complex exercises in pure visual rhythm in films which do not necessarily represent music literally but whose editing displays virtuoso patterns of repetition and variation – such as Celovek s Kinoapparatom

[The Man with a Movie Camera] (SU 1929, Dziga Vertov), STAROE I NOVOE [The Old and the New] (SU 1929, Sergei Eisenstein) or even Ivens' DE BRUG (NL 1928) or REGEN (NL 1929). Indeed the very term 'city symphony' shows the active role that musical analogies played in many documentaries of this period. Therefore, if the autonomous art of the cinema dwells in the creation of rhythm through visual means – composition, movement in the frame, camera movement and patterns of editing – we can follow a complete arc from films which show no objects through to films like Vertov's, which were dedicated to showing life as it is, or Eisenstein's films portraying the process of revolution.

The variety within this shared musical preoccupation likens the art cinema of the 1920s to an intricate jazz improvisation with an enormous range of soloists on diverse instruments, but all attuned to a central throbbing rhythm. Here lies the potential richness of the equivocal nature of an 'autonomous cinema', as opposed to one observing rigid definitions. For Liga audiences the autonomous film could encompass the endless permutations of Fischinger's line dances, Eisenstein's clearly articulated call to revolution, or Vertov's communist decoding of reality. Autonomy did not absolutely rule out either representation or even a political statement.

Perhaps the deepest controversy within the 1920s avant-garde cinema turned on film's role as a political tool, a means of revolutionary change, and therefore a tendentious, expressive and communicative medium, as opposed to a conception of 'autonomous' cinema which maintained that the purely aesthetic form of film constituted its essence. For many members of the 1920s avant-garde the most important aspect of the art of the cinema lay in its political and revolutionary possibilities, a view that became increasingly powerful towards the end of the decade, as the increasingly politicized statements on film of Ivens and Richter make clear. The Soviet filmmakers embodied and spread this viewpoint. At the Congrès international du cinéma indépendant, Béla Balázs maintained that the independent film movement must privilege film's social role, and therefore must be able to communicate to a wide audience, while Hans Richter defended the abstract film not immediately accessible to mass audiences. These contrasting definitions of alternative film reveal the fault line over which the avant-garde cinema had been constructed. But during this period there was not yet an absolute dichotomy between formal experiment and revolutionary purposes.

Filmliga, for instance, remained aesthetically driven, rather than politically defined, stressing the aesthetic nature of film, including the

Soviet films, as opposed to other more politicized Dutch film organizations. It was the nature of film 'as film' that the Liga pursued rather than film as the conveyer of information or even argument. L.J. Jordaan lamented in the magazine *Filmliga* that film must also be rescued from its own polyvalence and diverse uses: '[Film] can walk on its hands and call up apparitions, it teaches at Sunday School and dances the Charleston, it fights venereal disease and leers at dirty old men ... in short it can do anything – but be itself'.[4] But if Filmliga, in its discourse, primarily pursued the path of film's autonomy, its programmes did not avoid political, tendentious films altogether. And within later Liga programmes, political films were not restricted to revolutionary films. A number of films sponsored by fairly diverse political or social organizations were shown in the Liga programmes and the early Uitkijk seasons, explicitly without endorsing their respective politics or policies. These included not only Soviet films, but also Ivens' WIJ BOUWEN (NL 1930), commissioned by labour union Algemeene Nederlandsche Bouwarbeidersbond, Jan Hin's KENTERING [Capsizing] (NL 1932) on the Roman Catholic labour union struggle, and FAKKELGANG [Torch Walk] (NL 1932, Max de Haas) on the temperance movement. Besides the tendentious pleading of all these films on the part of their sponsoring organizations and causes, their stylistics also show (in varying degrees of mastery and aesthetic success) the strong influence of the avant-garde, with sequences of rhythmic editing, unconventional framings and close-ups, as well as visual effects or metaphoric montage (e.g. the bizarre drunken orgy in FAKKELGANG, the montage of the stock market and the assembly line in KENTERING).

Distortion and Defamiliarization: Reality and the Everyday

Perhaps the most fundamental oxymoron of the 1920s avant-garde lay in its equal pursuit of visual distortion or unfamiliar imagery and the documenting of everyday life. Liga programmes were just as likely to show the abstract films of Ruttmann and the experiments in slow motion, anamorphic distortions and extreme soft focus of Epstein, Dulac, Man Ray and others, as on-location documentaries on Hoogstraat in Rotterdam (Andor von Barsy's HOOGSTRAAT [High Street], NL 1930), the beach at Oostende (Henri Storck's IMAGES D'OSTENDE, BE 1929/30), or the weekday market in Berlin (Wilfried Basse's MARKT IN BERLIN [Market in Berlin], DE 1928). From the point of view of later theories of realism, this dual focus on everyday life and the distorting mechanisms of cinema appears nearly schizophrenic. But such apparent contradictions reveal the actual dynamics of this alternative cinema and the range of its sense of the cinematic.

The contrast between an abstract concern with rhythm and the mission of recording the everyday would not have seemed so sharp to any of the participants in 1920s alternative cinema: critics, filmmakers or viewers. The Liga programming, for instance, traced a direct connection between Ruttmann's abstract films and his city symphony BERLIN, DIE SINFONIE EINER GROßSTADT (DE 1927), as the opening of this film demonstrates, with rhythmic movement of abstract shapes giving way to the rhythms of a locomotive entering a modern metropolis. Many documentaries made at the time included experiments in visual rhythm and defamiliarized ways of filming people and the environment. Vertov's catalogue of the possible distortions available to the filmmaker in THE MAN WITH A MOVIE CAMERA provided the most thorough demonstration of the union between documentary and cinematic stylization, an example influential on Jean Vigo and Boris Kaufman's À PROPOS DE NICE (FR 1929), or Deslaw's ROBOTS (FR 1932).

This creative interpretation of the camera's claim on reality might be the aspect of the 1920s avant-garde most difficult to recover and, therefore, perhaps the most valuable. Our contemporary sense of cinematic realism has been restructured by the films of the Italian neo-realists and the theoretical works of André Bazin, for whom realism stood at complete antipodes to what he would refer to as film 'tricks', the cinematic devices of montage most importantly, but also superimpositions and other visual effects. Not only did the avant-garde culture value these devices as essential elements of autonomous film art, they did not see them as opposed to realism. In fact, one could claim that on-location, direct observational filmmaking, the sort of filming found in the documentaries of Ivens, Vertov, Kaufman, von Barsy, Basse, Ruttmann's BERLIN, Marcel Carné's NOGENT, ELDORADO DU DIMANCHE (FR 1929) or even Edgar G. Ulmer and Robert Siodmak's MENSCHEN AM SONNTAG (GE 1929) was simply another element of an alternative and autonomous film language. This on-location documentary filming contrasted with the studio-bound filming of commercial feature films, but was not seen as inherently contradictory or opposed to an elaboration of other devices of film language.

We find again a theoretical opposition which in practice, as styles of filmmaking, set up dialectical relations between films rather than maintaining mutually exclusive dichotomies. In some ways these antinomies are resolved if we realize that these apparently opposed techniques shared an opposition to the form of the commercial feature film. The Filmliga attacked conventional assumptions about what a film was (and different leading members launched their attacks on different aspects): certain types of narrative, characterization, acting, stars and a particular organization of space, time and visual portrayal that had become both dominant and fully encoded in commercial cinema over the previous decade. The cinema could be contested from a number of angles.

An International Avant-Garde, and the Need for Water

The congress at La Sarraz proclaimed the international character of the independent cinema as being as essential to the movement as its independence from commerce or its devotion to 'human significance'. Even the commercial cinema of the late silent era involved enormous international cooperation, as stars (Emil Jannings in Hollywood, Louise Brooks in Berlin), directors (Dreyer in France, Ruttmann in Italy, Ivens in the USSR, Murnau and Eisenstein in Hollywood), and even cameramen and set designers (Hungarian Rudolph Maté and German Hermann Warm working in France on LA PASSION DE JEANNE D'ARC (FR 1927/28, Carl Theodor Dreyer – perhaps the most international film of the period) moved across borders with an ease that the arrival of sound imperilled. Stylistic exchanges also took place, such as Charles Rosher observing Germanic lighting in Berlin and demonstrating to German cameramen the principles of Hollywood glamour lighting; or Soviet cutting becoming a model for Ivens in Holland and influencing politically committed filmmakers in Germany. This international exchange was the product of film as a global commodity in an era of high capitalism, rather than the universalistic ideals articulated by the avant-garde. But the nature of commodities had results that capitalism could not foresee or restrain in terms of the circulation of ideas and film styles. Essential to this was the distribution of films across borders, a basic aspect of international film business, but one which was seized upon by the film society movement as a promise of a universal film culture.

Examining the programmes of the Studio des Ursulines, the London Film Society, the Belgian Film Society, the Ciné-Club of Geneva, and Filmliga, one is struck by the overlap in programming. The same films by Cavalcanti, Epstein, Dulac, Richter, Dovzhenko, Seeber, Ruttmann, Deslaw, Man Ray, Room, Eisenstein, Metzner, Basse, Storck, Ivens and others were shown in nearly every venue. For example, one of the lesser-known films that played the film society circuit, the Chinese film

FUHUO DE MIGUI [The Rose of Pu-Chui], directed by Hou Yao, was first shown in the Studio des Ursulines in Paris, then in the Ciné-Club of Geneva, and then in the 1930 Filmliga series.

The international aspect was not restricted to projecting films. Filmmakers, too, circulated. The Liga hosted Germaine Dulac, René Clair, Jean Painlevé and Jean Dréville from France (as well as Brazilian Alberto Cavalcanti, working in France for the Liga's first official programme); Hans Richter and Walter Ruttmann from Germany; Charles Dekeukeleire from Belgium; Eisenstein, Pudovkin and Vertov from the USSR (as well as Ivens lecturing on his trip to the Soviet Union and presenting fragments from recent Soviet films). In addition, Jean Mauclair from Studio 28, one of the Parisian ciné-clubs, lectured in 1929 at the opening of Filmliga's third season and inauguration of the Uitkijk on the international cooperation between film clubs and the exemplary role Filmliga had played in this networking.

Indeed, Filmliga exerted its strongest international influence as a linchpin in the European system of film societies. From the beginning, it looked beyond its borders for models, especially to Paris, whose Studio des Ursulines provided an important paradigm for programming. And with Mannus Franken in Paris and Joris Ivens in Berlin, relaying information back to Amsterdam about the availability of films and filmmakers and making personal contacts when needed, the Liga seemed to stand midway between these two European capitals in terms of influence. The Liga journal regularly included reports from foreign countries (as well as occasional articles in French, German and English) not only on film production, but on the film societies in various places, from Berlin to New York City. At the La Sarraz congress, Filmliga was held up as a model when the congress discussed the project of an official international union of film clubs. Filmliga served as a model for an international organization because it was not only a single local society, but a national network, with branch organizations across The Netherlands. The magazine *Close Up*, the English language magazine published in Switzerland dedicated to the autonomy of film art and the principles of the film society movement, praised Filmliga as exemplary, noting, 'This tiny country that has no cinema industry shows a serious interest in film that many larger countries might well envy'.[5]

Even though many films were widely shown, there were, of course, national differences. *Close Up* criticized the Parisian film clubs for their excessive affection for American films (a criticism the Filmliga must have shared). The London Film Society seemed to build programmes more around feature films with a series of shorter films supporting a longer central film. The Liga avoided this feature-centred programming more than any of the other film societies, frequently programming a large number of shorter films, or presenting only fragments of feature films, articulating a programming philosophy that I will return to later. But beyond local differences, did the international film society movement define a shared avant-garde aesthetic through their programmes? The antinomies that I described appear, in varying proportions, in all the film society programmes I have examined. All showed the complete gamut of films from abstract films to documentaries. All included films funded as promotions of products or companies. All of them included highly political Soviet films, as well as purely aesthetic experiments. Therefore, if there was an international avant-garde at the end of the 1920s, it tolerated a wide range of filmmaking styles (although some had greater tolerance for Hollywood feature films than Filmliga).

But if we seek not just diversity but try to uncover some central metaphors or devices shared by many different and differing filmmakers, some consistencies in the pursuit of the essentially cinematic come into focus. Perhaps the most fundamental of these was the pursuit of cinematic rhythm and a musical form as an analogy for film. Very few films shown in these programmes would lack at least a sequence which could be described as a visual symphony, even though the ways of understanding this analogy (or the sorts of music evoked) were extremely varied. But I would propose another less abstract, and perhaps less universal, guiding image for 1920s avant-garde film. Yuri Tsivian's treatment of the particular understanding of the 'uniquely cinematic' in the work of European filmmakers in the 1910s points out the exemplary role reflections in mirrors play.[6] This device had been impossible to use in theatrical staging, and its use in film accented the staging and framing constructed by the single viewpoint of the camera that fascinated directors like Bauer, Hofer and Blom. If I were to nominate a similar device for the international avant-garde film of the late 1920s it would be the filming of water.

This may sound somewhat capricious and over-specific compared to a more obviously structural preoccupation such as rhythm. However, during the period commentators already remarked on the preoccupation with water by experimental filmmakers. For example, a satirical article in *Close Up* in 1929 provided a guide to making experimental films, and declared 'you want water'.[7] Water supplied a wide range of metaphors for the unique qualities of film and was a fluid enough medium to contain its protean forms. The 1910s preoccupation with mirrors reflects its concerns with balanced positioning and doubled compositions. A reflection within a shot drew attention to framing and the ambiguous construction of scenic space through frames within frames, and opened a play with depth and surface, on-screen and off-screen space, as Tsivian has shown. The fascination found in 1920s films with the various forms of water sinks into the centre of *photogénie* and the new freedom of visual composition (torn out of the scenic space of the 1910s) explored by the avant-garde through closer framing, rhythmic editing and camera movement. The film image and new forms of editing had dissolved the solidity of scenic space, and the liquidity and flow of water provided a powerful correlative of this new freedom.

Water cannot be framed. It flows beyond and around the borders of geometry. It can be placid and therefore clear and transparent, but also (more often in these films) in motion, and the range of its flowing plasticity produces a variety of visual effects. Its metamorphic power flows unbounded. It can become a series of concentric echoing waves, evoking an abstract play of form, for instance in IN DER NACHT, where patterns of rippling water seem to directly reproduce (and transform into) the abstract animation of the OPUS-films. But water ripples can also set up an almost infinite play with sunlit reflections, found in an almost endless series of films: ROMANCE SENTIMENTAL; DISQUE 957; PIEREMENT; BAUMBLÜTENZEIT IN WERDER [Tree Blossoming Season in Werder] (DE 1929, Wilfried Basse); DE TREKSCHUIT (NL 1933, Mannus Franken / Otto van Neijenhoff); KAIN I ARTEM; LA CHUTE DE LA MAISON USHER [The Fall of the House of Usher] (FR 1928, Jean Epstein); À PROPOS DE NICE (FR 1929, Jean Vigo); and BRONENOSEZ POTOMKIN [Battleship Potemkin] (SU 1925, Sergei Eisenstein). Images of people swimming and boating particularly give rise to this treatment of the fluid medium as a mode of rippling reflection: MENSCHEN AM SONNTAG; JAGD AUF DICH [Hunting You] (DE 1930, Ernst Angel), STACHKA [Strike] (SU 1925, Sergei Eisenstein). Furthermore, water plays with visuality as a medium to be seen through: refracting, reflecting and distorting the world into a shaky, tenuous vision filled with surprises. Rain or water purling down a window provides a visual theme most gloriously in Ivens' REGEN (certainly one of the most powerful and original explorations of the water imagery of the 1920s), but also in Dulac's DISQUE 957 as well as ARABESQUE (which also uses the play of water spray and refracted light). The frothing of rapidly flowing water provoked childhood memories in VISAGES D'ENFANTS (FR/CH 1924, Jacques Feyder), and expressed the unstoppable force of revolution in MOTHER, fructifying irrigation in TURKSIB (SU 1929, Victor Turin), the spring thaw in the Soviet Union in VESNOI [In Spring] (SU 1929, Mikhail Kaufman), the power of the Soviet in constructing hydroelectric dams (Vertov's MAN WITH A MOVIE CAMERA) and Eisenstein's THE OLD AND THE NEW, or even the fury of repression in the fire hoses of STRIKE. Last, but far from least, comes the poetics of ocean waves breaking onto the shore with its sub-themes of whipped froth and rippled sand, especially prevalent in the films of Belgium and the Netherlands: Storck's IMAGES D'OSTENDE, HISTOIRE D'UN DÉTECTIVE (BE 1929, Charles Dekeukeleire), Ivens' and Franken's BRANDING and, perhaps the greatest exploration of the run of surf and froth, Ivens' ZUIDERZEE (NL 1930). This is by no means an exhaustive list, and one would want to include here J.C. Mol's microscopic films revealing the floating denizens of a water drop. These examples demonstrate the very liquidity of this theme, its ability to take so many different shapes and forms of visuality and to evoke such varied associations. As an image for the art of the cinema, it stresses its protean nature, its sense of power in movement as well as in stilled reflection. As a metaphor for vision it expresses the medium of sight as a gamut ranging from the placid mirror-like reflections in ROMANCE SENTIMENTAL through to Dulac's refractions, Turin's frothing mountain streams, and Ivens' angry sea.

Gilles Deleuze has proposed a mode of liquid perception as an aspect of his 'movement-image', the mode of cinema which he primarily associates with the silent era. He beautifully describes the abstracting power of water in the cinema: 'water is the most perfect environment in which movement can be extracted from the thing moved, or mobility from movement itself'. Unfortunately, he prematurely restricts this aspect to what he calls the French school, and misses its role as an international image, a common shore for 1920s avant-garde film. But he understands that water imagery acts as more than an elemental or symbolic substance in the cinema. As he says, 'water was the promise or the implication of another state of perception: a more than human perception, a perception not tailored to solids … A more delicate and vaster perception, a molecular perception tailored to a "cine-eye"'.[8] I would claim that water reflects a new sense of visual composition, dispensing nearly entirely with the cube of scenographic space, seizing montage fragments which flow into each other according to diverse rhythms and purposes. Whether organized as an exploration of a railway bridge in operation, the symphony of a great city, or the chronicle of a day at the beach, 1920s avant-garde films in all genres reflect these new 'liquid' modes of stylistic organization in contrast to both the art cinema that preceded it – the German expressionist cinema, more closely tied to the styles of the 1910s with their use of deep space and reflections; and the contemporary Hollywood cinema, with its development of seamlessly continuous scene dissection.

My point here is not to boil down the varied practices of the avant-garde into one all-absorbing medium, like Hegel's characterization of Schelling's system as 'the night in which all cows are black', but rather to stress again its varied manifestations within a common aspiration. The imaging of vision as somehow liquid, at turns transparent, frothing, reflecting or refracting, serves as a metaphor for this alternative cinema, able to express lyricism or political dynamism, translucent images of the everyday or shimmering opalescent, soft focus dreams and visions.

Programming as Experiment

I want to turn from a shared international vision of the new art of cinema back to the specific experiences offered by the Filmliga and their programmes, particularly in its first seasons. Filmliga gave its members an identity through a common purpose based on a corpus of films which, as varied as they might be, were all related to the goal of rescuing film from the cinema. We could term this broad corpus of films 'Liga-like' films, a term used self-consciously and humorously in the Dutch titles supplied by the Liga in its presentation of a German film JAGD AUF DICH in which a group of filmmakers try to come up with a radical new way of making films, different from the 'kitsch' which surrounds them. But the individual programmes did more than screen such films; they shaped and *tutored* audience experiences of this new art form and attuned them to its possibilities. Placing films together in a single programme, as elements of the event that made up a Liga show, provides one of the strongest examples of the social practices of film exhibition, richly repaying a thorough analysis.

The Austrian avant-garde filmmaker Peter Kubelka, a master of precision editing, often maintains that 'it is between the frames that cinema speaks'.[9] In approaching the film programme we could say that it is between the films that a programme enunciates itself. The film programme, understood as creative force, works like a film editor, only instead of joining shots or specific frames, it joins films. Charles Musser has shown that in the earliest era of film exhibition this creative role of the film exhibitor as editor was very literal, as exhibitors determined the order of shots and the succession of films shown. Further, As Yuri Tsivian discovered, some early audience members at least playfully experienced the succession of short films in an early film programme as a single super-text, carrying associations from one film to the next.[10] Arranging a programme was a creative act in film exhibition. Even in the era of the silent feature and the picture palace, as Richard Koszarski reveals, the programme of short films, musical performances and live acts was often considered more important than the specific feature film shown; theatre managers were willing to re-edit the feature in order to fit it into a programme.[11]

In some ways, with the coming of the feature, the film programme became more conventional (which does not mean it was less important to audiences). The succession of short films that preceded the feature generally followed strongly inscribed conventions of genres and order. Even the regular film programmes at the Uitkijk followed a rather rigid order: a cartoon, a short comedy and/or a short documentary, and then the feature film. Although the features were often unusual and the short films seem to have been carefully chosen (although one Liga writer strongly objected to the Uitkijk's choice of a Max Fleischer cartoon as support for GRASS [US 1925, Merian C. Cooper / Ernest B. Schoedsack]), such programming basically followed the same template as most commercial theatres.[12]

But Filmliga organized programmes differently, accentuating their difference from the cinema. Menno ter Braak, writing in the inaugural issue of *Filmliga*, made it clear that rescuing film from the cinema demanded an analysis and reform of the film programme. He found this nearly virgin territory; the French ciné-clubs offered some models, while the commercial cinema only groped towards forms that were sometimes useful, sometimes counterproductive. The commercial cinema offered a number of films and unrelated elements, put together with no motivation or intention other than pure entertainment. It was the very chaos of different sorts of films jumbled together, along with other non-filmic acts, that the Liga would combat, with programmes that as much as possible were carefully arranged and sensitive to the way one film played against another.

In a later issue of *Filmliga*, L.J. Jordaan, inspired by a phrase he found in Léon Moussinac's book on Soviet cinema, amplified the Liga's distaste for the idea of the film programme as a form of entertainment. Moussinac declared that the film theatre must divorce itself once and for all from its music-hall legacy, eliminate 'attractions' from its programme, and follow the principle of not confusing genres. Moussinac and Jordaan particularly objected to non-film acts. As Jordaan puts it, 'No more MOTHER followed by the Song of the Volga performed by a ventriloquist – no more POTEMKIN followed by the tunes of Kees Pruis – no more MÉNILMONTANT followed by performing geese'.[13] New principles of programming would rescue film from the morass of entertainment, clearly separating film and mere amusement.

The semiotic violence behind the definition of film art asserts itself. Film must be 'detached from the environment that has vampirized it ... remove film from the world of amusement!' This is not simply a process of definition but a call to battle: *'de strijd om de film'*. Film's rescue from the commercial film programme of diverse attractions comes from its need to discover its own autonomy. The lesson is clear: film is not cinema, and to decant or refine its true essence, to liberate it from enslavement to demeaning tasks, one must take it out of the cinema theatre and create a laboratory environment, in which a series of experiments, pursued without thought of profit, will finally produce the quintessence of film, unalloyed with baser elements. The Filmliga served as that laboratory. The programmes became those experiments.

The importance of the experimental model must be stressed. It is precisely here that the Liga asserts its avant-garde nature, and its difference from the more traditional forms of artistic presentation. Unlike the concert hall, which performed a well-established canon, or the art museum, which exhibited established and priceless masterpieces, Filmliga (like contemporary avant-garde venues in the other arts) presented experimental works, whose value lay in innovation and exploration rather than established achievement. In contrast to conservative art exhibition ideology, Filmliga proclaimed outright that there were not yet any masterpieces of filmmaking and, even, few truly fine works. But any works that were striving to separate themselves from the cinema, and trying to find film's unique path as an art form, would find a home at the Filmliga. This stance not only 'separates film from amusement', but differentiates Filmliga's more clinical and probing attitude towards the new art of film from the enthusiastic cinephilia that dominated the French ciné-clubs.

This experimental attitude operates, for instance, in the Liga's attitude towards musical accompaniment. Although most programmes were presented with the fairly standard musical accompaniment of selections from the nineteenth-century romantic repertoire, the occasional deviation from the convention caused its members to reflect on the role musical accompaniment played, and the possibility of foregoing it. The Filmliga introduced the music of modern composers such as Debussy, De Falla, Strawinsky and Gershwin in the cinema, often using gramophone records – another departure from common practice. And in Rotterdam, Eisenstein's Strike was accompanied by 'concrete' music performed with hammers, chains, drills, and other hardware.[14] Occasionally Filmliga programmes, or parts of them, were screened in complete silence. Indeed, in the Liga's very first programme excerpts from Le Train sans Yeux (FR 1927, Alberto Cavalcanti) were presented without music. Afterwards, writing in *Filmliga*, Constant van Wessem pronounced this a 'successful experiment'. But he immediately indicated that this was partly due to the unique nature of this film in which 'the very disappearance of music enhanced the emotions'.[15] Most films, he claimed, could not do without music which provides a contact between the viewer and the film. Battleship Potemkin, he asserted, lost half its power without Meisel's score. But van Wessem's most interesting comment came from his feeling that the excerpts from Cavalcanti's film did after all receive a sound accompaniment: the clattering of the film projector provided a perfectly evocative counterpart to the images of trains and their mechanical rhythms.

In the Liga's third season, B. van Lier offered an extended consideration of the problem of film music, based very much on the Liga's distinction between the 'film' and the 'cinema', and the experience of Liga screenings. Based on the avant-garde obsession with film rhythm, van Lier declared that musical accompaniment often became one of the impure elements that the autonomous art of film had to struggle against. Film music provided in commercial theatres, which showed conventional narrative films, merely followed the story. However, in an art film, which possessed its own autonomous rhythm, musical accompaniment could be the film's 'worst enemy': 'The spectator is forced to undergo two disjointed rhythms, sliding along each other: that of the film and that of the music. The film is not being accompanied, but damaged. The continuity of filmic rhythm is being broken artificially; the power of its autonomy is being curtailed and cannot be experienced wholly by the spectator'.[16] Van Lier cited Liga screenings where music had spoiled a film's rhythm, such as the piano accompaniment to Ivens' Heien (NL 1929), which never matched the film's powerful rhythm. Sequences of no music during a screening of Dreyer's La Passion de Jeanne d'Arc showed that silence most certainly could be endured. 'The public, when it is really interested in the artistic meaning of the film, will be easily educated to appreciate silence. And it is the task of the Filmliga in my opinion to protect a pure autonomous development of film and undertake extensive, thorough experiments in this direction'. It does not seem that the Liga undertook a silent exhibition policy. But the importance of this intervention by van Lier comes not only from its originality and its argument for a presentation policy consistent with the Liga's principle of an autonomous art of film. His perception of the Liga as an experimental environment, where new types of programming and presentation could be tested and where previous screenings served to develop new ideas and approaches, reveals the adventurous nature of the organization.

The Liga programme acted like a laboratory apparatus in the discovery and isolation of pure film from the raw ore of the *bioscoop*. As opposed to a random heaping up of diverse attractions, Liga programmes would be sensitive to the unique qualities of each film within its programme, and place it accordingly. As ter Braak stated in his manifesto on the programme: 'one would want to liberate the film-of-the-night from the fool's procession of comedies, from the lingerie of the fashion film, from the grinning sports champion of the newsreel'. Ter Braak also stressed the experimental nature of Filmliga's programmes, part of the Liga's process of discovery. Previous discoveries of the beauty of cinema had come via 'haphazard surprises'. With the Liga's programmes 'we have to see what is interesting and what has been able to hold its own aesthetically'.[17]

However, the goal was not at all to provide a flattering setting for a single feature film ('One cannot demand that in an exhibition of pictures all attention is caught by one piece'). Rather, Filmliga wanted to provide a place where all films can be tested by a critical audience, albeit encouraging sympathy for the experimental and the unconventional (as ter Braak put it, the film programme's main duty was 'to extend a warm welcome, without respect of persons, to the experiment, the eternal now'.) Ter Braak acknowledged that the commercial film programme had acted as 'an unconscious pioneer'. What needed to be retained from the commercial programme was the idea of diversity, but diversity of a new sort. 'The film program has to distinguish itself from the motley anarchy by an *organized diversity*'.[18]

This 'refinement of diversity' highlights the tension between the traditional and the avant-garde sides of the Filmliga equation. Ter Braak expresses this in a statement that seems to move from modernist concerns to more traditional values within a single sentence: 'The film programme, a succession of various dynamic "*image field compositions*" has to be arranged expertly, so that the compositions complement each other and alternate in dignified coherence'.[19] While the experience of the programme as a dynamic diversity of surfaces recalls the formal vocabulary of the cubists or De Stijl (The Style), the attainment of 'dignified coherence' might mollify more traditional viewers. The Liga performed a balancing act between a variety of viewer positions and expectations, the very diversity of which acted as a source of its energy, purpose and method.

Learning by Contrast: The Alchemy of Comparison

The 'programme as experiment' policy often shaded into programming as pedagogical process, educating the audience to new viewing habits. Particularly in its early seasons, Filmliga constructed programmes *à thèse* to demonstrate the nature of pure film. In his initial statement on the aesthetics of the film programme, ter Braak had indicated that the Liga programmes must trace film's path of development, even, as he puts it, its 'ordeal' – its primitive stages as filmed stage plays with extravagant gestures and consequent lack of mastery of composition. While the first official Liga programme had tended more towards a 'dignified coherence', composed entirely of films by Alberto Cavalcanti, the second programme moved towards diversity and contrast. The programme notes published in *Filmliga* declared: 'This second programme is built on opposites'. The range of this programme draws our attention. It began with Guido Seeber's advertising film KIPHO-FILM (GE 1925), then presented 'ten minutes of pre-War film', consisting of two Pathé 'primitives', PARDONNE GRAND-PÈRE (FR 1908) and L'OBSESSION D'OR (FR 1906). LES MIRACLES DU CINÉMA, a documentary on the making of newsreels, followed, with shots of a succession of disasters, then Cavalcanti's RIEN QUE LES HEURES (FR 1925) and finally René Clair's ENTR'ACTE (FR 1924).The mixture of genres (advertising, actuality, trick, primitive drama, experimental narrative, Dadaist avant-garde with slapstick overtones) jumps out.

Was the purpose of this programme to show the full gamut of film-making, excluding the classical narrative feature? Yes and no. What individual members took away from the programme will never be determined with finality. A programme like this must have been exhilarating and a bit baffling, very different from a commercial cinema programme, but possibly more anarchistic than the programmers intended. For the programmers there was a logic beneath this madness. For instance, the screening of pre-war films may seem to indicate a discovery of the avant-garde possibilities of 'the cinema of attractions' that existed before the feature film and narrative structure became dominant. The rediscovery of Méliès by experimental filmmakers like Hans Richter and his fêting by French ciné-clubs was contemporaneous with the Filmliga. However, the pre-war films were intended to play a different role in this programme. For the Liga programmers, PARDONNE GRAND-PERE, the filmed stage play that betrayed cinema's true mission, represented 'bad cinema'. The film was introduced by programme notes with mockery of its out-moded conventions: '... the killing tree – hunger ... misery ... oh, my child! – love heals everything'.[20] Rather than reviving the lost paradise of early cinema, these films served as examples of what ter Braak termed film's 'pre-historical mistakes ... gestures gymnastically striving desperately for expressivity'.[21] Even a devoted fan of early cinema and Pathé (such as I am) has to admit that PARDONNE GRAND-PERE is a pretty bad film. But the ironic tone of the film notes for L'OBSESSION D'OR (such as reference to 'true-to-nature Pathé colour' for its stencil colouring) indicate that this rather delightful trick film may have been viewed with the same contempt. Of course, a position between contempt and admiration – a sort of condescending delight – was possible, and one must assume again that audience members may have experienced a range of reactions. Liga screenings released a range of film experiences into their audiences, startling a cinema public which had been settling into increasingly standardized fare at commercial cinemas.

The contrasts programmed into this matinee were varied: contrast in genre, contrast in historical periods, and even, as the programme notes indicated, contrast between two films about Paris, RIEN QUE LES HEURES and ENTR'ACTE. Seeing these two acknowledged masterpieces of the French avant-garde back to back provides an interesting experience. Both invoke and frustrate conventional narrative: Cavalcanti's film follows a series of characters via elliptical narratives as they progress through a single day, while Clair's film stages a slapstick chase as its final sequence. Both digress from their narrative centres: Cavalcanti into views of city life, and Clair into explorations of pure form and motion (the variety of visual jokes interspersed, like the bearded ballerina, as well as formal associations – the accelerating trajectory of the chase barrelling into shots taken from a roller coaster). It would seem from the comments published in *Filmliga* after the programme that organizers preferred Cavalcanti's relatively realistic concerns ('he has a nose like a detective for the tragedy of the banal') to Clair's Dada (ter Braak called the film 'no more than a reasonable joke').

The organized diversity of the programme demonstrated another principle of Filmliga's concept of the autonomous art of the cinema: the relative unimportance of the 'subject'. Commercial theatres used music to emphasize the story of the film, while art films had other organizing principles. As modern painting had liberated itself from depiction, cinema needed to divest itself of the literary confines of the subject. Comments in *Filmliga* characterized their second programme as 'a reaction against the cine-novel, against the "subject"'.[22] This second matinee traces a trajectory arching from the pre-war films whose role, the same article said, was 'to ridicule the subject-for-the-subject', to Clair's film with its long stretches of pure visual dynamism without a scrap of narrative logic. Even the fairly conventional newsreel form of Les Miracles du Cinema becomes part of the experiment in the context of this programme. It demystifies the cinema by revealing how films are made, showing a newsreel crew being put together and obtaining difficult shots. Its melange of diverse shots – cutting from volcanoes erupting to crowds rioting, from whaling ships to racetrack collisions – seems to anticipate the Dada associations of Entr'acte, focusing less on the incidents as subjects than the cinema's ability to be everywhere, see everything, and juxtapose it.

Comparison and contrast formed the basic tools of Liga programming, both within single programmes and across the seasons. By these means the nature of film art would be experienced, tested and debated. That these comparisons were not simple, but strove to defamiliarize the viewer's experience by seeking out common elements between uncommon films displays the dynamics of Liga programming. The fifth matinee of the first season, for instance, stretched from Grass, the semi-ethnographic exploration documentary on Persian herdsmen, to Man Ray's Emak Bakia (FR 1926), a Dadaist film collage with no traceable narrative or informative logic. These two diverse films were bridged by Handelsbladfilm (NL 1927, Cor Aafjes), another newsreel-like compilation which intertwines a documentary of the gathering of the news for a daily newspaper with a montage of contrasting images from around the world (e.g. from the peace conference in Geneva, to troops in mountainous Morocco, to a street scene in India, to crowds cheering Mussolini, to the French female tennis champion, to a ship at sea sinking). To find a thread through this diversity becomes less a conservative gesture of containment than a creative act of great ingenuity. The programme notes informed Liga members that 'With Grass and Emak Bakia the Liga aims among other things to give a view of the development of photographic possibilities; because both films are superior examples of that'.[23] While nearly any viewer would see these two starkly contrasting works as films from different worlds, the Liga encouraged the audience to find photographic similarities, asking them to see past disparities in treatment and to envision the frontiers of film art. Knowing EMAK BAKIA would be a hard sell for most members, the Liga strove to place it in several contexts for comparison. A later issue of the journal stressed that Man Ray's film was an indispensable link between the absolute film of Walter Ruttmann and the 'surrealist' film of René Clair. Programmes, through the announcements in *Filmliga*, provided a network of references for viewers so that no film existed in isolation.

If Liga members were encouraged to see extremely different films as equally important achievements in film art, differentiations within apparently similar styles of filmmaking were also pointed out. The abstract films of Eggeling and Richter, shown in the seventh programme of the first season, were contrasted by Henrik Scholte with Ruttmann's abstract films shown in the season's third programme. Comparing Richter and Eggeling to Ruttmann was, for Scholte, more important than the films' individual quality, since he claimed Ruttmann's films were much stronger in rhythm and dynamics. The point is not the value of Scholte's conclusion (which is probably not shared now by most scholars of the avant-garde), but his view of Liga programmes as a way to employ the 'comparison factor'. Equally creative was the programming of J.C. Mol's microscopic film UIT HET RIJK DER KRISTALLEN (NL 1927) with Eggeling and Richter's absolute films, posing this 'pedagogically intended film' as *'presqu' absolu'*. The crystalline forms of Mol's 'scientific film' streaking across the screen in an accelerating geometry, building and expanding on the play of forms, reveal themselves as forms in motion, abstract rhythms within a dark space, rather than demonstrations of the typical crystal forms of soda or silver nitrate. Again, ostensible 'subject' gives way to a perceptual discovery of form and motion, genre distinctions collapse against the pressure of cinematic discovery. When Filmliga finally succeeded in showing Ruttmann's BERLIN in its second season (an earlier showing of it with Ruttmann present had been blocked by Tuschinski, who was showing the film in his commercial picture palace), it was preceded by his short abstract films (which *had* been shown earlier) precisely to enable viewers to see the relation between the abstract films and the documentary, the programme notes stating, 'the combination of the two factors will be fascinating'.[24] Filmliga also employed the hard edge of pure contrast. They programmed the Soviet film KATORGA (SU

1928, Yuli Raizman) to be followed by Joris Ivens' (unfortunately lost) SCHAATSENRIJDEN (NL 1928, SKATING) and ETOILE DE MER (FR 1928, Man Ray). The programme notes indicated the motivation here was contrast, pure and simple. 'In this programme we present a curious opposition: the deadly seriousness of the Russian Raizman, the cerebral jest of Man Ray. We hope their differences will contribute to accentuating the various possibilities of an autonomous film art!'[25]

Far from reining in the possibilities of an 'autonomous art of film', Filmliga sought to locate its extremes, praising this programme in particular for its 'cross-sectional qualities' and adding, 'It is still extremely fascinating to see the extremes of film art and to be able to observe that those extremes both represent possibilities for the future and the realities of today. No dogmatic restriction to the true and the false, but comparison, directed by a critical eye, will make our stand indisputable: the film in all its purity'.[26] Purity but not limitation; comparison as a means of discovering a common purpose behind variety – these are the watch words of Liga programming notes.

Programming as Surgery: The Uses of Fragments

If comparison was the primary experimental process employed by Liga screenings, it was matched by another practice that accents the Liga's unique programming even more clearly. Filmliga frequently screened fragments of films rather than their entirety. This would seem to fly in the face of the international film society principles. For instance, an article in *Close Up* in 1928 entitled 'How I would Start a Film Club' gave as one of the basic principles for all such organizations that all films would be shown 'in their original version as cut by the directors'. The article championed film societies as an alternative screening situation where films were neither shortened capriciously by commercial distributors who trimmed scenes in order to fit them into their programmes, nor tendentiously cut by government censors weeding out immoral, scandalous or revolutionary content. The Liga absolutely shared these concerns. However, the preservation of the original intent of the director posed a more complex question for the Liga. Their programming was activist and creative, retaining something of the early exhibitors' claim to be a participant in the film creative process, and, even more, the experimenter's desire to transform and test the original film material. It was also a source of controversy among Liga members.

The issue was discussed in detail in *Filmliga*, with L.J. Jordaan asserting the 'right to cut'. Jordaan deplored the mutilation of films 'by various profane hands', and declared the film's original form should be considered sacrosanct (at least *in abstracto*). But, in actuality, Jordaan claims, there are few films which are perfect enough to merit this right. He asks: 'How many films can claim because of their intentions – I'm not even saying: because of their result – the right to integral screening? How many filmmakers have made products while assuming naively that not a single metre would be cut?' This issue became especially acute concerning older films (although often made only a few years earlier). Jordaan supported his claim for a 'right to cut' by the rapid progress of film art: 'How many films, whatever their significance might have been before, can still be accepted in their entirety? Take Grune's DIE STRASSE, Wiene's RASKOLNIKOV, Gance's LA ROUE, L'Herbier's FEU MATHIAS PASCAL ... all films that were events in their time; but who still feels the necessity to undergo the superfluous fuss in which the few parts that maintain themselves drown?' Jordaan concluded by proclaiming 'that for the principle of not cutting – defended as is evident from the questionnaire, by many Liga members – the time is not yet ripe'.[27]

There is a great deal to ponder here around this issue, which touches so centrally on the Liga's view of itself as an experimental process. The Liga's lack of cinephilia stands out – it is unthinkable to proclaim the 'right to cut' at the Cinémathèque française in the 1950s. The canon of film history, the aura of the auteur – such concepts do not determine Liga policy. Rather than attempting to preserve or rediscover the past, the Liga claims to be preparing the way for the future, while the past for Jordaan 'is paved with mistakes and fragmentary lucky things ... especially with mistakes!' Jordaan invokes a metaphor even more powerful than laboratory experiments – the surgeon's scalpel: 'the knife goes in – and a healthy organism is freed of a cancerous growth'.[28] The true gold of the future of film must be refined from the dross of the past, or cut away from its moribund body. The Liga stands like a fearsome midwife at an emergency caesarean delivery. The Liga takes an active role, acting as a creative force in ushering in a new era of cinema, even when the filmmakers themselves cannot separate their wheat from chaff. This remained, as Jordaan indicates, a matter of debate within the membership. The Liga had circulated among its members the questionnaire he refers to after their first season, in order to learn audiences' reactions to the programmes. Apparently a slight majority objected to the use of excerpts.

Although old films were excerpted most frequently, programmers also used scissors when presenting contemporary films. Ivens presented fragments of Soviet films he brought back from his trip to the Soviet Union (given to him by the filmmakers, presumably because bringing back whole films was difficult), and NAPOLÉON (FR 1927, Abel Gance) was presented through 'the most important excerpts'. Gance represented for the Filmliga a problematic director (as did Marcel L'Herbier and Jean Epstein). Acknowledging the power of passages in his films, they also deplored his lack of control. The Liga could intervene by showing excerpts: 'if one wants to really experience the poetry of the rhetoric, a proper selection is necessary'.[29] Sometimes excerpts were self-selected, as when Germaine Dulac sent sequences from her feature film LA FOLIE DES VAILLANTS (FR 1926).

A number of films considered problematic were nevertheless shown in their entirety. NOSFERATU (GE 1922, F.W. Murnau), for example, was shown as a whole, even though the programmers thought only certain scenes showed cinematic quality. Apparently the screening was a disaster. *Filmliga* felt it 'was by far the weakest of our series, and, we hope, will remain the weakest'.[30] In the questionnaire circulated at the end of the season, not one person ranked the film highly. The journal still referred back to this 'disaster' a year later when they discussed another unsuccessful screening, this time of Feyder's VISAGES D'ENFANTS. Feyder's film was shown in its entirety, the programme notes indicated, because 'last year's questionnaire requested the film's integral screening, we decided not to cut'.[31] In evaluating the programme, ter Braak claimed a year later, 'After NOSFERATU last year, this second programme of our second season left the audience generally unhappy'. The integral screening of Feyder's film seemed almost to have been intended as a demonstration of the superiority of screening excerpts. Ter Braak chirruped, 'it is clear from the showing of this film that those who in last year's questionnaire demanded integral screenings have been proved wrong'.[32] After that, the leadership resumed the screening of fragments. Comparison may also have played a role in this screening, since Feyder's feature was programmed with fragments from Dulac's most recent film. In this juxtaposition, VISAGES D'ENFANTS was described as 'older work' compared to Dulac's work. That the Feyder film, from 1923, was already understood by Filmliga as an antique indicates how quickly they felt the art of cinema had evolved in five years.

This express-lane view of history of cinema was a major justification for the screening of fragments. Berthold Viertel's film DIE PERÜCKE (GE 1924) was barely three years old when it was screened in early 1928 in the first Liga season. But the programme notes devoted to it placed the film definitively on the other side of a great divide in film history. 'The bathetic and romantic style of this masterly composed work has been replaced with a different way of viewing film. In the short history of cinematography one could call this style "classical", which might mean: past, but therefore in no way surpassed. We present these excerpts as a kind of rehabilitation, if only post mortem'.[33] Metaphors of autopsy and grave robbing make it clear that the Liga not only viewed themselves as the midwives of a cinema of the future, but the undertakers of the cinema of the past. But this progressive view of history assumed aesthetic principles. For instance, Robert Wiene's RASKOLNIKOV (GE 1923) was criticized not so much as an outmoded film, but as an inconsistent one. In fact, Jordaan preferred the 'more passionate and daring' older film by Wiene, DAS CABINET DES DR CALIGARI (GE 1919). RASKOLNIKOV's vacillation in its use of expressionist devices rendered it a film only worth screening in parts, as Jordaan found the film 'as a whole intolerable'.[34]

Programming excerpts assumed and entailed theoretical and aesthetic principles, deriving from the Liga's announced experimental nature. The mission of Filmliga to 'educate the audience' found a pedagogical method in screening fragments, a process, as the programme notes make clear, of demonstration. The selection of excerpts accented what is worthwhile in a film, those aspects redeemable as 'film', while the unshown parts were relegated to the past or to the cinema. Pedagogic programmes demonstrated Filmliga's serious purpose and its antipathy to entertainment. Liga programming not only operated surgically on a film, set it in a network of comparisons, pruned and refined it; it also acted on the audience, transforming their habits of viewing. One learned something about the autonomous art of the film from a Liga programme, or it was not worth attending.

But screening excerpts may also have drawn on an avant-garde love of the fragment and the incomplete, a modernist orientation with roots in the German Romanticism of the Schlegels and Novalis. The typically avant-garde aesthetics of the fragment led to modernist collage, futurist syntax, surrealist games or the pastiche style of poets ranging from Ezra Pound to Blaise Cendrars. Once again the inherent tension of Filmliga appears. The pedagogically exemplary excerpt has a different effect from the modernist fragment. For instance, at the Bauhaus in the late 1920s random bits of celluloid collected at the commercial cinemas in Dessau were spliced together, then projected, with the audience deciding whether the fragments were shown backwards or forwards.

This absurdist Dadaist practice would seem at antipodes to the careful pruning of significant and aesthetically worthy fragments at the Liga. But were the effects entirely unrelated? Students at the Bauhaus soon applied their interest in splicing fragments together to their instructor László Moholy-Nagy's experiments in montage and film rhythm. Although Filmliga programming had a different intention, the distance between a random order and the creation of new, non-narrative systems of relations between shots could easily be bridged in practice.

Many of the films shown at Filmliga explored the zone between the ordered and the random, most obviously Dada- or surrealist-inspired films by Richter, Man Ray or Dekeukeleire. But the exploration of the montage of diverse elements can also be found in such non-fiction compilation films as LES MIRACLES DU CINEMA, HANDELSBLADFILM, or the compilation that Liga member Willem Bon made of old newsreels. The aesthetics of montage – so central not only to many (if not most) of the films programmed by the Liga, as well as to their actual construction of programmes – depended on the play between the fragment and a larger structure. As an element of both modernist aesthetic practice and of the experience of modernity (e.g. the contrasts and juxtapositions of urban life chronicled in Ruttmann's BERLIN and other city symphonies), montage entailed a delight in fragmentation and rapid transitions. Like all the modernist movements of the 1920s, Filmliga meditated on and mediated this new experience and its aesthetic equivalents, in turns glorifying it and attempting to contain it through traditional values.

While montage can be seen as one of the essential elements of the avant-garde in all arts, film provided the strongest examples. Part of the appeal of the fragment to Liga programmers came from cinema's unique control of time – a sense that film's most autonomous possibilities might be best displayed through its ability to cut temporal flow into minute pieces. The film fragment, via the nature of the cut, works through interruption. There is a certain enigmatic fascination that results from fragmentation in film due to its abrupt curtailment of an unfolding temporal logic. The freedom of montage, the assembly of fragments, pointed towards the path that film must take to discover its own rules. Filmliga programmed fragments because their incomplete nature broke the hold of narrative logic and the 'subject'. This withholding of the pleasures of the story or subject from the audience may have provoked the objection to excerpts voiced by some Liga members. But the ideological core of the group strongly defended the practice. Scholte, responding to complaints about the screening of fragments from DIE PERÜCKE, argued, 'We have been reproached that by presenting excerpts we have hindered the comprehensibility of the content. But the "story" was printed in our programme and does not concern us anyway'.[35]

Filmliga was founded not only to screen films that were hard to see otherwise, but to discover and teach new ways to see films. Essential to this was a disdain of simple narrative comprehension. Although Filmliga programmed many narrative films, it also mounted a frontal attack on the hegemony of the story film as represented by the classical Hollywood feature. The alternatives to this form were numerous, and Filmliga contrasted their varied range to the conventions repeated constantly in the Hollywood product. The abstract film, the highly political and generally unpsychological Soviet films, the absurdist melange of Dada and surrealist films, the visual associations and symbolism of the French impressionists, the images of the dynamics of everyday life of the city symphonies and other documentaries – all of these forms sought organizing principles divorced from conventional, character-based narratives. New film forms demanded a new audience, and Filmliga programmes tried to break old habits of movie watching while building a new awareness of the art of the film.

The Promise of Film: A Visual (and Dutch?) Art of Description

In the 1920s the international film society movement began a process of legitimation for the relatively new film medium and its even more recent claims as an art form. Filmliga programmes, the discourse circulated in its journal, its public lectures and discussions – all carved out a place for film alongside other art forms. While Filmliga often valued aesthetics over politics, and seemed anxious to make the new art seem more traditional, they were nonetheless driven by a vision of film's possibilities as a force of transformation, as a new way of experiencing and representing the world. While the world view of Filmliga remained eternally poised between the more conservative project of legitimation and the avant-garde subversion of tradition, it always promoted film as something novel, a medium whose future was more important than its past, and as a force that opened new horizons.

As much as simply appreciating and making available the various novel forms of that avant-garde filmmaking employed in the late 1920s, Filmliga strove to fashion a new film spectator, a new creation necessary for a new art form. Was there a specific attitude towards film, towards the promise Filmliga sensed in film, that we can trace beneath the rich variety of forms it programmed? I believe that we can find in the filmmaking the Liga encouraged, and in the spectatorship it fostered, an alternative conception of cinema's promise, one which unites its avant-garde impulses and its concern for traditional values.

Filmliga shared essential traits with the international avant-garde film culture, but it also showed unique orientations. Nothing in the Liga programming was contradictory to the avant-garde of the time, but it did emphasize certain elements more than others in a very particular way which reflects a uniquely Dutch film culture. I enter here on more speculative territory, based on analysis of Liga programming, but moving into realms of interpretation. Following the example of film scholar Ben Brewster, I have put the interpretation at the end of this chapter, so that readers can take it or leave it.

I base my reading of the legacy of Filmliga partly on the early work of Joris Ivens, one of the most important founding members of Filmliga, although he was generally cast as technical adviser (and through the resources of his father's optical and photographic supply company, Capi, contributed greatly to Filmliga's ability to preview, examine and project films). Ivens' contributions to the Liga journal remain rather modest: notes on aspects of film technique, a report on cinema from Berlin, accounts of his own films and of his Soviet trip, rather than theoretical articles or critiques of films. However, I claim that the films Ivens made in the Netherlands – De Brug, Regen, Branding, and the various parts of Wij Bouwen, all of which were shown in the Liga's early seasons and were products of Filmliga's experimental vision – are as important 'Liga texts' as any published articles or programme notes by ter Braak, Jordaan, Scholte and others. Scholte at one point proclaimed that, with the increase in the number of Dutch filmmakers submitting work, the Liga could 'divide itself up into an active and a viewing section'.[36] As he indicated, it was Ivens' De Brug which opened this doorway and put Filmliga principles into practice.

Thinking of Ivens' early films as active contributions to Filmliga is not meant to limit them to this context. But the Liga had a hand in their creation. De Brug demonstrates Filmliga principles that cinema had to discover and explore its own language founded on dynamic composition and rhythm of editing. Ivens' characterization of De Brug as 'conscious laboratory work' illuminates the common purpose of Liga screening and his filmmaking. Both were involved in discovery, exploration and experiment rather than more traditional ideas of realizing

Figure 3.1 Dynamic compositions in a 'conscious laboratory work':
DE BRUG [The Bridge] (1928, Joris Ivens). [Deutsche Kinemathek]

(or exhibiting) masterpieces. Both saw their work as steps towards a realization of cinema's promise for the future.

De Brug and Regen are not only masterpieces of the avant-garde cinema of the 1920s, embodying and demonstrating the attainment of a unique cinematic language; they are unique meditations on the promise of cinematic vision. Note the difficulty of fitting them into any previously existing genre. Clearly they are not fictional dramatic films, nor abstract films. They are important films within the history of documentary, but partly because they transformed the form. As documentary films they create a new relation to that term so disdained by the Filmliga, the 'subject'. While De Brug certainly gives an extraordinary account of the railway bridge in Rotterdam, no viewer would describe it as simply an explication of the workings of the bridge (indeed, Ivens reports that audiences in the Soviet Union complained about the film's lack of information). Instead, it records visually the rhythms and forms, motions and varying perspectives of this industrial technology, capturing the modes of vision and seeing occasioned by this structure as much as it represents the bridge itself. Or, rather, this film demonstrates the impossibility of separating the visual experience of a modern structure from its essential existence.

The criticism this film often received as a purely aesthetic experiment deserves some discussion. Béla Balázs launched perhaps the nastiest of these criticisms, claiming that Ivens was an impressionist who 'dematerialized' his subjects and created something closer to the abstract film than a true documentary. None of Ivens' camera set-ups, Balázs complained, 'has anything to do with either the purpose of the bridge or its industrial qualities'.[37] Balázs' understanding of the film, while negative, shared a common perception with the positive description of the film by many critics and historians (including ter Braak, Germaine Dulac and the reviewer in *Close Up*) as a 'symphony', an exploration of the rhythms and motions of the bridge which attained the symbolist aspiration to the ideality of music, so central to the film culture we have been examining.

Certainly this analogy describes one aspect of the film. But if Ivens 'dematerializes' this gigantic machine-bridge it is by means of another relatively tiny machine, the hand-held Kinamo camera. Ivens highlights his own novel apparatus in the first shots of the film as he aims the camera directly into the lens of another (or into the audience, depending on which end of the film chain you think of). Ivens' film does not record a romantic, subjective, aesthetic impression of a bridge. Dulac's Arabesque, for instance does 'dematerialize' her images into pure shimmering light through a rather literal employment of the musical analogy. But, instead of mist, refracted sunlight, and faceted reflections, DE BRUG plunges into an industrial environment and the new modes of perception that a massive machine structure allows, encourages and even demands. One machine sees another here, the camera's precision in view points and editing capturing a uniquely modern experience of this uniquely modern structure.

DE BRUG exploits the visual possibilities of modern industrial construction which, unlike the ideals of domesticity or monumental edifices, remains open to the world rather than enclosed and cloistered. DE BRUG stands as a major work of the modernist movement of the 1920s but the source here is not the painting, poetry or theatre which inspired the cinematic avant-garde in most countries, but architecture, a key modernist influence in the Netherlands. The Filmliga intersected with modern architecture in many ways and this interaction partly defines the unique Dutch understanding of modernist cinema. A full exploration of this interaction, however, lies beyond the scope of this chapter on programming, other than to note that Liga programmes highlighted films on modern architecture: Pierre Chenal's films BÂTIR (FR 1931) and ARCHITECTURES D'AUJOURD'HUI (FR 1931) both focused on Le Corbusier, as well as Ivens' own, somewhat less inspired, NIEUWE ARCHITECTUUR. But DE BRUG is not a film whose 'subject' is architecture. Ivens' captures Filmliga's vision of the promise of cinema as an engagement with modernist vision, through the common concern of avant-garde film and modern architecture with new modes of experience opened up by technology and technological environments.

Far from a poetic, dematerialized impressionism, DE BRUG explores the new vision allowed by a new sort of construction. The Eiffel Tower at the end of the nineteenth century scandalized traditional artists while it inspired modernists like Seurat and Delaunay with a structure which exposed and demonstrated its construction and material laws. As Sigfried Giedion in his 1928 manifesto for the new architecture, *Building in France, Building in Iron, Building in Ferro-concrete*, describes: 'In the air-flooded stairs of the Eiffel Tower, better yet, in the steel limbs of a *pont tranbordeur*, we confront the basic aesthetic experience of today's buildings: through the delicate iron net suspended in mid-air stream things, ships, sea, houses, masts, landscape and harbor. They lose their delimited form: as one descends, they circle into each other and intermingle simultaneously'.[38] Could any art other than film convey this new experience of visual simultaneity? Giedion seems here to provide a sketch of Ivens' film of the Rotterdam lifting bridge. Ivens extends the celebration of modern architectonics to the Rotterdam railway bridge, exploring not only its reorganization of space, but through cinematic time, demonstrating how it works, its processes and rhythms. Contrary to Balázs, what Ivens records is neither the simple functioning of the bridge, nor a subjective impression of it, but a new social mode of vision, penetrating, organizing fragments in a blending of space and time.

No other avant-garde film to this point had so thoroughly explored a single site, creating a thorough investigation of its visual properties. While the musical analogy describes something of the exhilarating experience of this film, the ambition of synesthesia seems utterly lacking. Instead we experience one of the great documents of the modes of vision that modern industry and engineering made possible. I would maintain that DE BRUG does not create a subjective lyricism of the sort Dulac or Epstein pursued, nor a political analysis *à la* Vertov. But there is an exposition here of visual discovery and perceptual exploration, a discourse on method leading to a visually based knowledge, the ultimate fruit of film's promise. Ivens said 'I had realized that only a creative and prolonged observation would permit me to capture the complexity and richness of the reality facing me'.[39] The modern world and its new environments present a series of non-traditional experiences. Ivens' film participated in the ambition of the modernist movement to discover a means of representation that could answer this challenge. But more, he strove to discover film not simply as a mode of representation or even of demonstration, but of visual knowledge and understanding.

I would claim that Filmliga, particularly when focused through its most extraordinary fruit, the early films of Joris Ivens, was involved in discovering in film a new way of seeing the world; new participation in this modern world was made possible in film through the technological eye of the camera and the juxtaposition of images allowed by the editing table. This was congruent, of course, with the ambitions of the international avant-garde, perhaps most coherently theorized and articulated in the films and writings of Dziga Vertov. But whereas Vertov's vision was organized primarily by political theory, yielding, as he put it, 'an abstracted "I see"',[40] Ivens remains determinedly immanent, close to the surface and tactility of things.

Ivens self-consciously makes the process of sight the true 'subject' of his films behind his ostensible subjects of a railway bridge or the rain in Amsterdam. While REGEN, co-directed by Mannus Franken, is less obviously modernist in its topic (and more apparently 'impressionist' or poetic, as Ivens himself described it), the film remains engaged in a search for an understanding of a phenomenon, the visual knowledge the cinema opens up. REGEN accumulates metaphors of vision through its many shots of seeing through semi-transparent media, the windows covered with rain, the reflections caught in puddles, the blurred focus the downpour casts over the distance. At the same time, we never lose sight of the fact that this is rain falling in a modern city, and Ivens' sense of urban geography and rhythms is more finely honed than Ruttmann's click-clack mechanisms of contrast. While the temporal form of REGEN follows the onset, climax and diminution of a storm (synthetically made up in editing, of course, from numerous rainfalls over many days), its space, its sense of a larger whole into which each single moment fits, comes from the city and its intersections of streets, canals, houses, side-walks and the people who circulate through them. Ivens pursues more here than a meteorological lyricism, as his analogies between different rhythmic shots reveal. He commented on perhaps the most memorable moment in the film – the little girls running wrapped in a blanket to protect themselves from a soaking: 'the skipping movements of their legs had the rhythm of raindrops'.[41] This exploration of analogy, created not through the literal transcription of poetic images (such as we often find in Dulac) but through a close observation of the everyday in order to uncover a common rhythm uniting the life of the city, reveals Ivens' practice as the intersection between the everyday documentaries pro-grammed by the Filmliga and the attempts at film poetry they also fea-tured. Ivens grasps the direct connection between visual observation and transformation in which poetry comes from clarity of perception, rather than the romantic soft-focus and diffusion of the French school.

Ivens' films probe the core of Filmliga's faith in film, the promise for the future they sought from the medium: that film constituted a new way, not only of portraying but of discovering the world. This approach to film as a new means of investigation and revelation can be found in a number of theoretical writings of the 1920s and 1930s, including Epstein, Balász, Kracauer and Benjamin. It demanded new modes of making films and new modes of watching them. The almost millennial promises that film and new modes of spectatorship held for Filmliga helps to explain their suspicion of the Hollywood film. The Hollywood film was kitsch because it simply lolled a viewer into a fantasy without using visual devices to sharpen their perception or increase their knowledge of the world. Not only, as Vertov wailed, was the fictional film fake, it wrapped its viewer in a world that new forms of visual knowledge could not penetrate. Absorption in a story, involve-ment with characters, were pleasures Filmliga combated not only by programming non-narrative films but also by fragmenting fictional films which had visually inventive moments, in order that the visual experience would triumph over the telling of a tale or exposition of the subject. Filmliga sought a new visual regime, one bound up not simply with aesthetic pleasures or cinephilia, but with the thrill of experiment and the promise of a new knowledge.

The Filmliga's experimental programming and Ivens' 'laboratory work' of his early films recall Svetlana Alpers' discussion of a particular aspect of Dutch art of the seventeenth century, which she calls the 'art of describing'.[42] In contrast to the dramatic, theatrically inspired, Albertian composition of the great paintings of the Italian renaissance, Dutch art pursued a mode of representation that was resolutely empirical and obsessed with new powers of vision. This was embodied, for instance, in Antonie van Leeuwenhoek's microscope, Constantijn Huygens' experiments with lenses and the camera obscura, and, we could add, his son Christiaan's invention of the ultimate ancestor of the cinema, the magic lantern. As opposed to the dramatic scenography of the Italians, the Dutch sought out the visual experiences of the everyday. A union between knowledge and sight also entailed a strongly immanent involvement with the appearance and surface of things. Alpers' reading of Dutch art has been both seminal and controversial in art history, and my purpose here is not to invoke her as an authority but rather as a keen observer of the nature of visual knowledge and its intimate relation to the opening up of new realms of imagery and experience.

Ivens provides the central instance of this cinema of description. He eschewed the dramatic structure of the Hollywood film (even in his fictional narrative collaboration with Franken, BRANDING). But while influenced by Vertov, he remains much closer to the surface of things, to the sensual aspects of daily life, fully immanent in a physical world (even in an overtly political film like BORINAGE). Perhaps nowhere is his pursuit of a visual, or even better (like his Dutch forebears) of an 'optical' knowledge clearer than in his description of his abandoned IK-FILM undertaken in the late 1920s. This film sought to use the camera as a means of conveying a character's subjectivity through an extended use of what is now called a point-of-view shot. In adapting this subject, Ivens pursued a dominant theme in the avant-garde film tradition, the visual portrayal of subjectivity. The expressionist sets of CALIGARI and RASKOLNIKOV, the superimpositions, moving camera and soft focus of Dulac, Epstein and Dekeukeleire, even the rapid montage of Gance and Metzner, all attempted to find visual correlatives for mental states.

But this interiority does not seem to be Ivens' main purpose, at least in his description of the film. Ivens concentrated on the exact type of lenses, the carefully regulated sort of camera mount that would give a precise recreation of human *optical* experience. He abandoned the experiment, but the unique way he approached it reveals a sensibility attuned to the actual act of visual perception and the way it encounters the world, as opposed to the creation of subjective characterization or the psychological possibilities that other filmmakers pursued.

The core of the promise that film offered to the Liga lies in this pursuit of visual knowledge and the new access that film offered to the world. Thus, their fascination with the everyday does not contradict their interest in visual experiment and distortion. Their antipathy to Hollywood is not simply cultural snobbery (although it may have been that as well) but a belief that detouring vision into fictional illusionist fantasy blunted film's capacity to uncover the secrets of the world.

For Ivens, of course, this mode of filmmaking was an early stage of development, one which awaited a political awakening to truly fulfil itself. The 1920s avant-garde would ultimately shipwreck on the shoals of politics, in the form of the totalitarian regimes of Hitler and Stalin which put a sudden stop to formal experimentation, as well as in the growing conviction of many key figures of the avant-garde that only political analysis could yield the sort of understanding of the world they sought – Ivens and Richter primary among them (encouraged, of course, by the examples set by Vertov and Eisenstein). The avant-garde in all media in the 1920s had embraced the idea that new forms and media – from photography to photo-montage to cinema to typography to radio to architecture – could not only portray a new world but hasten its realization by challenging and transforming perception. The experience in the 1930s of worldwide depression and the growth of totalitarianism transformed the world, so that this promise remained either a hollow one or an abandoned project yet to be fulfilled.

Ivens' early films chart this faith in the visual exposition as well as its ultimate disillusionment. The film which Ivens says took him out of the avant-garde, his documentary for the construction union Wij Bouwen, retains, in its strongest segments, a Liga-like approach (and these segments were programmed by Filmliga). The masterpiece of this uneven film is, of course, Zuiderzee. There is much to be said of this film portraying the founding myth of Dutch national identity, the wresting of land from the sea. What I would stress, however, is that while its rhythms and compositions may be less formalistic than De

BRUG, they still exemplify his absorptive description of the process he is recording and observing.

The anecdote Ivens tells in his autobiography about showing ZUIDERZEE in the Soviet Union illustrates the unique knowledge that film could convey. After a screening, a Soviet worker objected that Ivens must have lied when he described his background as middle class, since ZUIDERZEE conveyed the work process in precisely the way a worker experienced it. Ivens, instead of being insulted by the accusation, realized the compliment to the film and explained how he had immersed himself in the processes of labour, carrying stones, moving supports, in order to realize how to film them properly. Whether or not the anecdote is literally true, it conveys the unique involvement of this film (and Ivens' earlier films as well) in capturing processes in all their manifest visuality, physicality and *gestural* nature. The power of this extraordinary film comes not only from its capturing of the epic battle of the elements, but from its faith in the promise of cinema as a new form of representation which could capture, and convey, the actual *experience* of labour, its effort and skill, and the physical and bodily processes. Visuality in Ivens, as in seventeenth-century Dutch art, plunges the viewer into the physical feel of things, their tactile surfaces, heft, weight and balance.

The visual promise offered by the film, whose different aspects are scattered through the varied types of films shown by the Filmliga, remains difficult to articulate in words, and not only because of the problem of translation from imagery to language. Film claimed to be the powerful means to convey not only the look of the world, but its feel, its tactility, its rhythms and physical efforts and delights. This view of film remains in some ways a forgotten promise, one which the Liga bring us back to. Take the modern suspicion of the visual in French culture.[43] This school of thought identifies vision with the panoptical gaze: a vision that is detached, perspectival, abstracting and domineering. In spite of an effort by French theorists to apply this to cinema, the experience of films such as those of Ivens demonstrates that the cinematographic apparatus does not by necessity visualize the world this way. A different, bodily immanent way of seeing, alert to movement and transformation, experiencing the world from a shifting perspective, rhythmically organized by human projects and bodily skill was explored in Ivens' early films. It was dreamed of by other filmmakers as well, and the Filmliga sought to define and encourage it. I feel this vision of film offers an alternative visual tradition to the panopticon and the Albertian system.

But Ivens' films from the Liga period also show that the cinema was in no way a utopian device that automatically delivered this visual richness. It was embedded in a technological world which ultimately, rather than achieving utopian goals, denigrated and destroyed this dignity of labour. Ivens' film on returning from the USSR, PHILIPS RADIO, financed and sponsored by the Philips Radio company, presents a very different world from the skilled physical labour challenging the elements in ZUIDERZEE. Here the human worker is caught within a web of industrial processes that is repetitive and spatially abstract. The very nature of factory space with its constantly moving conveyor belts, assembly lines and delivery systems, fixes the human gesture into a mechanical schema. Moments of traditional craft, such as the glass blowing that was so much a part of the Dutch handicraft culture celebrated in the painting of the seventeenth century, here seem imprisoned within a competition with machinery that is able to perform the same tasks more rapidly, but less beautifully. Ivens has indicated that he intended the film as a critique of the Philips plant – but this did not reflect statements he made during production.[44]

Leftist critics such as Léon Moussinac did read the film as a critique of the dehumanization of the worker under capitalism. However, viewing the film one senses an intense ambivalence. Ivens' camera portrays a dehumanizing system in complete contrast to the labour in ZUIDERZEE. Projected back to back, the two films seem to reveal – as no other form could – the transformation of work in the twentieth century. But PHILIPS RADIO also seems to participate in this technology, to caress it, to be attuned to it, to glide with the machines, to pulse with their rhythm, especially in relation to the celebratory music on the soundtrack. Film here seems seduced into abstraction, however much its bad conscience drags against this momentum. The world of bright illuminated glass tubes and bulbs, and the ease of movement, endow the film with a sense of mystery (what are those strange experiments those scientists carry out?) that contrasts sharply with the immediately comprehensible processes in ZUIDERZEE (the earth and rocks sink, the water rushes but is ultimately confined, and the human arm and back accomplish it).

The promise of visual knowledge sought by Filmliga was threatened already by its contradictory position within technology. Would it be a tool that could render the world and its people and processes visual, graspable, making viewers experience them in new ways, participating in their daily life and its rhythms, *feeling* as well as seeing, or experiencing seeing as feeling? Or was the world at this very point withdrawing from sight, becoming deceptive in its visual configurations in a manner that cinema would not be able to grasp directly – becoming, in Godard's terms, no longer a just image, but just an image?

Ivens himself provided the most bitter critique of the failure of the promise sensed in the Zuiderzee film in his starkly political essay film NIEUWE GRONDEN [New Earth] (NL 1933). Here Ivens reveals that the promise of new fertile land, of harvests enabled by human labour wrestling with the sea, was betrayed by a worldwide economic slump in which agricultural products no longer received a fair market price and were dumped or burned – even though, incidentally, this slump did not affect the new land conquered from the sea in ZUIDERZEE. The wasting of potential glares at us from this film, not only in the images of burning grain and spilled milk, but in the way the powerful images from Ivens' earlier film no longer say what they seemed to say. The knowledge and power they once held has been betrayed as well, as the images are no longer edited in order to make us participate in this creative labour, but instead these gestures are rendered meaningless, now part of a political and economic system that their labour cannot influence. As the labourer's work has been rendered pointless, the images too are drained of their immanent significance, are hollowed out by the new editing patterns Ivens devises which he himself described as being structured like a joke, rendering this heroic effort nonsensical. The world itself changed as it moved into the 1930s, and the utopian promise of direct participation through film in the nature of the world was rendered opaque. I experienced the ultimate stage in this process during the summer of 1998 researching Liga films, when I saw in Amsterdam cinemas an advertising film which intercut Iven's ZUIDERZEE footage with carefully lit shots of muscular male models posed next to machinery in order to sell Amstel beer. The *reductio ad absurdum* of film's ability to be re-edited to create new meanings was realized. Any image can mean anything, the power of a unique vision becomes a trendy 'look' channelled into the exciting of commodity desire; the process of labour simply spells: thirst = beer. After all, they are just images…

I do not wish to sound simplistically moralistic in decrying this beer advertisement. It reveals something fundamental about the nature of the film image, an insight about its inherent ability to synthetically produce meaning, a discovery that ultimately derives from the montage experiments of Kuleshov and Eisenstein, an axiom of the 1920s discovery of a new cinematic language. Filmliga must strike us as in some ways misguided in its exclusion of the popular from the nature of cinema, it elitist belief in an art untainted by commerce. Cinema always leads us into the heart of darkness: the industrialized modes of production, the role of technology, the dominance of financing – all of these are part of the dialectic of film history and, I would claim, film art, and can never be simply ignored. But they are *part* of a dialectic, and there remains a need to preserve and highlight other aspects of film, such as the search for visual meanings and knowledge beyond fashioning legible signs in the construction of a story, the conveying of information, or the exciting of consumer desire. I can only feel in debt to those who grasped this promise of cinema as it flickered up, as the moment of its peril, and perhaps extinction, approached. If it can never be fulfilled simply, this promise of new means of visual knowledge still hovers around us.

Notes

1. Noël Carroll. 1988. *Philosophical Problems of Classical Film Theory.* Princeton, NJ: Princeton University Press, 29.
2. Yuri Tsivian. 1996. 'Two "Stylists" of the Teens: Franz Hofer and Yevgenii Bauer', in Thomas Elsaesser and Michael Wedel (eds), *A Second Life: German Cinema's First Decades,* Amsterdam: Amsterdam University Press, 264–77, here 264.
3. Quoted after Ansje van Beusekom. 1998. *Film als kunst. Reacties op een nieuw medium in Nederland, 1895–1940,* Amsterdam: Unpublished Ph.D.
4. L.J. Jordaan. 1928. 'Film en "amusement"', in *Filmliga,* October, 4f.
5. *Close Up,* Jan. 1929, 70.
6. Tsivian, 'Two "Stylists" of the Teens'.
7. 'Rules for the Amateur', in *Close Up,* May 1929, 246.
8. Gilles Deleuze. 1986. *Cinema 1: The Image Movement,* London: Athlone, 77 and 80.
9. Peter Kubelka. 1990. 'La theorie du cinéma métrique', in Christian Lebrat (ed.), *Peter Kubelka,* Paris: Expérimental, 62.
10. Tsivian, 'Two "Stylists" of the Teens', 264–77.
11. Richard Koszarski. 1990. *An Evening's Entertainment: The Age of the Silent Feature Picture, 1915–1928,* New York: Scribner.
12. This is not to deny the interest such programs may have had, especially its range of different modes of representation within genres, from animation to documentary to feature length fictional film.
13. Jordaan, 'Film en "amusement"', 4f.
14. According to eye witness B. Stroman; see N.J. Brederoo (ed.). 1979. *Film en beeldende kunst, 1900–1930,* Utrecht: Centraal Museum, 7.
15. Constant van Wessem. 1927. 'De film met of zonder muziek?', in *Filmliga* 2, October, 7f.
16. B. van Lier. 1929. 'Filmkunst en "muzikale" begeleiding', in *Filmliga,* November, 11f.
17. Menno ter Braak. 1927. 'De aesthetiek van het filmprogramma', in *Filmliga* 1, September, 2ff.
18. Ibid., emphasis added.

19. Ibid.
20. Anon. 1982. 'Tweede voorstelling. Programma', in *Filmliga 1927–1931. Met een inleiding door Jan Heijs* (Reprint), Nijmegen: SUN, 57f.
21. ter Braak, 'De aesthetiek', 2ff.
22. Menno ter Braak. 1927. 'Onze tweede matinee', in *Filmliga* 3, November, 2ff.
23. Anon. 1982. 'Vijfde voorstelling. Programma', in *Filmliga 1927–1931*, 117f.
24. Anon. 1982. 'Zevende programma', in *Filmliga 1927–1931*, 391f.
25. Anon. 1982. 'Zesde programma', in *Filmliga 1927–1931*, 371f.
26. Menno ter Braak. 1929. 'Ons zesde programma', in *Filmliga*, March, 83f.
27. L.J. Jordaan. 1929. 'Over Amerika, een Parijsche film en het recht van coupure', in *Filmliga*, April, 97ff.
28. Ibid.
29. Anon. 1982. 'Zevende programma', in *Filmliga 1927–1931*, 391f.
30. Henrik Scholte. 1928. 'Onze vierde matinee', in *Filmliga*, January, 4.
31. Anon. 1982. 'Tweede voorstelling. Programma', in *Filmliga 1927–1931*, 295f.
32. Menno ter Braak. 1928. 'Ons tweede programma', in *Filmliga*, November, 27f.
33. Anon. 1982. 'Zevende voorstelling. Programma', in *Filmliga 1927–1931*, 161f.
34. L.J. Jordaan. 1928. 'Onze negende matinee', in *Filmliga*, April, 3f.
35. Henrik Scholte. 1928. 'Onze zevende matinee', in *Filmliga*, March, 2f.
36. Henrik Scholte. 1930. 'Onze vierde voorstelling', in *Filmliga*, February, 54f.
37. Béla Balázs. 1984. *Der Geist des Films. Artikel und Aufsätze, 1926–1931*, Munich: Hanser, 126.
38. Siegfried Giedion. 1995. *Building in France, Building in Iron, Building in Ferro-concrete*. Santa Monica, CA: Getty Center for the History of Art and the Humanities.
39. Joris Ivens. 1969. *The Camera and I*. Berlin: Seven Seas, 29.
40. See Dziga Vertov. 1984. *Kino-Eye*, Berkeley: University of California Press.
41. Ibid., 37.
42. Svetlana Alpers. 1983. *The Art of Describing: Dutch Art in the Seventeenth Century*. Chicago: University of Chicago Press.
43. Martin Jay. 1993. *Downcast Eyes: The Denigration of Vision in Twentieth-Century French Thought*. Berkeley: University of California Press.
44. Hans Schoots. 1995. *Gevaarlijk leven. Een biografie van Joris Ivens*. Amsterdam: Mets, 91f.

Chapter 4

WHEN WAS SOVIET CINEMA BORN? THE INSTITUTIONALIZATION OF SOVIET FILM STUDIES AND THE PROBLEMS OF PERIODIZATION

Natalie Ryabchikova

The birthday of the cinema is traditionally celebrated on 28 December, in commemoration of the first public séance by the Lumière brothers in Paris in 1895. While the Russian film community, along with the rest of the world, participated in the festivities that marked cinema's centennial, the Day of Cinema that is celebrated every year in Russia is 27 August, which was the date in 1919 when Vladimir Lenin signed the decree allowing the nationalization of all photo and film trade and production – so, like the date of Russian Orthodox Christmas, it does not correspond to that of the rest of the world. At present the historic event behind the Day of Russian Cinema seems to be forgotten in popular discourse and goes unquestioned in the discourse of film studies. The 90th anniversary of the decree in August 2009 was not celebrated at all. Instead, in the autumn of 2008, the 'Centennial of Russian Cinema' was commemorated, counting from the theatrical release of 'the first Russian film', PONIZOVAIA VOL'NITSA [aka Sten'ka Razin] (dir. Vladimir Romashkov, 1908). The oblivion into which Lenin's decree has sunk over the recent decades is in stark contrast to the years of the Soviet Union, when it was considered the point of origin of all Soviet cinema. For example, in 1944 the head of the Committee on Cinema Affairs, Ivan Bol'shakov, began his lecture on '25 Years of the Soviet Cinema', by saying: 'The chronology of the Soviet film art begins on 27 August, 1919 … The decree has laid out the foundations of the Soviet cinema as an area of Socialist culture that is being led and governed by the Soviet state'.[1]

This uncontested date, 27 August, which at first marked the beginning of the Soviet cinema but has now come to designate the 'birth' of Russian cinema in general, does not answer, but instead complicates, the question 'When was Russian/Soviet cinema born?' The 'date of birth' reflects less the moment of Soviet cinema's nascence, and rather the period when the date itself was established through the work of Soviet film scholars. It is possible to say that Soviet cinema, that is, the traditional narrative of its history, was born between 1925 and 1935. Moreover, as the following notes towards the history of the Soviet film studies show, the narrative of Soviet and Russian cinema is at least as much a product of genuine historical research as it is a sign of the Soviet cultural politics of the 1920s and 1930s. The traditional history of Soviet cinema is inextricably connected to its historiography, and the history of the discipline and its institutionalization can show why the Soviet film history evolved the way it did.

The Birth of Soviet Cinema

The date of the birth of the new Soviet state was established as the date of the Bolshevik coup: 25 October (7 November, according to the new style) 1917. The first celebration of that event happened only one year later. As James von Geldern notes, 'Holidays were … instrumental to revolutionary history. The February Revolution was sparked by an International Women's Day demonstration; and later in 1917 the Bolsheviks used Petrograd Soviet Day, declared by themselves on October 22, as a dry run for taking power'.[2] A simultaneous tendency of bringing new events into line with previous ones, creating a narrative 'backwards' (in the words of the leading Marxist historian Mikhail Pokrovsky, 'history is politics projected onto the past'), helps to explain the fact that Soviet cinema ended up being almost two years younger than the Soviet state. Moreover, until 1925 there could be no talk about the age or the date of birth of either an industry or an art that in effect did not exist.

In the spring of 1924, Nikolai Lebedev, a young journalist and member of the Bolshevik Party who only two years previously had turned his attention to film, compiled a book called *Kino: ego kratkaia istoriia, ego vozmozhnosti, ego stroitel'stvo v sovetskom gosudarstve* [Cinema: Its Short History, its Possibilities and its Construction in the Soviet State]. He introduces it as 'the first Soviet attempt at systematization of the meager available sources [on cinema] for the general reader'.[3]

Lebedev's first general narrative of the Soviet film history includes nationalization of 1919 as only one of several episodes in a chapter entitled 'Cinema after October'. Stating that by the end of 1919 film production had completely stopped and that following the decree of 27 August 1919, 'the All-Russian Photo and Cinema Committee carried out the nationalization of all film companies', Lebedev goes on to enumerate what exactly this nationalization brought to the Soviet state: 'several dozen distribution offices with their stock of already worn-out films, a couple of dozen small film studios, several laboratories for development and printing and a couple of million metres of different films on the negative stock'.[4] He then concludes: 'In effect, this nationalization did not bring us any good at that time'. According to Lebedev, there was no film stock and no 'revolutionary-minded' filmmakers to create any pictures; and the enormous amount of expropriated property and film prints needed so many resources for their preservation that there was no money left for actual production.[5] Calling the attention of the party to the matters of cinema, as he did at that time in a number of articles in *Pravda*, *Izvestiia* and *Kino*, Lebedev acknowledges that up to the very moment of the book's writing 'cinema has been left to the mercy of fate', that is, to its own devices.[6]

Less than a year later, on 1 January 1925, an editorial appeared on the front page of the trade newspaper *Kino-nedelia* (Cinema Week), entitled 'A 5-year Anniversary that Has Passed Unobserved'.[7] On this first day of the new year the editorial reminded its readers:

> On 27 August 1924, it was five years since the publishing of the Sovnarkom of RSFSR's resolution 'On the Transfer of Photo and Cinema Trade and Industry Under the Jurisdiction of People's Commissariat of Enlightenment'. ... *Later* this resolution was carried out. ... *It is well known that for the next several years the implementation of the film industry's nationalization has not produced the desired results and has not led to the creation of a Soviet film production industry* due to a number of objective reasons.
> Now, however, when Soviet cinema has begun to move forward ...; when the Soviet film production industry exists and is getting stronger every day, we need to remember *the already forgotten decree* that laid the first stone into the foundation of the Soviet film construction.[8]

These passages lay out exactly why the date of 27 August 1919 had suddenly begun to acquire importance – because new political and economic developments had finally brought cinema to the fore. The editorial was published right next to the lead article, 'To the New Year of 1925', which announced the merging of the existing film organizations into

Figure 4.1 Nikolai Lebedev. [Laboratory for the history of Russian cinema in VGIK]

the new joint-stock company named *Sovkino*. This company was given monopoly over all film-related export and import operations, while all film activities were absolved from tax in order to 'finally finish building the foundation that has already been laid for propaganda and cultural and educational cinema'.[9] The article proclaimed that 'To Soviet cinema the year 1924 has brought achievements, which the first six years that have passed since the October revolution, failed to bring'. The author of the article connected the long-awaited government measures (including consolidation of film importation, production and distribution, as well as economic incentives finally given to the industry) directly to the fact that 'the attention of the Party, which cinema needed so much over these past years, has finally started to manifest itself'. This in turn brought to mind 'the already forgotten decree'. Moreover, the attention of the party, as Soviet film history was now beginning to be narrated, had always been there. In contrast to Lebedev's description, the decree of 1919 in the *Cinema Week* article was already interpreted as 'the cardinal step of the Soviet power that gave cinema entirely into the hands of the state'.[10]

These documents show that the desire to construct a coherent narrative of the party's attention to the industry did not initially belong to the party itself. It was born from within the film community that by 1925 could boast of some noticeable achievements and could therefore seek approval and legitimization from the party and the state (along with much needed subsidies).[11]

Lenin's death in January 1924 acted as a catalyst, among other things, for the writing of a multitude of memoirs. His every word seemed to be in need of recording for posterity. In 1925 a documentary filmmaker turned film historian, Grigorii Boltianskii, published a book called *Lenin i kino* (Lenin and the Cinema), in which he collected all available materials that documented Lenin's attitude to cinema. Among them was a letter written to Boltianskii by the Commissar of Enlightenment, Anatolii Lunacharskii. In the letter Lunacharskii cited Lenin as saying: 'of all the arts, cinema for us is the most important'.[12] This reported pronouncement, together with other facts that established Lenin's connection to cinema, was then used to create prestige for the industry itself.

It took another ten years, however, for the date on which Lenin's decree was signed to become firmly established as the starting point of the Soviet film history narrative. It finally happened due to another string of cinematic achievements that the industry administrators were able to connect to Soviet cinema's own anniversary.

The twentieth anniversary of the revolution of 1905 and the tenth anniversary of the October Revolution of 1927 were marked by the production of films (several of them officially commissioned) that dealt with the country's revolutionary history. This history culminated with October 1917, which also began the new Soviet era.[13] By the fifteenth anniversary of the October Revolution, celebrated in November 1932, cinema could not boast of any major recent achievements.[14]

By 1934, however, Glavnoe upravlenie kinofotopromyshlennosti (GUKF, the State Directorate for the Film and Photo Industry), had been formed with direct subordination to Sovnarkom of the USSR, and the situation had begun to brighten up. The head of GUKF, Boris Shumiatskii, arranged the participation of the Soviet delegation at the Venice Film Festival of 1934; the release of CHAPAEV (SU 1934, Georgii and Sergei Vasil'ev), coordinated with that year's October celebration, and the organization of the Moscow International Film Festival scheduled for the early 1935. He then suggested another event that would demonstrate to the higher authorities the recent achievements of 'the most important of all the arts'. Using a logical operation similar to that of the *Cinema Week* editors of a decade earlier, Shumiatskii wrote the lead article in the anniversary issue of the main trade magazine, *Sovetskoe kino* (Soviet Cinema): 'We can celebrate our anniversary not only because we have existed for 15 years, but also because in our 15th year we have achievements, of which we can and should be proud'.[15]

Film scholars were given the task to support this pronouncement with facts and figures. Nikolai Iezuitov, a film critic and historian, wrote in a book prepared to coincide with the celebration of Soviet cinema's fifteenth anniversary:

> Spring, summer and autumn of 1934 were marked by the new steady advance of our cinema. Soviet films received much appreciation at the international exhibition in Venice [the Venice Film Festival]. They demonstrated the ideological and artistic power of our art, as well as its key position in world culture ... We are standing at the threshold of Soviet cinema's new period of growth; and the growth of 1926–29 will seem weak and pale by comparison, a mere rehearsal for the true blossoming of the cinematic art ... Everything is ready for this advance. The Party, the Government and the Soviet society have fostered film professionals, surrounded both the industry and its workers with attention. They have always taken care of cinema as a tool for communist propaganda, and therefore they have created for it the favourable conditions that can only be created in one state in the world – the socialist state.[16]

The Institutionalization of Film Studies and the Creation of the Soviet Film History

The final establishment of Soviet cinema's point of 'origin' was just one task (albeit perhaps the most pressing one) of the historiographic activity that had begun by 1934 within the emerging field of national film history. Its consolidation and institutionalization were ultimately due to the same historicizing process that made Lenin's decree the progenitor of THE BATTLESHIP POTEMKIN (SU 1925, Sergei Eisenstein) and CHAPAEV, and that turned his words about 'the most important of all the arts' into Soviet cinema's raison d'être.

The narrative of Soviet film history had to be created in order to show the progress of Soviet cinema towards its proudly acknowledged achievements – and this has become the impetus for the discipline's creation. To establish the historical narrative the question of periodization had to be tackled first – and so it became the focus of the first Soviet film historians' activity in the first half of the 1930s.

The definitive history of Soviet cinema was demanded by the industry itself (as part of the process of its legitimization), and also by the need to train new cinema professionals who would be taught the inherent difference between the nature of Soviet cinema and that of the bourgeois cinema of the West. That is why, after several abortive attempts, the most successful project of the institutionalization of film studies, with its subfield of film history, was carried out in the main educational institution for cinema in the Soviet Union.

Just as with the film industry itself, the development and institutionalization of film studies began independently of the direct involvement of party or government, and only acquired official support by the mid-1930s. The more or less systematic study of the theory and history of cinema (and, specifically, Russian cinema) began in the mid-1920s. In 1924, the year during which Nikolai Lebedev released his book, and the first 'anniversary' of Soviet cinema went unnoticed, a *kinokabinet* (Film Cabinet) was created within the intricate system of the State Academy of Artistic Sciences (GAKhN) in Moscow.[17] In 1929 GAKhN was renamed State Academy of Art Studies (GAIS), and the Film Cabinet became its Film Section.

In late 1925 a *kinokomitet* (Film Committee) was established at the State Institute of the History of Art in Leningrad.[18] Its publications included important translations of cinema books by Léon Moussinac, Béla Balázs and Rudolf Harms, but the most famous one was the Formalist foray into cinema, the 1927 volume *Poetika kino* (The Poetics of Cinema) with articles by Iurii Tynianov, Viktor Shklovsky and Boris Eikhenbaum.[19] Boris Likhachev, a theatre actor and director, one of the very first Russian film historians, worked in the Film Committee on his book *Cinema in Russia (1896–1926)*.[20] The activities of the Leningrad film scholars, as is evident from their publications, were somewhat eclectic, but their main interests lay in foreign cinema and in the general theory of cinema.[21]

While GAKhN of the 1920s was primarily theory-driven as well, its new incarnation, GAIS, was more invested in the problems of the recent cinema history. The work of the Film Section of GAIS on creating the history of Soviet cinema was initially timed to coincide with the fifteenth anniversary of the October Revolution. In this, members of the section took their cue from the 'Instruction for Collecting and Processing of Materials for "History of the Civil War"'.[22] This grandiose project of collecting memoirs about the events of 1917–1921, initiated and supervised by the writer Maxim Gorky, was to be finished, according to the announced plan, by 1 March 1932.

Likewise, the production plan of the History Group of the GAIS's Film Section for Year 1931 stated:

Taking into consideration Soviet cinema's enormous importance as a factor of the class struggle of the proletariat, our group sets as its first and primary goal to prepare material on the history of Soviet cinema in its development in connection to the construction of Socialism and in its struggle with class-antagonistic ideological influences. This material should be as comprehensive and as scientifically arranged as possible by the 15th anniversary of the October Revolution in 1932.[23]

The title of GAIS's appeal to all interested and cognizant parties was 'We Need to Create the Marxist History of Soviet Cinema'. It proclaimed the importance of history for the present and future cinema work, which would often be reiterated several years later:

It should be clear for any of us, that without the proper historical perspective we cannot fully evaluate the work that has been done and cannot envision the ways of its future development. Meanwhile, we have not really studied the history of Soviet cinema, and so we do not know it well enough. This especially concerns its earliest period, when the old, Russian, private cinema was being liquidated and the first proletarian cinema industry was being build. We do not know all the details of this struggle, of the laying out of the basis of the work that led to the achievements of Soviet cinema and to its taking a prominent place in world cinema. Now we must urgently fill in this gap. On the eve of the 15th anniversary of October we must carry out this task in order to have more or less comprehensive and arranged material on the history of Soviet cinema, equipped with the analysis of the Marxist–Leninist dialectics.[24]

The accumulation of materials of different kinds (original documents, photographs, periodic literature, and memoires), which began at GAIS, was in line with the concurrent efforts of Grigorii Boltianskii to collect existing film prints and to organize a film museum.[25] The work was complicated by the necessity of studying material 'in the light of Marxism' simultaneously with its accumulation. Another task was 'the drawing up, based on the collected and examined material, of the Marxist–Leninist methodology of studying the history of cinema and engaging on a wide scale in the struggle against vulgar anti-Marxist tendencies in the treatment of historical facts of cinema'.[26] In order to do that the Film Section planned to engage scholars from the Society of Marxist Historians in its work.

The GAIS group on cinema history was headed by Feofan Shipulinskii, a pre-Revolutionary journalist and an active member of the All-Russian Photo and Cinema Committee since 1919, one of the pioneer Russian film historians, whose specialization was foreign cinema. Because the group was working within the framework of the fifteenth anniversary of the October Revolution, for them Soviet film history began in 1917, not on 27 August 1919. It was provisionally divided into three periods: '(1) Soviet cinema in the Civil War period (1917–1921); (2) Soviet cinema in the NEP period; (3) Soviet cinema in the period of socialist reconstruction [up to 1930]'.[27]

This periodization of cinema history corresponded to the social and economic periodization of the country's recent history. The research, according to the plan, was to begin with the earliest period, but the Film Section had only managed to start collecting documents and organizing group interviews of 'old' cinema professionals and administrators when its work was stopped by the transfer of GAIS to Leningrad in 1931. Some of the already collected documents were sent there as well, while others, together with the personnel that stayed in Moscow, were transferred to another institution, NIKFI (All-Union Institute of Scientific Research in Cinema and Photography).[28] Research in film history and theory continued there in the Historical-Archival Cabinet of the Sector of Methodology, Methods and Organization of Film Production. This new cabinet was organized and headed by Veniamin Vishnevskii, a graduate of the Moscow Institute of Literature and Arts, who had been working in GAKhN and GAIS as a freelance researcher since 1927.[29] His initial desire was to write a book on the theory of cinema, but he quickly realized that theory was impossible without the thorough knowledge of the film history and dedicating his life to the work in filmography, bibliography, and chronology. At NIKFI, Vishnevskii had even less time for serious work than he had had at GAIS. In the autumn of 1933, his *kabinet* was transferred again, together with the whole Sector of Methodology, this time to GIK (Gosudarstvennyi institut kinematografii [State Institute of Cinematography]).[30] There, a new Research Sector (nauchno-issledovatel'skii sector, or NIS) was organized, and historical work had to begin anew geared to the new celebration – the fifteenth anniversary of Lenin's decree.

The State Institute of Cinematography was established in Moscow only four days after the Nationalization decree, on 1 September 1919, as the First State Film School (Pervaia gosudarstvennaia shkola kinematografii, or GShK). Although initially the school was designed for training actors and later for directors, its curriculum included courses on 'Cinema Technique' and 'The Basics of Cinema'. The latter course was taught by the film director Vladimir Gardin, who was one of the

Figure 4.2 Veniamin Vishnevskii. [Laboratory for the history of Russian cinema in VGIK]

school's organizers and its first head.[31] Feofan Shipulinskii was also among the school's organizers.[32] By the early 1930s, in addition to his work at GAIS, he was the head of the department of Cinema History and Theory at GIK, and a member of the institute's Research Bureau.[33] There remain, however, very few documents of the research work conducted at the institute before the transfer of the Methodology sector from NIKFI.

Shortly before the transfer, Nikolai Lebedev, the author of the 1924 *Cinema* book, came to teach at GIK after a stint as a documentary filmmaker and a period of studying Marxist social sciences at the prestigious Institute of Red Professors. Lebedev started teaching courses on documentary film in the 1931/32 academic year, and by August 1934 he had risen to the position of the institute's director. He then concentrated his considerable energy on turning the institute into a locus of film education and research.

In October of 1934 the institute was reorganized into a graduate school for directors and cameramen, and was renamed Vysshii Gosudarstvennyi Institut Kinematografii (Higher State Institute of Cinematography, or VGIK).[34] Research work was to become an even more essential part of this new institution. The Research Sector started operating officially on 1 January 1934 and was composed of four sections: screenwriting, organization of production, educational cinema and general film studies.[35] The Historical-Archival Cabinet of NIKFI became the basis for the Section of General Film Studies, headed by a collegium that included Lebedev, Sergei Eisenstein and Béla Balázs.[36] The work of the sector was expected to be conducted more systematically and on a larger scale than that of GAIS and NIKFI. Having just graduated from the Institute of Red Professors, Lebedev was aware of the recent developments in the field of history and in the social sciences in general, and he was also well versed in the parlance of the day. So, in the autumn of 1934, with his usual effusiveness, he declared an extensive programme of the research in film history and theory that needed to be carried out in connection with 'the needs of the corresponding areas of cinema practice'.[37] In his opinion, these areas were educational cinema, newsreel, scientific cinema, cinefication, and maintenance of cinema theatres network, as well as the 'general film studies' that included film history.

As a means of creating 'the scientific history of cinema in all its political, economic, technical, ideological and aesthetic connections and mediations', apart for collecting and processing all kinds of documents, he named the establishment of a specialized library, a film archive and film museum; the compilation of bibliographies, filmographies and indexes, as well as the publication of documents and memoirs, '[a] nd finally – the production of surveys, theoretical works on cinemas of individual counties, on individual artistic movements and major individual artists'.

This work was initially to be conducted with regard to Western cinema practice and scholarship. During the 1920s and the early 1930s not only Soviet film practitioners but also film critics were most closely connected with their Germany-based colleagues. German magazines and technical manuals were collected by individuals and institutions, and books and articles on German cinema and its stars were published in scores. After several trips to Germany, in 1927 Nikolai

Lebedev wrote a book arguing that the form of *Kulturfilm* could be applied to Soviet cinema to revive its propagandistic potential.[38] In the early 1930s, Soviet film scholarship benefited from the contributions of several prominent emigrants from Germany. Film theorist Béla Balázs, whose 1924 book *Der sichtbare Mensch, oder die Kultur des Films* was translated into Russian twice and created a large discussion in the mid-1920s, moved to the Soviet Union in 1931. He found work at the Scriptwriting Department of GIK while reworking his 1930 book *Der Geist des Films* into a new Russian-language edition. The book, with a new chapter on Socialist Realism, came out in 1935. Georg Lukács, while active mostly in literary criticism, took part in at least one discussion, organized at GIK in 1934, which was dedicated to film adaptations of classical literary works.[39] His and others' speeches were intended for a collective volume, which unfortunately never appeared in print. Publishing difficulties that plagued the institute also prevented the publication of already-translated foreign books on film theory, including Paul Rotha's *The Film Till Now*.[40] Another notable GIK connection to Western film scholarship was Léon Moussinac, Sergei Eisenstein's personal friend and author of a book on Soviet cinema, *Le cinéma soviétique* (1928). He visited the Soviet Union several times in the 1920s and 1930s, and took part in theoretical disputes in professional Soviet film press. These international contacts, however, grew weaker as the latter decade progressed.

One of the first tasks that the VGIK's Research Sector faced was the creation of an auxiliary research apparatus. In particular, Veniamin Vishnevskii, continuing the work he had begun at GAKhN/GAIS and NIKFI, compiled a filmography of Soviet films (1917–1934; later he expanded it up to 1945) and a filmography of pre-revolutionary films. He also started his long-term project of chronological tables on the history of Soviet cinema (1917–1945). This work became the basis of all subsequent work in filmography and film history chronology in the Soviet Union, leading to the publication of such seminal editions as Gosfilmofond's film catalogue, and several volumes of *Letopis' rossiiskogo kino* (Russian Cinema's Annals).

To tackle the mammoth task Lebedev set, it had to be divided into parts. Lebedev found himself facing the same necessity to break the section's work down based on historical periods, as had the film historians before him. The division carried, of course, not only practical importance, but ideological as well. For example, pre-revolutionary cinema was not considered to be of any help to the practical work of the current moment, and so there was no talk of seriously studying it.

At best, as is made evident by GAIS's research plan, it could be studied as an arena of class struggle. At worst, the mythical origin of Soviet cinema cancelled the previous period out in its entirety.[41]

At the end of December 1934, the Research Sector organized a conference dedicated to the fifteenth anniversary of Soviet cinema. There, Lebedev presented his project of cinema history periodization, which, as he was careful to note, was a preliminary one. It was more detailed than the rough scheme proposed by GAIS in 1931, and therefore did not fully follow the basic periodization of the socio-political history of the country, which was already established at the time as the succession of the Revolution, war communism, restoration period, reconstruction period, etc. Lebedev maintained that although this version could serve as a rough blueprint, the periodization of cinema history had to take into account the specifics of the medium itself. Nevertheless, both the history of the country and the history of cinema were assumed to develop 'based on the general laws of the development of class struggle and the growth of productive forces'.[42] This Marxist method presupposed that the driving forces in the history of cinematography were, first and foremost, 'the general movement of the class struggle and the growth of the forces of production in the country', and only then the conditions and tendencies of the productive forces within cinema industry itself, the measures taken by the party in the realm of culture, the influence of other arts, and 'the role of individuals in history'.[43] The six periods of cinema history that Lebedev outlined for 1917–1934 took into account both political and economic processes and the succession of technical and aesthetic priorities within the industry. The first period, which lasted from the October Revolution to the decree of August 1919, was called by Lebedev Soviet cinema's 'prehistory'. The second period, 1919–1921, roughly coincided with the period of the Civil War. The third one was the 'period of organizational and economic restoration of the cinema industry' (1921–1924). The fourth period, presented as 'the period of growth and blossoming of cinema' (1925–1929) coincided 'with the end of the restoration and the beginning of the period of reconstruction'. The fifth period, 'of technical and ideological reconstruction', lasted from the end of 1929 to the end of 1932. Finally, the sixth period, which began from the end of 1932, was termed 'the beginning of the new period of growth', echoing Nikolai Iezuitov's assertion.[44]

Lebedev's periodization, which broke the fifteen years that elapsed since 1919 down into roughly three-year sections plus the 'prehistory', strove to reflect internal industry processes in their connection to the more general processes at play in the history of the country. The main content of each period, in accordance with the laws of Marxist dialectics, was presented in terms of class struggle. Even the 'period of growth and blossoming' (1925–29), when looked at more carefully, turned out to be an arena of struggles that repeated countrywide processes on the miniature scale. Their enumeration is truly daunting:

> The struggle of the cinema dealers of the old kind who had planted themselves in the distribution branch, against Soviet films that allegedly held no interest for the viewers; the same people's struggle for the pseudo-Soviet petit-bourgeois film against films with revolutionary topics; the struggle of film distributors against the special film theatres networks catering to workers and peasants as allegedly 'unprofitable'; the struggle of saboteurs within film management against building our own technical basis (production of film stock and equipment), as measures that were too difficult to implement; the struggle of Formalists against ideological pictures for the masses and for experimental films, films for the chosen few; the struggle of national democrats in national film organizations against proletarian internationalism in art – these are the different forms in which bourgeois and petit-bourgeois influences manifested themselves within different areas of the construction of Soviet cinema.[45]

As nuanced and as conformist as this periodization was, it was still more appropriate for internal use, as a working draft. At the same time the fifteen years of Soviet cinema could easily be broken down into five-year periods, just like the whole socio-economic life of the country had been from 1928. This was most famously done at the time by Sergei Eisenstein in his article 'Sredniaia iz trekh' (The Middle of the Three) as well as in his speech at the All-Union Creative Conference of Soviet Film Workers.[46] The first two years following the creation of the Soviet state in this simplified version of cinema history received the definitive label of 'prehistory', and only ten of the remaining fifteen years were deemed important for practical use. As Lebedev himself declared at the conference, three weeks after his report to the Research Sector, 'only in 1924 Vertov released his feature-length film *Kino-glaz* [Cine-Eye]; in 1924 the FEKS group started their work, as well as Eisenstein. As for comrade Dovzhenko and others, they began even later. Therefore we can speak not of 15, but of 10 years'.[47]

Nikolai Iezuitov's already mentioned book, *Puti khudozhestvennogo fil'ma* (Directions of the Feature Film), had no uniform periodization governing its narrative. The book was divided into chapters that alternated 'trade' periodization based on the technological or aesthetic principles with periodization based on the general social and political landmarks of the USSR's recent history, such as 'The Time of the Civil War' (roughly 1918 to 1921) or 'The Victory of Realism' (from 1926, when the period of 'restoration' ended, to 1929). However, the 'general line' of his argument went straight from Lenin's decree to Stalin's personal involvement with cinema:

> The party's interest in cinema was not accidental; it was practical and it logically followed from the party's programme and tactics. It was not accidental that Lenin, while speaking to Lunacharskii, said that, 'of all the arts, cinema for us is the most important'. These words by Lenin expressed the party's attitude to cinema best. This attitude was consolidated in concrete guidance: Lenin's conversations with the leaders of the film industry during the first period of Soviet cinema's development; his advice, letters, and written instructions dealing with the questions of organization, ideology and technology, equipped cinema with necessary instruments; Stalin's instructions in subsequent periods helped it to move along the Leninist path, correcting its ideological and artistic mistakes.[48]

An art historian by training (he graduated from the Moscow State University in 1924), Iezuitov began to work at GAIS in 1930 and was transferred together with it to Leningrad, where he became the head of its Film Studies Division.[49] By the time his book came out, however, he was also employed by VGIK.[50]

It is interesting to note that Lebedev's (and, partially, Iezuitov's) treatment of pre-1919 as the 'prehistory' of Soviet cinema was opposed by those who had been active in the industry at that time, including the former head of the All-Soviet Cinema Committee, Nikolai Preobrazhenskii, who took part in many of the Research Sector's discussions.[51] For those who worked in Soviet cinema from 1917 to 1919, this period was rich in events – it was history, not some limbo into which the old Russian cinema had been thrown in order to be born anew by the stroke of Lenin's pen. Paradoxically, this period was the primary focus of historians' attention in the early to mid-1930s, the one they spent the most time investigating, collecting materials, and extracting interviews and reminiscences from people. One of the reasons for this specific attention was the obvious task of establishing the difference between Soviet, socialist, and pre-Soviet, bourgeois, cinema. The materials, however, suggested, that there was no clean break between the two cinemas. At the same time, the essential middle period of 1917–19 could only exist in official film historiography as 'prehistory', because otherwise there could be no fifteenth anniversary of Soviet cinema – and therefore no immediate reason to study it at all.

The Demise of Early Soviet Film Studies

In early 1935 the head of GUKF, Boris Shumiatskii, observed the work done by VGIK's Research Sector so far and in general approved of it: 'We did the right thing when on the eve of the 15th anniversary we started to interpret the historical paths of Soviet cinema, started to deal with methodological questions of our history'.[52] However, he judged the work that had been done so far to be completely insufficient:

> The weakness of one of the most important areas of our work – research activity – was revealed ... We can clearly see the backwardness of this area of work and its prevailing ideological confusion ... We do not remember and do not know our past, and what we do remember everyone interprets differently. Whereas now we must not have a hypothesis of our development but have an exact structure of the historical process, all the more so because this process has already been going on for fifteen years.

Since at that point even the director of VGIK could only advance hypotheses, and his colleagues were providing conflicting versions of periodization, the head of the cinema industry suggested in declarative form his own simplified and 'consolidated' periodization of cinema history. Without doubt, it was more in line with the current moment, since it proved that:

> The new cinema art of the country of the proletariat has as its source the victory of the proletariat in October. And we know for certain that the only right form of Soviet cinema's periodization is the periodization based on the basic phases of development and victories of our country: the period of *the Civil War*, the period of *restoration*, the period of *reconstruction*, and the period of the building of the classless *socialist society*.[53]

Film historians were quick to adopt these instructions. In March 1935, VGIK held several meetings with the specific agenda of 'creating the Soviet film history', at which Lebedev advocated a more general periodization.

Just like the Film History Section of GAIS before them, VGIK scholars started writing the history of the earliest periods first. The first part of the collective research project, 'History of Soviet Cinema', was scheduled for realization in 1935. It was to include the period of 1917–1921 and was titled 'Soviet Cinema of the Period of War Communism'. In 1936 the work was supposed to move on to 'Essays on the History of Soviet Cinema of 1922–1924'.[54]

In addition to the work done by Veniamin Vishnevskii and others on compiling filmographies and bibliographies, documents were again collected (including copies of documents from a number of Moscow and Leningrad archives that dealt with matters of cinema) and group interviews were conducted. Based on this preliminary research and simultaneous with it, several works dealing with the early period of cinema history were written by the end of 1936. They included Boris Martov's 'An Essay on the History of the Professional Movement of Filmmakers (1917–1921)' and one of the first Soviet dissertations in Film Studies, Vanda Rossolovskaia's 'Cinema on the Eve of the Great Proletarian Revolution'. Martov, who had been active in the industry before 1917, wrote a review of the dissertation, in which he was compelled to remind its readers (including, probably, the examination committee) of the scope and complexity of the task:

> It was necessary not only to plough through a pile of raw material scattered in old magazines, archives, books; not only to interview witnesses, to watch the existing films of the period and to interpret it all in connection to the general social and historical conditions of the period of war and the growth of the bourgeois-democratic revolution into the proletarian one … It was necessary to overcome a widely spread prejudice that the history of cinema only started in 1919 and there was nothing before the Revolution, and, therefore, there could be no talk about the critical assimilation of the experience of the past.[55]

Despite Martov's optimistic belief that the opinion of 1917–19 as 'prehistory' had been overcome or would be overcome soon through genuine historical research, in reality the simplified scheme of Shumiatskii prevailed, while the state support for historical research proved to be short-lived. Rossolovskaia's book was the only one from the entire project envisioned by Lebedev which actually saw the light of day. It was published in early 1938 under the title *Russian Cinema in 1917: Materials Towards its History*, probably because it was treated as yet another anniversary edition (the twentieth anniversary of the October Revolution). Soon after its publication, however, its author was arrested and spent years in Gulag.[56] As a result, all mention of the book and its author was forbidden in the Soviet press and in classrooms. The arrest was most likely connected to another area of Rossolovskaia's work: her stint in the script department of the Mosfilm studios, where she reputedly was close to the director of the studios Elena Sokolovskaia. Sokolovskaia, an old Bolshevik, was arrested on charges of espionage and membership of a counter-revolutionary organization in October 1937, and was shot in August of the next year. Its immediate reasons notwithstanding, Rossolovskaia's arrest was another indication among many that the empirical study of recent history had become complicated, if not downright impossible.

In 1934–36, several party decisions about the reworking of school history textbooks were issued. The unification of the narrative of the country's recent history was completed in 1938 when the *Short Course of the History of VKP(b)*, personally supervised by Stalin, came out, and the main archives were transferred into the system of the People's Commissariat for Internal Affairs (NKVD).[57]

GAIS was liquidated in 1936 and the Institute of Red Professors met with the same fate in 1938. On 22 September 1936, Nikolai Lebedev was removed from his position as director of VGIK. For three more months he remained the chair of the Department of Film History, until on 9 January 1937 he was fired from this position as well.[58] A month and a half later, State Directorate for the Film Industry (GUK, which had succeeded GUKF) issued an order to reorganize the Research Sector at VGIK. In effect, it was liquidated as well, and research work was transferred to individual departments. A new coordinating organ, the Research Division, was created under the direction of Nikolai Semenov, the former head of the Research Sector, and the dean of the Department of Screenwriting. This decision, however, seems to have remained on paper only. Some of the VGIK professors were also fired, including, for example, Lazar' Sukharebskii, who had been teaching courses on scientific and educational films. It was discovered that his works contained 'material that indicated his attempt to transport harmful bourgeois pseudo-scientific "theories" into Soviet cinema'.[59] Feofan Shipulinskii had been dismissed even earlier, after vicious attacks in the press on his book about foreign cinema. He died in June 1942. Boris Martov died even earlier, in May 1937. Other professors were arrested, including the talented cameraman and theoretician Boris Nil'sen. Vishnevskii and Iezuitov continued to work, but the scope of their research was much more limited from then on. Nikolai Iezuitov finally moved to Moscow after the liquidation of GAIS in Leningrad, and became the chair of the Department of Film History as VGIK. He died in the Second World War several years later.

The sustained institutionalized activity of the study of film history (as well as theory) was interrupted for a good ten years. Each anniversary of 1919, meanwhile, was accompanied by new brochures and collections of essays on the history of Soviet cinema. They continued to connect the historical narrative to Lenin's decree.[60] At the same time, the periodization of the past was always tied to the current political and industrial situation, constantly reworking and rewriting cinema's history. What suffered in this process was, of course, the past itself – the ongoing historical process with events, people and films that did not fit the established conceptions and therefore had to be excluded, glossed over, hushed up (like the names of executed or exiled filmmakers, film administrators and film scholars, including Nil'sen and Rossolovskaia).

Historian Viktor Listov suggested in the early 1990s that the traditional division of the history of Soviet cinema into the silent and the sound periods was, in fact, geared to hide the serious crisis in cinema at the turn of the 1930s that resulted from the industry's transfer into the system of VSNKh. This decision, taken in accordance with the general process of industrialization, was an attempt to strengthen the technical, production side of cinema. The ideological and aesthetic sides were considered, at best, secondary in importance. Looking past the established periodization, according to Listov, could finally yield some explanations for facts that could not be explained otherwise, such as the 'pause' in the careers of prominent filmmakers in 1931–33 that had traditionally been blamed on the 'long and difficult period of adaptation to the coming of sound or by individual features of this or that director's work'.[61]

Only in recent decades have Russian film historians begun to doubt the absolute value of the date of 27 August 1919, and the boundaries between pre-revolutionary and post-revolutionary cinema, or between Soviet cinema and the cinema of emigration.[62] Film historian Naum Kleiman suggested calling the whole period from the late nineteenth century until the mid-1920s 'early Russian cinema'.[63] This seems most appropriate, since it finally calls attention not only to the continuity of the historical process in contrast to the long tradition of breaking it apart, but also to the historiographic activity of the Soviet film historians and the Soviet state; to the activity of constructing the narrative of Soviet film history, and to the circumstances of its construction; and to the figures of the first Soviet film historians and the institutions in which they worked.

Notes

1. Ivan Bol'shakov. 1944. *25 let sovetskogo kino*, Moscow, 3.
2. James Von Geldern. 1993. *Bolshevik Festivals, 1917–1920*, Berkeley: University of California Press, 7. On the celebration of the first October anniversary, see ibid., 40–41, 74–79.

3. Nikolai Lebedev. 1924. *Kino: ego kratkaia istoriia, ego vozmozhnosti, ego stroitel'stvo v sovetskom gosudarstve*, Moscow, 7.

4. This and the next quotation are from ibid., 97.

5. Ibid., 95–96.

6. Ibid., 97.

7. At the time, the newspaper was published jointly by the Leningrad film company *Sevzapkino* and the International Workers' Aid organization, *Mezhrabpom*, established by the German communist newspaper mogul Willi Muenzenberg and actively involved in the film industry restoration since the inauguration of NEP in 1921.

8. '5-letnii iubilei, proshedshii neotmechennym'. *Kino-nedelia* 1 (1925), 1. Emphasis added.

9. This and the next two quotations are from: 'K novomu 1925 godu'. *Kino-nedelia* 1 (1925), 1.

10. '5-letnii iubilei' *Kino-nedelia* 1, 1.

11. See Kristin Thompson. 1992. 'Government Policies and Practical Necessities in the Soviet Cinema of the 1920s', in Anna Lawton (ed.), *Red Screen: Politics, Society, Art in Soviet Cinema*, London and New York: Routledge, 19–41.

12. Grigorii Boltianskii. 1925. *Lenin i kino*, Moscow-Leningrad: Gos. izd-vo, 19.

13. As historian Frederick C. Corney remarks, these films 'were all told as parts of the tale of October. All were mythic artifacts of the broad cultural process of creating this foundation event', Frederick C. Corney. 2004. *Telling October: Memory and the Making of the Bolshevik Revolution*, Ithaca, NY: Cornell University Press, 184.

14. Apart from the difficult transition to sound, it was undergoing major institutional changes. The industry was partially freed from the supervision of Narkompros and was included into the system of VSNKh [Supreme Council of the National Economy] in 1930, and then turned over to the Commissariat of Light Industry. Still, because the two umbrella organizations were preoccupied with more important tasks of state-wide industrialization, cinema was not getting enough attention from either. Again, like in the mid-1920s, it desperately needed financing in order to expand the distribution network and to move to large-scale manufacturing of film equipment and raw stock, not to mention the transition to the new sound technology. See Richard Taylor. 1979. *The Politics of the Soviet Cinema, 1917–1929*, Cambridge and New York: Cambridge University Press, 200–201.

15. Boris Shumiatskii. 1934. 'K chemu obiazyvaet nas iubilei'. *Sovetskoe kino* 11/12, 12–13.

16. Nikolai Iezuitov. 1934. *Puti sovetskogo fil'ma*, Moscow, 148, 151.

17. Rostislav Iurenev. 1977. *Sovetskoe kinovedenie*, Moscow: Vsesoiuz. gos. in-t kinematografii, 10.

18. Stella Gurevich. 1998. *Leningradskoe kinovedenie (Zubovskii osobniak, 1925–1936)*, Saint Petersburg: Rossiĭskiĭ in-t istorii iskusstv, 5.

19. See Richard Taylor (ed.). 1982. *The Poetics of Cinema*, Oxford: RPT.

20. Gurevich, *Leningradskoe kinovedenie*, 98–104. The first part of Likhachev's book, which dealt with the period 1896–1913, was published in 1927; the unfinished second part (1914–1916) appeared more than thirty years later, in 1960.

21. Ibid., 81–92.

22. 'Instruktsiia po sobiraniiu i obrabotke materialov po *Istorii grazhdanskoi voiny*'. Clipping from *Izvestiia*, n.d., n. pag. 490. Laboratoriia otechestvennogo kino, VGIK, Moscow.

23. 'Proizvodstvennyi plan gruppy istorii kino-sektora GAIS na 1931 god'. 1931. TS. 490. n. pag. Laboratoriia otechestvennogo kino, VGIK, Moscow, 1.

24. 'Sozdadim marksistskuiu istoiiu kino'. 1931. TS. 490. n. pag. Laboratoriia otechestvennogo kino, VGIK, Moscow.

25. Dziga Vertov. 1959. 'Tvorcheskaia deiatel'nost' G.M.Boltianskogo', in *Iz istorii kino: Materialy i dokumenty* 2. Moscow, 66–69, here 66. These attempts were repeated throughout the 1920s and the 1930s, but ultimately remained fruitless.

26. 'Sozdadim marksistskuiu istoiiu kino'. 1931. TS. 490. n. pag. Laboratoriia otechestvennogo kino, VGIK, Moscow.

27. 'Protokol zasedaniia gruppy istorii ot 3/II 31'. 1931. TS. 490. n. pag. Laboratoriia otechestvennogo kino, VGIK, Moscow.

28. It was organized in 1929 and mostly dealt with research in cinema technology. See Viktor Fomin and Aleksandr Deriabin (eds). 2004. *Letopis' rossiiskogo kino: 1863–1929*, Moscow: Materik, 663.

29. V. Myl'nikova. 1990. 'Istoriia izdaniia odnoi knigi (Perepiska A.A. Khanzhonkova s V.E.Vishnevskim)', in *Minuvshee: Istoricheskii al'manakh 10*, Paris: Atheneum, 415–64, here 419–20.

30. Veniamin Vishnevskii. 2000. 'Istoriia gosudarstvennogo instituta kinematografii v khronologicheskikh datakh', in Marat Vlasov (ed.), *K istorii VGIKa. Kniga I (1919–1934)*, Moscow: VGIK, 8–20, here 10.

31. Vlasov. *K istorii VGIKa. Kniga I*, 24.

32. Shipulinskii headed the school for a year in 1920–21 and taught there from September 1919 until the middle of the 1930s, in the later period giving lectures on foreign film history. See Rostislav Iurenev. 2004. 'Byla ni byla!', in Marat Vlasov (ed.), *K istorii VGIKa. Kniga II (1935–1945)*, Moscow: VGIK, 296–305, here 302–3.

33. Vlasov, *K istorii VGIKa. Kniga I*, 139, 141.

34. Vishnevskii, 'Istoriia gosudarstvennogo', 8–20, here 20.

35. 'Rabota NIS GIKa'. *Sovetskoe kino* 10 (1934): 71–72, here 71.

36. Ibid., 73.

37. This and the next quotation are from Nikolai Lebedev. 1934. 'O nauchno-issledovatel'skoi rabote v oblasti kino'. *Sovetskoe kino* 10, 43. Emphasis in the original.

38. Nikolai Lebedev. 2002. 'Kul'turfil'ma na Zapade i u nas. Glavy iz neizdannoi knigi'. *Kinovedcheskie zapiski* 58, 382– 406.

39. Vlasov, *K istorii VGIKa. Kniga I*, 213.

40. Ibid., 213, 357. The publication of Rotha's book was stopped when it was discovered that the translated manuscript stated that Soviet directors had to adjust their aesthetic principles to the political dictates of the Bolshevic Party and that Eisenstein and Pudovkin could no longer use their superior technique of filmmaking to express their own attitude to life. According to the newspaper report, which exposed NIS's negligence in choosing this particular book for translation, the typed copy of the translation had been used by students of VGIK even before it was sent to the publishers. See Sh. Akhushkov. 1935. 'Dobru i zlu vnimaia ravnodushno ...', in *Kino* 13, 4.

41. For instance, in the 1934 anniversary issue of the magazine *Sovetskoe kino*, Lev Nikulin, a pre-revolutionary screenwriter, who during the Soviet years was mostly active as a novelist, declared: 'One of the wonderful manifestations of the spirit of the October Revolution is the birth of Soviet cinema. Isn't it amazing that on this empty spot, among the crudeness, vulgarity, squalor, and the artistic impotence

of Russian pre-revolutionary art, there could appear the highest, consummate specimen of world cinema?'. Lev Nikulin. 1934. 'Vzgliad nazad'. *Sovetskoe kino* 11/12, 124–25, here 124.

42. Nikolai Lebedev, 'Osnovnye etapy razvitiia sovetskogo kino', 21–25 December, 1934. TS. 17989, 6. Laboratoriia otechestvennogo kino, VGIK, Moscow, 5.

43. Ibid., 6.

44. Ibid., 7–35, passim.

45. Ibid., 24.

46. See Sergei Eisenstein. 2010. 'Speeches to the All-Union Creative Conference of Soviet Filmworkers', in Richard Taylor (ed.), *Selected Works. Volume III. Writings, 1934–47*, London: I.B. Tauris. 16–41; Sergei Eizenshtein. 1934. 'Sredniaia iz trekh', in *Sovetskoe kino* 11/12, 54–83.

47. *Za bol'shoe kinoiskusstvo*. Moscow: Kinofotoizdat (1935), 137.

48. Iezuitov, *Puti sovetskogo fil'ma*, 9.

49. This new section was created on the basis of GII's *kinokabinet*. For the discussion of this process and for the characterization of Iezuitov, see Gurevich, *Leningradskoe kinovedenie*.

50. His invitation was one of the first documents written by Lebedev in his capacity as the institute's director. Although Lebedev's initial offer included making Iezuitov the head of VGIK's Research Sector, it was apparently declined, because in November 1934 the scholar became employed only as a lecturer in cinema history and theory, initially commuting from Leningrad once a month. See Nikolai Iezuitov's personal file, Archive VGIK. L. 5–8.

51. Lebedev, 'Osnovnye etapy razvitiia sovetskogo kino', 38–39.

52. This and the next quotation are from 'Shestoe proizvodstvenno-tekhnicheskoe soveshchanie – ianvar' 1935. Doklad B. Shumiatskogo', in *Za bol'shoe kinoiskusstvo*. Moscow, 1935, 170.

53. Ibid., 171. Emphasis in the original.

54. Nikolai Branitskii. 2004. 'VGIK na pod"eme', in Marat Vlasov (ed.), *K istorii VGIKa. Kniga II* (1935–1945), Moscow, 288–92, here 289 and 291.

55. Boris Martov. 1936. 'Otzyv o rabote V.S. Rosolovskoi *Kinematografiia v 1917 godu*', in Vanda Rosolovskaia. Kinematografiia nakanune Velikoi Proletarskoi Revoliutsii. TS. 16881. Laboratoriia otechestvennogo kino, VGIK, Moscow, 165.

56. V. Myl'nikova, 'Istoriia izdaniia odnoi knigi (Perepiska A.A. Khanzhonkova s V.E.Vishnevskim)', 415–64, here 419.

57. Viktor Listov. 2007. 'Ostorozhno, arkhivy …' in Viktor Listov, *I dol'she veka dlitsia sinema*, Moscow, 140.

58. Vlasov, *K istorii VGIKa. Kniga II*, 75. The circumstances of Lebedev's removal from VGIK, which was prompted in part by his falling out with Shumiatskii, need to be further researched.

59. Ibid., 79.

60. See, for example, Ivan Bol'shakov, *25 let sovetskogo kino*.

61. Viktor Listov. 1992. 'Kino: iskusstvo ili promyshlennos't?', in *Teoreticheskie chteniia pamiati S.I.Iutkevicha*, Moscow, 74–75.

62. Viktor Listov. 1995. *Rossiia. Revoliutsiia. Kinematograf*, Moscow: Materik, 59–76.

63. Quoted in ibid., 43.

PART II

NETWORKS OF EXCHANGE

Chapter 5

Eastern Avatars

Russian Influence on European Avant-Gardes

Ian Christie

In fact, the avant-garde in cinema, as in literature and theatre, is a fiction. Whosoever assumes to count himself among those timid revolutionaries is simply playing the game of 'if the cap fits, wear it'.
— Robert Desnos, 'Cinéma d'avant-garde'[1]

The history of avant-gardism offers an instructive challenge to those who like to know where they stand. The concept is frankly contentious, and to be meaningful really requires qualification in terms of 'when, where and for whom'? Above all, it's a relative term, defining artists in relation to what is not considered or self-defined as avant-garde – the tradition or body of work they are reacting against; the new direction they are taking, with its attendant risks and likelihood of failure; and also relative to the point of view of the observer. What is often forgotten is that where we stand, in history and locality, has a bearing on what we may consider avant-garde.[2] Avant-gardes typically tend to be local and temporary, even if their fame lives on in history. 'Avant-garde' is also typically a label conferred retrospectively, or from afar, which is likely to be contested vigorously by those to whom it has been applied, largely because of the inbuilt implication of elitism.[3]

Another controversial historiographic issue in studying avant-gardes is the question of influence. For artists in revolt and seeking the new, to be considered under the influence of others is often anathema, no matter how convincingly historians may trace such lines of influence.

Meanwhile, for others, claiming descent from a revered ancestor, however dubiously, may be vital. This chapter addresses some of these problematic aspects of defining avant-gardes in film, with an underlying argument that the proliferation of such avant-gardes during the 1920s and 1930s, throughout Europe and America, owed much to the dynamic role of a 'modernizing' Russia, both before and after the revolutions of 1917. Its thrust, however, is against over-simplification, against seeking single causes, and against 'freezing' the history of avant-gardes into a ghostly double of entertainment cinema.

One of the paradigm examples of repudiation of avant-garde status by those who seem most obviously to constitute an avant-garde is the Soviet 'montage' filmmakers of the 1920s. For the young filmmakers of the Soviet era, intent on creating a revolutionary cinema that would contribute to shaping the 'new man' of Bolshevik ideology, any suggestion that they were engaged in art for art's sake would have been anathema, as would the implication that they were only aiming at a narrow elite audience. 'An experiment, intelligible to the millions' was the slogan debated in 1929 by the leading Soviet filmmakers Leonid Trauberg and Sergei Eisenstein, as they faced a demand from the state that 'new forms of artistic language' should also be 'intelligible to the millions'.[4] Trauberg's and Eisenstein's responses differed: the former admitted that many experimental Soviet films, including his own, were 'crude' and 'not very agreeable', at the same time mocking the demand for popular intelligibility; while Eisenstein and Alexandrov insisted that their new film, THE GENERAL LINE [Generalnaja Linija] (1929), would not 'flabbergast people with puzzling stunts', and so would be 'however contradictory ... an experiment, intelligible to the millions'.

The work that these filmmakers staked their reputations on in 1929 was certainly challenging. Trauberg and Kozintsev's THE NEW BABYLON [Novyy Vavilon] (1929) celebrated the Paris Commune uprising of 1871 with a biting irony that used the popular culture of the 1870s as social critique, taking Marx at his word when he applied the term 'phantasmagoric' to French politics of the mid-nineteenth century.[5] And the musical score they commissioned from the young Dimitri Shostakovich parodied Offenbach operettas to offer its own critique of the bourgeois government's brutal crushing of the Commune. In contrast, Eisenstein's much-delayed film about the contemporary revolution in the Russian countryside emerged under a new title, THE OLD AND THE NEW [Staroe I nowoje], as an uninhibited hymn to the poetry of agricultural machinery, and to the life force represented by a communally owned bull.

There was also a planned accompaniment that would have combined music of many kinds with sound effects, often used ironically. But, like the orchestral score for New Babylon, this proved too complex for the era, and was never recorded.

Both films were, in effect, soon forgotten, condemned by their problematic status at the moment when synchronized sound was sweeping the world, Their makers' immensely ambitious conceptions of musical counterpoint would not be appreciated until decades later; and posterity would instead categorize their earlier films as 'avant-garde' – Adventures of Oktyabrina [Pokhozdeniya Oktyabriny] (1924), The Devil's Wheel [Chyortovo koleso] (1926), The Overcoat [Shinel] (1926), in the case of Kozintsev and Trauberg, working collectively as the 'Factory of the Eccentric Actor';[6] Strike [Stachka] (1925) and Battleship Potemkin [Bronenosets Potemkin] (1925) in Eisenstein's case – while deciding that their subsequent work, Kozintsev and Trauberg's Maxim trilogy (1934–38) and Eisenstein's Alexander Nevsky (1938), conformed to the requirements of 'socialist realism' and 'revolutionary romanticism'. Within the USSR, both were commended for fulfilling their duty to produce popular and inspiring works. But elsewhere, these 1930s films would contribute to a diagnosis that the early Soviet avant-garde has been crushed and replaced by an enforced populism, while Kozintsev and Trauberg and Eisenstein were seen as having forsaken their early 'formalist' exuberance to become 'responsible' realists.[7]

Whether this was 'good' depended on who was making the judgement in successive decades; whether they accepted the value of 'socialist realism', or deplored the suppression of an early Soviet avant-garde culture – which was likely to depend on their political attitude towards the USSR. By the 1970s, however, after the widespread politicization of 1968, a wholesale re-evaluation was under way among Western 'new leftists', intent on reclaiming first Eisenstein, then Kozintsev and Trauberg, as avant-garde artists who had been coerced into conformity. Eisenstein's first feature, Strike, was rediscovered, along with his playful debut, Glumov's Diary [Snevnik Glumova] (1923), a short skit on popular mystery thrillers that clearly sprang from the same carnivalesque world as Kozintsev and Trauberg's first FEKS films.[8] These were hailed as manifestations of 'Eccentrism', a politicized offshoot of Futurism, and along with Vertov's Man with a Movie Camera [Celovek s kinoapparatom] (1929) – another film from the transitional year of 1929 – became canonic examples of a 'revolutionary avant-garde' during the period between 1968 and the collapse of the East European communist bloc in 1989.

This was indeed the period when 'avant-garde' acquired a fundamentally new meaning. No longer associated with 'art for art's sake', as it had been during the reign of 'symbolism' and of the Ballets Russes, it was transformed into the ideology of a progressive art intent on disconcerting and ultimately politicizing its audiences, as it had been briefly in the 1930s. Filmmaker-theorists of the 1970s, such as Wilhelm and Birgit Hein in Germany,[9] and Peter Wollen and Malcolm LeGrice in Britain,[10] constructed their own histories of avant-garde film, which included early Eisenstein and Vertov, now set alongside the Fernand Léger of BALLET MÉCANIQUE (1924), and other self-referential work that seemed to point towards the main concerns of 1970s film artists – most of whom preferred to be known as film-*makers*, even if they were willing to accept the new connotation of 'avant-garde', which neither Vertov nor Eisenstein would have done.

What we can see here is a selective reshaping of the history of early Soviet cinema, which privileged the one-time outsider, Vertov, over Eisenstein, while stressing the provocative and even educative role of 'form' over revolutionary 'content' in a wider range of 1920s films. We might say that the activists of the 1970s were seeking to gain status by associating themselves with canonic work of the past, but at the same time they were redefining what counted as 'avant-garde'. Seeking to end a polarized perspective on the past, Peter Wollen's 1975 overview of 'the two avant-gardes' distinguished a painterly and a theatrical tradition, implying that these were but two routes to the same goal, to unlock film's potential for a 'reciprocal interlocking and input between painting, writing, music [and] theatre' which, historically, had characterized the avant-gardes.

Wollen's pivotal article did much to set a new, more inclusive agenda for understanding avant-garde film, linking it with the better-known avant-gardes in other media that constitute what is generally termed 'modernism'. At first sight, film appears to have little place in these, if we consider only the familiar avant-garde 'classics' that all date from the 1920s. However, as I have argued elsewhere, there are good reasons for considering the 1910s as a period of aspiration or 'proto cinema', when many artists contemplated using film or analogous forms, with some producing work that has since disappeared.[11] But equally, the 1920s avant-garde classics include a number of films from members of the Dada and surrealist groups, both of which vigorously rejected any association with what they saw as an institutionalized 'avant-garde'. Probably the most virulent opposition was that of Luis Buñuel and Salvador Dalì, authors of the canonic surrealist film UN CHIEN

ANDALOU (1929), who insisted that their work amounted to a 'call for violence' and rejected any aesthetic evaluation, in line with surrealism's refusal to be considered as an 'art movement'.

Buñuel had worked with Jean Epstein, a leading director and theorist of the French film avant-garde, whose work he claimed to despise, and the surrealists were equally hostile to Jean Cocteau, whose early career owed much to collaborations with Diaghilev. In retrospect, we may wonder how seriously these antagonisms should be taken. Although couched in terms of principle, were they not also fed by personal animosities and by competition for status? The French film avant-garde, represented by Abel Gance, Marcel L'Herbier, Jean Epstein and Germaine Dulac between about 1923 and 1929, may have been the only group to have willingly espoused the term,[12] but would itself be rapidly eclipsed, only to be rediscovered in the 1960s,[13] while UN CHIEN ANDALOU, despite all the protests of its makers and of latter-day surrealists, has come to be considered a paradigm of avant-garde film.[14]

The conventional view of avant-garde history, which we might call the 'linear consecutive' model, identifies the twentieth-century avant-gardes as successors of an earlier series, beginning with romanticism, and continuing with the symbolist and naturalist movements of the late nineteenth century; both of the latter were then challenged in the 1900s by the first modernist avant-gardes, cubism and futurism. This is not necessarily wrong in chronological terms, but it begs important questions of influence and appropriation, and suggests a progression which Wollen tried to undermine by invoking Viktor Shklovsky's figure of art advancing in 'knight's moves'.[15] One major influence, which has been consistently underestimated, was the impact of a series of encounters with Russian modernism, which reached Western Europe, and ultimately the United States, in three overlapping waves.

The first of these was led by Serge Diaghilev's Ballets Russes, which toured internationally from 1909 to 1929 and beyond, and offered a new vision of integrated choreography, set design and music, all drawing on the emergence of a hybrid Russian modernism in the early 1900s, which combined Western influences with Russian folk art. Indeed, the process of appropriation was even more complex, since it was a privileged access to post-impressionist painting, especially that of Matisse and Picasso, being avidly bought by Russian collectors in the early 1900s, which helped to shape the visual culture out of which the Ballets Russes grew. One of these wealthy industrialists, Sergei Shchukin, began opening to public view his massive collection, which included works by Renoir, Monet, Cézanne and Gauguin, as well as fifty Picassos and two large wall paintings specially commissioned from Matisse, *La Danse* and *La Musique* (1909–10). The link between these rhythmic, boldly simplified works and the revolutionary ballets that established Diaghilev's reputation, notably *The Rite of Spring* (Le Sacre du print-emps, 1913) has often been noted, but the complex underlying cultural dynamics are equally significant.

Russia developed its own series of avant-garde movements between 1900 and 1912, moving from symbolism and art nouveau to its own distinctive versions of futurism and cubism, culminating in the manifesto *A Slap in the Face of Public Taste*, published by the Hylea group in 1912.[16] While the main thrust of this, and of the group's provocative public stance – a precursor of Dada and surrealist 'performance art' – was 'futurist', and geared to modernity, it also undoubtedly owed something to the revival of interest in Russian folk art, which was in turn an influence on Diaghilev's composers and designers. The Ballets Russes enjoyed its first major successes in Paris, in 1910–11, with *The Firebird* and *Petrushka*, two ballets based on Russian folk stories which launched a 'neo-primitive' idiom in design, music and choreography that made a deep impression on jaded Western audiences. These were, simultaneously, exotic and 'modern', and their fusion of the component arts and crafts into a challenging yet unified work undoubtedly set a pattern for future cross-arts collaboration. While post-Wagnerian symbolism had defined the vanguard in art for two previous decades, the Ballets Russes would set a new standard from 1909 onwards. Its success, however, was not in Russia, where the cubo-futurists represented a leading edge of avant-garde activity, mainly in poetry and painting, but also in a modernist operatic performance, *Victory over the Sun* (St Petersburg, 1913), and even a collective film, DRAMA IN THE FUTURIST CABARET (1914), which may count as the earliest recognizable avant-garde film.[17] Diaghilev's 'Russianness' appealed to Paris, and soon to London and New York, while his avant-garde compatriots at home (who would have despised his fashionable audiences, as they did most of their Russian contemporaries) were embarking on 'the ship of Modernity' in search of 'the New First Unexpected'.[18]

There can be little doubt that it was the Ballets Russes which had an early and lasting influence on modernism around the world, while the Russian futurists would remain little-known until they mutated into the short-lived constructivist movement of the early Soviet era, amid a new network of competing avant-garde groups in this period. In fact, the outbreak of war in 1914 had already stranded Diaghilev and his company in France, confirming their exilic status. And it was their 1917 Paris production *Parade* which brought together the extraordinary combination of Jean Cocteau (scenario), Pablo Picasso (curtain, sets and costumes), Erik Satie (music), Leonid Massine (choreography) and Guillaume Apollinaire (programme note), and in doing so laid the basis for much subsequent cross-arts performance, including that of the Dada and surrealist groups.

Without this as a model and a recent memory, there might well not have been the Dada soirée *Relâche* (1924), which included René Clair's film Entr'acte, now a treasured record of the Parisian avant-garde and, together with Sergei Eisenstein's Glumov's Diary, among the earliest surviving examples of an 'artist's film'.[19] The lasting influence of the Ballets Russes is harder to chart, especially in relation to film, since dance history has tended to ignore the parallel course of film history, despite their often symbiotic relationship. Some examples will illustrate the problem. One of the last dancers recruited to Diaghilev's company, Rupert Doone, went on to co-found in London in the early

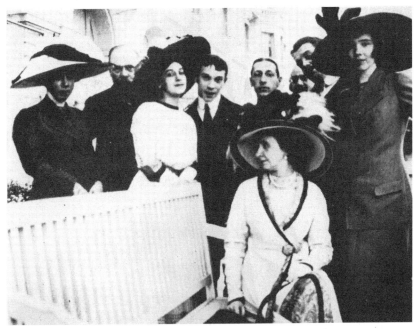

Figure 5.1 Sergei Diaghilev's Ballets Russes created a vogue for Russian avant-garde art in Paris before the First World War, which helped the young Jean Cocteau to launch his multi-media career with a series of ballet scenarios for the impresario, including *Parade* (1917). [Author's collection]

1930s the Group Theatre, which commissioned plays from T.S. Eliot and W.H. Auden, while Doone himself appeared in Len Lye's film RAINBOW DANCE (1936), one of the earliest avant-garde works to experiment with colour. Meanwhile, in Los Angeles, the young Kenneth Anger (b.1927) apparently took dance lessons with Theodor Kozloff, a one-time Diaghilev dancer, who had defected to the movies after being introduced to Cecil B. DeMille in 1917, for whom he appeared in a number of films, after THE WOMAN THAT GOD FORGOT (1917).

Another Kozloff pupil, better documented than Anger, was Agnes DeMille, niece of Cecil, who gratefully acknowledged Kozloff as her first teacher after she became a choreographer in the 1930s. DeMille's ballet *Rodeo* was premiered in 1942 by the Ballets Russes de Monte Carlo, a Diaghilev successor company, before she went on to choreograph *Oklahoma!* on Broadway and later for its film adaptation. Other crossover figures in America would include the filmmaker-dancer Maya Deren, often considered the founder of American avant-garde film with her seminal short films made between 1943 and 1948, and Yvonne Rainer, another dancer-turned-filmmaker, who translated 1960s New York performance art into film. Through this dance history, which criss-crosses with avant-garde film history, the enduring legacy of Diaghilev can be traced.[20]

However distant these contacts, it seems clear that the name of Diaghilev remained potent during the decade after his death in 1929. Michael Powell and Emeric Pressburger were (separately) inspired by his legacy, which eventually led to their homages in THE RED SHOES (1948) and THE TALES OF HOFFMANN (1951), both starring Diaghilev's protégé Leonide Massine. Diaghilev, and the legitimacy that his Russian roots lent to his dancers and choreographers, continued to play a seminal role decades after his death – with a mystique no doubt enhanced by his refusal to allow the filming of any Ballets Russes performances.

Second Wave: First Avant-Garde?

The French film avant-garde of the 1920s was to a considerable extent also a beneficiary of Russian influence, even though it is often dated from the impact of Cecil B. DeMille's THE CHEAT (1915), shown in France as FORFAITURE in 1916.[21] The First World War had stranded Diaghilev and many of his collaborators in Western Europe, and after the Bolshevik revolution of 1917 these were joined by a second wave of Russian emigrants, which included the successful film producer Iossif Ermolieff, who re-established his company in Paris in 1920. After Ermolieff left for Germany in 1922, his associate Alexandre Kamenka launched the Albatros film company, which would provide the nearest thing to an institutional base for the French film avant-garde of the 1920s, employing many of its actors, designers and directors, while injecting a Russian exoticism – not unlike Diaghilev's impact on dance – into French production of the decade. Jean Epstein, the leading film-maker-theorist of the avant-garde group, made four films for Albatros in the mid-1920s, beginning with the spectacular LE LION DES MOGOLS (1924), written by and featuring Ivan Mosjoukine, the company's most famous star. Mosjoukine also took the lead in a co-production between Albatros and Cinegraphic, Marcel L'Herbier's production company, which yielded the only major screen adaptation of Luigi Pirandello, his novel THE LATE MATHIAS PASCAL [Feu Mathias Pascal] (1924). But the lasting influence of Albatros on French production, and on cinema in general, was more pervasive.

Dominique Païni has described how he envisaged that a study of Albatros (whose archive belongs to the Cinémathèque Française) would reveal a 'struggle' between the 'legacy of the end of the nineteenth century – symbolism, art nouveau – and the constructivist wave of the 1920s ... a struggle between "Red and White Russias"'.[22] In the event, as he notes, François Albera's erudite study of the impact of Albatros goes considerably further. Besides suggesting that the 'Russian orientalism' fostered by Albatros offered a kind of 'passage to modernity' (which Païni compares with the role of negro art in cubism), Albera claims that the work of the company's set designers, who included Lazare Meerson, Boris Bilinsky and Alexandre Lochakoff, and its great poster artist Jean-Adrien Mercier, brought about a transition from the weighty décor associated with 'film d'art' into a more modern style, influenced by cubo-futurism and the prevailing climate of 'style moderne'.

The influence of the 1925 Paris 'Exposition des arts décoratifs' on cinema has often been noted – usually in connection with L'Herbier's somewhat stilted L'INHUMAINE (1923), which featured contributions by Robert Mallet-Stevens and Fernand Léger – but Païni and Albera argue convincingly that it was through the personnel assembled by Albatros, who increasingly were not Russian, and included the directors René Clair, Jacques Feyder and Alberto Cavalcanti, that many of the currents of 'modernity' present in Paris in the 1920s eventually found their way into cinema. The new cult of 'décor', which the exhibition helped to foster, created a sensitivity to design which was first demonstrated in

Figure 5.2 Ivan Mozzhukhin was a leading star of Russian cinema before he emigrated after the revolutions of 1917, and lent glamour to 'White Russian' productions such as FEU MATHIAS PASCAL [The Late Mathias Pascal] (1926), based on a novel by Luigi Pirandello and directed by one of the key figures in the French avant-garde, Marcel L'Herbier. [Author's collection]

the Albatros studio at Montreuil, but would have a much wider influence in the years to come. Thus the atmospheric décor of 1930s 'poetic realism' can be traced back to the decade-long process of assimilation and exchange fostered by Ermolieff, Kamenka and the Russian artists they brought to France.

Third Wave: 'The Soviet Example'

What I have called the 'third wave' of Russian impact abroad is one of the best-known cases of 'influence' in film history, and has been widely acknowledged since the earliest publications in this field.[23] From 1926 onwards, the films of Pudovkin, Eisenstein, Vertov and Dovzhenko began to attract both notoriety and admiration throughout Western Europe, and further afield, in the United States and in Asia. In addition to the films, which were often banned or cut, the filmmakers' writings proved inspirational; and their presence at screenings in Germany, the Netherlands, France and Britain further added to the excitement generated by what was quickly perceived as a movement. Malte Hagener has made the important point that these travels have usually been charted in individual (and incomplete) biographical terms, rather than in a 'synthesizing fashion' which would make clear their collective significance.[24] If we attempt this synthesis, building on his valuable concept of a dynamic network, it would appear that the veneration of 'Soviet cinema' became the foundation of an institution-alized concept of avant-garde film, which took shape as commercial cinema underwent its wholesale conversion to synchronized sound between 1928 and 1930. And despite the Russians' professed keen-ness to experiment with sound in non-naturalistic ways, as declared in the Eisenstein–Alexandrov–Pudovkin 'Statement' of 1928 and demon-strated in Vertov's ENTHUSIASM (1930), they were, at least temporarily, co-opted into a rearguard action to 'defend' silent film by those intent on resisting it.

There are many ironies in this reception and perception of Soviet cinema and its ideology. One is simply chronological: BATTLESHIP POTEMKIN was nearly four years old by the time it was finally seen in Paris and London in late 1929, and Eisenstein had already moved far beyond it in his ambitious montage constructions in OCTOBER (1927) and THE OLD AND THE NEW, influenced by the recent reading of Joyce's *Ulysses* and by his contacts with the psychologists Alexander Luria and Lev Vygotsky; but he was typecast as the creator of POTEMKIN. His plan to synchronize THE OLD AND THE NEW in London failed to attract commercial support,[25] and although recorded comment on the film's screenings is scant, its apparent pantheistic fervour seems to have antagonized many. Huntly Carter, who had been an early enthusiast for the 'new spirit' in Soviet theatre and film, judged it 'unsuited for consumption by British Labour', condemning it as 'inconceivably old-fashioned' and 'a mess of primitive magic and ritual', unlikely to stir British workers 'to economic action'.[26]

Significantly, Eisenstein denied any involvement with the experi-mental sound short ROMANCE SENTIMENTALE (1930) that he had made with Alexandrov in Paris, which actually fitted better with the 'impres-sionist' aesthetic of the Dulac-Chomette French avant-garde than with the prevailing conception of Soviet montage, and seems only to have met with negative responses when it was shown.[27] This left Vertov's militant ENTHUSIASM as the only practical demonstration of an experi-mental asynchronous approach to sound that was seen – and this too was long known only in anecdotal terms, from when Vertov insisted on blasting his Film Society audience with the soundtrack of ENTHUSIASM played at 'an ear-splitting level'.[28] ENTHUSIASM was, however, admired by a leading 'sound-resister', Chaplin, when he saw it during that same London visit.[29] and Grierson wrote: 'I have never set eyes on a film that interested me more', adding, however, 'or that demanded more solid criticism'.[30] This matched his celebrated rejection of Vertov's MAN WITH A MOVIE CAMERA as 'not a film at all ... a snapshot album ... that dithers about on the surface of life',[31] which would pass into received history, until it was challenged by the rediscovery and re-evaluation of Vertov that began in the 1970s.

Although there are many well-documented verdicts on the impact of the Russian 'third wave', it would be wrong to conclude that there was any unified Western response to 'Soviet cinema' during 1926–31. Indeed, as the Soviet regime embarked on Stalin's much-vaunted Five-Year Plan, the Soviet filmmakers tended to be seen more as its cultural ambassadors. Only Eisenstein seems to have entered into the more traditional avant-garde spirit of playful improvisation, with his enthusiastic participation in the collective parody film made at the Independent Cinema congress in Switzerland, STORM OVER LA SARRAZ [Sturm über La Sarraz] (1929), followed by an appearance in another group film conceived by Hans Richter in London.[32] And here, again, the anecdotal has often loomed larger than any broader historiographic attempt to gauge how influential Russian montage might have been – and indeed whether its influence was confined to avant-garde circles.[33]

To do this, we need to consider the different kinds of impact resulting from the screening of Soviet films, translations of their makers' theoretical writing and personal appearances – the combination of which presented a novel phenomenon, quite different from ordinary promotional press conferences by film directors and stars. The results would vary considerably in different countries. In Germany, Soviet cinema enjoyed its first international success in 1926, and continued to be strongly supported by Willi Münzenberg's pro-Soviet organizations until the early 1930s, when it was cut short by the rise of national socialism. In the case of Britain, which will be considered in more detail here, the impact of Soviet cinema in a relatively concentrated period between 1928 and 1931 has long been considered crucial to the creation of a film intelligentsia and the British documentary movement.[34]

Access to the new Soviet films had been frustrated by censorship bans everywhere since 1926, reinforced by political intervention, with Germany the only country where POTEMKIN could be seen publicly, albeit in a censored form. In Britain, Pudovkin's THE MOTHER [Matj] (1926) and THE END OF ST PETERSBURG [Konets Sankt-Peterburga] (1927) were shown in October 1928 and February 1929 respectively, at the members-only Film Society, and POTEMKIN finally had its premiere, also at the Film Society, in November 1929. All of these would subsequently be seen at other film societies, as these were established elsewhere in the U.K. over the next five years. And the continuing struggle to see and show Eisenstein's films would also become a formative experience for many, linking film with involvement in revolutionary politics, through such groups as Kino and the Worker's Film and Photo League.[35] But as Henry Miller has revealed, Pudovkin's THE MOTHER, THE END OF ST PETERSBURG and STORM OVER ASIA [Potomok Gengis Khan] (1928,) were all shown widely and publicly in Britain during 1930, under local authority dispensation.[36] To some extent this may have been *because* they were silent, and thus attractive to many cinemas not yet wired for sound; yet the apparent demand for such screenings also testifies to an interest in Soviet film that must be considered wider than the metropolitan avant-garde.

Claims have often been made for the influence of Soviet montage on the emerging British documentary movement: notably on Grierson's own DRIFTERS (1929) and on his protegé Basil Wright's SONG OF CEYLON (1934). Wright later wrote that 'the only people who went to town on the 1928 "Statement on Sound" were the British documentary filmmakers of the early 1930s under the influence of Grierson and Cavalcanti'.[37] Wright explained that this was partly because the British filmmakers worked within similar technical limitations, as if to excuse the influence of montage thinking on his and several of Len Lye's films for the next phase of the documentary movement, as the GPO Film Unit (1933–40). But there were also clearer, if less widely seen, examples of both political and aesthetic impact on British filmmakers. BREAD (1934), made for the Communist-backed Kino group, attempted to raise class consciousness by showing a desperate man punished for stealing a loaf of bread. The film's obvious use of the Soviet-style montage editing would probably have been familiar to its intended audiences, since Kino had been active in showing POTEMKIN non-theatrically.[38] More ambitiously, although still on a semi-professional level, Norman McLaren and Helen Biggar's HELL UNLTD (1936) challenged the armament industries that were encouraging governments to prepare for war. With its ingenious combination of live-action, models and diagrams, this remains one of the most impressive examples of Eisensteinian montage stimulating a creative response, following McLaren having seen POTEMKIN at the Glasgow Film Society.[39]

Writings by the Soviet filmmakers have also been credited with a wide and lasting influence, and the fact that two important texts appeared almost simultaneously in English translation in October 1928 undoubtedly added to this impact, especially after the frustrating wait to see any of the writers' films. The jointly signed 'Statement on Sound', by Alexandrov, Eisenstein and Pudovkin, appeared in *Close Up*, a 'little magazine' with a limited, though elite circulation; while Pudovkin's

'Film Technique', translated by Ivor Montagu from a German version, appeared in the second issue of a new magazine, *Film Weekly*, which claimed a massive sale of 250,000 for its first issue.[40] Both of these were destined to have a long career, with the Statement often anthologized; Pudovkin's text was published as a booklet in the following year, and has remained in print virtually ever since.

But how influential were they? The Statement had a special relevance, and poignancy, in late 1928, appearing as Europe was witnessing the first American 'Talkies' – THE JAZZ SINGER (1927) and THE SINGING FOOL (1928) – and filmmakers were coming to terms with the obvious popular success of these. For those opposed on aesthetic principle to recorded sound, such as the 'Pool' group who published *Close Up*, the Statement may have offered some comfort, but only if read selectively. For others, it offered a first blueprint for creative approaches to linking image and sound, taken up by Wright, Lye and others. However, its influence must be judged much less than Pudovkin's *Film Technique*, which was not only an immediate success, but has continued to inform filmmakers through the decades, despite being written within the 'silent' period. Stanley Kubrick paid tribute to it in a 1969 interview, speaking of his own self-education in film around 1950:

> The most instructive book on film aesthetics I came across was Pudovkin's *Film Technique*, which simply explained that editing was the aspect of film art form which was completely unique, and which separated it from all other arts forms. The ability to show a simple action like a man cutting wheat from a number of angles in a brief moment, to be able to see it in a special way not possible except through film – that this is what it was all about. This is obvious, of course, but it's so important it cannot be too strongly stressed. Pudovkin gives many clear examples of how good film editing enhances a scene, and I would recommend his book to anyone seriously interested in film technique.[41]

The impact of Pudovkin's essay was heightened by his addresses to audiences on his two visits to Western Europe, in 1928 and 1929. On the second of these, in London in February 1929, he spoke after a screening of THE END OF ST PETERSBURG to an audience that included 'nearly twenty English film directors', including Anthony Asquith, George Pearson and Adrian Brunel.[42]

If Eisenstein was the most eagerly awaited of the Russian visitors in Western Europe, his writings, other than the manifesto-style Statement, would not have anything like the broad appeal of Pudovkin's text. Kubrick records in the same interview that he 'didn't

really understand Eisenstein'; and many who attended Eisenstein's
series of lectures in London in 1929 found themselves similarly per-
plexed. Basil Wright recorded the anticipation: 'There we were, with
notebooks and pencils, thinking passionately about Film, Film, the
great new art form ... There was he, with blackboard and chalk, about
to expound the inner, the Eleusinian mysteries of Film Art'.[43] What
the audience heard, however, ranged across an immense intellectual
and cultural landscape, including Japanese Kabuki plays, Darwin,
Daumier, Stefan Zweig, Zola, Ben Jonson, Joyce and many more figures
who illustrated Eisenstein's belief that 'film montage was the cinematic
aspect of a particular form of expression used by artists in other media'
(ibid.). Wright was certainly not alone in finding this 'disappointing,
a little shocking', since it seemed to contradict the general direction of
all 1920s film theory, towards identifying the 'specificity' of film. Not
until the first edited collection of Eisenstein's essays, *The Film Sense*,
appeared in 1942, followed by two further collections, would the range
of his thought about film and its place among the other arts become
apparent – and even then, it was far from clear to those merely seeking
instruction in film practice.

Between the early essays and the eventual appearance of his first
sound film, ALEXANDER NEVSKY, followed by the interrupted dyptich
of IVAN THE TERRIBLE (1944/45),[44] Eisenstein would become a problematic figure for many, especially within successive avant-gardes: he was
often considered to have betrayed the radicalism of his early montage
position, as his theoretical and cultural interests widened. But even
though this became the dominant view, we should also remember that,
among others attending Eisenstein's lectures and reading his early
essays, there were different responses. The future production designer,
Ralph Brinton, for instance, was already an architect when attending
Eisenstein's London lectures provided him with an epiphany, which
led him to abandon architecture for film design.[45] Dallas Bower, a
pioneer sound recordist in the late 1920s, was another who responded to
Eisenstein's aesthetic challenge, producing his own manifesto, *Plan for
Cinema*, in 1936, and later commissioning a radio version of ALEXANDER
NEVSKY for the BBC in 1941, before becoming a major influence on
Olivier's HENRY V (1944).[46]

The period of acute 'Russian influence' on film, as felt in Britain
and other Western countries between 1928 and 1931, has come to be
seen as a *coupure*, a paradoxical point at which the aesthetic of 'silent
film' reached its climax, only to be superseded by the new paradigm of
sound film. While it was once common to place Soviet cinema on the

side of the vanquished silent paradigm, as we have seen, it was in fact the Soviet filmmakers who pointed forwards, identifying paths that sound film might follow, as well as offering lessons in filmic construction that remained valid long after the painful transition to sound had been achieved. But what can also be deduced from a wider perspective on the successive waves of 'Russian influence' is a recurrent pattern of 'formal challenge', combining the old and the radically new, and an insistence on the essentially hybrid nature of what might be termed 'modern spectacle'.

The challenging synthesis that Diaghilev first created in the Ballets Russes, followed by the insertion of Russian melodrama into French modernism that Ermolieff and Kamenka achieved in the mid-1920s, and the Eisensteinian vision of montage as a structuring principle in all art – first sketched in a temporary classroom in London in 1929 – all of these can be seen as belonging to a long-running process of cultural exchange, in which 'Western' art is assimilated by Russian culture, before being re-transmitted to its original sources as a renovating discovery.[47] The cultural theorists Viktor Shklovsky, Mikhail Bakhtin and Yuri Lotman all contributed to interpreting this process in terms of 'defamiliarization', 'dialogism' and cultural semiotics. What remains within the history of film and film theory is to apply their insights more systematically.[48]

Notes

1. A typical Surrealist polemic against the contemporary French film avant-garde, by the poet Robert Desnos. 1929. 'Cinéma d'avant-garde', *Documents* 7 (December). Translated by Paul Hammond for Paul Hammond (ed.). 1978. *The Shadow and Its Shadow: Surrealist Writings on the Cinema*, London: British Film Institute, 37.

2. A review of recent books on Classical Greece by Victor Davis Hanson draws attention to the relevance of historians' own historical situation for their perspective. He notes that since the fall of the Soviet Union, the spread of consensual government has 'turned attention away from Marxist interpretations of the ancient economy [towards] a new interest in the vibrancy of ancient constitutional government'. *Times Literary Supplement*, 5 Oct. 2012, 11.

3. See my earlier discussion of these issues, for example in 'French Avant-garde Film in the Twenties: From Specificity to Surrealism', in Philip Drummond et al. (eds). 1979. *Film as Film: Formal Experiment in Film, 1910–1975*. London: Arts Council of Great Britain, 37–46; and in 'Histories of the Future: Mapping the Avant-garde', *Film History* 20(1) (2008), 6–13.

4. Leonid Trauberg. 1929. 'An Experiment Intelligible to the Millions'; and Sergei Eisenstein and Grigori Alexandrov. 1929. 'An Experiment Intelligible to the Millions', both reprinted in Richard Taylor and Ian Christie (eds). 1988. *The Film*

Factory: Russian and Soviet Cinema in Documents, 1896–1939. London and New York: Routlege, 250–51 and 254–57.

5. Kozintsev and Trauberg developed the shimmering visual style of their film under the influence of Marx's account of Louis Napoleon's attempted coup of 1851. Karl Marx, *The Eighteenth Brumaire of Louis Napoleon* [Der achtzehnte Brumaire des Louis Bonaparte] (1852).

6. On the FEKS group, see Ian Christie and John Gillett (eds). 1978. *Futurism/Formalism/FEKS: Eccentrism and Soviet Cinema, 1918–1936*, London: British Film Institute.

7. See 'Introduction. Soviet Cinema: A History and its Heritage', in Taylor and Christie, *Film Factory*, 9–10.

8. Eisenstein's Strike was not seen between its (limited) release in 1925 and its reappearance in Western Europe in 1957, in the wake of Khrushchev's denunciation of Stalin's record at the 20th Congress of the Soviet Communist Party. Glumov's Diary was discovered in the Soviet Documentary Archive during the 1980s, attached to a 1923 edition of Vertov's Kino Pravda.

9. Birgit Hein and Wulf Herzogenrath. 1978. *Film als Film. 1910 bis heute*. Stuttgart: Gerd Hatje.

10. Peter Wollen. 1975. 'The Two Avant-Gardes', *Studio International* 190(978), 171–75; Malcolm LeGrice. 1982. *Abstract Film and Beyond*. Cambridge, MA: MIT Press.

11. Ian Christie. 2001. 'Before the Avant-Gardes: Artists and Film, 1910–1914', in Leonardo Quaresima and Laura Vichi (eds), *The Tenth Muse*, Udine: Film Forum, 369–70; Ian Christie. 2006. 'Film as a Modernist Art', in Christopher Wilk (ed.). *Modernism: Designing a New World, 1914–1939*. London: Victoria and Albert Museum.

12. Noureddine Ghali claims that the earliest use of the term 'avant-garde' in relation to film is in a pseudonymous 1918 text: 'Metteurs en scène d'avant-garde, profitez de ce bel été pour vous attacher aux paysages vraiment français. Vos scénarios y gagneront en style, en élégance et en homogénéité' (signed 'La femme de nulle part'), reprinted in Noureddine Ghali et al. (eds). 1995. *L'Avant-garde cinématographique en France dans les années vingt: idées, conceptions, théories*. Paris: Paris expérimental, 32–33.

13. Henri Langlois, founder of the Cinémathèque Française, wrote an influential article about the 1920s avant-garde, linking it with the then contemporary *nouvelle vague*: H.L. 1968. 'La première vague', *Cahiers du cinéma* 202 (July–August); this was also used as the title of a two-part television film on the period by Noel Burch and Jean-André Fiesci, *La première vague* (1968).

14. According to Desnos: 'When René Clair and Picabia made Entr'acte, Man Ray L'Etoile de Mer, and Buñuel his admirable Un Chien Andalou, there was no thought of creating a work of art or a new aesthetic, but only of obeying profound, original impulses …' Desnos, 'Cinéma d'avant-garde', 36.

15. Viktor Shklovsky, *Knight's Move*, 1923.

16. Burlyuk et al. 1912. 'A Slap in the Face of Public Taste', in Christie and Gillett, *Futurism*; retrieved on 20 Oct. 2012 from http://www.unknown.nu/futurism/slap.html

17. This lost film is known only from surviving stills, which show the painters Mikhail Larionov and Natalya Goncharova with their faces vividly painted. See Taylor and Christie, *Film Factory*, 32.

18. Burlyuk, 'Slap in the Face'.

19. Like ENTR'ACTE, Eisenstein's short film, only rediscovered in 1977 and hence omitted from many accounts of 'the' canonical avant-garde, was made as an insert for his theatrical production, *Enough Simplicity for Every Wise Man/Wiseman*, in 1923.

20. On the dance connection, see Ian Christie. 2012. 'The Cinema has not yet been invented', edited transcript of a presentation at the Screendance workshop, Brighton, 2009, in *The International Journal of Screendance* 2.

21. On the immediate impact of THE CHEAT, see an article by Colette from August 1916: 'Every evening, writers, painters, composers and dramatists come and come again to sit, contemplate, and comment in low voices, like pupils'. Reprinted in Richard Abel (ed.). 1988. *French Film Theory and Criticism, 1907–1939*, vol. 1. Princeton, NJ: Princeton University Press, 128. Many avant-garde filmmakers would subsequently date their 'conversion' to seeing DeMille's film.

22. Dominique Païni. 1995. 'Albatros: révélateur du cinéma français', introduction to François Albera, *Albatros: des russes à Paris 1919–1929*, Paris: Cinémathèque française, 9.

23. C.A. Lejeune. 1931. *Cinema*. London: Maclehose, has a chapter on the new Soviet cinema, noting the 'irony' that it appeared just as 'the Talkies' made its example redundant.

24. Malte Hagener. 2007. *Moving Forward, Looking Back: The European Avant-garde and the Invention of Film Culture, 1919–1939*. Amsterdam: Amsterdam University Press.

25. There are contradictory accounts of where Eisenstein planned to produce a synchronized version of THE OLD AND THE NEW. Seton claimed it was in Berlin (Marie Seton. 1960. *Sergei M. Eisenstein: A Biography*. New York: A.A. Wyn, 125), while Leyda noted laconically that 'the promised funding for the London recording of OLD AND NEW was withdrawn' (Jay Leyda and Zina Voynow. 1982. *Eisenstein at Work*, New York: Pantheon, 38).

26. Carter is quoted more extensively in Ian Christie. 1999. 'Censorship, Culture and Codpieces: Eisenstein's Influence in Britain during the 1930s and 40s', in Albert J. LaValley and Barry P. Scherr (eds), *Eisenstein at 100: A Reconsideration*, New Brunswick, NJ: Rutgers University Press, 112.

27. Information about the contemporary screening of ROMANCE SENTIMENTALE is scant. Bulgakowa refers to a screening with POTEMKIN in Berlin and to screenings in France and England, all received negatively. Oksana Bulgakowa. 2001. *Sergei Eisenstein: A Biography*, Berlin: Potemkin Press, 103.

28. Recalled by Dickinson in Thorold Dickinson and Catherine de la Roche. 1948. *Soviet Cinema*, London: Falcon Press, 23.

29. Hagener, *Moving Forward, Looking Back*, 189.

30. John Grierson. 1966. 'The Russian Example', in Forsyth Hardy (ed.), *Grierson on Documentary*, London: Faber, 128.

31. Ibid., 127.

32. Both of the films are lost and known only from stills, with Eisenstein appearing as an armour-clad knight at La Sarraz, and as an English 'bobby' in London.

33. Henry K. Miller's thesis, *Where We Came In: The Origins of a Minority Film Culture in Britain, 1917–1940* (Birkbeck College, London, 2012), which I supervised, demonstrates that Soviet films, like many other foreign 'art' films of the 1920s, were more widely shown than is often supposed, and argues that linking their influence exclusively to the London Film Society is a founding myth of 'minority film culture'.

34. Rachael Low, for example, ends the introduction to her volume on British cinema in the 1920s with two pages devoted to Pudovkin's 'answers' to the decade's

'unresolved questions' about film theory, in Rachael Low. 1971. *The History of the British Film 1918–1929*. London: Allen & Unwin, 29–31. The anthology of Grierson's writings edited by Forsyth Hardy includes a substantial section entitled 'The Russian Example', cited above.

35. Don Macpherson and Paul Willemen (eds). 1980. *Traditions of Independence: British Cinema in the Thirties*. London: British Film Institute.

36. Miller, *Where We Came In*, ch. 7.

37. Basil Wright, *The Long View*, quoted in Christie, 'Censorship, Culture and Codpieces', 112.

38. A loophole in cinema legislation in the U.K. allowed uncertificated films to be shown 'non-theatrically'.

39. McLaren described the film as 'juvenilia' in the 1970s, but may well have been exercising caution, in view of Cold War attitudes towards former Communist Party members, as he had been. See interview with Norman McLaren, by Janick Beaulieu et al., in *Séquences* 82 (October 1975); trans. in Scottish Arts Council. 1977. *Norman McLaren*. Edinburgh, 11.

40. I also owe this detail to Henry K. Miller's research.

41. Interview with Stanley Kubrick (1969). In Joseph Gelmis. 1970. *The Film Director as Superstar*. Garden City, NY: Doubleday. Retrieved on 20 Oct. 2012 from http://www.visual-memory.co.uk/amk/doc/0069.html

42. Reported in the *Daily Express*, 4 Feb. 1929, 19. I am grateful to Henry K. Miller for this reference.

43. Basil Wright, 'Eisenstein's Lectures in London', a reconstruction, BBC Third Programme, 17 Dec. 1949, quoted in Seton, *Eisenstein*, 143.

44. Although shot and edited consecutively, IVAN PART 1 was released in 1944, while PART 2 was banned and remained unseen until 1958.

45. Ralph Brinton (1895–1975) worked as an art director from 1935, and is best known for his contribution to a group of British realist films of the late 1950s, including ROOM AT THE TOP, THE ENTERTAINER, A TASTE OF HONEY and LONELINESS OF THE LONG DISTANCE RUNNER. The revelation of his debt to Eisenstein appears in Laurie N. Ede. 2010. *British Film Design: A History*. London: I.B. Tauris, 97.

46. On Bower, see Christie, 'Censorship, Culture and Codpieces', 113–16.

47. This is one of the themes of Alexander Sokurov's film RUSSIAN ARK (2001), as he portrays the cultural significance of the Hermitage Museum's collections of Western Art.

48. For an attempt to use and trace the influence of Shklovsky's 'defamiliarization', see contributions to Annie van den Oever (ed.). 2010. *Ostrannenie: On 'Strangeness' and the Moving Image. The History, Reception and Relevance of a Concept*. Amsterdam: Amsterdam University Press.

Chapter 6

EARLY YUGOSLAV CINÉ-AMATEURISM

Cinéphilia and the Institutionalization of Film Culture
in the Kingdom of Yugoslavia during the Interwar Period

Greg de Cuir, Jr.

The International Union of Non-Professional Cinema (UNICA) was founded in 1931 with the goal of promoting non-commercial film, which was achieved by organizing yearly festivals and congresses. Five countries participated in UNICA's first international amateur film competition held in Brussels in 1931, among them the Kingdom of Yugoslavia. In his study on the emergence of film culture, Malte Hagener states that '[w]hile the movement of film societies evolved slowly but steadily over the 1920s, there was a sudden upsurge and boom of film societies in the time between 1928 and 1931'.[1] This upsurge marked the flowering of a phenomenon that can be called 'cinéphilia', which would have a dynamic impact on the development of an advanced film culture throughout Europe. This was particularly true in a country like Yugoslavia, where cinéphilia and the culture surrounding it ultimately engendered a diverse national film industry from a very grassroots, 'amateur' level.

Ciné-club culture was expanding in the interwar period in Europe, eventually leading to the creation of the International Federation of Ciné-Clubs in 1947 in Cannes, which is still functioning today. This association has the stated aim to organize film societies (or ciné-clubs) worldwide in an effort to create alternative distribution of quality films across borders, to convene international juries at film festivals, and to make film societies acknowledged as an important cultural factor.[2] Partly as a result of the work of ciné-clubs, the medium of cinema gained a history; films became artefacts worthy of study, exhibition and preservation.

The wartime generation of ciné-enthusiasts that came of age in ciné-clubs (after the pioneering interwar generation) was the first generation of 'film students', because they grew up with an awareness of, and sensitivity to, a tangible film history. It is no coincidence that this generation sparked the numerous new waves that flourished across the world in the postwar period and beyond, as their films reflected a progressive form that was born from an intimate awareness of the medium. In contrast, the pioneering interwar generation of cinéastes existed alongside the widespread notion of films as disposable products and not as works of art. Therefore, the children of cinema, who were able to learn from and appreciate the works of past masters, came from a place of privileged knowledge: the ciné-club. This was the generation for which the cinema was much more than a vocation – it was a religious devotion. Ciné-club culture is 'amateur' culture in the true, original Latin sense of the term: one who loves.

Ciné-club culture made an early appearance in the territory of Yugoslavia, then the Kingdom of Yugoslavia (and shortly prior to that, the Kingdom of Serbs, Croats and Slovenes). In 1928 in Zagreb (Croatia), Dr Maksimilijan Paspa founded a ciné-section within Zagreb Photo Club.[3] Paspa was the president of Zagreb Photo Club, which was originally incarnated as Zagreb Amateur Photo Club in 1892. He had acquired his first ciné-camera in 1925 – a 9.5 mm Pathé-Baby, which was produced by Pathé as part of an amateur film system for home use.[4] The founding of the Zagreb Photo Club ciné-section occurred amid a general climate of early cinéphilic activities in the city. As reported in the second issue of the journal *Film*, in 1925, the Zagreb Sociological Society organized a conference on film under the initiative of Dr J. Šterna. This conference focused (among other things) on the economic conditions for producing film in Yugoslavia, thus considering the establishment of a national film industry. Also, later that year in the journal *Film*, an announcement was published on the establishment of a ciné-section within the Red Cross Youth Society in Zagreb. The society stated an aim to collaborate with other cultural institutions that were dedicated to enabling film activities.

Another of the founding members of the Zagreb Photo Club ciné-section was Oktavijan Miletić, who worked closely with Paspa. Oktavijan was the son of the celebrated theatre director and critic Stjepan Miletić. The younger Miletić had a celebrated career himself,[5] and would eventually be called 'the first Yugoslav filmmaker to reach the highest creative levels of international cinema ... and the first whose films were screened and awarded prizes throughout Europe'.[6] For the initial four years of existence of this ciné-section, Paspa and Miletić directed all of the films that were produced (fifteen in total). It almost seems that in this initial four-year span, Paspa and Miletić were the only two members of the ciné-section, or at least the only two active members. However, membership would soon grow, as well as the number of films that were produced each year.

It is significant to note that, from the outset, the Zagreb Photo Club ciné-section was chiefly concerned with production. By contrast, the Zagreb Sociological Society engaged in pedagogical activities and research, and the Zagreb Red Cross Youth Society ciné-section seemed to be focused on promotional and cultural action. The Zagreb Photo Club ciné-section was an artisanal film club, which can be seen as a clear departure from the early ciné-club model popular in France and elsewhere in Europe, in which film screenings were a central purpose. This emphasis on the craft of filmmaking created a heritage that the many ciné-clubs in Yugoslavia continued over the years, and which ultimately provided the basis for a functional professional film industry.

In 1931 the Kingdom of Yugoslavia (represented by the Zagreb Photo Club ciné-section) participated in the first international amateur film competition of UNICA in Brussels. These sorts of transnational contacts with other European institutions would continue to grow, mainly through the space of film festivals and competitions, which were a new phenomenon in the 1930s.[7] In fact, due to this early activity, we can say that Yugoslavia was a pioneering force helping to drive the development of European film culture. Paspa served as a jury member at the UNICA competition; also, Miletić won an award for his animated film AH, BJEŠE SAMO SAN! [Unfortunately, It's Only a Dream!] (1930). Miletić's film would go on to win another award that year at the film competition hosted by Photokino-Verlag GmbH, Berlin. These were among the first of many international film awards for the club.

Yugoslavia became a member of UNICA in 1933.[8] At this time, Zagreb Photo Club was also a member of the Institute of Amateur Cinematographers in London. Also in 1933, Paspa won first prize at a London international film competition organized by the Institute of Amateur Cinematographers for his film PRIRODA U NARAVNIM BOJAMA [Nature in Escallop Colours] (1933) – the first colour film made in Yugoslavia.[9] As can be seen, amateur film culture was at the forefront of technological shifts in the nascent Yugoslav film industry. With these international successes, membership in the club was growing and the first films from new directors began to appear regularly, including films by Aleksandar Paspa and Leon Paspa (brothers to Maksimilijan). From 1932 to 1935, the ciné-section produced a total of forty films, made by five different club members (the three Paspa brothers, Miletić, and Ljudevit Vidas).[10]

Amateurism was spreading quickly. As Petar Volk notes, '[f]ilm was one of the most attractive symbols of the modern age, especially in the 1930s'.[11] He further remarks that '[d]ocuments from 1940 state that there were around one hundred amateur cameras in use in the country'.[12] The year 1935 proved to be an important one in the history of ciné-club culture in Yugoslavia. Zagreb Ciné-amateur Club was founded on 20 November, with Maksimilijan Paspa elected as its first president and Miletić as the first vice-president. Other functionaries on the ciné-club staff included a secretary, a treasurer, a librarian, a curator, and advisory board members. Regular activities of the club (continuing with those practised by the ciné-section) included bi-monthly meetings, amateur film projections, lectures on production techniques, and further educational endeavours on the subject of filmmaking. 'For a long time the ciné-club was the only formalized educational institution in the area of film'.[13] As a result, many future Yugoslav professionals in the field came through the ranks of the ciné-clubs as a sort of training ground.

Earlier, in the autumn of 1935, Zagreb Photo Club had organized a large photography exhibition featuring Slavic photographers, while the ciné-section had organized a parallel exhibition as the first pan-Slavic film competition.[14] Pan-Slavism, a movement for the unification of Slavic peoples throughout Europe, had origins in the nineteenth century. It should be remembered that upon its birth in 1918, Yugoslavia was given the name 'Kingdom of Serbs, Croats and Slovenes'. The name was changed in 1929 to 'Kingdom of Yugoslavia' amid the backdrop of violent internal tensions in the country. Internal strife continued to increase throughout the 1930s, and it can perhaps be seen that a (relatively progressive) pan-Slavic ideal at this time was preserved and celebrated within the artistic community, if nowhere else. This was certainly true among the members of the avant-garde community in Belgrade and Zagreb in the interwar period, as many of them were communists and would constitute the ranks of the multi-ethnic Yugoslav Partisans during the Second World War, who fought for a united Yugoslav socialist republic (against the Croatian Ustasha, Serbian Chetniks, and German Nazis).

Ciné-amateurs from Yugoslavia, Czechoslovakia and Poland entered their work in the All-Slavs Film Competition in Zagreb in four competitive categories: Slavic folklore; Slavic travelogues and cultural films; fiction films; and colour films in any theme or genre. Co-production support for this film competition was provided by the Prague Pathé-club and the Polskie Towarzystvo Fotograficzme (Polish Society of Photography in Warsaw).[15] This is just one example of the different collaborations that Zagreb Ciné-amateur Club had with other amateur organizations in the world, including relations with Klub der Kinoamateure in Vienna and Bund der Filmamateure in Berlin.

Regarding these latter partnerships, Zagreb had always shared a close relation with Vienna in the context of the Austro-Hungarian Empire. It was very common for film magazines to publish certain articles in German (particularly in an area like Zagreb, or the North Serbian province of Vojvodina), even after the fall of the empire. This practice culminated in the wartime newsletter *Njemačke slikopisne novosti* (German Cinematographic News), published in Zagreb from 1942 to 1944, constantly featuring news about German films. German was one of the many languages spoken in the densely diverse territory of Yugoslavia, and German films were extremely popular on local movie screens throughout the interwar period and into the war years. Although Germany became Fascist in the 1930s, it should also be remembered that upon the invasion of Yugoslavia by the German armed forces, Croatia (with Zagreb as its capital) in effect became a puppet state of the Nazi regime, and a nascent link between Berlin and Zagreb was further nurtured, albeit relatively short-lived.

Also in 1935, the films of the Zagreb Ciné-amateur Club dominated at the UNICA congress in Barcelona, winning prizes in each of the four categories: FAUST (1933) by Miletić in the fiction film category; TUNOLOV NA JADRANU [Tuna Fishermen on the Adriatic] (1933) by Ljudevit Vidas in the documentary category; MORE – JADRANSKA IDILA [Adriatic Sea Idyll] (1934) by Miletić in the genre film category; and NATURE IN ESCALLOP COLOURS (1933) by Maksimilijan Paspa in the colour film category.[16] In 1936, Paspa and Miletić had films in competition at the 4th Biennale of Cinematographic Art in Venice, with Miletić winning a top prize for his film NOCTURNO (1936).[17]

NOCTURNO was written, directed and shot by Miletić in the 9.5 mm format. It is the story of a man obsessed with detective novels, who finds himself in what at first appears to be a murder mystery, soon revealed to more likely be one of his many fantastic dreams. The film is a strange hybrid of the horror genre and what would come to be known as 'film noir', melding the iconography of both into a mélange that in retrospect seems to be prescient of the style of Hollywood filmmaking that would develop in the 1940s. Its heavy use of shadow and low-key lighting owes a debt to German expressionism, also evidenced by the German inter-titles and the German-language covers of the main character's favourite thriller serials. In addition to winning a silver medal for his film, which amounted to a de facto best short film and best amateur film award at the Venice Biennale, Miletić also won first prize with NOCTURNO at the All-Slavs Film Competition in Zagreb.

NOCTURNO was the final film that Miletić shot in the 9.5 mm format, which means that for all intents and purposes, this was his last amateur film (as this small-gauge format was closely linked with amateur use) and served as a closing statement for this particular stage of his career. Miletić would move into the ranks of professional filmmaking from this point on, shooting reportages for foreign producers and also the occasional large-format short fiction film. One example of these professional short subjects is the romantic comedy film ŠEŠIR [The Hat] (1936), which was produced by Zora Film on 35 mm and was also Miletić's first sound film. This is a surreal romantic comedy that utilizes a dreamlike structure in telling the story of a man looking for love, and also the hat that accompanies him on his journey. At this stage in his career, Miletić had been making films for almost a decade and was a well-polished cinéaste. One can tell this from the clarity and flow of his visual expression and also the inventive use of editing, including a virtuous command of trick photography.

Miletić would go on to become a very important and pioneering professional filmmaker. He directed the feature-length film LISINSKI in 1943 (it premiered in 1944) – at the same time NEVINOST BEZ ZAŠTITE [Innocence Unprotected], the first feature-length film in Yugoslavia, was made by Dragoljub Aleksić (in Serbia). After the liberation of Yugoslavia from German occupation, Miletić began working as a cinematographer. In 1947, during the initial year of feature film production in the new Socialist Yugoslavia, he shot ŽIVJEĆE OVAJ NAROD [This Nation Will Live] for director Nikola Popović. Subsequently, Miletić began collaborating with a young Dušan Makavejev on his early professional documentaries as cinematographer, including the following films: SLIKOVNICA PCELARA [The Beekeeper's Scrapbook], KOSNICE PUNE SMIJEHA [Beehives Full of Laughter], BOJE SANJAJU [Colours are Dreaming] and PROKLETI PRAZNIK [Cursed Holiday] – all completed in 1958 and all produced in Zagreb. For almost the entire remainder of his career, well into the 1970s, Miletić worked as a cinematographer, often on various documentaries.

Ciné-enthusiasm in Yugoslavia also extended to publishing, and a large number of magazines and journals existed to celebrate and propagate film culture. Between 1919 and 1941 there were about a hundred different film magazines being published in the country.[18] The first such magazine was *Kinematografski glasnik – Organ za zaštitu i promocije interesa jugoslavenske kinematografije* (Cinematography Herald – An organ for the preservation and promotion of interest in Yugoslav film), founded in 1919 in Zagreb, but its title was almost immediately changed to *Film*.[19]

Two other journals were published at this time that carried the title *Film*. One was published in Belgrade with a premiere issue that appeared in 1923. The Belgrade *Film* was a weekly, edited by A.M. Popović and published in a small newsletter format. This newsletter consisted of articles on popular films and stars (usually Hollywood), as well as some pieces on the domestic film situation. In 1925, in Zagreb, another journal called *Film* appeared.

The Zagreb *Film* (not to be confused with the edition that first appeared in 1919) was founded and edited by the cinéaste Boško Tokin. Not only that, but it seems Tokin wrote most all of the content that was featured in the small-format publication. Every issue opened with an essay written by him that contemplated such issues as the poetry of film, techniques for shooting film, the domestic film situation (which was usually seen as bleak, and in need of prodding), translations (by Tokin) of foreign film theorists and critics, and other areas of aesthetic and practical concern. Tokin's *Film* also featured short film scenarios written by him that came complete with illustrations, short stories by various authors, and other attempts at creative content. When seen in relation to other film journals of the time, which were usually focused on generic news items of interest about global Hollywood and European film stars and directors, Tokin's *Film* offered the earliest serious criticism on film that appeared in Yugoslavia. His work betrayed a creative ambition that can be called cinéphilia in written form. Other magazines that appeared throughout the 1920s and 1930s were *Kino* and *Kinematograf* in Zagreb, *Filmska zvezda*, *Kroz film*, and *Naš film* in Belgrade, *Filmska revija* in Sarajevo, and many more.

In 1932 a monthly journal called *Foto revija* was founded in Zagreb by members of Zagreb Photo Club.[20] The journal was published from 1932 to 1940 and often publicized news and activities related to members' photography work as well as their filmmaking output. In 1937 the

Figure 6.1 Tokin's *Film*. [Marinko Sudac Collection]

journal devoted a larger space for ciné-amateurs, under the title *Kino smotra*.[21] This was where announcements about the many accomplishments of the ciné-section were published, as well as articles about the techniques of filmmaking and ciné-amateurism in general.

Perhaps the most unique example of an interwar film journal in Yugoslavia was *Togo*, first published in 1939. The journal was founded as an initiative of the new royal society and operated under the watch of King Petar II, who acceded to the throne in 1934 at the age of eleven when his father, King Aleksandar I, was assassinated. *Togo* was named after a small black Scottish terrier that followed King Petar around. The journal itself was as quirky and playful, as its title suggests. With glossy magazine pages filled with pictures and production stills, the journal was composed of a series of brief notes on film viewing, usually focusing on popular Hollywood product. All of the writers that published in the journal (school-aged friends and associates of King Petar) used offbeat pen names such as 'Tree', or 'Penelopa', which was the pseudonym that King Petar wrote under. The journalist Pavle Tokin (of relation to Boško Tokin) wrote under the pen name 'Nikot Ajap' – his own name spelled backwards. Another Tokin family member, Djura, published under the pen name 'Dju-Dju'; surely the Tokin family was the first family of film criticism in Yugoslavia! *Togo*, and the fledgling film company named after it, ceased operations in 1940 after only four issues, as King Petar was forced to flee the country following the Axis invasion in 1941.

* * *

Ciné-enthusiasm in Belgrade (Serbia) developed alongside that in Zagreb, as the two cities had always been united in a national context during the time of the two Yugoslavias – with Belgrade as the capital and largest city, and Zagreb as the second largest. Belgrade Cinephile Club, the first ciné-club in the city, was founded on 27 February 1924.[22] The aims of the club were to propagate film art, to affect the tastes of the public through writing books about film, and to create film programmes. Belgrade Cinephile Club opened the first film library in the city and also hosted lectures on film art.[23] Membership in this pioneering club quickly ballooned to around three hundred people; among the founding members was Boško Tokin, Serbia's first film aesthetician.

Tokin was born in Romania in 1894 and got his start in journalism at a young age. He was the film section editor for the weekly *Nedeljne ilustracije* in Belgrade, and he began writing theoretical pieces on cinema as early as 1920. For the Belgrade magazine *Progres* in October 1920, he wrote a two-part essay called 'Towards a Cinematographic Aesthetic', which has been called the first aesthetic reflection on film in Yugoslavia.[24] This essay was a summary of a series of Tokin's theoretical studies which were published under the title 'Essais d'une esthétique cinégraphique' in the French journal *L'Espirit nouveau*.[25] In 1925, Tokin left for Zagreb to found and edit the magazine *Film*. Just as Miletić can be thought of as an international film artist (and Yugoslavia's first), perhaps we can think of Tokin as the first transnational film critic in the country.

Tokin was part of a unique strain of avant-garde ciné-amateurism in Yugoslavia. One of the most influential of the numerous interwar avant-garde movements was zenithism, founded by Ljubomir Micić, and described as something akin to abstract expressionism. The aim of zenithism was to 'Balkanize Europe' with Eastern barbarism and irrationality. Tokin was one of the three original co-signers of the 'Manifesto of Zenithism' in 1921. He often wrote criticism under the pen name 'Filmus', and he also 'designed some cinematically conceived photo-collages and cherished the genre of "cinematographic poetry"'.[26] These extra-cinematic experiments were also practised by other members of the zenithist movement, in addition to a number of avant-garde artists in Yugoslavia who were fascinated by the liberating and subversive potential of cinema as an art form.

Figure 6.2 Zenithist Manifesto. [Marinko Sudac Collection]

Tokin's activities, and others like it, have been described by Pavle Levi as 'cinema by other means'. This 'other means' is characterized by a severing of cinema from the material base of the apparatus itself. As Levi defines it in his book on alternative filmmaking: 'the practice of positing cinema as a system of relations directly inspired by the workings of the film apparatus, but evoked through the material and technological properties of the originally nonfilmic media'.[27] The Serbian avant-garde theorist Branko Vučićević (whose work Levi follows and expands upon) called the unique method of ciné-writing practised by Tokin and others 'paper movies'.[28] This descriptive concept grew from the thought that everything can be a film, or 'the production of written texts *a priori* [can be] designated as films proper'.[29] One can call amateur cinema a 'cinema by other means' in some sense, as it often diverges from mainstream cinematic practices, in economic and aesthetic terms. Surely avant-garde cinematic writing and ready-made collages are closely linked with amateur film culture, as a number of these exercises grew from the ideological and physical space of ciné-clubs.

In 1924, Tokin wrote and co-directed a film with Dragan Aleksić (another founding member of Belgrade Cinephile Club) called Budi Bog s nama, or ili Kačaci u Topčideru [God be with Us, or Albanian Outlaws in Topčider Park], which was described by Petar Volk as a burlesque film in the style of a Harold Lloyd comedy.[30] This film, though incomplete (and considered lost), was the first instance of the Yugoslav avant-garde undertaking an effort to create cinema by traditional means; it can also be considered the earliest venture into amateur ciné-club filmmaking in Yugoslavia. Like Tokin, Aleksić was a film critic, as well as a leader of the Dadaists in Yugoslavia. In Zagreb in 1921, he was a co-editor of the film magazine *Kinofon*[31] before returning to Belgrade. Aleksić published film criticism in this magazine and also in the avant-garde zenithist journal *Zenit* (founded by Micić and first published in 1921 in Zagreb). This fluidity between theory and practice would prove to be characteristic of the Belgrade cinéastes, as many wrote criticism alongside their filmmaking activities. Also, as evidenced, there was a steady stream of transnational cooperation among cinéastes in Yugoslavia – from the first flowering of ciné-enthusiasm in the 1920s through the postwar period and the rise and fall of Socialist Yugoslavia.

On 12 February 1928, the Belgrade Cinephile Club joined forces with the University of Belgrade-based Academic Drama Group to form the Kingdom of Serbs, Croats and Slovenes Cinephile Club.[32] The goal of this club was to promote the realization of domestic films, though not necessarily to actively produce them. In 1930 the Yugoslav Film Club was founded with the continued purpose of prioritizing domestic film in something of a promotional manner.[33] Two years later, in 1932, the Yugoslav Film Society was formed, which became one of the first building blocks towards constructing an industrial film system.[34] This became likely when the emphasis turned to actual film production within the organization, perhaps best symbolized by the gradual shift in nomenclature from 'club' to 'society'.

In 1933, the Yugoslav Film Society produced AVANTURE DOKTORA GAGIĆA [The Adventure of Doctor Gagić], a fiction film directed by Aleksandar Čerepov. Čerepov was a Russian theatre actor and director who worked in the Russian Cultural Centre in Belgrade. In 1931 he opened a private film school in Belgrade, and his students often collaborated with him on the production of his feature films. It is not evident whether there were ties between the Yugoslav Film Society and the Russian Cultural Centre, though the possibility that they enjoyed a working relationship certainly exists.

At this early stage of ciné-club culture in Yugoslavia, members tended to be bourgeois citizens who were able to afford the costs of production, either through membership fees or donations.[35] For example, Maksimilijan Paspa was a dentist, and Oktavijan Miletić grew up in a privileged artistic environment, with a father who was the manager of the Croatian National Theatre. The club members included businessmen and professionals of all types, such as Ljudevit Griesbach, who ran a photography and cinema supply shop called 'Griesbach and Knauss' that financially supported the ciné-club. Zagreb Ciné-amateur Club also counted among its sponsors the Zagreb City Building Society. Hagener offers the idea that '[t]he ciné-clubs on the whole remained high-brow and elitist'.[36] This would continue to be the case in Yugoslavia until after the Second World War and the formation of a socialist republic.

For the most part, the people who came through Zagreb Ciné-amateur Club were apolitical. As noted by club member Mihovil Pansini, who initiated the radical avant-garde movement 'antifilm', the films produced there and later in Zagreb Ciné-club in the 1950s were 'small holograms of [personal] reality'[37] detailing the unique way in which the filmmakers spoke about themselves rather than the (political) era they lived in. According to film critic and club member Hrvoje Turković, this was a clear anticipation of the new wave of personal, auteurist cinema which began emerging in the Yugoslav film industry in the early 1960s.[38] However, when the Yugoslav Black Wave appeared by the mid-1960s, the films in this movement often took direct aim at politics and the surrounding social reality.

Although operating as 'ciné-amateurs', Paspa and Miletić represented the opening of the professional age of Yugoslav cinematography. 'Amateur documentaries and other films at that time were
equal and sometimes superior to institutionalized, professional film'.[39]
The term 'amateur' is a bit inconclusive here, as the line separating
it from professionalism was very thin due to the advanced quality
of the films produced and the rigorous organizational structure of
the club itself. 'Non-commercial' is perhaps a more exact phrasing (as
described in the aims of UNICA), meaning that these ciné-club films
were not bought and sold on the open market. Or, as the president
of the Yugoslav Photo/Ciné League would define it in 1957, amateur
film was 'film which is not used commercially, its author receiving no
compensation for the idea or the work'.[40] In any event, Miletić began
his career in professional/commercial filmmaking while he was still
involved with the club. Continuing with his pioneering efforts, his
debut film LISINSKI was the first (feature-length) Croatian sound film.[41]

Film production continued at a regular pace in Zagreb Ciné-amateur
Club during the early years of the Second World War, although only
one film was made in 1942 and none were made in 1941 or 1944.[42] Of
course, these years of scarcity coincided with the climaxing of the war:
in 1941 the Axis invasion achieved victory over the Royal Yugoslav
Army, which led to the founding of the Nazi-controlled Independent
State of Croatia, with Zagreb as its capital; 1944 was when the Allied
invasion of Normandy took place, which for all intents and purposes
was the beginning of the end of the war.

After the liberation of Belgrade and the declaration of a socialist
federal republic in Yugoslavia, a film industry was very quickly organized in the reborn country. The Committee for Cinematography was
formed in 1946, with the writer Aleksandar Vučo placed in charge. He
immediately composed a multi-point manifesto outlining the rigid
tenets to which Yugoslav films were to adhere.[43] Vučo was one of
those interwar communists (and later Yugoslav Partisans) who were
active in the avant-garde arts, practising a 'cinema by other means'.
For example, in 1930, Vučo and his surrealist colleague Dušan Matić[44]
produced an abstract, framed wooden assemblage called 'The Frenzied
Marble' that was 'organized into successive rectangular, screen-like
formations, creating the overall impression of a filmstrip'.[45] Now on the
side of conservative dogma, forsaking his earlier experimental leanings, Vučo's decree highlighted the fact that cinema was an effective
means through which the League of Yugoslav Communists perpetuated their collective myths and ideology: 'Films were for reflecting the

development of a distinctive socialist art based upon the principles of national realism (a Yugoslav variant of socialist realism)'.[46] However, ciné-clubs were able to remain free from dogmatic ideological intervention and continue to function as an open space for filmic expression and experimentation – however, this was not always the case when certain ciné-clubs ventured into commercial feature film production.[47]

Also in 1946, and of great significance, the Central Committee of the Yugoslav Communist Youth League founded an initiative designed to administer technical training for amateurs in a number of fields – a sort of 'enlightenment' process designed to make various technologies accessible to the citizenry and to 'further culture in the population'[48] (though some feel this was a deliberate counteractive gesture to quell potential dissent by securing a marginalized space for radical experiments and critique). As a result, the Belgrade Society of Photo Amateurs was founded, whose tasks, among others, included developing ciné-amateurs. This Communist Youth League initiative was officially organized under the Commission of Techniques and Sport, which in 1948 gave birth to a workshop-like series called 'Narodna tehnika' (People's Technology) – this created a number of leagues, including the League of Photo Amateurs, which in 1949 changed its title to the Yugoslav League of Photo/Ciné-amateurs. The Belgrade Photo/Ciné-amateur Club was founded on 11 September 1950[49] as an organization under the auspices of the larger Yugoslav League of Photo/Ciné-amateurs, and the legendary Belgrade Ciné-club was founded on 27 May 1951[50] as an offshoot of the Belgrade Photo/Ciné-amateur Club.

If Zagreb Ciné-amateur Club remained a free space in the early years of Socialist Yugoslavia, and also seemed to maintain a somewhat 'tame' documentary focus in their films of the late 1940s. In 1945, a few films were produced that clearly toed an official socialist ideological line, such as KONGRES USAOH-A [United Anti-Fascist Croatian Youth Congress] by Nikola Tanhofer (who in the next decade would move into directing feature-length genre films) and OSLOBOĐENJE ZAGREBA [The Liberation of Zagreb] by Ivo Žgalin. Beyond films such as these, ciné-club production in the 1940s did not necessarily have an overt focus on national/socialist realism but rather explored newsreel-like subjects such as weekly sports reports, travelogues and operas. No data exists on the operations of Zagreb Ciné-amateur Club from the immediate postwar period into the early 1950s, nor does documentation exist on any official termination of the club. However, films produced in this period by club members were considered to be part of the output of Zagreb Ciné-amateur Club by default. In any event, the club as a formal institution seemed to disappear around this time, amid the general restructuring in the national cultural landscape.

When it comes to the institutionalization of film culture, it seems apparent that Yugoslavia developed a national film industry out of the seeds of the ciné-club movement.[51] The ciné-clubs served not only as a production model but also an artistic ideal, with their emphasis on freedom of expression, in addition to their success in winning awards at numerous international film festivals. Ciné-clubs set an example with regards to establishing international collaborations, and this was a lesson not lost on the Socialist Yugoslav film industry in the 1960s, which was notable for numerous large co-productions with both European and Hollywood film studios.

Cinéphilia, which is a gateway to ciné-amateurism, can then be read as a key formative impulse with regards to constructing a national cinema. It can be argued that all filmmakers are amateurs at one point or another – whether they incubate this amateurism in the space of ciné-clubs, film schools, or professional production. Therefore, a nuanced understanding of, and appreciation for, ciné-amateurism highlights the very building blocks of cinema as an apparatus, an industry and an art form.[52] Ryan Shand has argued that '[t]he aesthetic history of amateur cinema is now waiting to be written'.[53] While this is true and a very relevant task at hand (although not one that can be realized in the space of this study), the institutional history of amateur cinema is still in need of thorough investigation, in all of its diverse national contexts, including in relation to the development of national cinemas. The present chapter has moved in this direction with regards to the Yugoslav experience.

As has been demonstrated by their interconnected histories, ciné-club culture was built on comradery and cooperation. Club members regularly worked on each other's films and supported each other's efforts. These working relationships often lasted a lifetime, frequently blossoming into familial bonds. As filmmaker and original Belgrade Ciné-club member Marko Babac said, '[i]t was beautiful to be among people who were pleasant, unique, original, witty … and who loved the same thing – film'.[54] This love crossed all national and ethnic lines in Yugoslavia, as members frequently visited neighbouring clubs and continually struck up new partnerships.[55] Ciné-clubs formed a network through which various cinéastes communicated and interacted all over the country and beyond, drawing the framework for a dynamic ciné-nation in the process.

Notes

1. Malte Hagener. 2007. *Moving Forward, Looking Back: The European Avant-Garde and the Invention of Film Culture, 1919–1939*, Amsterdam: Amsterdam University Press, 96.
2. http://www.filmklubb.no/IFFS.php (retrieved 11 July 2010).
3. Duško Popović (ed.). 2003. *Kinoklub Zagreb 1928./2003./ Zagreb ciné-club 1928/2003*, Zagreb: Hrvatski filmski savez/Kino klub Zagreb, 22.
4. Ibid., 21.
5. See Greg de Cuir, Jr. 2012. 'The Nocturnal Affairs of Mr Miletić: Oktavijan's Career, Genre Hybridity, and Ciné-amateurism in Yugoslavia', in *Small-gauge Storytelling: Discovering the Amateur Fiction Film*, ed. by Ryan Shand and Ian Craven, Edinburgh: Edinburgh University Press.
6. 'Obrazloženje za "nagradu Vladimir Nazor" Oktavijanu Miletiću/Announcing Oktavijan Miletić for the "Vladimir Nazor Award"'. *Filmska kultura* 62 (1968): 66–67.
7. However, the monthly trade journal *Jugoslavenska filmska revija*, in issue 11–12, 1923, features an advertisement for the German film PETER DER GROSSE [Peter the Great] (1922) by Dimitri Buchowetzki, which states that the movie won first place in an international film exhibition in Turin.
8. This first term lasted until 1939, after which the country rejoined from 1953–98. UNICA conferences were held on Yugoslav soil twice: Zagreb in 1965 and Dubrovnik (Croatia) in 1988.
9. Popović, *Kinoklub Zagreb*, 24.
10. Ibid., 54–56.
11. Petar Volk. 1986. *Istorija jugoslovenskog filma* [The History of Yugoslav Cinema], Belgrade: Institut za film/Partizanska knjiga, 75.
12. Ibid.
13. Hrvoje Turković. 2003. 'Kinoklub Zagreb: Filmsko sadište i rasadište' [Zagreb Ciné-club: The Seeds and Development of Film], in Popović. *Kinoklub Zagreb*, 12.
14. Vjekoslav Majcen. 2003. 'Hrvatski neprofesijski film: 70 godina kinoamaterizma u Hrvatskoj (1928–1998)' [Croatian Non-Professional Film: 70 Years of Ciné-Amateurism in Croatia (1928–1998)], *Hrvatski filmski ljetopis* 29.
15. Ibid.
16. Vladeta Lukić. 1952. 'Amaterski film kod nas i u svetu' [Amateur Film at Home and in the World], *Film* 24: 4.
17. Majcen, 'Hrvatski neprofesijski film'.
18. Dejan Kosanović. 2011. *Kinematografija i film u Kraljevini SHS/Kraljevini Jugoslaviji 1918–1941* [Cinematography and Film in the Kingdom of Yugoslavia 1918–1941], Belgrade: Filmski centar Srbije, 46.
19. Ibid.
20. Majcen, 'Hrvatski neprofesijski film'.
21. Ibid.
22. Volk, *Istorija Jugoslovenskog filma*, 73.
23. Ibid.
24. Kosanović, *Kinematografija i film*, 171.
25. Ibid.
26. Pavle Levi. 2012. *Cinema by Other Means*, Oxford: Oxford University Press, 13.
27. Ibid., 27.
28. Branko Vučićević. 1998. *Paper Movies*, Belgrade-Zagreb: Arkzin & B 92.

29. Ibid., xiii.
30. Volk, *Istorija Jugoslovenskog filma*, 74.
31. The second issue of *Kinofon* featured the German director and actor Harry Piel on the cover, along with cartoon images of Charlie Chaplin.
32. Volk, *Istorija Jugoslovenskog filma*, 74.
33. Ibid., 75.
34. Ibid.
35. Turković, 'Kinoklub Zagreb', 13.
36. Hagener, *Moving forward, looking back*, 91.
37. Mihovil Pansini. 2003. 'Pet razdoblja Kinokluba Zagreb' [Five Eras of Zagreb Ciné-club], in Popović, *Kinoklub Zagreb*, 5.
38. Turković, 'Kinoklub Zagreb', 14.
39. Hrvoje Turković. 2009. 'Paralelni, alternativni i subkulturni opstanak – neprofesijski dokumentarizam u Hrvatskoj' [Parallel, Alternative and Sub-Cultural Survival – Non-Professional Documentary Filmmaking in Croatia], in *ZagrebDox – International Documentary Film Festival/Međunarodni festival dokumentarnog filma 2009*, Zagreb: Factum.
40. Popović, *Kinoklub Zagreb*, 33.
41. In the 1930s, a ciné-section for producing travelogues was formed in Sljeme Mountain Society, which included members of Zagreb Photo Club, such as Ljudevit Griesbach. In 1931 they produced an ethnographic film called *Durmitor*, directed by Branimir Gušić and his ethnologist wife Marijana Gušić-Heneberg, detailing the road from Zagreb to the top of Mount Durmitor in Montenegro. This seventy-minute film was accompanied by a gramophone record soundtrack and presented in theatres as a 'mountain sound film' (from Majcen's 2003 'Hrvatski neprofesijski film' in *Hrvatski filmski ljetopis* 29).
42. Ibid., p. 57.
43. The first of the four key points in this manifesto stated that 'films should be based on the principles of socialist realism, avoid abstract experimentation, and offer clear effective communication' (see Greg de Cuir, Jr. 2011. *Yugoslav Black Wave: Polemical Cinema from 1963–72 in the Socialist Federal Republic of Yugoslavia*, Belgrade: Film Center Serbia.
44. Dušan Matić would later serve as the dean of the Academy of Theater and Film Art in Belgrade from 1953–59 (see Vladimir Petrić, Alojz Ujes and Dragan Anđelković. 1971. *Almanah: dvadeset godina akademije za pozorište film radio i televiziju* [Almanac: Twenty Years of the Academy of Theatre, Film, Radio and Television], Belgrade: Umetnička akademija u Beogradu).
45. Levi, *Cinema by Other Means*, 27.
46. Daniel J. Goulding. 1985. *Liberated Cinema: The Yugoslav Experience*, Bloomington: Indiana University Press, 2.
47. As was the case with the Belgrade Ciné-club and their production *Delije* [Tough Guys] (1968) by Mića Popović, which was unofficially banned for exhibition and never given a theatrical release.
48. Turković, 'Paralelni, alternativni i subkulturni opstanak'.
49. Marko Babac. 2001. *Kino-klub 'Beograd'* [Belgrade Ciné-club], Belgrade: Jugoslovenska kinoteka, 7.
50. Ibid., 12.
51. As Turković alludes to in the very title of his article 'Zagreb Ciné-club: The Seeds and Development of Film'.

52. Ciné-amateurism has been theorized by such writers as Patricia Zimmermann (*Reel Families: A Social History of Amateur Film*, Bloomington : Indiana University Press, 1995); also Ryan Shand in his unpublished doctoral dissertation *Amateur Cinema: History, Theory, and Genre (1930–80)*. The landmark essay 'For an Imperfect Cinema' by Julio García Espinosa also contains applicable theoretical tools for penetrating the phenomenon of ciné-amateurism, from a decidedly more political and (just as important) Latin American (i.e. non-Western) perspective. However, Espinosa positioned 'imperfect cinema' in opposition to polished mainstream cinema, which he felt was reactionary. In this sense, ciné-amateurism as an 'imperfect' aesthetic is an ideal to be realized, rather than a means to an end (professional or otherwise).

53. Ryan Shand. 2008. 'Theorizing Amateur Cinema'. *The Moving Image* 8(2): 36–60.

54. Miroslav Bata Petrović (ed.). 2008. *Alternativni film u Beogradu od 1950. do 1990. godine* [Alternative Film in Belgrade from the Years 1950 to 1990], Belgrade: Dom kulture studentski grad, 40–41.

55. For indications of this creative networking in the era of Socialist Yugoslavia, see my essay 'Yugoslav Ciné-Enthusiasm: Ciné-club Culture and the Institutionalization of Amateur Filmmaking in the Territory of Yugoslavia from 1924–68', in *Romanian Review of Political Sciences and International Relations*, edited by Ion Bulei, Vol. VIII, No. 2, 2011.

Chapter 7

Soviet–Italian Cinematic Exchanges

Transnational Film Education in the 1930s

Masha Salazkina

The development of film education in Europe in its formative stage in the 1920s and 1930s was largely state-supported. Thus, it does not come as a surprise that it was both shaped by and formed part of the state nationalist modernizing agendas of industrialization, rationalization of labour and institutional practices, and mass education which characterize the social and political history of the first half of the twentieth century. In this way, the new media was integrated into the consumerist capitalist (technological, economic and political) hegemony of modernity, and of state nationalist projects. The development of national cinemas as well as both film education and the use of film in education formed an important part of a project to create a literate, governable population, whether domestic or colonial. This approach has recently been placed at the centre of scholarly discourse, providing a much needed social and political corrective to the narratives of artistic genius, heroic avant-garde and enlightenment commissars of film culture.[1]

Such a sobering view of film culture, however, needs to fully account for the fundamental heterogeneity of this phenomenon as subject to internal dialectics and conflicting internal pressures. As the new media became the locus for the new forms of social control, its institutional development generated an apparatus that often resisted its very logic. Despite – and sometimes because of – its privileged status vis-à-vis the hegemonic social and economic forces, the structures of film production, exhibition and distribution provided unforeseen lacunae, alternatives and possibilities. Film education in particular became a natural front of struggle between different visions of what cinema was, and what it could become. The ideal of film education from its earliest developments is constituted through a complex internal dialectic. It was simultaneously a way to control the masses and emancipate them; to bring the industrial production and aesthetic labour under strict organizational and rational control, and to free it from commodification and reification; to extend ideological control over film production and exhibition, and to create an engaged and participatory audience culture.

And while film education, like most forms of mass education, was largely a project governed by appropriate logic of nationalism, its institutional, discursive and artistic practices often depended on international circulation, in particular as the sphere of film education can be taken to include not only places of film instruction such as institutes, universities and centres but a broader range of cultural sites, formal and informal, ranging from cine-clubs to publications in newspapers and journals, and art exhibitions. Most of those sites were part of a broader international network of exchanges, translations and explicitly supra- and transnational organizations and projects which developed parallel to the national film education institutions. These various institutional structures not only co-existed, but shaped each other, forming a tight network, thus making clear distinctions between 'official' and 'alternative' or 'informal' cultural spheres quite problematic. Thus, for example, the gradual institutionalization of cinema and its accompanying discourses of film theory and film criticism were, indeed, closely linked to the legacies of the international avant-garde cultures, while at the same time serving the goals of the nation state.

These tensions can be revealed with particular clarity through an analysis of the relationship between Soviet and Italian film educational institutions in the late 1920s and early 1930s. Both countries had broken decisively with classical liberalism, albeit in different ways. This period was foundational in Italy, leading to the formation of the film educational structures which shaped both its pre- and postwar production. In the Soviet Union, during this period, its international status as a model for successful experimental film culture was solidified. The history of Italian and Soviet film cultures has a strong relevance to the institutionalization of cinema studies, and their role in this process could be argued to rival that of France – both Italy and the Soviet Union provided a significant critical and theoretical apparatus which shaped the curriculum of many postwar film educational institutions internationally. Both also became important centres for the training of filmmakers in the postwar period, especially for the aspiring ciné-astes from Latin America, Africa and Asia. Much of this apparatus was shaped in the course of the 1920s, 1930s and 1940s – and despite the often held assumption of the cultural autarky of both totalitarian states, it was a transnational process.[3]

In correspondence to the policies of modernization aggressively pursued by both states, many of the Soviet–Italian cinematic exchanges in the 1920s and 1930s centred around problems that arose in non-commercial cinema (educational, political, scientific and industrial) and the organization of the film industry around experimental educational projects. On the institutional level, these exchanges took places through the International Institute of Educational Cinematography, and culminated, symbolically, in the Venice Film Festival's inclusion of Soviet films. The Soviet film institute, (V)GIK, served as a model to which the founders of the Experimental Centre of Cinematography in Rome looked when developing their own programme. While direct exchanges were limited, Italian institutional and cultural discourses and practices relied heavily on Soviet examples, creating a rich site for transmission and translation of Soviet cinema and theory in Italy during the first phase of the fascist regime, from the 1920s up to the Spanish Civil War. The spaces for this cultural circulation were almost entirely situated outside of commercial structures, and while fully aligned with a Fascist Italian state that expressed a lively interest in cinema as an instrument of propaganda, nonetheless enjoyed a semi-autonomous status and effectively engaged in – and sometimes succeeded in creating – an active and participatory film culture. The nodes of this culture were: ciné-clubs and GUF's (university fascist youth clubs which both screened and produced films); educational and research centres such as the International Institute of Educational Cinematography, the National Film School (which would later become the *Centro Sperimentale di Cinematografia*); the journals associated with these institutions: *Revue internationale du cinema educateur*, *Intercine*, *Cinema*, and *Bianco e nero*; and, to some degree, even the Venice Film Festival (which was founded by the director of the International Institute of Educational Cinematography). All of these sites of exhibition, discussion and training were interconnected, and all remained in close contact with Soviet materials and promoted them in their practices.

Since Italy – unlike Germany, France or the U.S. – was not at the centre of Soviet political interests, this relationship remained largely one-sided, and so when official relations were broken off in 1936, its very existence was subsequently downplayed in the cultural histories of both countries. The leading figures from this time had little reason, in the postwar years, to recall the Fascist–Communist detente. Only recently historians have begun to uncover the full extent and importance of the Italo-Soviet dialogue, which now seems foundational to the development of some of the key film institutions in Italy. In this chapter, I take up the theme to show how the Soviet model was referenced and reproduced in the early days of the International Institute of Educational Cinematography and the Experimental Centre for Cinematography in Rome.

L'IICE

L'Instituto Internazionale di Cinema Educativo (L'IICE, the International Institute of Educational Cinematography), was founded in 1928 under the auspices of the League of Nations and was based in Rome until 1935. It served as the first major forum for an international discourse in the domain of promoting and supporting documentaries for educational purposes, according to its mission statement.[4] During its brief existence, L'IICE was active on a number of different fronts: it organized several film and photography exhibitions, including the Venice Film Festival; between 1929 and 1934 it sponsored a monthly journal, published in five languages; it carried out a series of massive international surveys on film and education; and it even financed an encyclopedia of cinematography that was eventually aborted. Rudolf Arnheim, a member of L'IICE, began writing his seminal *Film Art* as part of this project.[5] Such figures as László Moholy-Nagy and Germaine Dulac were also involved with the league's institute.[6] At the same time, key figures in L'IICE also occupied governmental positions in Mussolini's state-run film propaganda units. More surprisingly, recent research has shown that the older scholarly assumption that L'IICE meant to serve as a liberal alternative to communist-oriented cultural cosmopolitanism (i.e. communist internationalism), however tainted with its associations with the Fascist government, is false, as L'IICE's ultimate plans included the inclusion of the Soviet Union in its projects.

Luciano De Feo, L'IICE's director, tirelessly searched for ways to involve Soviet organizations in the running of the institute, writing letter after letter of invitations to the Soviet officials. These contacts were enacted through the Soviet Society for the Cultural Ties Abroad (VOKS), a para-governmental organization with representatives around the world (including Italy), as well as through the Soviet Embassy in

Italy.[7] Luciano De Feo's efforts were eminently understandable, since the Soviet Union was evidently the most advanced country in using the state's power to implement the development of cinema as a tool of education, and this extended to making cinema the object of scholarly study in academia in the 1930s.[8] True, other film schools existed in Germany and France, and isolated film courses were being taught in U.S. universities, but only Soviet cinematic education was conceived on a truly broad scale, within a larger humanities framework. It was conceived to integrate not only craft training and film appreciation, but it also related film to the study of aesthetics at large, while at the same time insisting on film as a distinct scholarly discipline.

Thus, under the surface of an anti-Bolshevik discourse in the European cinema cultures of both the fascist states and the democracies, the Soviet film institutions were imitated by those in the film culture concerned with the potential and aesthetics of film. Sergei Eisenstein in particular became not only an international sensation and a constant point of reference for the cinematic left from the late 1920s on, but also served as an important cultural mediator (in particular through his long trip abroad in the late 1920s/early 1930s), who established long-lasting ties with key figures of international film culture such as Ivor Montagu, Léon Moussinac, Georges Sadoul, Alberto Cavalcanti and Jay Leyda.[9] Much later in the course of the 1930s and 1940s, he became a much greater player in the institutional development of Soviet film education than has been traditionally acknowledged.[10] However, in the period under discussion, L'IICE lacked direct contacts with any Soviet cultural figures of note, and repeatedly turned to the Soviet film officials and state bureaucrats for participation in their initiatives.

A decade of correspondence exists that flowed between De Feo and the Soviet organizations, which document the extent of De Feo's relentless intermediary work in trying to transplant the Soviet model by creating a modus vivendi between Soviet film institutions and L'IICE. Thanks to his efforts, a great deal of printed material from the Soviet Union was published in the journals associated with the institute: *Revue internationale du cinema educateur* (RICE), *Intercine* and even *Cinema*, which at its inception in 1936 was also affiliated to the institute.

The very first issue of *Review internazionale del cinema educatore* (the Italian-language version of RICE), included a piece by Vladimir Erofeev and another by cameraman Nikolai Strukov, both Soviet filmmakers. The first piece concerned the making of Erofeev's ethnographic documentary in Afghanistan, which discussed the importance of making sure that documentaries are 'founded on real facts and phenomena which give the exact idea of the world and contribute to the broadening of the intellectual horizons of the spectators'. The latter detailed the making of a scientific film about meteors.[11] It is worth noting that this emphasis on forms of exploration – geopolitical and scientific – point to the shared colonial interests and ambitions of the Soviet and European counterparts.

De Feo selected these articles from the monthly bulletins of films and publications which VOKS sent him at his request. He had expressed a specific interest in 'cultural, scientific [and] educational films – in particular those about the rationalization of labour and agriculture'.[12] VOKS provided these lists, and acted as an intermediary for the articles to be published in RICE and *Intercine* between 1929 and 1932.[13] De Feo also continued to send out questionnaires to members of the Soviet film industry regarding its organization of labour, but to no avail; despite clear interest on the side of some of the Soviet counterparts, these requests never made their way through the labyrinth of the Soviet cultural bureaucracy. De Feo was more successful in getting the collaboration of the Soviet embassy and VOKS for screening Soviet films in the embassy in Rome, which happened regularly in the early 1930s.[14] Encouraged by such interest, in 1930–31 VOKS' Italian Section repeatedly requested the main organization in charge of film production at the time, Sovkino, to help to promote Soviet cinema in Italy, stating that there is 'enormous interest in Soviet cinema and culture in Italy'.[15] VOKS' proposal was to establish an Italo-Soviet society of cultural ties, as well as increase the commercial exhibition of Soviet films in Italy. However, the international office (*Narodnyi Komitet po Inostrannym Delam*) rejected the suggestion, while the international trade section (*Intorgkino*) even failed to appoint a direct representative in Italy, delegating all its business through its Berlin section, which effectively occluded Italy.[16]

Despite these failed attempts, VOKS' Italian section floated the idea of organizing an international exhibition of the achievements of Soviet cinema, which would take place in Rome in May 1932 and then continue to other European locations. The plan received official approval in February 1932, and Sovkino started its preparations. The exhibit took up De Feo's expressed interest in educational film, and in the organization and development of the film industry through the planned economy. Among other topics touched upon were: the Soviet's film educational structures – that is, film institutes – including a detailed explanation of the educational structure of VIK; the system of interconnectedness between theory and practice, and research; ciné-clubs and various forms of film exhibition; and advances in Soviet film technology and film art.

The exhibition was planned to encompass ten sections, including those on the cinemas of the Soviet republics – Ukraine, Georgia, Armenia, Azerbaijan and Turkmenistan – whose studios were ready to send out its materials (both films and informational bulletins). A special section was to deal with developments in Soviet sound technology.[17] Right before the start of the exhibition, the Soviets offered to send the newest newsreels shot in Moscow during the May Day parade, the start of Dnepromstroi, which would be edited specifically for the purposes of the event. *Intorgkino* also proposed sending its sound films to be included in the screenings, as well as a selection of silent films 'for those interested in questions of film art'.[18] By all accounts, this exhibition would have been the largest and most ambitious showcase of the Soviet film industry and culture outside the USSR, and without a doubt it would have had significant impact on the international film culture. However, this time the Italian side balked. When the plan was approved, the representative of VOKS in Italy wrote a letter to De Feo outlining the idea of the exhibition and suggesting its affiliation with L'IICE. De Feo, however, was involved in the organization of the first Venice Film Festival, planned for that same year, 1932. As a counterproposal, he suggested the inclusion of Soviet films in the festival, as well as an official visit to the Soviet Union by the representatives of the Italian film industry, including De Feo himself – this subsequently took place in July of that year.[19]

As a result, three Soviet films – Alexander Dovzhenko's ZEMLIA [Earth] (1930), Nikoilai Ekk's PUTIOVKA V ZHIZN [The Road to Life] (1931), and Olga Preobrazhenskaia and Ivan Pravov's TIKHII DON [And Quiet Flows the Don] (1931) – were included in the first Venice International Film Festival organized by De Feo in 1932. Ekk's film in particular received the Audience Referendum Award for 'the most convincing directorial work', and was met with considerable critical enthusiasm.[20] Consequently, after long bureaucratic delays, in 1934 Stalin permitted a group of Soviet filmmakers and functionaries to attend the second International Film Festival in Venice, where they presented over ten films, ranging from documentaries such as Vertov's TRI PESNI O LENINE [Three Songs of Lenin] (1934) and Shafron and Troyanovsky's CHELIUSKIN (1934) to literary adaptations, GROZA [Thunderstorm] (1934, Vladimir Petrov) and PYSHKA, aka BOULE DE SUIF (1934, Michail Romm,), musical comedy such as VESELYE REBYATA [Jolly Fellows] (1934, Grigori Alexandrov) and Dovzhenko's ill-fated

IVAN (1932). Some of the films were shown as work-in-progress such as NOVYI GULLIVER [The New Gulliver] (1935, Aleksandr Ptushko). As a result, the Soviet Film Industry (rather than any individual film) was even given an award for achievement in cinematographic production, with Mussolini himself mentioning CHELIUSKIN as a model heroic documentary.[21]

Despite this seeming political approval and critical success, very few of these films garnered wide distribution; when they were exhibited in Italy, it was mostly in the context of private clubs and university groups, which formed a widespread network of venues for non-commercial film exhibition. But while Soviet films lacked a popular Italian audience, especially in contrast with American cinema (despite Mussolini's limitation of American film exhibition) among the inner circle of filmmakers, Soviet cinema became the cornerstone of cinematic education in 1930s.

L'IICE failed, in the end, to surmount the political obstacles to involving the Soviet film industry and its film education institutions in its world congress on educational cinema or the encyclopedia of the history of cinema. In fact, L'IICE was caught in an ultimately untenable political situation in the 1930s, which is why its ambitious projects were, for the most part, shelved. However, I would argue that the attempt to open relations between the European and Soviet cinemas played a large part in the diffusion of certain themes and programmes on the international film culture. The legacy of L'IICE includes the use of international film festivals as major sites of non-theatrical cinematic exchanges, and the formation of various film archives which led to the establishment in 1938 of the International Federation of Film Archives (which included the MOMA,[22] Cinémathèque Française, Reichsfilmarchiv, and the U.K. National Film Library).[23]

Although, as this précis of L'IICE's engagement with the Soviet models of didactic filmmaking shows, the institution's turn towards Soviet filmmaking was of rather limited consequences to the broader Italian film culture of the time, it had subtler effects among the core of the Italian film community. Surely the most important development in the cinematic landscape of interwar Italy was the founding of the National Film School, which eventually became known as *Centro Sperimentale* in Rome, and this was definitely inspired by the Soviet film educational structures. When Mussolini's government categorically rejected the Soviet proposal to give Soviet films a wider distribution, they forced those who wanted to show and discuss Soviet cinema to find non-commercial venues for the showing and discussion of these films. And these venues were mostly of interest to cinéphiles, critics, and those in the film industry.[24] So, in an ironic 'return of the repressed', Soviet cinema became the cornerstone of the cinematic education in 1930s Italy, primarily through the work of the Centro Sperimentale di Cinematografia.

The Centro

The role that the Centro has played in the history of Italian cinema is well known. But of equal historical and cultural importance is the fact that it functioned at the crossroads of an international cultural dialogue, and it did so both in the Fascist period and the postwar period.

The Italian national film school was initially the brain child of Anton Giulio Bragaglia, one of the key figures of Italian futurism, who had long-standing ties to the Russian and Soviet avant-garde (in particular to Vsevolod Meyerhold). In 1930, when Bragaglia proposed establishing a national film school to the state agency dealing with mass media in Fascist Italy (Corporazione dello specttacolo), he backed up his idea of a school based on the 'European example' which would bring together artistic experiment and academic research by referring to the already existing Soviet schools, specifically the School of Screen Arts in Leningrad, and to Trauberg and Kuleshov's experimental studios, as well as to the Moscow State Institute of Cinematography (GIK, later VGIK). The three pillars of Bragaglia's proposal were centred on actor training, teaching and practice, with the teaching to be based on (1) theoretical culture, (2) experimental application of scholarly ideas, and (3) practical artistic work.[25] The Bragaglia proposal resulted in the funding of the National Film School (Scuola Nazionale di Cinematografia), which was opened in Rome in 1932.

In 1934, when the Fascist regime moved to give the state more control over film, the Scuola was re-formed as Centro Sperimentale di Cinematografia. Luigi Chiarini, who at that point was best known as a literary and cultural critic and follower of Giovanni Gentile's neo-Crocean fascist idealist ideology, was appointed as its head. Chiarini brought his friend Umberto Barbaro with him, and the two of them would be largely responsible for the Centro's programme and for the film journal *Bianco e nero*, founded in 1937 under its auspices.[26]

In his institutional manifesto of 1934, Chiarini announced the theoretical platform of the centre, which conceptualized it as an instrument for a new realist cinema, making reference to the 'new realism' implicit in Pudovkin's use of montage.[27] Given Chiarini's background, the reference to Pudovkin appears to be an unexpected choice as his neo-Croceanism seems explicitly antithetical to the theoretical stance of the Soviet avant-garde. Moreover, Pudovkin's films were not in circulation in Italy at the time (except for some isolated screenings which took place at the Soviet embassy), nor had they been chosen for showing among the Soviet films seen at either the 1932 or 1934 Venice Film Festivals. How, then, did Chiarini know about Pudovkin?

The reference no doubt stems from Chiarini's involvement in the publication of the 1932 translation of Pudovkin's writings by Umberto Barbaro under the title *Il soggetto cinematografico*. Translations of Pudovkin's text were collected again in 1935 under the title of *Film e Fonofilm*, which went on to become one of the primary texts used in the curriculum at the Centro. In addition to Pudovkin, Barbaro and Chiarini gathered together texts by Eisenstein, Timoshenko, Balázs, Arnheim, Spottiswoode and Rotha for inclusion in the anthologies they produced for classroom use at the Centro: '*I problemi del film*', '*L'attore*' and '*L'arte dell'attore*'.

Chiarini and Barbaro were unlikely allies in the campaign to promote cinema's social and educational function as against its commercial use. This thesis is articulated through the meshes of their respective ideologies: Chiarini idealistically takes cinema as an expression of individual creation, which takes its place in the aesthetic education of the people; meanwhile Barbaro takes it as an instrument film to raise the consciousness of the masses concerning the society they function in, while at the same time mirroring the properties of commodity production in its own structure. Barbaro's cinema is two-sided – one forging class consciousness, the other marked by self-reflectivity. In Fascist Italy, then, the GUF and the Centro were meant to create a new generation of filmmakers within new institutional spaces that were structured by the emergent social and aesthetic discourse on film as both a popular and an aesthetically modernist medium, which in turn existed within the limits imposed by the fascist project. However, the institutional form that was created, with its emphasis on international film and its encouragement of debate, unintentionally undermined the ostensible content to which it was dedicated, the national aesthetic as the fascists officially conceived it. The pervasive influence of Soviet cinema was represented as much by early Soviet film writings as by the products of the Soviet film industry. In those writings, the Italians found a rhetoric and a theoretical standpoint that allowed them to embrace 'realism' and the anti-realist tendency of the European avant-garde. No theorist implemented this synthesis more thoroughly or influentially in the 1930s than Umberto Barbaro.

Umberto Barbaro and Vinicio Paladini

Umberto Barbaro was one of the first professors at the Centro, and he remained there until 1948 (briefly serving as its director in the postwar period). He was responsible for much of cultural and ideological diversity in the 1930s and 1940s.[28] A fervent Marxist, Barbaro translated Eisenstein, Pudovkin and Timoshenko, along with Balázs, Richter and Arnheim, and used Soviet cinema extensively in his teaching and in the essays he wrote for *Bianco e nero*, the official journal of the Centro (for which he served as editor). He saw the Soviet cinema explicitly as 'the starting point and as an example for the rebirth of Italian cinema'.[29]

Barbaro's knowledge of Russian and Soviet culture was broadly based. He began to translate Russian literature and write articles about Russian and Soviet literature and culture in the 1920s. Barbaro is important as a link between the Centro and the Soviet, as well as the Italian, avant-garde of the 1920s – a period when he associated himself with the movement of the leftist futurist artists in Rome. Barbaro's friendship and artistic collaboration with Vinicio Paladini was key to his engagement with the Soviet avant-garde. Paladini, who was born in Moscow to a Russian mother but raised in Rome, established a place in the cultural scene of Rome both as an avant-gardist and as a key intermediary in the dissemination of works by the Soviet avant-garde, in particular the constructivists and supremacists. He was also on good terms with Gramsci's *Ordine Nuovo* circle in Turin, where he participated in the 1922 leftist futurist show and contributed articles to *Avanguardia*, the official organ of the Federation of Young Socialists, a forum for debate on progressive culture and the role of art in socialism in the early 1920s.[30] Paladini's small press, *La Bilancia* (Libra), named after the Russian symbolist group of the same name, published not only manifestos and essays by the Italian leftist avant-garde groups but also works on the Soviet art: for instance, in 1925 he wrote a long piece reviewing the exhibit of Soviet art at the art pavilion in Venice the previous year.[31]

From 1925 to the late 1930s, Barbaro and Paladini collaborated on a number of avant-garde projects: first within the futurist framework (with Giacomo Balla, and in Bragaglia's Teatro degli Indipendienti in Rome), after which they inaugurated a new group of 'Imaginismo' (a peculiar fusion of futurism, constructivism and surrealism, with particular emphasis on the circus and Luna Park aesthetic), until moving, in the late 1920s, towards cinema and the rediscovery of 'realism' and 'art based on reality', references filtered through the experience of the Soviet avant-garde. In 1923–24, together with Barbaro, Paladini published in the near-anarchist (but sympathetic to the Soviet Union) journal *Fede!*, where he continued to develop his ideas about the revolutionary role that could be played by an intellectual and artist in society who merged with the proletariat.[32] Given this image of the engaged intellectual, it is not surprising that Barbaro and Paladini saw the Soviet avant-garde as the model for marrying experimental techniques to the radical political programme in Italy. Paladini also produced a number of works in the style of the Soviet constructivism, often referring to himself as 'fotomonteur', and his theatre of 'Futurist Mechanical Ballet' which was not only emblematic of the futurist ethos of the time but also explicit about the machine as both a vehicle and a metaphor for the communist revolution, a mediation between the artist and the industrial production process. Reversing the bourgeois aesthetic distaste for the dehumanizing effects of industrialization, Paladini took industrial production (the machine) for the very image of the art of the future, creating an image of modernism understood not in relation or opposition to realism, but as a reaction to and against bourgeois commodity culture, with its total separation of production and consumption, and its consequent creation of a passive audience.[33] In 1927, Paladini entered a contest for set design organized by Blasetti's famous journal *Cinematografo*, with sketches clearly modelled on Alexander Exter's work (which he praised in his review of the Russian pavilion).

The next year Paladini made a trip to the Soviet Union where he met figures in the Soviet film industry and discussed intersections between Constructivism and cinema. He was fascinated by the Soviet movement of factography. Returning to Rome, he published a series of articles about his trip, including the theoretical reflections that it inspired.[34] In 1928–29, Paladini and Barbaro published more articles, evidently in response to Alexei Gan's recent essays on constructivism in cinema and to works by Pudovkin and Vertov, testifying to the temporary fusion of Italian leftist futurist positions with Soviet constructivist and productivist ethos.[35] It is in the 1928–29 series that we see the argument for documentary and 'reality-based' cinema take root; this kind of film is argued for as a 'pure' cinema (that is, one in which film exhibits its uniquely cinematographic qualities rather than deriving its form and content from other arts, i.e. literature and theatre) that takes up the task disseminating the ethos of modern art 'among the masses of workers and peasants'.[36] He also tried to establish regular correspondence with Vertov, whom he had apparently met during his trip, as part of the project of translating Vertov's writings. However, there is no evidence of Vertov ever having responded to Paladini's eager letters.[37] Paladini continued working with Barbaro on various film projects, both theoretical and actual productions, until the late 1930s – for instance, on the sets of Barbaro's 1937 film L'ULTIMA NEMICA. However, unlike Barbaro, Paladini was unable to find a niche for himself in 1930s Fascist Italy – despite Barbaro's (failed) attempts to get him involved in the Centro. In the late 1930s Paladini chose to emigrate to the United States, bringing to a close his career in architecture and set design. Barbaro, however, moved forward and deepened his preliminary engagement with the Soviet film theory by incorporating it into the Centro's articulation of the new Italian realist aesthetic. The proto-history of this engagement is found in the futurist and constructivist models of avant-garde of the 1920s, in which the parameters were formed that coded Barbaro's encounter with Pudovkin's writings, within which Barbaro elaborated his theoretical approach and pedagogical practice. Throughout his life, Barbaro remained loyal to the insight that cinema presented a unique capacity for fusing the aesthetic and the political, thus remaining an essential reference, in modernity, for the forging of a 'critical consciousness'. For him, cinema was above all a practice.

Barbaro's gift was in assimilating and synthesizing seemingly disparate aesthetic and ideological approaches under the title of a realism that had freed itself from the bourgeois mimetic moment of the nineteenth century. This position is perhaps best expressed by Barbaro in the introduction to his translation of Béla Balázs, to whom Barbaro attributes traits that, as Gian Piero Brunetta argues, could equally be applied to Barbaro himself:

> Work for him was an unbreakable union of theoretical and practical activity, not merely a way to understand and explain the world but a contribution to its transformation. [Work] was a free and full expression and expansion of a man solidly tied to other people with the same orientation … an exemplary life of a man both free and social, i.e. fully human.[38]

In the light of this intention, Barbaro took up Pudovkin's writings as a secret weapon against the prevailing Crocean idealism (whose champion at the Centro was Barbaro's colleague and protector, Chiarini). This idealism, extending into the twentieth century themes that had been generated in the romantic age of the nineteenth century, understood art in terms of individual expression that transcended the routines of everyday life without attempting to change them in any critical or systematic way. In fact, the descent into practice would inevitably ruin the aesthetic stance. Evidently, under this aesthetic programme, cinema's revolutionary potential is diverted into an affirmation of social hierarchies, and film theory is exhausted by connoisseurship – the writing appreciations and evaluations. This reproduced the role allotted by the commercial cinema system to the critic in mass media, as a sort of intermediary between the apparatus of publicity and the consumer.[39] What Barbaro found in Pudovkin above all others was a way of looking at the construction of the art object which performed a double demystification, stripping away the individualistic notion of the auteur and marking the process of its production – its institutional setting, its network of distribution, and its reception (in so far as the art object can apprehend it). However, Barbaro's conclusion did not undermine the organizational role played by the film director, but, on the contrary, carved out a role for cinema education as the process by which the film director was taught how to create a critical distance from his naïve, classbound visual and narrative impulses. As Pudovkin states in one of his earliest essays:

> A film factory has all the characteristics of industrial production. The leading engineer can do nothing without his experts and workers. Their mutual efforts will come to nothing if workers were to limit themselves to the mechanical execution of their narrow functions. Collective work is what makes every part of the work a living and organic part of the larger goal/ task. The nature of filmmaking is such that the more people take a direct and organic involvement, the more varied their involvement in the work, the better the final product of this process – the film – becomes.[40]

Pudovkin also emphasized the collective nature of the filmmaking practice. His insistence on the importance of a script needs to be understood as a way of centralizing the work of the collectivity, which takes filmmaking out of the director-centric orbit (that is, out of spontaneous subjectivity) and emphasizes the contradictions between the era of individualist subjectivity and the revolutionary future of collective subjectivity. 'It is not a lone director who is called upon to resolve such creative task [as the making of a film requires]. Only a collective/community united by a shared idea and a unified understanding of a goal/ task (*zadachi*), creative and controlling itself (*sam sebya kontroliruyuschii*) can do such a work [of real filmmaking]'.[41]

Pudovkin took filmmaking to be a distinct form of collective labour, all the parts of which are linked to the twofold collective social goal of creating socially relevant art and putting it in contact with a mass audience. But the transition from script to filming had to be further mediated through the collectivity of self-reflexive cinematic production ('creating and controlling itself') in order to remain coherent. Barbaro must have found this to be exactly the kind of thing he was searching for as he constructed an ideology of the new Italian cinema, which did not sever its connection with mimetic realism, but did attack the idealist/passive form of it. It was 'technical' enough to account for the medium specificity of cinema, it understood film's popular nature, both in its creation and its reception, and further understood those characteristics that made it a distinct form of industrial production and consumption among the medias and then, by a final leap, redeemed the figure of the artist not on bourgeois individualist terms, with its cult of the genius, but on class-based terms, with its transparent need for some critical organizing force. What central planning was to industrial policy, the director would be to the production of film.

For Barbaro, then, the natural consequence of this understanding of realism was that it became a term for the transformative function of cinema: art 'is not limited to making an interpretation of the world, but intends to actively transform reality'.[42] This quote mirrors almost exactly the Soviet factographic discussion of realism where '[factography] had nothing to do with the naïve and lying verisimilitude of bourgeois realism's aesthetics of resemblance. Rather its interventionist, operative aesthetic called upon the producer not simply to depict life, but to create it anew in the process'.[43] This point is sometimes buried under the criticism of the 'political ineffectiveness' of neorealism as politically engaged cinema; however, it was Barbaro's politicized representation of neorealism in terms of the potential of cinematic apparatus – rather than describing a specific film style – that strongly influenced the global set of theorists and practitioners of political modernism of the 1950s and 1960s (including figures such as Gillo Pontecorvo, theorists and cinéastes of Cinema Novo in Brazil, and of Cuban Imperfect Cinema).[44]

However, unlike most of these subsequent political filmmakers and theorists, for whom Eisenstein exemplified Soviet cinema, Barbaro always preferred Pudovkin to Eisenstein's theories of montage, which he considered insufficiently materialistic. This preference is further reflected in the institutional canon of the Centro, where Pudovkin was assigned as standard reading for the students throughout the 1930s. Pudovkin was a greater realist for Barbaro because of his more 'pragmatic' attitude towards filmmaking as a collective activity, which required a different kind of the organization of the production, placing the issue of aesthetic labour at the centre of the discussion. But a different aspect of Pudovkin's 'pragmatism' was the more practical nature of his writings on cinema – their accessibility and concern with specific cinematic problems, which made them easily applicable as a model for a particular didactic and pedagogical critical practice that the Centro embraced. Pudovkin's approach to filmmaking was preferable due to the fact that it could easily function as a didactic text for cinematic education, almost a manual for the future filmmakers, which was particularly important to the educational mission of the Centro and another aspect of the fusion between theory and practice through education.

Pudovkin's aesthetic position mediating the earlier avant-garde stance with the new rhetoric of realism provided a correlate to ideas afloat in both fascist and leftist circles.

Thus Pudovkin's texts – via Barbaro's interventions – came to provide a productive and polemical reception field in the cinematic culture of Fascist Italy, and re-catalysed the cinematic debates. At the core of this dialogue is the problem of the commodification of the work of art and its alienation from society and politics, and the use of institutionalized film education to bridge this gap.

In this opposition to commercialization of cinema we can see three different approaches unfold: Chiarini's fascist art cinema, Barbaro's version of engaged realism outside the studio system, and De Feo's didactic cinema for the modernization of the nation. The terms of this debate remained the same, while emphasis on one or the other of these issues depended on the divergent and often contradictory and competing elements of the larger film culture, be it the state, organizations, critics or the filmmakers themselves. Established in close, if sometimes unacknowledged, dialogue with the Soviet forms of institutionalized film education and its theoretical apparatus, the debates concerning the relationship between film and the state, and film and commerce, demonstrate not the presumed affinities between the totalitarian states but rather underscore the fundamental internal contradictions and dialectics which underwrite the development of film education in the first half of the twentieth century.

Notes

Parts of this chapter are revised and adapted from Masha Salazkina. 2012. 'Moscow–Rome–Havana: A Film Theory Roadmap', *October* 139 (Spring), 97–117.

1. See Dana Polan. 2007. *Scenes of Instruction: The Beginnings of the US Study of Film*. Berkeley: University of California Press; Malte Hagener. 2007. *Moving Forward, Looking Back: The European Avant-garde and the Invention of Film Culture, 1919–1939*. Amsterdam: Amsterdam University Press; Lee Grieveson and Haidee Wasson (eds). 2008. *Inventing Film Studies: Towards a History of a Discipline*. Durham, NC and London: Duke University Press; Lee Grieveson and Colin MacCabe (eds). 2011a. *Empire and Film*. London: Palgrave Macmillan and British Film Institute; Lee Grieveson and Colin MacCabe (eds). 2011b. *Film and the End of Empire*. London: Palgrave Macmillan and British Film Institute.
2. Hagener, *Moving Forward, Looking Back*.
3. This scholarly position was recently challenged by Katerina Clark. 2011. *Moscow, the Fourth Rome: Stalinism, Cosmopolitanism, and the Evolution of Soviet Culture, 1931–1941*. Cambridge, MA: Harvard University Press.
4. See Christel Taillibert. 1999. *L'Institut International du cinématographe éducatif. Regards sur le rôle du cinéma éducatif dans la politique internatonale du fascisme italien*, Paris: L'Harmattan; Zoë Druick. 2008. '"Reaching the Multimillions': Liberal Internationalism and the Establishment of Documentary Film', in Grieveson and Wasson (eds), *Inventing Film Studies*, 67–92; and Zoë Druick. 2007. 'The International Educational Cinematograph Institute, Reactionary Modernism, and the Formation of Film Studies', *Canadian Journal of Film Studies / Revue canadienne d'études cinématographiques* 16(1), 80–97.
5. For more on Arnheim's role, see Jürgen Wilke. 1991. 'Cinematography as a Medium of Communication: The Promotion of Research by the League of Nations and the Role of Rudolf Arnheim', *European Journal of Communication* 6(3), 337–53.
6. Druick, 'The International Educational Cinematograph Institute', 88.
7. On VOKS, see Michael David-Fox. 2011. *Showcasing the Great Experiment: Cultural Diplomacy and Western Visitors to the Soviet Union, 1921–1941*. Oxford: Oxford University Press, 40.
8. See the contributions by Natalie Ryabchikova and Duncan Petrie in this volume.
9. See the contribution by Ian Christie in this volume.
10. See Naum Kleiman and Antonio Somaini (eds). Forthcoming. *Sergei M. Eisenstein: Notes for a General History of Cinema*, Amsterdam: Amsterdam University Press.
11. Vladimir Erofeev. 1929. 'A proposito del film 'L'Afganistan'. Il mio passato e il mio avvenire', *RICE* (July), 65; Nikolai Strukov. 1929. 'Alla ricerca del meteorite nella taiga', *RICE* (July), 69–72.
12. GARF (State Archive of the Russian Federation), f. 5283, op. 7, d. 543.
13. GARF f. 5283 op. 2 d. 62.
14. Such as, for example, the screening of Turksib (1929, Viktor Turin) in Rome in February 1932. GARF f. 5283 op. 1a d. 168.
15. Ibid.
16. Ibid.
17. GARF f. 5283 op. 11 d. 175.
18. Ibid.
19. For details, see Stefano Pisu. 2010. 'L'Urss e l'Occidente: L'Unione Sovietica alla Mostra del cinema di Venezia negli anni Trenta', *Bianco e nero* 567 (May–August), 93–109.
20. Guilio Caseare Castello and Claudio Bertieri (eds). 1959. *Venezia 1932–1939. Filmografia critica*. Rome: Bianco e nero, 243–55.

21. Ibid., 253.
22. Jay Leyda, who was Eisenstein's student in VGIK in the 1930s, was directly involved in the development of MOMA's film library and a number of its other film-related projects. See Haidee Wasson. 2005. *Museum Movies: The Museum of Modern Art and the Birth of Art Cinema*, Berkeley: University of California Press, 81.
23. See the contribution by Malte Hagener in this volume.
24. For more on the importance of the ciné-clubs alongside the activities of Centro Sperimentale for the emergent neorealist filmmakers, see interview with Carlo Lizzani, in Vito Zagarrio. 2004. *Cinema e fascismo: Filmi, modeli, immaginarii*. Venice: Marsilio, 266–67.
25. Ernesto G. Laura. 1976. 'CSC dal fascismo allo stato democratico', *Bianco e Nero* 5(6), 4–29.
26. For Chiarini and the CSC, see also the contribution by Francesco Pitassio and Simone Venturini in this volume.
27. Luigi Chiarini. 1934a. *Cinematografo*, Rome: Cremonese. Quoted in Laura, 'CSC', 12.
28. Gian Piero Brunetta. 1969. *Umberto Barbaro e l'idea di Neorealismo (1930–1943)*. Padua: Liviana.
29. Quoted in Gian Piero Brunetta. 1993. *Storia del cinema italiano, v.2, Il cinema del regime 1929–1945*, Rome: Editori riuniti, 170 (translations MS).
30. Gunter Berghaus. 1998. *Italian Futurist Theater, 1909–1944*. Oxford: Clarendon, 417–18.
31. Vinicio Paladini. 1925. *Arte nella Russia dei Soviets: il padiglione dell'U.R.S.S. a Venezia*. Roma: La Bilancia.
32. Giovanni Lista. 1988. *Dal futurismo all'immaginismo: Vinicio Paladini*. Bologna: Il cavaliere azzurro, 22.
33. Vinicio Paladini. 1928. 'Cinematografo e teatri in Russia sovietica', *Cinemalia* 2(8) (15 April), 23–24.
34. For an articulation of this aspect of modernist art, see Walter Adamson. 2007. *Embattled Avant-Gardes: Modernism's Resistance to Commodity Culture in Europe*. Berkeley: University of California Press.
35. See Vinicio Paladini. 1928. 'Estetica cinematografica', *Cinemalia* 2(19) (1 Oct–1 Dec), 35; and Vinicio Paladini. 1928. 'Cinematografo dal Vero', *Cinema-teatro*, 15 sett.
36. Quoted in Umberto Carpi. 1981. *Bolscevico immaginista. Comunismo e avanguardie artistiche nell'Italia degli anni venti*. Naples: Liguori, 165–66.
37. RGALI f.2091, op.2, d. 351.
38. Gian Piero Brunetta. 1972. *Intellettuali, cinema e propaganda tra le due guerre*. Bologna: Patron, 149.
39. It is ironic, however, that Barbaro himself, especially in the postwar period, became just that kind of critic, evaluating the films based on his own very narrow ideological criteria of 'critical realism' against the 'excesses of formalism', following the Zhdanovite line of the Communist Party.
40. Vsevolod Pudovkin. 1974. 'Kollektivizm – baza kinoraboty', in V. Pudovkin, *Sobranie sochinenii v trekh tomakh*, Volume 1, Moscow: Iskusstvo, 129 (translation MS).
41. Vsevolod Pudovkin, 'O scenarnoi forme', in *Sobranie*, 47.
42. Ibid., 28.
43. Sergei Tret'iakov. 1931. *Feld–Herren: der Kampf um eine Kollektiv–Wirtschaft*. Berlin: Malik, 23; quoted in Devin Fore. 2006. 'The Operative Word in Soviet Factography', *October* 118 (Fall), 101. For more on the relationship between factography and

cinematic realism, see Joshua S. Malitsky, 'Ideologies in Fact: Still and Moving-Image Documentary in the Soviet Union, 1927–1932', *Journal of Linguistic Anthropology* 20(2) (Fall), 352–71.

44. For an elaboration on this argument, see Masha Salazkina. 2012. 'Moscow–Rome–Havana: A Film Theory Roadmap', *October* 139 (Spring), 97–117.

Chapter 8

THE AVANT-GARDE, EDUCATION AND MARKETING

The Making of Non-theatrical Film Culture in Interwar Switzerland

Yvonne Zimmermann

This chapter examines the emergence of film culture in the 1920s and 1930s as an outcome of an informal network of various institutional strands – among them the avant-garde – that shared ideas and practices about film and cinema as an instrument for social interference. In the following, the cinematic avant-garde is considered along with educational and corporate milieus to uncover the intersections, cooperation and alliance of the art film movement with coalitions whose contributions to non-theatrical film culture have largely gone unnoticed in cinema studies. To illustrate this point, we only need to look at two historical events that both happened to take place in Switzerland. The first instance made it into all serious film history books as the culmination point of the European interwar film avant-garde: the First International Congress of Independent Cinema (le 1er Congrès international du cinéma independent) in La Sarraz. In September 1929, Madame Hélène de Mandrot hosted at her castle near Lausanne the *Who's Who* of the cinematic avant-garde of the day. Among the participants were Béla Balázs, Hans Richter and Walter Ruttmann, Léon Moussinac, Robert Aron, Alberto Cavalcanti, Sergei Eisenstein and Eduard Tissé. Never before and never since have so many protagonists of the interwar avant-garde assembled at one place. And the moment of their meeting could not have been more crucial, marking the climax of the movement before its dispersing in different ideological and artistic directions. According to Freddy Buache, film historian and for many years director of the Swiss Film Archive, the La Sarraz Congress is 'the grand date of cinema history in Switzerland'.[1] And for Hervé Dumont, Buache's successor at the Swiss Film Archive and a film historian too, it is 'probably the most important cinema event to have ever taken place on Swiss territory'.[2]

The second instance, the First European Educational Film Conference in Basel, has gone virtually unnoticed in past and present film historiographies, even though this meeting was two years ahead of the one at La Sarraz and outnumbered it both in terms of attendees and of nationalities represented. This assembly of many important figures in European film pedagogy of the 1920s was organized by Gottlieb Imhof, director of the Educational Film Centre in Basel (founded in 1922) and a leading figure in the transnational educational film movement of the interwar period.[3] From 7 to 12 April 1927, about 170 representatives from twenty-one countries gathered in the city on the Rhine, among them, from Italy, Luciano de Feo, director of the Istituto Luce in Rome, from Germany, Professor Felix Lampe, director of the Bildstelle des Preussischen Zentralinstituts für Erziehung und Unterricht, and Walther Günther, co-editor of the cinema reform journal *Der Bildwart*, as well as members of the League of Nations.[4] The participants discussed the development of transnational cooperation in producing, collecting, exchanging and disseminating knowledge on film as a teaching tool and its use in the classroom. It was considered that a network of information should lay the foundation for transnational production and circulation of educational films. Imhof put it this way: 'We cannot negotiate about production and distribution before we have clarified generally the range of possible uses of classroom film'.[5] At the conference, a daily bulletin was published and several educational film programmes were screened. The debates resulted in the introduction of a permanent educational film committee with eleven expert commissions that prepared the foundation of the European Educational Film Chamber with its office in Basel in 1928. Hence, the First European Educational Film Conference was a milestone in the process of institutionalizing film as a pedagogical tool.

The two events – one famous, one largely forgotten – served as platforms both to discuss measures to increase film knowledge and to build transnational circulation and exhibition networks. In the pursuit of these aims, both the avant-garde and the educational film community mainly operated outside the film industry and beyond commercial cinema circuits in the non-theatrical sector. In a larger perspective, the fate of both groups was overshadowed by socio-political developments in the 1930s that, in the case of the avant-garde, led to a 'functional differentiation' (Malte Hagener).[6] Within the educational film movement, Fascist Italy contested Switzerland's leadership in the field. Fuelled by nationalist intentions and personal rivalry, and with the help of political interventions, Italy set up the International Educational Cinematograph Institute in Rome in 1928 as a counter institution to the Educational Film Chamber in Basel.[7] The movement was drawn into the turmoil of the political and ideological crisis of the 1930s.

From (Avant-Garde) Monoculture to Polyculture

The Educational Film Conference is a poignant example of film historiography's selective emphasis on certain institutional fields, whereas others fall into oblivion. The French cinema journal *Archives* dedicated a detailed documentation to La Sarraz Congress, diligently edited by Roland Cosandey and Thomas Tode.[8] No such documentation exists for the Basel conference, even though the reconstruction of the international repertoire of educational films screened on this occasion would generate a compelling corpus for further studies – to say nothing of the impact of that conference on the institutionalization and production of classroom films in different countries.

Film scholars today more often than not ascribe the 'invention' of film culture to the avant-garde movement of the 1920s.[9] Most notably, the avant-garde was instrumental in gaining the bourgeoisie's acceptance of cinema as an art form. This limited understanding of film as art has been so influential to this day that the first years of film culture are generally associated with the avant-garde and an eclectic art film diet served to the fastidious palate of the intelligentsia. Film culture is thus reduced to an elite avant-garde culture.[10]

The two congresses clearly show that film knowledge was produced and disseminated in more than one field. Film culture was not (avant-garde) monoculture, but 'polyculture'. Various institutional initiatives turned film culture into a heterogeneous landscape in which film culture took multiple shapes. To single out the avant-garde as the sole representative of film culture not only obscures the manifold programmes launched in other institutional fields in the 1920s and 1930s to educate audiences with film and about film – among them the schools, corporations, unions, the church, and the state – but the monofocal accent on the cinematic avant-garde also conceals the distinct features of the avant-garde itself.

The most popular (and lucrative) of all strands of film culture – commercial cinema and its specific practises of producing, exhibiting and consuming films as well as its discourses around film and cinema – serves in the following as the counterpart to a different kind of film culture that emerged in the 1920s. Efforts – some new, many revived after the First World War – to use film and cinema for other than entertaining purposes were enforced in multiple institutional contexts. They led to the institutionalization of an *alternative* film culture in which film was not a commodity to make money, but an instrument to be used for a variety of other purposes, specifically to produce and disseminate knowledge and to influence audiences. Films were inscribed in particular institutional contexts and rendered useful as an instrument for governmental programmes of scientific, economic, political, social and cultural management. This kind of film culture was obviously 'useful culture', to take up Tony Bennett's concept of culture in which the governmental utilization of culture for specific ends is central to the definition and constitution of culture.[11] Most notably, this type of 'non-commercial' film culture evolved beyond commercial cinema in the non-theatrical sector as an 'alternative' to theatrical film culture.[12] The emergence of this 'other' film culture in the 1920s can be described as the institutionalization of non-theatrical film in Europe. To analyse film culture then means to explore non-theatrical film practices.

In this chapter, Switzerland serves as a promising paradigm for the making of non-theatrical film culture in the interwar period. The focus is on three different institutional fields: the avant-garde, the educational film movement and corporate film culture, and on their shared techniques and practices of producing and disseminating knowledge with and about film in the non-theatrical sector. At first sight, these three milieus seem most disparate: the first having an aesthetic agenda, the second a pedagogical brief and the third financial interest. Yet, to an astonishing extent, these institutional fields were allies in film culture in that they used similar means in order to reach their respective goals. The three strands of non-theatrical film culture examined here converged and culminated on the occasion of the Swiss National Exposition in Zurich in 1939. The exhibition visibly evidences the institutional diversity of the medium in the late 1930s and allows the mapping of the multiple institutional strands of film culture at the moment of its establishment in all social contexts. The depiction of full-blown non-theatrical film culture at the Swiss National Exposition provides a basis for the analysis of the practices of building film culture shared by the avant-garde, pedagogues and private enterprises. The aim is to identify distinct features of non-theatrical practices and to contribute to a better understanding of European film culture in the interwar period as a comprehensive educational programme – both *with* film and *about* film – for governmental and other purposes.

To integrate the avant-garde in this survey and to relate it to educational and corporate film culture means a change in perspective: the cinematic avant-garde is not considered in the context of art, but as one strand among other strands of non-theatrical film culture. Situating the avant-garde in the heterogeneous landscape of non-theatrical film culture and reviewing it from this angle makes it necessary to reconsider also the status of the film medium within the movement. The thesis I purport in this chapter is that avant-garde films were not primarily intended as works of art, but as instruments to reform cinema with the goal of changing society. In other words, avant-garde films were 'useful films', or functional art, if you will, conceptualized as functional tools for social utilization. On this pragmatic level, the avant-garde, the educational film movement and private enterprises were allies.

Mapping the Strands of Film Culture: The 1939 Swiss National Exposition, Zurich

The Schweizerische Landesausstellung (Swiss National Exposition), in popular parlance called 'Landi', took place in Zurich from 6 May to 29 October 1939. Inaugurated as a showcase of national achievements in art and industry, in history and politics, it coincided with the outbreak of the Second World War and the mobilization of the Swiss Army on 1 September 1939. In this menacing political context, the exposition turned into a reassuring symbol of the nation's power and readiness to defend itself with arms and spirits (thus the term *Geistige Landesverteidigung* which could be translated as 'Spiritual National Defence' referring to the fostering of each and every thing that was reckoned to be 'typically' Swiss). The exhibition registered 10.5 million admissions (the country had a total population of four million then) and was the most popular public event that had ever been held in Switzerland. It was also a crucial moment in the history of film and cinema in Switzerland in that it exposed the different roles and functions film and cinema had acquired in society at that time.[13]

The medium was on display in three distinct ways.[14] First of all, a proper section was dedicated to the *Filmwesen* (film industry) where film itself was a subject to be exhibited, i.e. where the medium displayed itself. A movie called WIE EIN FILM ENTSTEHT [How a Film Is Made] showed the making of a movie in four parts. Four projectors alternately projected the four parts to the darkened half of the pavilion that looked like an illuminated aquarium and was therefore called 'Filmaquarium'.[15] The section also covered information on film production, distribution, exhibition, legislation and press to complement the cinematic self-portrayal.

Secondly, film played an outstanding role as an exhibition medium: it served practically all sections as a means for exhibiting all kinds of subject matters that could not adequately be exhibited as fixed objects or graphical presentations. This was, to quote Marcel Gero, director of the exposition's Film Office, 'the proper and grand mission of film' at the exposition.[16]

Thirdly, film was part of the cultural programme of the exposition. A 'best of' domestic feature film productions, including box-office smash hit FÜSILIER WIPF [Fusilier Wipf] (Hermann Haller, Leopold Lindtberg, CH 1938) and FARINET OU L'OR DANS LA MONTAGNE [Farinet or the Gold in the Mountains] (Max Haufler, CH 1939), was screened in the Zentralkino which, with three hundred seats, was the largest of the movie theatres at the exposition. The programme also comprised co-productions like RAPT (Dimitri Kirsanoff, FR/CH 1933) and foreign films, among them William Wyler's Brontë adaptation WUTHERING HEIGHTS (US 1939), the feature-length documentary DER WEISSE TOD IM HIMALAYA [White Death in the Himalaya] (DE 1935), produced by Transocean Film Co. Berlin, and six so-called *Kulturfilme* (cultural documentaries) which Martin Rikli, a Swiss citizen, had directed for Ufa Germany.[17] This selection of films, most popular with the audience, was to enrich the exposition's artistic programme. Cinema was thus put on a par with established art forms like theatre and music.

The Swiss National Exposition in Zurich recognized, displayed and used the film medium as art, as an industry, and as a means of communication. Film had officially turned into a cultural and economic factor and was omnipresent at the exposition: in fourteen sections, 303 films were projected in nineteen cinemas (with 1,760 seats in total) and at eleven open projection sites. The total quantity of films screened amounted to one hundred thousand metres. Virtually all institutional fields took the opportunity to present themselves in moving images. The exposition was a platform where the paths of different milieus crossed and the strands of film culture converged: social organizations, corporations and business associations, public undertakings such as the Swiss Federal Railways and the Swiss Post Office as well as educational institutions contributed films. In the Kino Soziale Arbeit (cinema of social work), a large variety of non-profit organizations propagated their religious, pedagogical, social and health messages in about sixty films. The avant-garde was present with works by Hans Richter and Alberto Cavalcanti, all sponsored by Swiss corporations and associations. During his exile in Switzerland from 1937 to 1941, Richter made seven films in collaboration with private enterprises, five of which were screened at the exposition.[18] DIE BÖRSE ALS BAROMETER DER WIRTSCHAFTSLAGE [The Stock Exchange as a Barometer of the Economic Situation] (1939), commissioned by the Zurich Stock Exchange on the occasion of the 'Landi', explained in twenty minutes the evolution, functioning and importance of the stock exchange in order to restore the confidence of private investors in this institution. DIE BÖRSE was programmed in the prestigious Zentralkino and was awarded 'best film' at the exposition. The slapstick comedy HANS IM GLÜCK [Hans in Luck] (1938) starring Emil Hegetschweiler and Alfred Rasser (both vernacular stars) as well as German actress Therese Giehse, celebrates the benefits of accident insurance. Sponsored by SUVA, the Swiss National Accident Insurance Fund, Richter's seven-minute homage to Charles Chaplin was one of five films that were shown in the Kino Privatversicherung (cinema of private insurance).

Figure 8.1 DIE BÖRSE ALS BAROMETER DER WIRTSCHAFTSLAGE [The Stock Exchange as a Barometer of the Economic Situation] (1939, Hans Richter). [Ciné]

Two of Richter's films were commissioned to represent the chemical industry in Basel in the exposition's Kino Chemie (cinema of chemistry). The first one, DIE GEBURT DER FARBE [The Birth of Colour] (1939), was a joint venture between the four chemical corporations Ciba, Durand & Huguenin, Geigy and Sandoz. The film demonstrates step by step in thirty minutes the industrial production of coal tar dyes. It is a creative variation on the classical process film narrative and an experiment in colour:[19] the opening and closing scenes of the otherwise black and white film were shot in Dufay Colour (a mosaic screen additive system). In his film treatment, Hans Richter explains the artistic concept as follows: 'Part four has to show the application. It does not suffice to present nicely dyed pieces. What has to be expressed and what has to create an impression in this part is above all the artistic organization of colour. There has to be resonance: a symphony of colour'.[20] Richter was called in as an expert at a late stage of production when almost all footage had been shot and both Eoscop Basel (the former production company) and the sponsors were at their wits' end. Richter's task was to 'edit this material into a movie fit to screen'.[21] Richter's working with pre-existing footage in a standardized film genre on the one hand, and his experimenting with colour and animation to render fabric patterns of dyed garment into abstract forms on the other, shows the aesthetic range of the cinematic avant-garde in intersection with private enterprises at the end of the 1930s.

The second film by Richter to be screened in the Kino Chemie was EINE KLEINE WELT IM DUNKELN [A Small World in the Dark] (1939), sponsored by Geigy. What starts like a biological lesson on moths turns into a demonstration of the industrial moth repellent Mitin. The twenty-minute film helped to launch the product innovation, yet the advertising campaign (including Richter's film) was a failure in communication: it promoted Mitin as an over-the-counter product whereas in fact it was only available for industrial wool treatment. The flop encouraged Geigy to establish a marketing department in 1940.[22]

RIVALEN AUF PARSENN [Rivals at Parsenn] (1938), the fifth film by Richter shown at the exposition, remains lost to this day. According to contemporary articles, this 'nice little ironic rendition' promoted skiing in Davos.[23] It was screened in the Kino Tourismus (cinema of tourism) in a series called *Wie der Ausländer die Schweiz sieht* (Switzerland seen from abroad). This series included three further *Kulturfilme* by German director Herbert Dreyer sponsored by the Swiss National Tourist Office and the Swiss Post Office in the mid-1930s: AUS DEM LAND DER RÄTOROMANEN [From the Land of the Rhaeto-Romans] (1935),

TESSINER HERBSTLIED [Autumn Song from the Ticino] (1935), and ÜBER WINTERBERGE IN FRÜHLINGSTÄLER [Over Wintery Mountains into Spring Valleys] (1936), all of which had been theatrically released in Germany and other European countries.[24] The series also comprised three films by Alberto Cavalcanti, himself a representative of the French avant-garde in the 1920s: MEN OF THE ALPS, FOUR BARRIERS and WE LIVE IN TWO WORLDS, all produced in 1937 by the celebrated Film Unit of the British General Post Office and sponsored by Pro Telephon Zurich, an institution devoted to the marketing of technological communication means. Also directed by Cavalcanti and sponsored by Pro Telephon was LINE TO THE TSCHIERVA HUT (1938). This film was screened in the Kino PTT (cinema of the Swiss Post Office) in the section Verkehr und Transport (traffic and transportation). It shows the laying of a telephone cable in the Alps to connect the Tschierva Hut with Great Britain and the world. Cavalcanti's Pro Telephon films, all 'documentaries' in Grierson's sense, promote new communications media and infrastructure to overcome the 'first world' of nationalism and to create a 'second world' of international trade and communications. The contemporary 'documentary' label did not preclude experimentation: in WE LIVE IN TWO WORLDS for example, Cavalcanti treats sound so creatively that according to Patrick Russell, the 'weird experiments with echo, repetition and amplification take the film to the edge of science fiction'.[25] In this respect, Cavalcanti was no exception: many of the documentaries produced under Grierson for the British Empire Marketing Board and the British Post Office were highly creative (and formative for documentary, both in Europe and the United States) in 'treating actuality' in terms of narrative structure, storytelling, and the use of sound and of voice in particular.

With sponsored short films made by avant-garde filmmakers, the cinematic avant-garde was present in virtually all sections of the Swiss National Exposition, thus reaching out into practically all areas of life in the late 1930s. The film medium made institutional milieus incessantly overlap: resolute classroom films such as DIE LACHMÖWE [The Black-Headed Gull] (Ernst Rüst, 1930) produced by the Schweizerische Arbeitsgemeinschaft für Unterrichtskinematographie (SAFU), the Swiss Working Committee for Classroom Films, were screened in the Kino Haus der Tierzucht (cinema of animal breeding). In the same location, a film on farming by the industrial food producer Maggi was programmed. And last but not least, Nestlé looked after the children: in Nestlé's Kinderparadies (children's paradise), the food corporation took professional care of the visitors' offspring and provided bread and circuses for just one Swiss franc a day. The entertaining programme included Punch and Judy as well as short documentaries and cartoons. These screenings served the corporation to recruit members for the Fip-Fop Club, a film club for children aged five to fifteen that Nestlé had founded in 1936.[26]

Advertising Non-theatrical Film Culture: Teaching how to Teach (with) Film

The exposition worked not only as a platform, but also as an incentive for film culture: out of the 303 films screened, 180 had been commissioned on this very occasion.[27] The demand for film created by the event boosted native film production. An advisory board was established in preparation for the exposition, to help exhibitors to produce, select and exhibit their films. The board viewed, discussed, corrected and approved or rejected approximately 750 films before handing the case over to a film jury of three people: chairman Karl Naef, artistic director of the exposition, Edwin Arnet, film critic at the daily newspaper *Neue Zürcher Zeitung*, and a member of the party the examined film belonged to. The jury treated 330 dossiers, and watched 58 films of which 16 were refused. Exhibitors were motivated to voluntarily withdraw 'insufficient works' to keep the official number of rejected films low.[28]

With the advisory board and the film jury, the exposition performed activities that would be key to building film culture in the 1920s and 1930s: it imparted film knowledge to potential sponsors and taught them how to use the medium. Thereby, the exposition also set the standards for judging films as good or bad. Interestingly enough, in virtually all institutional milieus, film culture emerged as an educational programme that in the first instance addressed the potential *users* of film before addressing the *consumers* (i.e. audiences). Instructing institutions on the nature and possible utilization of the medium was an essential part of the pronounced lobbying that characterized the emergence of film culture in every institutional milieu; advertising film in the public sphere to gain public acceptance of the medium was another. Teaching teachers how to teach with film was *the* mission of Ernst Rüst, long-time director of the SAFU founded in 1929. In the early 1920s, Rüst developed a rigorous didactic conception of classroom film based on Pestalozzi's doctrine of *Anschauung* that he tirelessly promoted in innumerable lectures at congresses (among them the First European Educational Film Conference in Basel in 1927), and in publications for fellow professionals.[29] Rüst was appointed Professor for Photography at ETH Zurich (the Swiss Federal Institute of Technology) in 1928, and used his technical equipment and staff to launch the in-house production of classroom films. The aforementioned DIE LACHMÖWE, a patient cinematographic study with fixed camera of the brood care of the black-headed gull was, in 1930, the first SAFU production. Rüst conceptualized a model lesson on the black-headed gull with slides and film in order to train fellow teachers how to use still and moving images, in particular as teaching tools in the classroom.[30] In writings and lectures, Rüst incessantly categorized, theorized and historicized classroom film to achieve both institutional and public acceptance of his concept.[31]

Rüst had pedagogical conviction, whereas others were also driven by monetary interests when promoting the implementation of film in all areas of life. More often than not, film lobbyists were also film providers, and creating a demand for a certain kind of film (and work and income for oneself) was not the least motivation for imparting film knowledge to possible sponsors. On that score, avant-garde filmmakers Hans Richter and Franz Heinemann were of kindred spirit. Heinemann was a private lecturer at the ETH lecturing on the usages of film in science and university education from 1922 to 1928, when Rüst took over and continued the lectures until the late 1930s.[32] The ETH was one of the first institutions to include film in its curriculum, and it was the birthplace of probably the longest-living film club in Europe.[33] Heinemann was not only an academic lecturer, but also a journalist and the co-founder of Uto Film AG Zurich, a production company devoted to the cinematic promotion of Swiss science, industry and art. In 1924, Heinemann not quite selflessly published *Der Film in der Schweiz. Privatwirtschaft. Zeitgemässe Anregungen* [Film in the Swiss Private Sector of the Industry: Modern Stimuli].[34] This brochure elaborated on the lecture 'Der Industriefilm in seiner Technik, Werbekraft und nationalen Bedeutung' [The Industrial Film, Its Technology, Persuasive Power and National Significance) that Heinemann gave in 1922 on the occasion of the first film screening at the Schweizerische Mustermesse Basel, a trade fair founded in 1917. Heinemann criticized Switzerland for having fallen behind in the promotion of the national economy compared to other countries, and called for a systematic 'selling' of Switzerland with film to develop new markets. To reach this goal, Heinemann recommended the production of 'industry films' that would represent a whole sector of the industry instead of individual corporations. It took five years for Heinemann's lobbying to fall on fertile ground when the Schweizerische Zentrale für Handelsförderung, the Swiss Office for Business Promotion, OSEC (Switzerland Global Enterprise, or S-GE, today) was founded in 1927 and the systematic production and dissemination of films on various branches of industry was launched. Five OSEC films, all produced in cooperation with private corporations, were screened at the exposition in 1939 in the Zentralkino. Dedicated to agriculture, aviation, hydro-electricity, textile industry and export business, the films promote the national economy, yet they became figureheads of the entire country and helped to build national identity at home and abroad. Many corporations acquired film expertise from OSEC and its director Albert Masnata, who instructed the (non-film) industry 'on the principles of efficient film marketing'. In the article 'Le film – moyen de publicité' [Film as an Advertising Medium] published in 1929, Masnata classifies and defines advertising film genres into three classes, advertising films in the strict sense (i.e. commercials, documentaries and newsreels) and provides a handbook for sponsors on how to produce and use the medium for advertising purposes.[35] Masnata also founded the Swiss film producers' association in 1934 with the aim to professionalize native film production in order to improve the quality of OSEC and other 'propaganda' films, and he became a key figure in national film politics in the late 1930s. The activities of people like Masnata and Heinemann, Richter and Rüst clearly show that even though non-theatrical film culture emerged in distinct institutional fields, it evolved in a hybrid environment in which people, artefacts and practices constantly transgressed lines, migrated and circulated, thus making milieus intersect, overlap and to some extent converge. Non-theatrical film culture spread as a network that spanned institutional fields.

'Co-producing' Audiences

The avant-garde in the 1920s also set out to teach; exploring the whole range of purely cinematic expression, the movement demonstrated how cinema could be freed from theatre and literature, and turned into an independent art form. But in order to exploit the medium's formal potentials and challenge narrative cinema, the avant-garde needed support – in other words, they needed an audience. In *The Struggle for the Film*, Hans Richter writes 'that a product without consumers is valueless and that therefore the consumers must be co-'produced' with the commodity'.[36] Richter refers here to commercial advertising practices in private industry, yet, from a historical materialist point of view, this holds equally true for film. Since films are valueless without audiences, making films is not enough. Audiences have to be made, even more so in the case of avant-garde 'product innovations', as these new experiments needed new audiences. The way Richter puts it makes it quite clear that audiences are not 'found' but have to be 'co-"produced"' – in other words, they have to be created actively. In a few institutional contexts audiences were just 'there' by compulsion, as in the classroom; but in most instances, emerging film culture had to build audiences beyond commercial cinema and create public spheres for film exhibition, consumption and discourse to take place.

As has been well researched for the avant-garde, film clubs and specialized theatres first opened up in Paris in the early 1920s, followed by the Film Society in London (1925–1939), the Dutch Filmliga (1927–1933), the German Volksverband für Filmkunst (1928–1931) and the Swiss Le Bon Film (1931–today), to name just a few of the emerging avant-garde screening organizations.[37]

While the avant-garde specialized in stimulating the self-organization of audiences in membership organizations, other institutions in the quest for audiences launched travelling film shows. In the educational sector, it was the Schweizer Schul- und Volkskino (Swiss School and People's Cinema, SSVK) that since its foundation in 1921 had brought 'good' films (read: non-fiction) in the sense of the *Kinoreformbewegung* (cinema reform movement) to children and adults, even in remote mountain regions that lacked commercial movie theatres. Until the late 1920s, the SSVK had organized approximately 1,100 screenings every year in five hundred to eight hundred boroughs in collaboration with local school and municipal authorities, parishes, trade and business associations, and women's and charitable organizations.[38] The SSVK built up a vast international film library of educational films in the broadest sense, which included scientific and classroom films as well as cultural, industrial and other sponsored films. As a non-profit organization, the SSVK became the centre for non-theatrical distribution of educational films in the country for more than five decades.[39]

In private industry, it was primarily the food and consumer goods industries that specialized in creating non-theatrical audiences, mainly of children and housewives, through travelling film shows for advertising purposes. These free itinerant screenings of corporate films to promote brands were a major factor in film culture in Switzerland from the early 1920s to the late 1950s, and even challenged the supremacy of the SSVK's travelling film lecture service.[40] Itinerant advertising in the industry can be traced back to travelling slide lectures. The Maggi Food Corporation, for example, launched slide-illustrated lecture tours at the turn of the twentieth century to bridge the gap between consumers and producers that had resulted from industrialization and urbanization in the second half of the nineteenth century. The lectures advised malnourished factory workers and farmers on nutrition and on industrially processed food provided by Maggi. In 1921, the corporation replaced the coloured slides with moving images to illustrate the lectures on Maggi's farming and food processing. And in 1929, in-house *Heimatfilme* portraying the homeland's most attractive (mountain) regions and cultures were introduced to lighten up and conclude the programme, together with a soup tasting that proved very popular with audiences.[41]

Performing Non-theatrical Film Culture: *Dispositifs*

Exhibition is another feature that unites the seemingly disparate fields of avant-garde, pedagogical and corporate film culture. Compared with narrative cinema, non-theatrical film culture suggested not only alternative films in alternative locations, but also alternative modes of experiencing film. Or, in other words, it provided alternative *dispositifs*. The term *'dispositif'* was employed by French theorist Jean-Louis Baudry in the 1970s to describe the relation between screen, projector and spectator in a movie theatre. Revisiting Baudry's concept, historian Frank Kessler suggested using the original French term instead of the common English translation 'apparatus' in order to 'mark a shift from a psychological approach to spectatorship to one that frames the relation between the film, the viewer and the viewing context rather in terms of a historical pragmatics'.[42] Kessler's research area being early cinema, he argues that 'the cinema of attractions' (Tom Gunning, André Gaudreault) can be understood as a *dispositif* that is opposed to the one of classical narrative cinema. The term seems very useful to seize the manifold historical and contemporary configurations of institutional framing, exhibition practices, modes of address and the films themselves. In our case, looking at *dispositifs* helps to identify distinct features of exhibition practices within the various fields of non-theatrical film culture in the 1920s and 1930s.

Film culture unfolded not in one, but in a large variety of *dispositifs*, the Swiss National Exposition in 1939 being one of them. Notwithstanding

Figure 8.2 Paradigmatic dispositif of non-theatrical film exhibition. Illustration published in the SSVK brochure *Rationelle Film-Propaganda*, 1929.

different institutional framings, the various *dispositifs* of non-theatrical film culture largely drew upon the lecture tradition of bourgeois society and were informed by an overall educational impetus. This underlying pattern determined exhibition practices in virtually all institutional fields and is evidenced by the fact that non-theatrical film viewing was never a self-contained activity, but was always embedded in an instructive discourse that moderated between screen and spectator. More often than not, the spoken word of lecturers, live commentators and moderators guided the production of meaning and regulated film experience. Film did not 'speak' for itself but was mediated instead, thus becoming an object of reflection itself.

Without going into the details of the various *dispositifs* (as this has been done elsewhere),[43] suffice it to say that screenings in avant-garde film clubs, in classrooms and in travelling corporate film shows all had a pronounced 'performative' character by virtue of live presentations of lecturers, teachers or film commentators on the one hand and because of direct audience address and audience participation on the other. In opposition to individual spectatorship as the dominant reception mode of narrative cinema, film culture more often than not addressed spectators as collective audiences. The collective experience and its integrative practices underline the social character of film culture and account for its productivity in community building and in stimulating fan culture. Examples of emerging fan culture in the 1920s and 1930s are the circle of cinéphiles in the avant-garde context and in Nestlé's Fip-Fop Club: this animated children's club built sustained communities of creative 'produser' of film (and consumer) culture in Switzerland.[44]

Live performances of moderators and spectators turned each screening into a unique event. Non-theatrical film culture evolved as event culture; hence the prevalence of conferences and festivals, trade fairs and expositions as privileged sites of manifestation. With live performance, direct audience address and a predominant programme pattern of short films that occasionally also included other media and live acts, several features of the *dispositif* of early cinema lived on in non-theatrical exhibition long after cinema's narrative integration. Allowing for alternative media encounters and engagements different from those offered by commercial cinema to a large extent account for the proliferation, popularity and sustainability of non-theatrical film culture.

Training and Entertaining Audiences: Building Non-theatrical Film Expertise

Film culture, to mention another distinct feature, was to a large extent a film literacy project. Most obviously, it was the avant-garde movement that introduced audiences to the basics of film language by means of screenings and lectures, exhibitions like the Film- und Fotoausstellung ('FiFo') in Stuttgart 1929 and textbooks such as Hans Richter's *Filmgegner von heute – Filmfreunde von morgen*, published on the occasion of the

FiFo. As Malte Hagener and Ansje van Beusekom in their respective studies on avant-garde programming have highlighted, avant-garde screening organizations showed the cinematographic 'state of the art' as well as its history.[45] Even though the integration of older films from the period of early cinema into the programmes mainly served as a contrast to demonstrate the 'superior state of development' of contemporary avant-garde films, they helped to establish the idea that film was a medium with its own history that deserves to be written and preserved.

While avant-garde lessons in film aesthetics and history mainly addressed well-educated adults in urban centres, other institutional fields took systematic care of children's media education. In the 1910s, most Swiss cantons introduced a cinema legislation that denied children, aged under sixteen, admission to regular movie theatres, even if accompanied by adults.[46] Only special afternoon programmes authorized by regional censorship boards were approved. Yet these screenings did not meet with success, as schoolteachers had reservations about the cinema as an institution and preferred to incorporate the medium into the classroom. Therefore, children and teenagers under sixteen were virtually excluded from commercial movie theatres. As a consequence, child film socialization was relegated to non-theatrical spaces. The school, the SSVK and private corporations like Maggi and Nestlé filled the breach. In remote rural areas, the first films that children and sometimes even adults would ever see in the 1920s and 1930s were often brought to them by the food industry. Nestlé's Fip-Fop Club, to allude to a poignant example, was a comprehensive corporate film literacy programme designed to socialize children with the medium in order to 'train them as future customers'.[47] Nestlé's introductory course to film expertise included both knowledge and experience. Children were taught to discriminate 'good' films from 'bad' films so that they would be able to make the 'right' choices (both aesthetically and morally) when leaving the club and accessing cinema at the age of sixteen. The joys of experiencing Fip-Fop film shows and participating in the club's (fan) community introduced children to the delights of media consumption and attuned them to the gratifications of (commodity) consumption. Media education converged with consumer education, and went hand in hand with civic education. General Henri for instance, commander-in-chief of the Swiss Army during the Second World War, became an honorary member of the Fip-Fop Club in 1940, with the declared aim to teach children 'to become good patriots'.[48] Maggi in turn lectured children on national history and geography with the help of slides and

Figure 8.3 Fip-Fop audience in cinema Oriental in Vevey, 26 October 1938. [Archives historiques Nestlé, Vevey]

Heimatfilme. Within the institutional context of the industry, children received a thorough bourgeois education in film and through film – a training to be good media consumers in order to honour their civic duty and become good commodity consumers. The convergence of media entertainment and consumer education prepared the ground for a media-driven consumer culture in capitalist society, and demonstrates that training did not preclude entertaining. Instead, entertainment was a constitutive part in the building of film expertise within many fields of non-theatrical film culture – including the avant-garde.

The Avant-Garde and the Social Use of Film

Following Brecht's 'pleasure of learning', an emphasis on entertainment also accounts for Hans Richter's educational programme that he suggested in the late 1930s in *Der Kampf um den Film*. Published only shortly after Richter's death in 1976, and translated into English in 1986, *The Struggle for the Film* has received little attention by film scholars so far, even though the book quite accurately accounts for the politicization of the avant-garde in the 1930s. While Richter's *Filmgegner von heute – Filmfreunde von morgen* from 1929 can be read as an introduction to film aesthetics, *The Struggle for the Film*, finished ten years later, develops a theory of audience education that encompasses formal aspects of the medium and stresses the social function of cinema instead. According to Richter, cinema had acquired 'a new social mandate' as an art in the 1930s: 'art – and especially film art – is called on and able to perform an important social function in this way, namely, to bring the spectators into conscious contact with reality and to put into their hands or their heads the means whereby they can recognize their real interests and act accordingly'.[49] Richter's 'cinema of enlightenment' is written from the perspective of the audience, turning the book into an early theoretical contribution to the long-neglected field of audience studies, and clearly demonstrating the shift in the avant-garde from visual to social education. Richter's concern at that moment was to develop a film dramaturgy that could 'develop the audience's capacities for thought and judgement' and at the same time would 'completely satisfy the masses' need for spectacle and entertainment'.[50] This 'progressive cinema', as Richter called it, would 'intervene actively in the consciousness and emotional life of its spectators', with the ultimate aim of 'inducing us, the cinema audience, to think'.[51] The sponsored documentaries Richter made at that time for the Swiss National Exposition in 1939 can be seen as practical experiments with formal strategies for social education.

Richter's pamphlet makes two things clear: firstly, the avant-garde, dispersed as a movement but alive through representatives who carried on the ideas and ideals, had not ceased to experiment with film form in the late 1930s, as is manifested in Richter's strive for a 'progressive cinema' and his 'invention' of the 'film essay' as a new form of documentary film capable of revealing the functioning and functions of abstract concepts – institutions like the stock exchange that could not just be 'reproduced' by the camera, but had to be 'produced' by the interpretative, imaginative and instructive capacities of cinema.[52] Secondly, the avant-garde was fuelled by intentions that were not limited to art for its own sake, *l'art pour l'art* so to speak. Instead, aesthetics were put in the service of social and political aims in order to unite art and politics in the cinema. Like educational, classroom and corporate films, avant-garde films can therefore be conceived as 'useful films' or *Gebrauchsfilme*, to suggest a term that has been introduced recently in German-speaking film studies to describe films with a predominant instrumental character.[53] The term *Gebrauchsfilme* usually gathers all sorts of films outside the commercial mainstream and outside the art film canon. My contention however is that avant-garde works, usually situated in modern art, can also be conceived as 'useful films'. This approach suggests reconsidering the cinematic avant-garde in the context of media practices of the school, the (non-film) industry, the state and other institutional fields. In their concerted social use of film, not as a means to make art or money, but as a means to intervene on economic, pedagogical, social and political levels, the avant-garde, the school and the industry were allies in building and maintaining non-theatrical film culture as an educational programme to change society with the help of cinema.

Conclusion and Perspectives

It is hardly a coincidence that in several milieus, film culture became an object of history in the course of the disruptions of the Second World War. The founders, advocates and practitioners set out to write their own history 'from within': in 1941, Franz Heinemann suggested a detailed chronological account of emerging film culture in various institutional fields in Switzerland, including school and industry.[54] Hans Richter on his part presented the very first version of 'A History of the Avantgarde' in Europe in 1947 to an emerging avant-garde film community in the United States that was constructing its own genealogy and who welcomed Richter as a pioneer of abstract cinema and a forefather of experimental film.[55] While Richter's account had a sustained impact on film historiography (his delineation of the fate of the avant-garde in the 1930s, for example, is still official history), Heinemann's record was largely forgotten.

This chapter set out to explore contingent techniques and practices of building non-theatrical film culture in three different institutional milieus in the 1920s and 1930s. As we have seen, many activities usually attributed to the avant-garde such as advertising and theorizing, lecturing and historicizing film were not unique to the avant-garde movement, but were characteristic of a multifaceted non-theatrical film culture that emerged in the 1920s as an alternative to commercial cinema. Producing and disseminating film knowledge, creating non-theatrical networks of distribution and exhibition, co-producing audiences and communities, presenting alternative films, alternative programme patterns and alternative exhibition and reception modes (via performance and audience participation) and providing film expertise were common features of different institutional fields – features that helped to build non-theatrical film culture as a tool for economic, social and political purposes.

Depicting the avant-garde as one among many facets of non-theatrical film history might stimulate more interest in this field of study – one that has long been neglected by film scholars. Extending the scope of Tom Gunning's claim that the study of early cinema as the *period before* the emergence of the dominant classical cinema must always serve as a challenge to film history, I would also hold that the study of non-theatrical film culture as the *space beyond* dominant classical cinema can and must serve as a challenge which prompts us to revisit the nature of cinema.[56]

To reconsider avant-garde movies as 'useful films' or *Gebrauchsfilme* may not only reassess our understanding of the movement, but in a larger perspective may also draw more attention to film culture as purpose driven (whether disciplinary or subversively) in past and present media environments.

Notes

1. Freddy Buache (ed.). 1979. 'Cinéma indépendant et d'avant-garde à la fin du muet. Congrès de La Sarraz (1929) et présentation des films projetés au symposium de Lausanne (1–4 juin 1979)', in *Travelling* 55, Spring, 12.
2. Hervé Dumont. 1987. *Geschichte des Schweizer Films. Spielfilme 1896–1965*. Lausanne: Schweizer Filmarchiv, 116.
3. On Gottlieb Imhof and the transnational educational film movement, see Anita Gertiser. 2011. 'Schul- und Lehrfilme', in Yvonne Zimmermann (ed.), *Schaufenster Schweiz. Dokumentarische Gebrauchsfilme 1896–1964*, Zurich: Limmat, 431–47.
4. Ibid., 439. Walther Günther published a copious personal report on his participation at the conference; cf. W.G. 1927. 'Tagebuch', in *Der Bildwart: Blätter für Volksbildung* 5(6) (June), 343–56.
5. Gottlieb Imhof. 1927. 'Was bezweckte die Basler Lehrfilmkonferenz?', in *Der Bildwart: Blätter für Volksbildung* 5(8) (August), 512.
6. Malte Hagener. 2007. *Moving Forward, Looking Back: The European Avant-garde and the Invention of Film Culture 1919–1939*. Amsterdam: Amsterdam University Press.
7. On the International Educational Cinematograph Institute, see Christel Taillibert. 1999. *L'Institut international du cinématographe éducatif. Regards sur le rôle du cinéma éducatif dans la politique internatonale du fascisme italien*, Paris: L'Harmattan; Zoë Druick. 2007. 'The International Educational Cinematograph Institute, Reactionary Modernism, and the Formation of Film Studies', in *Canadian Journal of Film Studies / Revue canadienne d'études cinématographiques* 16(1), 80–97 (retrieved 25 Nov. 2011 from http://www.filmstudies.ca/journal/pdf/cj-film-studies161_Druick_studies. pdf).

8. Roland Cosandey and Thomas Tode. 2000. 'Quand l'avant-garde projetait son avenir. Le 1er Congrès international du cinéma indépendant, La Sarraz, Septembre 1929', in *Archives* 84 (April); retrieved 25 Nov. 2011 from http://www.cinematheque.ch/f/documents-de-cinema/cinema-et-avant-garde/archives-n-84.html.
9. Cf. among others, Jamie Sexton. 2008. *Alternative Film Culture in Inter-War Britain*. Exeter: Exeter University Press.
10. This perception does not do justice to avant-garde film clubs either, as their repertoire was not limited to avant-garde works, but included a diverse mixture of styles and genres. On the programming of avant-garde screening organizations, see Malte Hagener. 2006. 'Programming Attractions: Avant-Garde Exhibition Practice in the 1920s and 1930s', in Wanda Strauven (ed.), *The Cinema of Attractions Reloaded*, Amsterdam: Amsterdam University Press, 265–79; Ansje van Beusekom. 2007b. '"Avant-guerre" and the International Avant-Garde: Circulation and Programming of Early Films in the European Avant-garde Programs in the 1920s and 1930s', in Frank Kessler and Nanna Verhoeff (eds), *Networks of Entertainment: Early Film Distribution 1895–1915*, Eastleigh: J. Libbey, 285–94.
11. On 'useful culture' as an alternative way of understanding the relations between culture and power in modern societies, see Tony Bennett. 1992. 'Useful Culture', *Cultural Studies* 6(3), 395–408. Since culture is always inscribed within governmental strategies according to Bennett, commercial cinema and film entertainment are also part of useful culture.
12. In contrast to commercial cinema, the term 'non-commercial' refers to the predominant non-commodity status of films and film exhibition in the non-theatrical sector. More often than not, non-theatrical film screenings were non-profit or altogether free of charge for audiences. Before the First World War, non-theatrical exhibition was commercial, but started to become the non-commercial strand of cinema after the war.
13. The Swiss National Expositions in Geneva (1896), Bern (1914), Zurich (1939) and Lausanne (1964) were all important indicators and promoters of film and cinema in Switzerland. For a comprehensive account, see Zimmermann, *Schaufenster Schweiz*; specifically on the Bern Exposition see Roland Cosandey. 2000a. 'De l'Exposition nationale Berne 1913 au CSPS 1921. Charade pour un cinema vernaculaire', in Maria Tortajada and François Albera (eds), *Cinéma Suisse. Nouvelle approaches. Histoire – Esthétique – Critique – Thèmes – Matériaux*, Lausanne: Payot, 91–109; on the Zurich Exposition see Pierre-Emmanuel Jaques and Gianni Haver. 2004. 'Le cinema à la Landi. Le documentaire au service de la Défense nationale spirituelle', in Gianni Haver (ed.), *Le cinéma au pas. Les productions des pays autoritaires et leur impact en Suisse*, Lausanne: Antipodes, 97–110; on the Lausanne Exposition see Roland Cosandey. 2000b. 'Expo 64. Un cinéma au service du "scénario"', in *Mémoire vive. Pages d'histoire lausannoise* 9, 18–23; Alexandra Walther. 2007. *La suisse s'interroge ou l'exercice de l'audace*. University of Lausanne: unpublished master's thesis.
14. If not otherwise stated, the following account is based on Marcel Gero. 1940. 'Film', in Schweizerische Landesausstellung (ed.), *Die Schweiz im Spiegel der Landesausstellung 1939*, vol. 2, Zurich: Atlantis, 577–79.
15. The four parts, all in 16 mm, were titled: 1. *Die Vorbereitung* (the preparation), 2. *Die Aufnahme* (the shooting), 3. *Die Verarbeitung* (the processing), 4. *Montage und Fertigstellung* (the editing and finalizing). Parts 1 to 3 were silent and 50 metres each, while part 4 was 105 metres and had sound. At a projection speed of 24 i/s, the film would have had a duration of about 23 minutes. See Liquidation Committee of the

Swiss National Exhibition (ed.). 1942. *Schweizerische Landesausstellung 1939 Zürich. Administrativer Bericht.* Zurich, 123.

16. Gero, 'Film', 577.
17. A list of the films screened at the Swiss National Exposition is provided in Liquidation Committee, *Administrativer Bericht*, 116–23.
18. The two films *not* to be screened at the exposition are WIR LEBEN IN EINER NEUEN ZEIT! [We Live in a New World] (1938) on the fabrication of Ovaltine (sponsored by Wander) and DIE EROBERUNG DES HIMMELS / LA CONQUÊTE DU CIEL / THE CONQUEST OF THE SKY (1938), an actuality film on the 4th International Air Show in Dübendorf near Zurich in 1937 that, according to Rudolf Arnheim, takes 'pure avant-garde pleasure in photographic effect and in perplexing montage' (Rudolf Arnheim. 1939. 'Hohe Schule der Filmkunst', in *National-Zeitung* 255 (7 June), 5). On WIR LEBEN IN EINER NEUEN ZEIT!, see Pierre-Emmanuel Jaques. 2005. 'L'Ovomaltine et un cinéaste d'avant-garde. Hans Richter et le film de commande en Suisse', *Décadrages. Cinéma, à travers champs* 4(5), 154–66.
19. Since early cinema, the process or fabrication film is a highly standardized genre within the category of the industrial film, and typically demonstrates the trajectory from raw material to product and consumption, step by step. See Yvonne Zimmermann. 2011. 'Industriefilme', in Zimmermann, *Schaufenster Schweiz*, 241–381, esp. 266–85; Tom Gunning. 1997. 'Before Documentary: Early Nonfiction Films and the "View" Aesthetic', in Daan Hertogs and Nico de Klerk (eds), *Uncharted Territory: Essays on Early Nonfiction Film*, Amsterdam: Nederlands Filmmuseum, 9–24, esp. 17–18.
20. Hans Richter, 'Entwurf zu einem Kulturfilm. Die Geburt der Farbe', typescript, 13 December 1938, 4 (Firmenarchiv der Novartis AG Basel, Geigy, WE 14/1[5], Schweizerische Landesausstellung 1939, Dec. 1938 – Feb. 1939).
21. 'Protokoll über die Besprechung der Filmkommission vom 16. Dezember 1938', 1 (Firmenarchiv der Novartis AG Basel, Geigy, WE 14/1[5], Schweizerische Landesausstellung 1939, Dec. 1938 – Feb. 1939).
22. See Barbara Junod. 2009. 'From a Focus on Products to a Focus on Customers: The Advertising Policies and Practices at the Basel Headquarters', in Andres Janser and Barbara Junod (eds), *Corporate Diversity: Swiss Graphic Design and Advertising by Geigy 1940–1970*, Baden: Lars Müller, 32. On Hans Richter, Geigy and the chemical industry's use of film, see Yvonne Zimmermann. 2009. 'Target Group Oriented Corporate Film Communication: Geigy Films', in Janser and Junod, *Corporate Diversity*, 48–57.
23. Léo Sauvage. 1938. 'La Suisse. Patrie du film artisanal et du documentaire', *Cinémonde* 517 (15 September). Cf. also 'Un movement international se produit parmi les réalisateurs de films documentaires', *Paris-soir*, 16 May 1938; 'Ein deutscher Avantgardist in der Schweiz', *National-Zeitung* 232, 23 May 1939. Robert Blum is mentioned in *Paris-soir* as the composer of the film music. There are many variants of the title: DAVOSERFILM, DAVOS PARSENN, RIVALS AUF DER PARSENN; Frech version: LES RIVAUX DE LA PARSENN. A photo of the shooting is reproduced in Yvonne Zimmermann, 'A Missing Chapter: The Swiss Films on Hans Richter's Documentary Practice', in Timothy O. Benson (ed.), *Hans Richter: Encounters*, Los Angeles: Los Angeles County Museum of Art, 115. It shows two actors, a man and a woman, talking to each other in a chalet, as well as two men behind a camera and a boy (probably an assistant) sitting at a table. In the caption, the man at the camera is identified as Charles Métain. Hans Richter stands behind him.

24. In the administrative report, Aus dem Land der Rätoromanen is listed as Im Lande der Rätoromanen (cf. Liquidation Committee, *Administrativer Bericht*, 119). The titles quoted in the report often differ from the titles given in the opening credits of the respective film prints. Whenever available, this article quotes film titles according to the opening credits.

25. Patrick Russell. 2009. 'We Live in Two Worlds', in British Film Institute (ed.), *We Live in Two Worlds: The GPO Film Unit Collection*, vol. 2, London, 47 (booklet to the DVD edition).

26. Ro., 'Das Kinderparadies', *Neue Zürcher Zeitung*, no. 1892, 27 Oct. 1938, 7. See also Liquidation Committee, *Administrativer Bericht*, 121. On the Fip-Fop Club, see Yvonne Zimmermann. 2010. 'Nestlé's Fip-Fop Club: The Making of Child Audiences in Non-Commercial Film Shows in Switzerland (1936–1959)', in Irmbert Schenk, Margrit Tröhler and Yvonne Zimmermann (eds), *Film – Kino – Zuschauer. Filmrezeption / Film – Cinema – Spectator. Film Reception*, Marburg: Schüren, 281–303.

27. Gero, 'Film', 578.

28. Anon, 'Schweizerische Landesausstellung 1939 Zürich. Schlussbericht der Filmstelle', typescript, 26 Dec. 1939, 9–10, quotation 10 (Stadtarchiv Zürich, VII.80. Landesausstellung 1939).

29. In 1921, Rüst probably published his first article on the subject: Ernst Rüst. 1921. 'Der Kinematograph in der Schule', in *Zur Praxis der Volksschule*, supplement to *Schweizerische Lehrerzeitung* 4, 16. For more details on Ernst Rüst, his didactical conception of classroom film and the Swiss Working Committee for Classroom Films, see Anita Gertiser. 2011. 'Schul- und Lehrfilme', in Zimmermann, *Schaufenster Schweiz*, 447–70.

30. See Ernst Rüst. 1931. 'Die Lachmöwe: Lektion mit Lichtbildern und Film', in Arbeitsgemeinschaft für Filmunterricht (ed.), *Fünf Lehrproben aus der Praxis der Filmverwertung*, offprint form *Schweizerische Lehrerzeitung*, 76 (9 May 1931), 10–18.

31. See, for instance, Ernst Rüst. 1938. 'Die Arten des Films und ihr Bereich', *Neue Zürcher Zeitung*, 872 (15 May).

32. For more details on the emergence of film clubs in Switzerland, see Andres Janser. 2001. 'Es kommt der gute Film. Zu den Anfängen der Filmclubs in Zürich', in Vinzenz Hediger, Jan Sahli, Alexandra Schneider and Margrit Tröhler (eds), *Home Stories: Neue Studien zu Film und Kino in der Schweiz / Nouvelles approaches du cinéma et du film en Suisse*, Marburg: Schüren, 55–69.

33. The Filmstelle (Film Office) of the students' association of the ETH started collecting and exhibiting scientific films to be screened in the auditorium in 1922 before becoming one of *the* avant-garde and art film screening organizations in Switzerland. Still alive today, and devoted to the 'screening of extraordinary films' (retrieved on 12 Dec. 2011 from http://www.filmstelle.ch/aboutus) the Film Office invited Hans Richter in 1940 to give a series of five lectures on 'Der Kampf um den Film' [The Struggle for the Film] based on the book of the same name that Richter wrote during his exile in Switzerland: Hans Richter. 1976. *Der Kampf um den Film. Für einen gesellschaftlich verantwortlichen Film* (edited by Jürgen Römhild), Munich: Hanser; English translation: Hans Richter. 1986. *The Struggle for the Film: Towards a Socially Responsible Cinema*. New York: St Martin's Press.

34. Franz Heinemann. 1924. *Der Film in der Schweiz. Privatwirtschaft. Zeitgemässe Anregungen*. Zurich: Orell Füssli.

35. Albert Masnata. 1929. 'Le film – moyen de publicité', *Informations économiques / Wirtschaftliche Mitteilungen* 8(35) (18 October), 147. On OSEC, see Zimmermann, *Schaufenster Schweiz*; on Masnata in particular, see Pierre-Emmanuel Jaques. 2007. 'La

propaganda nationale par le film. Albert Masnata et l'Office suisse du d'expansion commerciale', *Revue historique vaudoise* 115, 65–78.

36. Richter, *The Struggle for the Film*, 142.
37. For a detailed account of the emergence of avant-garde screening organizations, see Hagener, *Moving Forward, Looking Back*, 77–120; on the situation in Paris, see Christophe Gauthier. 1999. *La passion du cinéma, cinéphiles, ciné-clubs et salles spéciali-sées à Paris de 1920 à 1929*, Paris: Ecole nationale des chartes: Association française de recherche sur l'histoire du cinéma; on the Filmliga, see Céline Linssen, Hans Schoots and Tom Gunning (eds). 1999. *Het gaat om de film! Een nieuwe geschiedenis van de Nederlandsche Filmliga 1927–1933*. Amsterdam: Bas Lubberhuizen; on the Film Society in particular, see Sexton, *Alternative Film Culture*; on Le Bon Film Basel, see Kaspar Birkhäuser. 1981. 'Fünfzig Jahre im Dienste der Filmbesucher und des guten Films', in Le Bon Film (ed.), *50 Jahre Le Bon Film*, Basel: Le Bon Film, 5–46.
38. See the 1929 brochure *Rationelle Film-Propaganda durch den Schweizer Schul- und Volkskino Bern und Zürich*, ed. Schweizer Schul- und Volkskino, Bern and Zurich.
39. On the SSVK, see Anita Gertiser, 'Schul- und Lehrfilme', in Zimmermann, *Schaufenster Schweiz*, 399–431.
40. See Yvonne Zimmermann. 2008. 'Training and Entertaining Consumers: Travelling Corporate Film Shows in Switzerland', in Martin Loiperdinger (ed.), *Travelling Cinema in Europe: Sources and Perspectives*, Frankfurt am Main: Stroemfeld/Roter Stern, 168–79.
41. On Maggi's use of slides and films, see Yvonne Zimmermann. 2006. 'Maggis Wandervortragspraxis mit Lichtbildern. Ein Schulmädchenreport aus der Schweiz', *KINtop* 14/15, 53–65; Yvonne Zimmermann. 2007. 'Heimatpflege zwecks Suppenpromotion. Zum Einsatz von Lichtbildern und Filmen in der Schweizer Lebensmittelbranche am Beispiel von Maggi', *Zeitschrift für Unternehmensgeschichte* 52(2), 203–26; Zimmermann, 'Training and Entertaining Consumers', 168–79.
42. Frank Kessler. 2011. 'Programming and Performing Early Cinema Today: Strategies and *Dispositifs*', in Martin Loiperdinger (ed.), *Early Cinema Today: The Art of Programming and Live Performance*, New Barnet: John Libbey, 138. See also Frank Kessler. 2006. 'The Cinema of Attractions as *Dispositif*', in Strauven, *Attractions Reloaded*, 57–69.
43. For *dispositifs* in avant-garde screening organizations, see Hagener, 'Programming Attractions' and van Beusekom, '"Avant-guerre" and the International Avant-Garde'; for *dispositifs* in the context of the industry and school, see Zimmermann, *Schaufenster Schweiz*; for the screening practices of labour organizations in Switzerland, see Stefan Länzlinger and Thomas Schärer. 2009. *'Stellen wir diese Waffe in unseren Dienst'. Film und Arbeiterbewegung in der Schweiz*, Zurich: Chronos.
44. On the Fip-Fop Club, see Zimmermann, 'Nestlé's Fip-Fop Club', 281–303.
45. Hagener, 'Programming Attractions'; van Beusekom, '"Avant-guerre" and the International Avant-Garde'.
46. See 'Bericht des Bundesrates an die Bundesversammlung über das von Herrn Nationalrat Dr. Zimmerli und Mitunterzeichnern im Nationalrat eingereichte Postulat betreffend Revision von Art. 31 der Bundesverfassung (am 26. Mai 1925)', *Bundesblatt* 77/2(22) (3 June 1925): 545–85.
47. Alfons Helbling, 'Jugendwerbung in der Schokoladen-Industrie NPCK', type-script, 7 June 1950, 1 (Archives Historiques Nestlé Vevey, NPCK, F 3/14). See also Zimmermann, 'Nestlé's Fip-Fop Club'.

48. Karl Lauterer [alias 'Euer Götti']. 1940. 'Unser General. Ehrenmitglied des Fip-Fop-Clubs', *Fip-Fop Zeitung* 3(2) (February), 2.
49. Richter, *The Struggle for the Film*, 131.
50. Ibid., 133.
51. Ibid., 133 and 164.
52. See Hans Richter. 1940. 'Der Filmessay. Eine neue Form des Dokumentarfilms', *National-Zeitung* (25 April), 192, reprinted in Christa Blümlinger and Constantin Wulff (eds). 1992. *Schreiben Bilder Sprechen. Texte zum essayistischen Film*. Vienna: Sonderzahl, 195–98. See also Hans Richter. 1955. 'The Film as an Original Art Form', *Film Culture* 1(1), reprint in P. Adams Sitney (ed.). 1970. *Film Culture Reader*. New York: Praeger, 15–20.
53. See for instance the two volumes of the cinema journal *Montage AV* 14(2) (2005) and *Montage AV* 15(1) (2006) dedicated to science films and to educational and industrial films; on industrial uses of media in Europe, see Vinzenz Hediger and Patrick Vonderau (eds). 2009. *Films that Work: Industrial Film and the Productivity of Media*. Amsterdam: Amsterdam University Press; on institutional uses of cinema in the United States of America, see Charles R. Acland and Haidee Wasson (eds). 2011. *Useful Cinema*, Durham, NC and London: Duke University Press.
54. Franz Heinemann. 1941. 'Ein Viertel-Jahrhundert schweizerische Kinematographie: 1915–1940. Frühe schweizer. Mittelpunkte internationalen Filmschaffens', in *Jahrbuch der Schweizer Filmindustrie / Annuaire de la cinématographie suisse*, 3–34.
55. Hans Richter. 1947. 'A History of the Avantgarde', in Frank Stauffacher (ed.), *Art in Cinema: A Symposium on the Avantgarde Film together with Program Notes and References for Series One of Art in Cinema*, San Francisco: Museum of Art, 6–21.
56. Tom Gunning. 2003. 'A Quarter of a Century Later: Is Early Cinema Still Early?', *KINtop* 12, 30.

PART III

EMERGENCE OF INSTITUTIONS

Chapter 9

INTERWAR FILM CULTURE IN SWEDEN

Avant-Garde Transactions in the Emergent Welfare State

Lars Gustaf Andersson

The possibilities of film art are unlimited, and its suggestive powers are immense. It is still in the beginning of its prosperity, so a wide field lies ahead. And we, who have lived for so long under the black banner of violence during the world war, should rejoice when facing something which we can expect will revolutionize the life of mankind.[1]

– Julius Regis, *Filmens roman*

This epigraph is from a chapter on the future of film art in *Filmens roman* (lit. 'The Novel of the Film'), a Swedish account of the history and aesthetics of film from 1920, written by the prolific crime writer and critic Julius Regis. His enthusiasm is shared by many of his contemporaries among critics and writers. As the critic Sven Stolpe put it in an article in the popular journal *Filmnyheter* some years later: 'Cinema is the art of the future'.[2] Paradoxically they upheld this optimism concerning the new medium in a decade when domestic film production was declining; the successes of the 1910s with directors like Victor Sjöström and Mauritz Stiller, and their adaptations of the national literary heritage, were already history. Svensk Filmindustri – the Swedish film production company, distributor and movie theatre chain, formerly known as Svenska Bio – was no longer dominating the market as before. The stars of the Swedish silent screen were migrating to Hollywood: Sjöström, Stiller, and most notably, Greta Garbo. New production companies were emerging, and above all, the American film industry had become the most important factor for the Swedish audiences. Yet, even if domestic production was in crisis, film culture itself was thriving, with movie theatres, film clubs and a burgeoning area of film criticism in daily newspapers and film journals, as well as in book-length studies.

The story of the expanding film art discourse, and the clash between diverse cultural structuring systems, has been told before. For the Swedish conditions the most important contributions are works by art historian Elisabeth Liljedahl and film historians Jan Olsson and Leif Furhammar.[3] The emergence of a Swedish art cinema institution can be sketched as narrative, where the film culture grows in importance and legitimacy. The first films to be produced, besides early documentaries and attraction films, are attempts in the spirit of *film d'art* by production company Svenska Bio in Kristianstad, dating back to 1909 with adaptations of some Swedish literary classics. There was some competition, from independent producers like Frans Lundberg and N.P. Nilsson; the latter produced the first adaptations of August Strindberg, FRÖKEN JULIE [Miss Julie] (1912) and FADREN [The Father] (1912), both directed by the first female director in Sweden, Anna Hofmann-Uddgren.

The ambitions within the growing film industry to gain acceptance within the literary culture of the time was in fact helped by the establishment of a governmental board for film censorship in 1911, the Statens Biografbyrå. Film censorship meant that standards were set for film production, something that was to benefit the industry and its need for legal norms in this field. It also meant that a discourse about art film was beginning to formulate.[4]

The film as art form made a symbolic entrance into the public sphere in January 1917, when TERJE VIGEN [A Man There Was] premiered, directed by Victor Sjöström with a script based on a poem by Norwegian poet and playwright Henrik Ibsen. In the leading newspaper in Stockholm, *Dagens Nyheter*, the film was reviewed by the distinguished poet and critic Bo Bergman, who in 1925 became a member of the Swedish Academy. This review has been interpreted as a significant breakthrough for the Swedish art cinema.[5]

Svenska Bio went in for a new strategy.[6] Dominated by directors Victor Sjöström and Mauritz Stiller, the company produced several literary adaptations, especially from novels and stories by Selma Lagerlöf; some of the most successful were HERR ARNES PENGAR [Sir Arne's Treasure] (1919, Stiller) and KÖRKARLEN [The Phantom Carriage/Thy Soul Shall Bear Witness] (1921, Sjöström).[7] In Swedish film historiography this period has been labelled 'The National Style' or 'The Golden

Age'.[8] Even if this label is contested, it is obvious that the Swedish film production, incarnated by Svenska Bio and its *dioscuri* directors, together with film critics and the film censors, structured an art film institution.[9]

That film culture in general had been institutionalized was evident by other phenomena, such as film journals, most of them popular or trade papers, but to some extent developing a field for discussion concerning film as art, and problems concerning film and politics, film and education, film and religion, and film and science. Much of this was to be retold and summarized by Julius Regis in the aforementioned *Filmens roman* – the first Swedish attempt, as early as 1920, to write the history of film in general.

The field of experimental film, or avant-garde film culture, was not institutionalized in the same way, but there were some critics that made efforts to introduce new ideas, and present new filmmakers. Sven Stolpe, who much later (in the 1950s) became well known as a conservative writer and literary critic, was among the most enthusiastic film critics during the 1920s. In *Filmjournalen*, one of the most popular film journals in Sweden ever, he wrote some general articles on film and cultural value, discussing the work of René Clair, arguing for a film school in Stockholm, and introducing the new Soviet cinema.[10] His partner in crime at *Filmjournalen* was Gerda Marcus, a journalist with close ties to the women's rights movement.[11] She wrote about Béla Balázs and *Der Sichtbare Mensch*, and was for a while stationed in Berlin, from where she reported about BRONENOSETS POTEMKIN [Battleship Potemkin] (1925, Sergei Eisenstein), as well as BERLIN, DIE SINFONIE DER GROSSSTADT [Berlin: Symphony of a Great City] (1927, Walter Ruttmann).[12]

The continental avant-garde concluded the decade with the meeting in La Sarraz. As Malte Hagener puts it: 'the avant-garde seemed to be on the verge of a breakthrough to a mass movement. Yet, the opposite was the case: the avant-garde fell apart and petered out'.[13] Despite this evaporation of the avant-garde, it survived in a certain sense and was sustained by the culture of cinéphilia.

The Swedish film avant-garde had by then been divided into two parts, one consisting of the practice in exile, personified by Viking Eggeling, and the other consisting of a growing theoretical and critical discourse in the homeland. The output in terms of film production was to stay very modest during the following years, in fact until the end of the Second World War, but the experimental film culture grew at the same time, with film clubs, critics, and an evermore conscious relationship to the international tendencies. And the 'avant-garde of the avant-garde' consisted in turn of the young writers, a new, urban generation, who championed a rather belated modernism.

Swedish modernism was reluctant.[14] Most of the Swedish contributions to the modernist movement seem to be the ones delivered *outside* Sweden; nevertheless they are significant, even from an international perspective. It is for example impossible to sidestep the name of Viking Eggeling, but there are several others to be mentioned. One can in fact speak about a sort of imaginary Swedish film avant-garde, situated in Paris and Berlin, and with very limited influence on Swedish film or art culture until long afterwards.

The interest in movement and colour and urbanity – pointing towards the art movements of the 1960s – was a common denominator for many of the young artists who tried to find ways of expression outside Sweden. One of them was Otto G. Carlsund. He was introduced to Fernand Léger in Paris 1924, and was accepted at *Académie Moderne* together with two other Swedish artists, the surrealists Erik Olson and Waldemar Lorentzon. Carlsund's most famous contribution to film art is that he assisted Léger in making BALLET MÉCANIQUE (1924).[15] The film – 'a sampling of avant-garde aesthetics' – has been of pivotal importance for other filmmakers.[16] As such it was obviously attracting some contemporary Swedish artists, like Carlsund, but it was not acknowledged in Sweden until the 1930s and 1940s when it was often screened at the various ciné-clubs.

Another significant Swede in Paris during the early 1920s was Rolf de Maré and his Ballet Suédois, which produced well over twenty ballets in close cooperation with contemporary artists, painters and filmmakers.[17] Two of the main artists in the troupe were Jean Börlin and Carina Ari. Börlin was a successful dancer who made a career for himself in Paris, while Ari – one of the stars at the Royal Opera in Stockholm – was, among other things, responsible for the choreography of the feature film EROTIKON (1920, Mauritz Stiller).[18] In Paris they joined under the guidance of de Maré. This group of artists was harassed by the Swedish tabloids; they were portrayed as traitors, and the homosexuality of de Maré was ridiculed in severe attacks. Like Carlsund, they found a refuge in Paris. Together they formed an exile culture of sorts, where they could cultivate, create and perform contemporary art. In Paris it was possible for this Swedish minority culture to incorporate and develop the new film medium in a way that had been impossible in Sweden. Several of the ballet productions were integrated with or inspired by film, as SKATING RINK (1922) with its resemblance to Chaplin's THE RINK (1917).[19] One of their productions was *Relâche* (1924) with choreography by Börlin, music by Erik Satie, decorations by Francis Picabia and – as an integrated part – a film by René Clair, ENTR'ACTE.[20]

ENTR'ACTE is sometimes categorized together with BALLET MÉCANIQUE as a Dada film, consisting of 'unconnected, wildly irrational scenes'.[21] Several of the dancers of the Swedish troupe appeared in the film, most notably Jean Börlin.[22] Rolf de Maré and his troupe returned to film in the production *Ciné-Sketch*, a celebration of New Year's Eve 1924, where Picabia and Clair collaborated in order to get the pace and rhythm of cinematography to appear on stage. In 1925, however, the Swedish Ballet was dissolved by its manager de Maré, and the adventure in exile was over.

Otto G. Carlsund, Jean Börlin and the Swedish Ballet of Paris functioned thus as a kind of mobile Swedish avant-garde in exile, performing briefly at the European art scene, but still close to the important events and figures. Another artist from Sweden, who contributed to the experimental film and avant-garde culture of the 1920s, was Viking Eggeling.[23]

During the years 1915 to 1917, Eggeling had started to work with the picture scrolls 'Horsiontal-vertikal orkester' (Horizontal–Vertical Orchestra) and '*Diagonalsymfoni*' (Diagonal Symphony). Hans Richter accompanied him and later recalled: 'In these scrolls we tried to build different phases of transformation as if they were phrases of a symphony or fugue'.[24]

The ambition of Eggeling and Richter was to create an abstract visual language, universal and boundless. Eggeling developed, inspired by contemporaries like Vasily Kandinsky, Kazimir Malevich and Raoul Hausmann, a theory of his own, which he formulated in some brief articles and notes. Another source of inspiration was French philosopher Henri Bergson whose *L'evolution créatrice* (1907) was published 1912 in a German translation. Among Eggeling's posthumous notes there is a manuscript, 'Film', which consists almost solely of quotations from Bergson. It was the hope of Eggeling to recreate '*la durée*', the flow of the present, through the cinematic medium. Through reduction he wanted to create a unique language: 'Artistic richness is not to be found in an arbitrary innovation, but in formal transformation of the most simple motifs'.[25]

Eggeling and Richter found at last some financial support from Ufa in Berlin in 1920, and Eggeling made a first version of a film, based upon 'Horizontal–Vertical Orchestra'. These experiments were described by Theo van Doesburg in an article in *De Stijl*, and were also related by

Eggeling himself in an article, 'Theoretical Presentations of the Art of Movement', which he published in 1921 in the Hungarian journal *MA*.[26] A Swedish journalist, Birger Brinck-E:son, describes the film in an article in *Filmjournalen* 1923, as about ten minutes long, consisting of two thousand drawings, and he characterizes the film as a 'symphony of lines'.[27] The musical analogy is found in Eggeling's own writings, and it is obvious that his aim was to create a visual counterpart to music.

'Horizontal–Vertical Orchestra' is lost, and was never shown in public. The support from Ufa was withdrawn after a while, and Eggeling had to produce his next film by himself, together with his assistant Erna Niemeyer. At the same time he broke with Richter. He suffered from illness as well as financial problems, but was able to finish his work. The film, which was to become *Symphonie Diagonale*, was made with a simple cut-out technique, where he used forms in tinfoil, filmed frame by frame.[28] On 5 November 1924, Eggeling had a private screening of the film, and on 3 May 1925 the film had its first public screening at Ufa-Palast in Berlin, together with films by Richter, Léger, Ruttman, Clair and others, all under the banner '*Der absolute Film*'. Sixteen days later Viking Eggeling died by septic angina, weakened by infections and a hard life.

Symphonie Diagonale is now part of the avant-garde canon and is acknowledged as an essential element in Swedish film history. But it was a long process before it became part of a Swedish heritage, as it was only after the Second World War, when Eggeling became a canonical figure for the young film lovers and filmmakers *in spe*. This can be exemplified with the important exhibition and festival 'Apropå Eggeling' which was held at the museum for modern art in Stockholm, Moderna Museet, in May 1958, where Eggeling was described as the main character in the Swedish film avant-garde.[29] Some years earlier, Peter Weiss had published his seminal book on avant-garde cinema, but he treats Eggeling somewhat harshly, mainly noting that his film was the first animated and abstract work, and putting a lot more emphasis on Clair and Léger, not to mention the German expressionists.

Otto Carlsund and Viking Eggeling were two artists who left Sweden for the continent where they (at least Eggeling) were acknowledged, while they were forgotten or left in the margins of culture in their native land. They were not outcasts, but they were not considered central until later on. There are several reasons for this delay of the cultural modernization process: it was partly due to the lack of an urban culture in Sweden, at least in comparison with Berlin and Paris; and for sure it also had to do with the relative homogeneity of Swedish culture and its protectionist strategies towards influences from the rest of the world.

When studying popular Swedish film journals from the beginning of the twentieth century, one can trace a specific ironic mode when confronting modernism. The American mainstream film culture was soon the matrix for the understanding of the film medium, and in cartoons and columns the filmic avant-garde of Europe was ridiculed in a harmless but still negative way. 'Cubism', 'expressionism' and 'futurism' were terms that were easily attached to everything incomprehensible and foreign.[30] This kind of context turned artists like Carlsund, Eggeling and de Maré into foreigners, and expelled them from the national public sphere.

'The avant-garde attitude' – to use a term coined by Deke Dusinberre – was to a great extent carried by the young writers.[31] Artur Lundkvist, Vilhelm Moberg and Erik Asklund belonged to a new generation of writers from the working class who, together with several others, formed a heterogeneous literary school, Arbetarlitteraturen (Workers' literature).[32] They had no common manifest, and no programme, but most of them were autodidacts, many of them earned their living as reporters, they were often oriented towards the labour movement, and they were eager agents for modernism and modernity. For these young intellectuals cinema was indeed the new art.

Artur Lundkvist was the most eloquent of these angry young men. He was involved in the journal *Fronten* (The Front), which under editor Sven Stolpe (and the distinguished publishing house Albert Bonniers) was to be an important stronghold for the new generation. A subdivision of the journal functioned as a book series, *Frontens bibliotek* (The Front Library) where Lundkvist in 1932 published a collection of criticism, *Atlantvind* (Atlantic Wind). *Atlantvind* contained introductory articles on American poetry, fiction and drama, a section on Swedish modernism, and a big section on cinema, 'the new art form', where Lundkvist in five essays wrote a brief history of film, introduced the American and Soviet cinema, discussed the problem of the talkies, and reflected on the cinema and its audience. In '*Från kinetoskopet till avantgardefilm*' (From the kinetoscope to avant-garde film) he claims that 'the just position of cinema in the culture, as a manifestation of the contemporary creative and spiritual life, can no longer wait'.[33] But he moves on from general cinéphilia, to a position where the important historical progress within European cinema is dependent on the avant-garde. Without explicitly mentioning psychoanalysis (which at this time was *on dit* among Scandinavian intellectuals), Lundkvist ends his essay by praising French surrealism; films by Buñuel and Dulac, 'all of them characterized by dynamic intensity, subconscious contact and a liberated, creative imagination. They are directly inspired by dreams and the life of instincts, and do maybe signify a new line of the coming art of cinema'.[34]

Svensk Filmindustri did in fact support two experimental shorts which together form the total output of experimental film production in Sweden during the 1930s, except for home movies and marginal experiments within mainstream cinema.[35] One of these shorts, *Gamla Stan* (Old Town) was co-written and co-directed by a writer's collective, consisting of, among others, Artur Lundkvist; the other one, *Tango*, was made by a young cinéphile, Gösta Hellström. These two shorts represent two lines of evolution within cinema, but neither of them had any successors until many years later.

The story, as it has been told, is that Eyvind Johnson, Artur Lundkvist, Erik Asklund and Stig Almqvist – all by that time well known as modern artists and critics – went to the offices of Svensk Filmindustri and told manager Olof Andersson that they wanted to do a short film. Fearing a lot of trouble from the angry young men, he let them use the facilities of the company.[36] Johnson wrote the script, while Almqvist, according to Lundkvist, was responsible for the direction.[37]

Old Town, shot mostly in the medieval parts of Stockholm, was made in the spirit of the continental urban film, with Ruttmann's Berlin film as the emblematic pattern.[38] Music (Eric Bengtson) and cinematography (Elner Åkesson) was handled by professionals, and it resulted in *une pièce bien faite*, not as norm breaking as the working group maybe intended. The film was screened at the art house cinema Sture, together with Dreyer's LA PASSION DE JEANNE D'ARC [The Passion of Joan of Arc] (1932). The film starts with a poem, and Lundkvist remembers:

> Asklund did recite the poem, in a proletarian fashion shirt, open at the neck, and with make-up that made him as beautiful as Gösta Ekman. We ourselves found that our film experiment had rather failed, but we learned a lot. We had gained knowledge about what a long way there was between the poet's imagination and the shooting of a film, how hard this way was and how worn out the vision was bound to be.[39]

The poem, in the film read by Asklund, was written by Asklund and Lundkvist together, and is an invocation to the 'old town' which is compared to a woman in different guises:

> Old Town –
> you are like an old woman:

your memories are all your beauty.
We have seen your stained walls,
your tramps, your shady hotels
where shadows of men stumble over the
worn out thresholds,
the deep wells of your alleys
where the sheet metal rusts and the mould crawls
green over the walls.[40]

The film then portrays this old lady over a day and a night, picturing the life of the tramps and fishermen and salesmen and street-girls, but also focusing on a young couple and their fragile love story. Continuously the modern city life breaks through, with cars and shop windows and running feet. The documentary or realist aspect of the film is sometimes very dominant, for example when the street sweepers clean the alleys in the morning; plain shots from a recognizable reality.

The film language of *Old Town* is mostly conventional, but sometimes there are experiments with camera angles and steep perspectives. A recurrent device is to create non-figurative patterns from everyday details: puddles with water, raindrops, clouds and reflections of the sun. Many of the symbols and characters that fill the short narrative are also congruent with the free-spoken 'primitivist' tendency within 1930s Swedish literature, where the sailor and the girl in the window are among the most obvious icons for a new urban sensuality. *Old Town* had fairly good reviews, and it is noteworthy that one critic, in Labour paper *SocialDemokraten*, later defined the film as avant-garde.[41]

The second experimental short to be launched by Svensk Filmindustri was *Tango*. At first glance it seems to be the absolute antithesis to *Old Town*; instead of documentary impressions of an anonymous collective in the proletarian alleys we are furnished with a melodramatic morality play in a high society setting, staged by some popular theatre actors of the day. Most interesting is maybe the director, Gösta Hellström, who was a representative for the early cinéphilia in a different way from the young writers who wrote and directed *Old Town*.

Gösta Hellström was one of the reporters of *Filmjournalen*, well known for his interest in the new Soviet cinema (but also reporting about the animations of Lotte Reiniger).[42] He started out as a journalist for *Göteborgs-Posten*, reporting from Hamburg, Paris and Moscow. He was appointed chairman for the student film club of Gothenburg University College in 1929, and soon organized the film import for all film clubs in Sweden. In Moscow he met Eisenstein and his entourage, and was wildly influenced by the new film theories. Svensk Filmindustri hired him in 1931 as assistant director to Gustaf Molander for the feature film En Natt [One Night]. It is commonly assumed that he had a great influence on the film and its 'Soviet style', and he wrote with great enthusiasm about the production.[43] He agitated for a montage view of the sound track. He loathed 'the synchronic devil' and wanted to get away from a routine-like naturalism in the handling of the sound.

Hellström was then appointed to direct the short *Tango*, based on his own script. Before the film had been screened he got the assignment as director for the popular comedy Sten Stensson Stéen från Eslöv på nya äventyr [New Adventures with Sten Steenson Stéen from Eslöv] (1932). In December 1932, one month after the public screening of *Tango*, he died of tuberculosis. The obituaries were plentyful, and many regretted the great loss that Hellström's death meant for Swedish film culture – at twenty-four years of age he was considered a sparkling hope for Swedish film.[44] His friend, the writer Stig Almqvist, had even hoped for a Swedish Billy Wilder or Robert Siodmak.

Tango is an extraordinary film within a Swedish context, and points out directions that were never to be followed in Swedish film aesthetics. The story deals with two lovers – a man and a married woman. They are suddenly disturbed by a burglar and the woman runs away home to her husband, while it is revealed to us that the burglar was hired by her lover. The setting is a functionalist apartment with high windows and steel furniture. A bird's eye view is used, sometimes in extreme measure. Details of the interior design and the exterior architecture are sometimes framed in close-ups that isolate them from the narrative, turning them into decorative elements. There are no classical Stockholm views as in *Old Town*; *Tango* is indeed staged within the walls of the studio.

The most intriguing formal element, though, is not the perspectives or the framing, but the use of the sound track. According to Hellström's sceptical views on 'the synchronic devil', but also in an attempt to make the film saleable internationally and easy to dub, you never see the person who talks, but only the one who listens. This device creates, at least for modern audiences, an almost bizarre syncopation of the soundtrack, a veritable but non-intended *Verfremdungseffekt* (alienation effect) of sorts.

In a kind of unintentional symmetry these two works contain two complementary tendencies within the international avant-garde; the hunger for reality and documentary as well as the lust for stylistic innovation – both in an urban setting. *Old Town* and *Tango* were, however, exceptions in a production climate dominated by the domestic popular genres.

There are a few productions made in Europe by Swedish production companies in cooperation with American and German companies, in order to make Swedish films abroad. The most ambitious enterprise was by American Paramount, who used the Joinville studios outside Paris and the Gaumont studios in Buttes-Chaumont. Around a dozen films were made, mostly comedies and melodramas, but they had very little impact in terms of actual reception, and failed immensely in terms of economy.[45] In fact, the most transnational project during the interwar decades is the cinéphile movement, characterized by an avant-garde profile and always putting forward the term *experimentfilm* as something valuable in the general exploration of film art.

An essential part of film history is the history of film reception – some of the most important works in a specific period may not have been produced within the local or national culture in question, but they still belong to the cultural context. This is evidently the fact with Swedish experimental film culture during its formative years. The domestic production of experimental film was marginal, but the experimental film discourse was thriving around a kernel of international works that gained in importance, and was discussed within film clubs and in film journals. It was in this public sphere that discourses were shared, launched and reproduced.

The reception is only available as a reconstruction, based on a spectre of fragile evidences and ephemeral memories.[46] The dominant historical facts are the institutional traces like screening programmes, legislations, film reviews and remnants of discussions and debates in journals and newspapers. With respect to these facts and suppositions it is possible to make at least a preliminary mapping.

The general discussion on film in the public sphere was not, however, oriented towards questions of new forms of filmic modernism; the main debate concerned, still, whether film could be considered as an art at all, and it focused on the supposedly low standards of Swedish film production. Writers like Vilhelm Moberg and Artur Lundkvist were engaged in the discussions in favour of film art, but were highly critical towards the dominant trends within Swedish genre films. During the 1930s, burlesque comedies and melodramas constituted the bulk of Swedish film production. The debate culminated in a public meeting at the concert hall in Stockholm in 1937, arranged by the Swedish Writer's Union under the headline 'Swedish Film – A Threat against the Culture'. The meeting was directly connected to the first performance some days earlier of the Swedish comedy PENSIONAT PARADISET [A Boarding House Named Paradise] (Weyler Hildebrand), a highly popular comedy which, however, was considered to be of particularly bad taste.[47]

The primary result of these discussions was a higher degree of involvement in the film industry by the professional writers; during the 1940s established novelists and poets were to be engaged as screenwriters. This can be understood as phases in the formation of a Swedish art cinema, which would finally get its prominent iconic figure in Ingmar Bergman, who from the 1950s and well into the 1990s personified Swedish art film as an institution.

But even if the promotion of experimental film art seems to be invisible in this more public agenda, the avant-garde film culture was discussed and advanced in the cinéphile context, based upon the film society movement. The Swedish film clubs, often called *Filmstudios*, constituted a network of local organizations which made it possible to import film and screen it at closed meetings, thereby avoiding the censorship regulations. The first film clubs were constituted within the academic context, often in close cooperation with students' unions. Film clubs were constituted in Stockholm, Uppsala, Gothenburg and Lund during the late 1920s and early 1930s, inspired by the French Ciné-Clubs.[48] A new branch of the movement started after the Second World War, when film clubs, not connected to the student organizations, were established all over the country, especially in the provinces, constituting the national union, the Sveriges Förenade Filmstudios (Swedish Federation of Film Societies).

The student film clubs screened the new films and created a critical context. A good example is the American film LOT IN SODOM (1933), directed by James Sibley Watson and Melville Webber. The works of Watson and Webber are among the earliest in the American film avant-garde. Even if their films were produced within a context that can be categorized as amateur, they had a great impact on European film culture.[49]

The film was treated by the Swedish governmental censorship board in August 1935, and was prohibited for public screenings, according to a clause in the Cinema Ordinance, which states that examiners at the censorship board 'shall not approve cinematic pictures, the showing of which is contrary to law or morality or is otherwise liable to have a brutalizing or agitating effect or to cast doubt on the concept of legality. Therefore, pictures depicting scenes of horror, suicide or serious crimes in such a manner and in such a context as to have such an effect shall not be approved'.[50]

But through the loophole of closed screenings, Lot in Sodom as well as several other prohibited films could have a Swedish reception, mainly at the student film clubs.[51] Through the film club movement and later the film journals, it was possible to see and discuss modern filmmaking, and put it into an avant-garde context. Slowly an experimental canon emerged. In spite of poor conditions for production of film, a discursive field could be established where it was meaningful to discuss in terms of 'avant-garde' and 'experimentalism'.

An illustrative example is the list of films screened by the film society of Lund (founded by among others Gösta Werner) during the spring semester of 1930: Rien que les Heures [Nothing But Time] (Alberto Cavalcanti, 1927), Un Chapeau de Paille d'Italie [An Italian Straw Hat] (René Clair, 1927), Oktiabr [October] (Sergei Eisenstein, 1928), Turksib (Victor Turin, 1929), Celovek s kinoapparatom [The Man with the Movie Camera) (Dziga Vertov, 1929), Le Jardin du Luxembourg [The Garden of Luxembourg] (Mannus Franken, 1929), De Brug [The Bridge] (Joris Ivens, 1928), and Regen [Rain] (Joris Ivens/Mannus Franken 1929).

Many of the screenings in Lund and elsewhere were accompanied by introductions or lectures. Independent and amateur filmmakers visited the film clubs, screened their works, and joined the discussions. Several of them would later become established filmmakers (like the omnipresent Gösta Werner).

The student film clubs started to build libraries; the film society of Lund was especially ambitious, and in 1934 issued a little booklet with an index and catalogue of the library, annotated by Gösta Werner.[52] The index contains 123 books, from Eugen Albán's *Charlie Chaplin* (Stockholm, 1928) to a special sound film issue by *Die Woche* (Berlin, 1931); it also lists some journal articles and subscriptions for several domestic and international film journals. This library grew over the years, and when the society closed down in 2011 it contained the second largest collection of film literature in Sweden after the library of the Swedish Film Institute.

In 1933, Svensk Filmindustri announced a competition for film scripts. Around seven hundred scripts were submitted. One of the scripts that received an honourable mention by the jury was the drama *En judisk tragedy* (A Jewish Tragedy), by novelist Gunhild Tegen. The script was never filmed, but the film society of Lund published it and declared it to be the first book in a new series.[53] The script was annotated by Swedish novelist Marika Stiernstedt, and in an appendix Gösta Werner contributed a bibliography of published film scripts.

There were also ambitions among some of the young film buffs to make film themselves, especially in Stockholm and Uppsala. The Stockholm students ran their own script competition, and did a lot of experimental filming; the results were presented at screenings together with works by Léger and Buñuel. In Uppsala, it resulted in the 'sub-standard gauge classic' IMPERFECTUM (1941), a melodramatic horror story in the campus settings of Uppsála, directed by Lars Swärd.[54] Lack of funds for investing in technique, however, slowed down this kind of filmmaking, even if some of the experiments were in fact sponsored by Svensk Filmindustri.

An important organization was Svenska Filmsamfundet (The Swedish Film Society), founded 1933 in Stockholm, with the objective of creating a national film archive. The society was important, as it published an annual summary of film in Sweden and internationally,

Figure 9.1 The working committee of Svenska Filmsamfundet during one of their first meeetings, in autumn 1933: Nils Beyer, Ragnar Allberg, Arne Bornesbusch, 'Robin Hood' (Bengt Idestam-Almquist), Gustaf Molander, Per-Axel Branner and E.W. Olson. [Swedish Film Institute]

and arranged lectures and screenings.[55] In 1935, it published a booklet on avant-garde directors, written by Arne Bornebusch, who was on his way to becoming established as a film director and screenwriter.[56] The book contains portraits of 'film poets', like Clair and Eisenstein, and it is symptomatic for the cultural agenda within the cinéphile movement. Together with the film club movement, the Swedish Film Society offered a public sphere for the experimental film, even if the aims were often more general in scope.

There were also other institutions, such as the cinema Sture (or Sturebiografen) in Stockholm, a part of the movie house division of Svensk Filmindustri, which was profiled into an art movie cinema. The expression 'Sture-film' was associated with art film, and many of the art films and experimental films that had a public screening during the 1930s had their first (and often only) performance there.[57]

During the 1930s, *Filmjournalen* was an influential film journal, with writers like Almquist and Stolpe introducing foreign films, and discussing film theory and film aesthetics. Stolpe introduced Béla Balázs and *Der Geist des Films*, and there were articles on animation experiments as well as on Soviet montage cinema.

The single most important agent here, however, was the magazine *Biografbladet*. The journal was founded in 1920, and lasted until 1952. It was originally a journal for film professionals, dealing with film business and technology, but was gradually transformed into one of the leading film journals in Scandinavia, containing aesthetic discussions, polemical reviews and statements, and – especially during the editorship of Gösta Werner – offering the young cinéphiles an arena where they could make an entrance into the public sphere. Gerd Osten and Peter Weiss turned *Biografbladet* into the mouthpiece for a new generation.[58]

Swedish film production was regulated by the government in two ways. There was the censorship board, initiated in 1911, and there was an entertainment tax which treated film the same way as variety and music hall shows – a heavy burden for the film production. (The taxation did not end until 1963 when the Swedish Film Institute was funded, based on an agreement between the state and the film companies.) But besides this, there was no state policy for film, and film production was never included in the debate on cultural politics. Film was defined as an 'industry' by the state, and the only sphere where it could be discussed as art in any meaningful way was the film culture, with its system of clubs and journals. The young writers and critics, many of them connected to the same labour movement as the reigning social-democratic party, created a cultural policy of sorts, in the shadow of the state apparatus. But the archival question was far too difficult to be solved by students, critics or labour-movement writers.

It may seem odd that the Swedish national state, with an archival history going back at least to the sixteenth century, and having a church with a long history of collecting documents and demographic facts, did not establish an archival policy for film and media until the end of the 1970s. In 1979 an archive was founded for films and recordings of television and radio, as well as gramophone records. The 'Arkivet för ljud och bild' (The Archive for Sound and Images) was later, in 2009, transferred to the National Library of Stockholm. The National Library is now responsible, through its department for audio-visual media, for the archiving of all moving images. At the same time, there is a film archive housed by the Swedish Film Institute. The institute is not a genuine public authority, but an agency regulated by a treaty between the state and the film producers, and its archive is to a certain extent conditioned by the companies and individuals who have deposited their reels and documents there. The institute, however, has since 1963 been the central archive for films and film-related documents.

In comparison with other European film cultures, the Swedish film archival institutions were thus very late. This does not mean that the archival question was absent during the interwar years when national film archives were founded in several European countries. Already in 1918 an organization was founded, Föreningen Film och Fonogram (The Film and Phonogram Society), which had as its purpose to collect and store recordings of sound and film.[59] In the organization's first and only annual report, the importance of archiving moving images was stated and it was declared that the main objective of the archive was to 'acquire and preserve Swedish films and phonograms of histori- cal, cultural and social significance'. This very ambitious and modern enterprise was supported by important authorities of the time such as the National Librarian, the head of the Royal Dramatic Theatre, and several scholars, businessmen and authors. The patron was Crown Prince Gustaf Adolf. The circumstances of the founding and closing down of this organization are not known, but in 1921 it was suddenly dissolved; very few of its documents remain, but one hypothesis is that the archives of Svensk Filmindustri were supposed to serve the purpose more effectively.[60]

In 1933, when the aforementioned Svenska Filmsamfundet was established, it also had as a central objective to collect films and documents. Through generous donations from film companies, publishing houses and individuals, this film society could start to collect books and other documents, and even film reels. This was a private enterprise, but with a certain official nimbus, since for example Prince Wilhelm (a brother of the crown prince and a prolific documentary filmmaker) was its patron. In 1938 it was decided that the archive could be housed at the Technical Museum in Stockholm, and it was accepted as a member of FIAF in 1946. The film companies supported the work by annual gifts. In 1964 the collection was finally transferred to the Swedish Film Institute.[61] This film archive, which functioned as an embryonic national film archive, and was to be an important collection for the Swedish Film Institute, was thus founded by cinéphiles, working in the public sphere but without governmental support.

The film culture of the Swedish interwar years was thriving through journals, film clubs and public events, and as in several contemporary European film cultures, the cinéphiles and avant-garde critics were paving the way for the institutionalization of film. The omnipresent state apparatus of the Swedish welfare state has roots way back in history, in the founding of the nation state in the early sixteenth century when, through the process of the Lutheran reformation, it became amalgamated with church. During the modernization of a former agrarian country into an industrial society, the state cooperated with popular movements and diverse civil organizations in order to promote cultural policy. The absence of a state policy for film can thus be seen as a paradox – there was an empty space where suddenly an avant-garde was able to operate and negotiate. It is noteworthy that the important question of an archival policy for film was raised within film clubs and by young writers and critics within the experimental or avant-garde film culture; they were also the ones who later tried to promote a national film school and a governmental responsibility for film art as part of the cultural heritage.

In 1932, Artur Lundkvist – who in 1968 was elected as a member of the Swedish Academy – formulated the position of the new generation thus:

> For the younger generation – the generation of cinema itself – it is natural to perceive film as a new art form, as important as other art forms. Often film is even seen as the most up to date and present means of expression, an art form created by development itself, and through its dynamics closely connected to our contemporary life. We can no longer wait for the just placement of cinema in culture as a manifestation of the contemporary creative forces and spiritual life.[62]

Notes

1. All translations are by author unless otherwise indicated.
2. Sven Stolpe. 1925. 'Filmen är framtidens konst', *Filmnyheter* 6(33), 1 and 15.
3. Elisabeth Liljedahl. 1975. *Stumfilmen i Sverige – kritik och debatt. Hur samtiden värderade den nya konstarten.* Stockholm: Proprius; Jan Olsson. 1991. 'I offentlighetens ljus – några notiser om filmstoff i dagspressen', in Jan Olsson (ed.), *I offentlighetens ljus. Stumfilmens affischer, kritiker, stjärnor och musik*, Stockholm: Symposion, 211–74; Leif Furhammar. 1991. *Filmen i Sverige. En historia i tio kapitel.* Höganäs: Wiken. These issues, and others outlined here, are also treated in Lars Gustaf Andersson, John Sundholm and Astrid Söderbergh Widding. 2010. *A History of Swedish Experimental Film Culture: From Early Animation to Video Art.* Stockholm: National Library of Sweden.
4. According to Annette Kuhn (1988. *Cinema, Censorship and Sexuality 1909–1925.* London and New York: Routledge), film censorship helped to create a public sphere for cinema, and also to create a discourse of the forbidden.
5. Olsson, 'I offentlighetens ljus', 268; Furhammar, *Filmen i Sverige*, 68.
6. Gösta Werner. 1981. 'Svenska Bios produktionspolitik fram till 1920', in Leif Furhammer (ed.), *Rörande bilder. Festskrift till Rune Waldekranz*, Stockholm: Norstedt, 160–86.
7. THE PHANTOM CARRIAGE, and especially the dream sequences by legendary cinematographer Julius Jaenzon, have in retrospect been seen as important steps in the development of an avant-garde aesthetics. See Carl Henrik Svenstedt. 2007. 'Halva historien', in *Film & TV* 1, 36–41.
8. See Bo Florin. 1997. *Den nationella stilen. Studier i den svenska filmens guldålder.* Stockholm: Aura.
9. For a critical view of the concept of 'Golden Age', see Tommy Gustafsson. 2007. *En fiende till civilisationen. Manlighet, genusrelationer, sexualitet och rasstereotyper i svensk filmkultur under 1920-talet*, Lund: Sekel.
10. Sven Stolpe. 1925. 'Modern film och gammal', *Filmjournalen* 25–26, 436; Sven Stolpe. 1926. 'Filmen och kulturen', *Filmjournalen* 11, 372; Sven Stolpe. 1926. 'En filmhögskola i Stockholm?', *Filmjournalen* 15, 490; Sven Stolpe. 1927. 'Den ryska filmen', *Filmjournalen* 2, 34; Sven Stolpe. 1927. 'Filmhjälten som blev Gud', *Filmjournalen* 8, 228.
11. Eva Kaijser. 2008. 'Gerda Marcus – "den stora tiggerskan" på Svenska Dagbladet', in Ami Lönnroth (ed.), *Empati och engagemang. En kvinnolinje i svensk journalistik*, Enhörna: Tusculum, 39–51.
12. Gerda Marcus. 1924. 'Den synliga människan eller filmens kultur', *Filmjournalen* 36, 707 and 720; Gerda Marcus. 1926. 'En rysk film som gör sensation i Tyskland', in *Filmjournalen* 9–10, 245; Gerda Marcus. 1927. 'Storstadens symfoni', *Filmjournalen* 17, 485.
13. Malte Hagener. 2007. *Moving Forward, Looking Back. The European Avant-garde and the Invention of Film Culture, 1919–1939.* Amsterdam: Amsterdam University Press, 34.
14. Peter Luthersson even argues that modernism proper never existed, at least not within literature. See Peter Luthersson. 2002. *Svensk litterär modernism: en stridsstudie.* Stockholm: Atlantis. A thorough account of the belated modernism is delivered by Bengt Lärkner. 1984. *Det internationella avantgardet 1914–1925* (Ph.D. dissertation), Malmö/Lund: Stenvall. He only deals marginally, however, with the conditions of film art.

15. Anders Wahlgren. 2007. 'Otto G. Carlsund – ett konstnärsliv', in Anders Wahlgren, Niclas Östlind and Helena Persson (eds), *Otto G. Carlsund 11.12.1897 – 25.7.1948. Konstnär, kritiker och utställningsarrangör*, Stockholm: Arena, 52. The significance of the cooperation between Léger and Carlsund is disputed. In Swedish accounts Carlsund is always mentioned as an important collaborator, but in international film literature he is more or less invisible. In a very thorough analysis of the production by Judi Freeman, the name of Carlsund is absent; instead she discusses the better-known collaborators Ezra Pound and Man Ray: Judi Freeman. 1996. 'Bridging Purism and Surrealism: The Origins and Production of Fernand Léger's Ballet Mécanique', in Rudolf E. Kuenzli (ed.), *Dada and Surrealist Film*, Cambridge, MA and London: MIT Press, 28–45. Furthermore, the most important person besides Léger is of course co-director Dudley Murphy.

16. Susan McCabe. 2005. *Cinematic Modernism:. Modernist Poetry and Film.* Cambridge and New York: Cambridge University Press, 198.

17. Erik Näslund. 2008. *Rolf de Maré. Konstsamlare, balettledare, museiskapare.* Stockholm: Langenskjöld.

18. Margareta Sörenson. 2007. 'Sverige och Svenska baletten', in Tomas Forser and Sven Åke Heed (eds), *Ny svensk teaterhistoria*, vol. 3, Hedemora: Gidlund, 46–56.

19. Näslund, *Rolf de Maré*, 292.

20. Moderna Museet. 1969. *Svenska Baletten/Les Ballets Suédois 1920–1925. Ur Dansmuséets samlingar*, Stockholm: Moderna Museet; Erik Näslund et al. 1995. *Svenska Baletten i Paris 1920–1925. Ballet Suédois*, Stockholm: Dansmuseet; Bengt Häger. 1989. *Ballets suédois*, Stockholm: Streiffert.

21. David Bordwell and Kristin Thompson. 1994. *Film History: An Introduction*, New York: McGraw-Hill, 195.

22. Börlin's career as a dancer was beginning to fade, and he wanted to start anew as a film actor. In LE VOYAGE IMAGINAIRE (1925, René Clair) he was promoted to a lead role as a clerk who travels in his dreams. He was also – together with other members of the Swedish troup – engaged in L'INHUMAINE (1924, Marcel L'Herbier), but he never successfully established himself in this new branch.

23. Peter Wollen. 2002. *Paris Hollywood: Writings on Film*, London and New York: Verso, 39–54; Louise O'Konor. 1971. *Viking Eggeling 1880–1925: Artist and Film-Maker. Life and Work.* Stockholm: Almqvist & Wiksell; Gösta Werner. 1999. 'Spearhead in a Blind Alley: Viking Eggeling's DIAGONAL SYMPHONY', in John Fullerton and Jan Olsson (eds), *Nordic Explorations: Film Before 1930*, London: J. Libbey, 232–35.

24. Hans Richter. 1949. 'Avant-Garde Film in Germany', in Roger Manvell (ed.), *Experiment in the Film*, London: Grey Walls, 221.

25. Fragment no. 6 from 'On the Spiritual Element in Man: On Different Methods of Composition', in O'Konor, *Viking Eggeling*, 96. See also R. Bruce Elder. 2007. 'Hans Richter and Viking Eggeling: The Dream of Universal Language and the Birth of The Absolute Film', in Alexander Graf and Dietrich Scheunemann (eds), *Avant-Garde Film*, Amsterdam: Rodopi, 3–53.

26. Théo van Doesburg. 1921. 'Abstracte filmbeelding', *De Stijl* 4(5), 71–75; see also Ansje van Beusekom. 2007a. 'Theo van Doesburg and Writings on Film in *De Stijl*', in Klaus Beekman and Jan de Vries (eds), *Avant-Garde and Criticism*, Amsterdam: Rodopi, 55–66; Viking Eggeling. 1921. 'Elvi fejtegetések a mozgómüvészetről', *MA* 6(8), 105–6.

27. Birger Brinck-E:son. 1923. 'Linjemusik på vita duken. "Konstruktiv film", ett intressant experiment av en svensk konstnär', *Filmjournalen* 4, 50.

28. The French title of the film is of Eggeling's origin.
29. Also in Denmark, Eggeling was used in order to promote experimental or avant-garde film culture. In 1951 Gallery Tokanten had an exhibition on Eggeling including film programmes with works by Hans Richter and Norman McLaren. The event was arranged by an association called 'International Experimental Film' (in fact the only event that the organization ever arranged) and had Hans Richter as Honorary President. See Helge Krarup and Carl Nørrested. 1986. *Eksperimentalfilm i Danmark.* København: Borgen, 30. An anecdote concerning the Eggeling heritage was told by Jonas Mekas: In 1979 a pencil drawing by Eggeling was donated to the Anthology Film Archives: 'The sale of this drawing, graciously arranged by another great Swede, Pontus Hultén, paid for one half of the purchase fee for the Second Avenue Courthouse, Anthology Archives' present headquarters'; see Jonas Mekas. 1991. 'A Word from the Curator', Jonas Mekas et al. (eds), *Swedish Avantgarde Film 1924–1990,* New York: Anthology Film Archives, 2.
30. See, for example, Gust. Magnusson. 1914. 'Futuristiska biografintryck', *Biografen* 2(22), 325–26, in which a cartoonist makes fun of the search for meaning in modern film, or the editorial comments to some collage-like drawings by artist Erik Aaes under the headline 'Expressionistiskt' in *Filmjournalen* 6 (1927) where the editor ridicules 'this all to self-assured expressionism'.
31. Deke Dusinberre. 1996. 'The Avant-Garde Attitude in the Thirties', in Michael O'Pray (ed.), *The British Avant-Garde Film 1926–1995,* Luton: University of Luton, 65–83.
32. The case of Vilhelm Moberg is interesting; he wrote scripts for film (and several of his novels were to be adapted into film), and it is claimed that he wrote a never-finished script for an experimental film, 'a *real* film', as his friend director Per Lindberg put it. See Bengt Forslund. 1998. *Vilhelm Moberg. Filmen och televisionen,* Stockholm: Carlssons, 37; and Anna-Karin Carlstoft Bramell. 2007. *Vilhelm Moberg tar ställning. En studie av hans journalistik och tidsaktuella diktning.* Stockholm: Carlssons, 130–33. This script, however, is not to be found in his archive at the National Library, Stockholm, and it probably never left his desk.
33. Artur Lundkvist. 1932. *Atlantvind.* Stockholm: A. Bonnier, 119.
34. Lundkvist, *Atlantvind,* 129.
35. Furhammar, *Filmen i Sverige,* 149–50; Carl Anders Dymling et al. (eds). 1944. *Svensk Filmindustri. Tjugufem år.* Stockholm: AB Svensk Filmindustri, 154–56.
36. Artur Lundkvist. 1966. *Självporträtt av en drömmare med öppna ögon.* Stockholm: Bonnier, 87. For a study of the production context, see Mikael Askander. 2003. *Modernitet och intermedialitet i Erik Asklunds tidiga romankonst.* Växjö: Växjö University Press 2003, 9–11; and Mikael Askander. 2001. 'Gamla stan. Reflektioner kring ett modernistiskt filmförsök', *HumaNetten* (2001), 8. Retrieved on 29 Aug. 2013 from http://lnu.se/polopoly_fs/1.26003!HumaNetten,%20Nr%208,%20v%C3%A5ren%20 2001.pdf
37. Eyvind Johnson. 2002. 'En film om Gamla stan. Förslag I. (stumfilm)', *Pequod* 31–32, 9–12; Lundkvist, *Självporträtt,* 88.
38. For an account of the City Symphony subgenre, see Alexander Graf. 2007. 'Paris – Berlin – Moscow: On the Montage Aesthetic in the City Symphony Films of the 1920s', in Alexander Graf and Dietrich Scheunemann, *Avant-Garde Film,* 77–91.
39. Lundkvist, *Självporträtt,* 88. Gösta Ekman (1890–1938), a very popular stage and film actor, most famous internationally for the title role in Faust (1926, F.W. Murnau).
40. Erik Asklund and Artur Lundkvist. 1931. 'Gamla stan', *Stockholmstidningen,* 25 October.

41. Moje Gren [Nils Edgren]. 1933. 'Filmpubliken kultiveras', *SocialDemokraten*, 3 April.
42. Liljedahl, *Stumfilmen i Sverige*, 271; Gösta Hellström. 1929. 'Djärva teorier som blivit glänsande praktik! En översikt av ryska filmen idag', *Filmjournalen* 20–22, 10–11 and 78; Gösta Hellström. 1930. 'En ukrainsk regissörskomet', *Filmjournalen* 14, 9 and 26; Gösta Hellström. 1930. 'Svart och vitt. Lotte Reiniger en sagoförtäljerska i silhuetter', *Filmjournalen* 4, 12–13 and 30; Gösta Hellström. 1930. 'En rysk realist. Alexander Room, den tredje av ryska filmens "tre stora"', *Filmjournalen* 5, 6 and 30.
43. Gösta Werner. 1979. 'En natt', in Lars Åhlander (ed.), *Svensk Filmografi 1930–1939*, Stockholm: Svenska Filminstitute, 93–95. See also Gösta Hellström. 1931. 'En natt – banbrytande?', *Filmjournalen* 11, 4–5 and 28.
44. Stig Almqvist. 1932. 'En brinnande entusiast. Gösta Hellström död – En verklig förlust för svensk film', *Filmjournalen* 51, 23; Stig Almqvist. 1947. 'Gösta Hellström – en ung filmentusiast. Till 15-årsminnet av hans bortgång', *Biografbladet* 4, 215–23; Ragnar Allberg. 1947. 'Gösta Hellström i vännernas krets. Några personliga minnen', *Biografbladet* 4, 224–27. Legendary film critic Bengt Idestam-Almquist ('Robin Hood') claimed many years later that with the death of Hellström 'the ambition for form in Swedish film [has also] died for several years to come': 1952. 'Svensk film genom tiderna', in Hugo Wortzelius and Nils Larsson (eds), *Filmboken: En bok om film och filmskapare*, Uppsala: Orbis, 161.
45. Per Olov Qvist. 1995. *Folkhemmets bilder: Modernisering, motstånd och mentalitet i den svenska 30-talsfilmen*. Lund: Arkiv, 30–36.
46. Janet Staiger. 1992. *Interpreting Films: Studies in the Historical Reception of American Cinema*. Princeton, NJ: Princeton University Press.
47. Eva Bjärlund. 1970. '30-talsdebatten om den svenska filmen', *Filmrutan* 4, 166–74; Furhammar, *Filmen i Sverige*, 127–28; Per Olov Qvist, *Folkhemmets bilder*, 106–41; Carina Sjöholm. 2003. *Gå på bio. Rum för drömmar i folkhemmets Sverige*, Stockholm and Stehag: Brutus Östling, 52–55; Tytti Soila, Astrid Söderbergh Widding and Gunnar Iversen. 1998. *Nordic National Cinemas*. London and New York: Routledge, 175–78.
48. Jan-Gunnar Lindström. 1938. 'Svensk filmstudiorörelse', in Bengt Idestam-Almquist and Ragnar Allberg (eds), *Om film. Svenska Filmsamfundets årsbok 1937–38*, Stockholm, 103–10; Gösta Werner and Per Olof Wredlund. 1952. 'Den svenska filmstudiorörelsen. Från pionjärår till studiecirkelsrutin', in Wortzelius and Larsson, *Filmboken*, 600–10; Bengt Bengtsson. 2007. 'Vad suckar gästboken? Uppsala Studenters Filmstudio som arena för konstfilmsinstitution och filmdebatt', in Per Vesterlund (ed.), *Mediala hierarkier*, Gävle: Högskolan i Gävle, 13–48; Hagener, *Moving Forward, Looking Back*, 77–120.
49. David James. 2005. *The Most Typical Avant-Garde: History and Geography of Minor Cinemas in Los Angeles*. Berkeley: University of California Press, 142; Hagener, *Moving Forward, Looking Back*, 231.
50. *Förordning angående biografföreställningar*, 1911.
51. Gösta Werner. 1952. 'Kortfilm, experimentfilm, dokumentärfilm', in *Filmboken*, 352.
52. Gösta Werner. 1935. *Förteckning over Lunds studenters filmstudios bibliotek*, Lund.
53. Gunhild Tegen. 1935. *En judisk tragedi*, Lund: Lindström. It was however the only title to be published in this ambitious enterprise.
54. Bengt Bengtsson. 2008. 'Filmstudion och drömmen om den stora uppsalafilmen: Uppsala Studenters Filmstudio som filmproducent och plantskola', in Erik Hedling and Mats Jönsson (eds), *Välfärdsbilder. Svensk film utanför biografen*, Stockholm: Statens Ljud- och Bildarkiv, 205–27.

55. Anon. 1944. 'Tio år – en cavalcade', in Ragnar Allberg, Arne Bornebusch and Bengt Idestam-Almquist (eds), *Filmboken. Svenska Filmsamfundets årsskrift 1944*, Stockholm, 17–38.

56. Arne Bornebusch. 1935. *De lever ett rikt liv. Filmdiktare.* Stockholm: Bonniers.

57. Kjell Furberg. 2000. *Svenska biografer*, Stockholm: Prisma, 63; Kurt Berglund. 1993. *Stockholms alla biografer*, Stockholm: Svenska Turistföreningen, 321–22; Bjärlund. '30-talsdebatten', 170.

58. In 1947, *Biografbladet* was even acknowledged in a review article in *Hollywood Quarterly* by Harry Hoijer, who saw *Biografbladet* as a 'serious film journal which should be of considerable interest to readers in the United States'. Harry Hoijer. 1947. 'Our Swedish Contemporary', *Hollywood Quarterly* 3(1), 100–101. Some of the issues that were reviewed by Hoijer were in fact bilingual, but the great bulk of articles over the years were in Swedish only.

59. Jon Wengström. 2008. 'Föreningen Film och Fonogram. The Forgotten Archive', *Journal of Film Preservation* 77/78, 77–81.

60. Ibid., 80.

61. Rune Waldekranz. 1982. 'Filmstudier och filmforskning. En orientering i internationell och svensk filmlitteratur', in Gösta Werner (ed.), *Svensk filmforskning*, Stockholm: Norstedt, 28–31.

62. Lundkvist, *Atlantvind*, 119.

Chapter 10

BUILDING THE INSTITUTION

Luigi Chiarini and Italian Film Culture in the 1930s

Francesco Pitassio and Simone Venturini

Fascism … is not a reactionary,
or regressive movement …
and is not hostile to modernity. …
Fascism is a revolutionary movement,
but not subversive or radical …
[it] does not tend to turn values upside down.

– Ardengo Soffici (1922)

Politics, Field, Apparatus

The 1968 Venice Film Festival was to be Luigi Chiarini's last. Having been responsible for the event since 1962, he resigned because of the protests of the leftist Italian filmmakers and students who were asking for a more prominent space for art films in the selection – protests that in a general climate of political turmoil also affected the festival. Chiarini, however, was effectively dismissed by the political apparatus that had appointed him six years earlier, as a result of the producers' pressure and of the discontent of the Venetian tourism industry. Luigi Chiarini had denied producers a role in curating the selection, and through his actions had reduced the presence of famous stars at the Lido, thus endangering the incomes of local business owners. The Roman intellectual's fate was a paradoxical one; in the 1930s he had been put in a position of power by the Fascist regime, and subsequently struggled to create a new film culture or to contribute to the training of a new generation of filmmakers.[1] This chapter aims at describing under which circumstances and through which strategies and means Luigi Chiarini could so significantly contribute to the formation of Italian film culture during Fascism. This cultural legacy was so relevant and enduring that more than forty years later Gian Piero Brunetta observed:

> In Italy, all the initiatives that were taken within film studies or to create specific professional structures can mostly be traced back to his person [Luigi Chiarini]. These initiatives were so important that in the postwar years no others could be compared with them in terms of the range of interests, the rigorous use of documents, the creation of a homogeneous cultural space.[2]

The chapter will follow two main paths. Firstly, we will reconstruct the intellectual field that Chiarini belonged to. Secondly, we will examine the apparatuses he used in his cultural policies. In outlining the intellectual field and its relationship with the field of power, we rely on Pierre Bourdieu's work. More specifically, we share the French sociologist's assumption that mechanisms of social reproduction guarantee a generational turnover and operate in different fields – among them, the intellectual one: 'Thus we are faced with several markets, with various individual market agencies competing. There is a structure in which rules, interests, and groups of interests compete: here is a field. Each field is relatively autonomous, since specific interests determine strategies that cannot be traced back to overall interests'.[3] The field is both historical and narrative; it is historically specific and it tells a story in its own right, on the struggle that took place in it:

> The field is a product of history which is itself a story ... The field is also a story. Among its qualities, the field has always an avant-garde and a rearguard: persons opposing each other in the name of a past and a future. This means that what is at stake in the internal struggle is just to know who will define the future of the field ... In this respect, the field implies the story. And the story is the struggle ... The law of the field is to push back in the past, the victory is the statement 'I am the future of your past', even if this future is a past.[4]

In the Italian intellectual field in the 1930s, Chiarini declared himself to be avant-garde, and successfully did away with competing conceptions of cinema, thanks to a complex combination of political, institutional and cultural factors. As a matter of fact, 'the intellectual field is included in a specific type of political field, that assigns to the intellectual and artistic fraction a determinate position'.[5] This social mechanism is possibly even truer when considering a totalitarian society like the one Fascism produced. Chiarini's actions will also be considered in relation to the apparatuses and practices legitimizing and articulating cinema's cultural identity. The concept of apparatus will be employed here to stress the material aspect of cinema's cultural memory.[6] Such a perspective enables us to observe Chiarini's actions within an 'economy of traces'.[7] Thus, we will consider the outcomes of his 'institutional' policies as an act of recording and writing the cinematic cultural tradition. We would like to emphasize three apparatuses that share a certain reflexivity and retrospective tension: the institution of historical and aesthetic criticism (*historical apparatus*, i.e. film history); the institution of training programmes (*pedagogical apparatus*, i.e. teaching film); and the preservation of documents (*archival apparatus*, i.e. film archiving).[8] The method that inspired Chiarini was an integrated one, combining[9] critical and historical research with pedagogical and archival methods. His publishing and teaching activities, the books he edited or promoted, the films he preserved or used, the film anthologies he directed or produced all complemented each other and helped to build one of the three apparatuses on which he based his policies.[10]

Intellectuals and Functions

The intellectual activities that made Chiarini such a pivotal figure of film culture took place in the cultural scene of 1930s Italy which was significantly marked by a general political attempt to rule culture itself, and thus garner the support of the intellectual classes. Having silenced the political opposition, the Fascist regime wanted to diminish the areas of dissidence, while using intellectuals as mediators between state and society. As the historian Gabriele Turi noted: 'In the fascist period, during which a modernization process by authoritarian means takes place in Italy, the State faces increased needs: beyond violence and coercion, it is forced to look for the consent of the masses and therefore attributes intellectual functions to "specialized categories", mediating between State and society'.[11] In order to reinforce the general consensus and at the same time justify and conceal its repressive policies, the Fascist regime focussed on the cultural sphere, significantly increasing the state's financial contribution to cultural affairs, and founding a number of new cultural institutions. In doing so, the Fascist regime on the one hand won the approval of many intellectuals from different backgrounds; on the other hand, it directly involved them by appointing them to powerful positions.

> Many contemporary observers missed Fascism's demonstrable skill ... of combining force and consensus in giving birth to institutions with the purpose of centralizing and organizing the most varied cultural forces; they also missed the tendency among many intellectuals ... of separating ... culture and politics, fooling themselves into hoping they would be able to continue nurturing the former even within the regime's institutions, without becoming politically 'contaminated'.[12]

This strategy produced the 'functional intellectual', who submitted himself to the state's highest needs. It is no surprise that at the time, such a figure was called an 'intellectual worker', implying that the function within the system is more important than the personal freedom of the individual. This process was associated with a general restructuring of society in the name of 'corporativism', a political doctrine that purported to be a true Fascist idea and a challenge both to capitalism and to the Soviet model. Its central theme was 'the attempt to absorb the different social articulations into the State ... Its jurists and theoreticians saw the project of a new juridical order based on corporativism as an innovative political project; at its centre was the state as the only subject that could legitimately create a society'.[13]

In the processes described above, Giovanni Gentile played a paramount role. Gentile was Minister of Education (1922–1924), author of the Manifesto of the Fascist Intellectuals (1925), president of the National Institute of Fascist Culture (1925–1937), and chairman of the scientific board of the *Italian Encyclopedia* (1925–1938).[14] Among the many noteworthy roles and functions the philosopher assumed in his dialogue with Fascism, Gentile was probably the most relevant theoretician of the totalitarian state, conceived as an entity that transcended individuals: 'Foundation of the Fascist doctrine is the idea of the State, of its essence, its duties, its tasks. In Fascism, the State is an absolute: individuals and groups are merely relative. Individuals and groups can be thought of only as part of the State'.[15] It is well known that the Sicilian philosopher wrote the preface to Luigi Chiarini's first cinema book.[16] Usually, what is stressed is Chiarini's early theoretical alignment with Gentile's positions, and particularly with his 'actual idealism'.[17] We will discuss this later on. For the moment, we would like to address the importance of this philosopher in determining Luigi Chiarini's activities as an institutional intellectual, a cultural worker who operated as an institutional agent, managed to institutionalize cinema, and who built some institutions essential to film culture.

Luigi Chiarini appears to have responded to two different demands coming from the field of power of his time, one ideological, the other institutional. On the one hand, the Roman intellectual embodied the regime's effort to modernize the nation, turning from more traditional literary criticism to the cinema. On the other hand, Luigi Chiarini identified his goals with those of the institutions he chaired, and achieved them through the establishment that he had helped to consolidate in the first place.

Fascism explicitly aimed at negotiating a palatable solution to the contradictions of modernity, translating foreign impulses and trends into vernacular art, promoting national cultural production abroad, mediating between recent experiments and the Italian humanist tradition. In this respect, Chiarini played an important role as a cultural operator, both before and after he devoted himself to cinema.[18] Moreover, cinema itself was a device of the modernization put in place by Fascism, which from 1934 onwards established a General Film Direction (Direzione Generale della Cinematografia), with the aim of supporting, coordinating and promoting national cinema. Within this overall effort, the establishment of a film culture appears to have been one of the main tasks, as Luigi Freddi explained in his 1933 report for the Press Bureau, an institution that answered to the Prime Minister's office:

> Such a diffused mentality, mocking the value of a specific [film] culture that is based on scholarship, and that is more valuable the more vast and profound it is, is retrograde and at odds with the examples coming from abroad; it is an anarchist, confused and unconscious mentality.[19]

Freddi's report expresses at least three aims: a need to modernize the film sector and bring it in line with current trends; a demand to regulate the national cinema, coordinating film culture with producers and the market; and a wish to create a specific filmic knowledge. All these goals were to help to bring about a national cinema, as Chiarini confirmed: 'The State's direct involvement, through *competent persons*, must mathematically guarantee that the *old film world* is doomed to disappear; it will be replaced with *new and fresh energies*. What is at stake here is the *artistic dignity of Italian cinema'.*[20] Thus we have here the themes we mentioned above: generational turnover, modernization, and nation.

Figure 10.1 Building the pedagogical apparatus: Luigi Chiarini (Rome, 1930s) surrounded by CSC students. [Centro Sperimentale di Cinematografia – Archivio Fotografico, Rome]

Modern Institutions

The first half of the 1930s was a period during which Italian film became the subject of a lively debate. For a long time, the medium had received relatively little attention; now, it began entering the cultural discourse, first at the margins, then moving towards its centre. Well-established cultural journals and magazines were now writing about cinema – prompted by new noteworthy art films such as those by Alessandro Blasetti – about cinema's transition to sound and about changes in the structure of film production. With a delay of almost ten years compared to the French, German or Russian debate, Italian intellectuals discovered cinema, began enquiring into its ontology and comparing it with traditional arts. For instance, between the 1920s and 1930s the well-established literary journal *La fiera letteraria/L'Italia letteraria* devoted a section exclusively to cinema;[21] and in the early 1930s a philosophical circle that also published a journal, *Il convegno*, organized a film club and published a supplement to the journal entitled *Cine-convegno*, with contributions inspired by the thought of Benedetto Croce, the most influential

Italian philosopher at the time.[22] A similar role was played by one of the main organs of the regime, the cultural magazine *Quadrivio*, founded by Telesio Interlandi, and belonging to the 'intransigent' area of Fascist culture. *Quadrivio*'s editor-in chief was none other than Luigi Chiarini, who remained in the position throughout the decade. Some essays that were published in this weekly introduced the European debate on cinema to an Italian audience, through references to Rudolf Arnheim, Béla Balázs, Sergej Ejzenštejn, Lev Kulešov, Vsevolod Pudovkin or Hans Richter.[23] Moreover, given its political relevance, the magazine helped to institutionalize cinema. It is not surprising that a whole issue was devoted to the medium in 1935, some months after the creation of the General Film Direction and before the appointment of Luigi Chiarini as director and general commissioner for the Centro Sperimentale di Cinematografia (CSC), the newly constituted film academy in Rome.[24] Chiarini implemented the general aims of Fascism in film culture: he coordinated, rationalized and promoted what had previously been a rather fragmented area. He was the right man in the right place, with a vast cultural background, managing skills and political acumen. The ultimate step that enabled Chiarini, the intellectual, to realize his ambitious goals was his appointment to the CSC. In his role as its general commissioner, Chiarini managed to perform various tasks and fulfil different functions, effectively acting outside the law, since the bill constituting the CSC was only passed in 1942.[25] As general commissioner, Chiarini designed curricula, supervised the film studies journal *Bianco e nero* and the volumes linked to the journal, and made suggestions for preservation policies to be implemented by the film archive that was part of the film academy. In addition, he continued to pursue his theoretical endeavours, outlined his aesthetic and political credo, and delineated his position within the Italian intellectual field.

Culture-Building: Film Theory as an Institution

Luigi Chiarini's attempt to create an Italian film culture was intertwined with his goal of promoting film aesthetics. This latter purpose was built around three ideas, namely to insist on the medium's artistic autonomy, to encourage a comparison with other art forms, and to highlight its political value.[26] From Chiarini's perspective, establishing cinema as an art form was the main priority: 'Most of the diseases that actually affect cinema derive from the fact that common sense does not consider it as an art in its own right'.[27] Within the Italian culture of idealism, the effort to establish cinema as an autonomous artistic genre required a demonstration of several things, namely turning its techno-logical base into a neutral factor, the identification of an anthropomor-phic entity responsible for endowing the artwork with meaning, an underlying unity of the work of art, and evidence of an organic inten-tion at its foundation. In the authoritative words of Giovanni Gentile, the technological obstacle was solved thus:

> In creation, the universe as antecedent is annihilated, or if you want, is transfigured: it becomes the artist's world, infinite. The technique ceases to be, and art begins ... The problem is solved by overcoming or annihilat-ing the technique: this is the spectacle where the audience no longer sees the mechanism that produces it; it is the man that the audience sees, there before its eyes, alive, not on the screen but in the world.[28]

Because man is a moral creature, the artist is responsible for the work of art; he is the source of its expressiveness and of the unity of content and form. As a matter of fact, artworks centre on the subject of morals, and this moral undercurrent conveys the artwork's identity:

> Morality, as we understand it today, ... constitutes a man's, the artist's very personality. They are the sum of the ideals he lives and struggles for, they are what makes him act in society, the impulse that pushes him to avail himself of the artistic form to give life ... to what he feels ... There is no film of any artistic value without a fundamental theme or thesis that represents almost its soul and deep motivation.[29]

Morals are an expression of individual perspective and feelings, and as such they need to be properly reflected in the work of art. In the words of Telesio Interlandi, the director of *Quadrivio* and, in later years, of the obscenely racist *La difesa della razza*: 'Today, the whole cinema is political, in the widest and noblest sense of the word, because it cor-responds to a specific life or world conception that the film's author wants to spread to the audience, with the declared or implied intention of seizing the audience's spirit and prompting it to identify with his feelings'.[30] At the same time, morals bridge the gap between subject and society, and determine the political value of the film. Thus, according to Gentile, morals realize the attitude of the individual, merging it with a transcendent organism, namely the state that rules society.

In pursuing his project, Chiarini wisely entered into a dialogue with categories, theoretical frameworks and thinkers that were fully anchored in Italian cultural life: firstly, Giovanni Gentile, and secondly, but no less significantly, Francesco De Sanctis. It should be further noted that rarely were two intellectuals as closely identified with the same institution, having both served as minister of education. Through Gentile, Chiarini adapted De Sanctis's notion of 'absolute form', 'the only form and the only content that count in art and are indivisible: the artist's feeling and its expression'.[31] Such references, and others stemming from the Italian humanistic tradition, enabled the Roman intellectual to introduce European film theoreticians and specific conceptions of the cinema to an Italian audience. Chiarini's project was not about constructing an original film theory; rather, he wished to blend national epistemological and political traditions with foreign contributions, both in a geographical and in a theoretical sense.

In order to achieve this goal, he launched an encompassing publishing project, translating recent theoretical contributions, encouraging a national debate on film, and recovering older writings on aesthetic theory that could inform contemporary reflection on cinema. The main organs were the monthly journal *Bianco e nero*, the first Italian journal entirely devoted to film studies, and the book series associated with the journal, *Edizioni di Bianco e nero*. This balance between traditional culture and film culture was also reflected in the CSC's curriculum, to which *Bianco e nero* and its book series were linked. Thus, Chiarini recovered the main themes of European film theory of the 1920s and incorporated them into a rather eclectic system. He explored issues such as film acting and the value of the close-up, drawing on the thought of Béla Balázs and Vsevolod Pudovkin;[32] the revelatory power of the cinematic image, inspired by the French debate on 'photogénie'; the comparison between film and theatre; the filmic reality as a reality in its own right that is commensurate with the medium's technical means, an echo of Rudolf Arnheim's positions;[33] and most of all, evidently inspired by the Soviet debate, film editing as the signifying practice that entitles cinema to the status of a fully fledged art form:

> There is a chance to realize the cosmic feeling we talk about when discussing art. *Cinematically*, therefore with a fully original form, independent of other art forms. Here, we need to determine the cinematic creative moment that can be identified with artistic creation. We mean the moment when we go beyond simple and mechanical reproduction and enter into the realm of art. In my opinion, such a moment occurs in a process that the industry has rather neglected and reduced to a mechanical operation: editing.[34]

Luigi Chiarini's achievement was to provide a fairly conservative Italian culture with new theoretical tools, heterogeneous as they may have been. This operation relied on the already mentioned blending of tradition, modernity and politics, a constellation that exactly describes the Italian intellectual field during the Fascist 1930s. For this reason, an anthology of theoretical writings edited by Chiarini and Barbaro assembles texts by such different writers as Balázs and Goebbels, Interlandi and Ejzenštejn.[35] What might today appear like a disconcerting association, or as mere political tactics, is actually the result of a specific culture at a specific stage – or it reflects the narrative of a field, to put it in Bourdieu's terms. Chiarini successfully struggled for cinema to become an institution, and to overcome a conservative concept of art as well as the short-sighted interests of the producers; this meant acknowledging cinema as an art form. But cinema was nevertheless a mass art, destined for popular diffusion; it was also an industrial one. These features induced the Roman intellectual to recognize the relevance of politics: cinema's aesthetic and largely communicative potential could be fruitfully realized as long as it remained subjected to moral control, thus becoming an instance of political expression. The industrial character of film was indeed a necessary evil: 'Film is art, cinema is an industry', as Chiarini famously observed.[36]

If cinema was connected to this origin, politics could provide redemption: the problem arose because of the constraints the free market placed on film production, and did not concern production per se.

> Industrial rationality affects the artistic creation, it limits, destroys, depresses … Industrial rationality encroaches on the artistic one from the outside, replaces it … Everyone knows that the industry is based upon *standardization* and *typification*, since its consistent law is to increase production.[37]

But Fascism was intended to solve modern aporias. In the realm of economics, its answer was corporativism, which Chiarini adapted for film production.

> Cinema's current deficiencies stem from the capitalist system. Now, this can be explained in other countries, but cannot be permitted in Italy, where corporativism has definitively outstripped capitalism. This means subjecting producers to regulations and including them in the life of the State, subordinating their interests to the general ones.[38]

Thus, the state controls and rationalizes the power of cinema, both in its trade and in its political meaning; it nurtures film as art, considering it to be a morally significant artwork, thus setting it apart from cheap commercial products such as Hollywood screwball or Central

European comedies. This clear aversion to a specific genre, and a preference for dramatic works and artworks, was echoed in postwar neorealist film production and criticism that constituted a true national film culture. Luigi Chiarini's project proved successful indeed.

Exhibiting History: Film History as an Institution

In order to establish cinema as an art, Chiarini had to provide it with an artistic past. Moreover, in order to establish Italian cinema as an art, an earlier period of glory had to be discovered. Therefore, a historical perspective on cinema must privilege a specific stylistic approach; for this reason, scholars must reflect on film texts. Cinema is an art, and as such embodies a nation; besides, according to Chiarini, cinema as an art is an Italian invention.

> Cinema has falsely been considered an international art, because of the universality of the visual language, and of the easy access this provides to international trade ... If one art exists where one can or should feel a peculiar national character, that is cinema ... Film as art was born in Italy; ... foreigners continuously drew on it.[39]

This perspective responded to a general political and institutional need. On 22 March 1935 an exhibition in Rome commemorated the fortieth anniversary of cinema. As a recent commentator observed, 'The fortieth anniversary of cinema officially marks the birth of film history [in Italy]',[40] celebrating 'not only the beginning of an institutional film history, but of a Eurocentric one as well'.[41] Generally speaking, the fortieth anniversary was the first time the institutional foundation of film culture in Italy was brought into full display. Through the monumental and spectacular forms typical of Fascism, the festivities helped to invent a tradition and asserted the historical supremacy of Italian cinema; thus, the history of cinema became socially consolidated. Lastly, the event gave legitimacy to the new General Film Direction and its main representatives: Freddi and Chiarini.

Chiarini composed some writings on this occasion, as well as editing a film anthology (together with Barbaro), that was screened as part of the celebration: *Selezione e comparazione cronologica di brani di film italiani e stranieri* (Chronological selection and comparison of clips from Italian and foreign films). Two features in Chiarini's writings have to be stressed in order to fully understand their function in the context of film history. Firstly, according to Chiarini, the state intervention coordinated by the General Film Direction finally led to the Italian film renaissance,[42] overcoming both 'practice' and 'intellectualism': two characteristics that had negatively affected Italian filmmaking and reflection. Secondly, Italian cinema possessed 'historical supremacy'. In the mid-1930s, around the time of the fortieth anniversary, Chiarini, with Umberto Barbaro and Corrado Pavolini – all then teaching at the CSC – 'invented' an Italian cinema tradition. This was based, thanks to textual collation, on film genres, style and language evolution. The overlapping of the these two themes – state intervention and film history – proves the twofold principle underlying Chiarini's institutional activity: on the one hand, a *project*, based on financial and managerial state support, to select and train a new generation of artistic and technical personnel; on the other hand, a *retrospection*, based on a historical-aesthetic tradition that constitutes a national film culture within and without the industry.[43]

The fortieth anniversary marked the regime's endorsement of some 'conceptual clouds' widespread in Italy between the 1920s and the 1930s,[44] followed by a period of substantial censorship,[45] and finally by their overcoming.

From a methodological perspective, it should be remarked that such an overcoming happens because of a new attitude towards film history: besides a *monumental iconography* and a *memorial hagiography*, film history also refers to a concrete preservation activity, as well as a first critical revision of the documentary traces.[46] Together with Barbaro, Pasinetti and Pavolini, Chiarini fully understood and supported the archival and philological trends that were emerging in the 1930s; this is evident in his writings, where concepts such as 'trace' and 'document' frequently come up. Chiarini was clearly aware of the principles that governed the institution and functioning of cultural memory.[47] But some considerations concerning the document/monument relationship might be in order when describing the *Selezione*, a collation that is not exclusively historical in nature, but is informed by theoretical ideas, connecting archival and film theory. This attempt to produce a filmed history should be related to two previous examples: firstly, the efforts to develop a film theory between the 1910s and the 1920s that resorted to a comparative study of images to prove a hypothesis; and secondly, the first film anthologies.[48]

Pasinetti's *Storia del cinema dalle origini a oggi* (Film History, from its Origins to the Present, 1939) provides further evidence of Chiarini's interest in comparative approaches. In his preface to the volume, he deplores the 'obstacles to viewing works of film', and the lack of

Figure 10.2 Building the conceptual apparatus – sober book covers for a film theory and history on the rise: Francesco Pasinetti, *Storia del cinema dalle origini a oggi* (1939), left; Luigi Chiarini, *Cinematografo* (1935), right.

'film archives or complete collections of the most important films'.[49] Moreover, commenting on Pasinetti's volume, Chiarini praises it for including information concerning 'the companies or institutions of film preservation'.[50] Thus an addendum containing information for tracing films responded to the needs of researchers and teachers; these were of the utmost importance to Chiarini, since he sought to provide film culture with a historical and documentary base.

Conventions and Experiments:
The Film Academy as an Institution

When the Fascist regime founded the CSC, it provided Italian cinema with a curriculum for its future artistic and technical personnel. The name of the academy was Chiarini's suggestion. Later on, the Roman intellectual declared: 'This institution ... is not exactly and solely a school, but a place for experimenting, researching, inquiring, and for film culture'.[51]

Together with the Cineguf (Fascist University Cinema Groups) and the Littoriali dell'arte (cultural competitions), the CSC cultivated the creative and intellectual resources of its members. But the CSC was not limited to its professional training mission, but was based on a wider pedagogical project.[52] As Chiarini then commented, 'therefore, the basis for all the courses ... will be historical and theoretical criticism ... Through this method, trends in film theory were conceived and promoted at the Centro Sperimentale di Cinematografia in Italy; today, these are a common heritage'.[53] From 1935 onwards, Chiarini put in place a curriculum that was 'based more on history than practice';[54] as a matter of fact, 'the turn in the school balance happened when the curriculum started including classes in general culture, beginning 1935';[55] at the same time, the school developed a plan 'to prepare and publish textbooks for all courses'.[56] In 1939, the CSC's curriculum included a class on 'Film Culture' on Mondays, and a screening of masterpieces on Saturday afternoons. In the first two years, 1935–1937, the classes in film history and film aesthetics made up 10 to 25 per cent of the total teaching time.

Another privileged feature of this vast educational project was the conferences that were realized together with the Cineguf. In 1939, conferences on film culture took place in Rome, Naples and Florence. During these events, CSC instructors and *Bianco e nero* contributors – Chiarini, Barbaro, May and Pasinetti – presented their research in film history and film aesthetics, gave talks on film education, and screened clips, anthologies and masterpieces.

Film Archive: Film as an Institution

Chiarini wanted the newly created film culture to have a historical perspective. This meant that the relevant historical documents had to be recovered and interpreted. In order to fully develop film studies and transmit the relevant knowledge, the creation of a film archive became essential. In 1934 people had already addressed such demands to the state, namely the Cineteca Nazionale (National Film Archive).[57] If Barbaro thought of the archive as a canon, and Pavolini as a collection, Chiarini from 1935 on conceived it as a tool serving higher educational purposes. The responsibility for programming and granting passive access to the film collection was delegated to the Cineguf.

The regulations governing access to the CSC's archive highlight its underlying cultural policy. In 1939 films were made available for individual screenings, and a full list of the archive's holdings was published. This amounted to an institutional statement that promoted 'active' access to the library and to the archival collections. In this respect, Chiarini's credo significantly differed from the policies of other institutions of film preservation, such as the Cineteca Italiana in Milan.[58] Chiarini never nurtured a fetishist conception of the film as an artefact. He instead thought of cinema as a range of examples, a thesaurus that could be drawn on; he did not think of it as a heritage or a precious treasure,[59] although he expressed his preferences and aversions clearly enough.

Film was a key feature of film culture in the 1930s;[60] Chiarini's thinking as well as his practical activities were based on a broad conception of film as an 'icon' and as a 'document'. Consequently, the film archive is just one aspect of a larger institution and apparatus, the General Film Direction; it is neither autonomous nor central for transmitting knowledge and expertise. Freddi and Chiarini wanted the CSC to perform this crucial function, and possibly also to be responsible for the archival work.

In conclusion, we might observe that the event that brought an end to this policy of film preservation was at the same time symbolic and concrete. On 17 November 1943 the German authorities confiscated more than three hundred film copies stored at the CSC: 20th Century Fox negatives and positives, short films, and some hundred titles that belonged to the CSC. The films never made it to their destination, Berlin.[61] One might consider the disappearance of films preserved in just one copy as a sacrifice, an act and a form of sacralization of the national cinema that transforms it into a myth and a monument.[62] In the postwar years the documentary approach to film history – profane, laical, public and open – was quickly abandoned, in favour of a perspective that was sacral, believing and, in some respects, private. A new film culture arose from the ashes of the old one.

Notes

This contribution was jointly drafted by the two authors. Together, they wrote parts 1 and 5; Francesco Pitassio wrote parts 2 to 4, and Simone Venturini wrote parts 6 and 7.

1. On the 1968 edition of the Venice film festival, see Luigi Chiarini. 1969. *Un Leone e altri animali*. Milan: Sugar; Stefano Della Casa. 2002. 'La contestazione a Venezia', in Gianni Canova (ed.), *Storia del cinema italiano. 1965–1969*, Venice: Marsilio, 356–57; Giacomo Manzoli. 2009. 'Il carnevale di Venezia', *Bianco e nero*, 70(563), 40–49.

2. Gian Piero Brunetta. 1972. *Intellettuali cinema e propaganda tra le due guerre*. Bologna: Patron, 158. See also Gian Piero Brunetta. 1993. *Storia del cinema italiano, vol. 2, Il cinema del regime 1929–1945*. Rome: Riuniti, 45–51. A general survey on the Roman intellectual is Orio Caldiron (ed.). 2011. *Luigi Chiarini, 1900–1975. 'Il film è un'arte, il cinema un'industria'*, Rome: Centro Sperimentali di Cinematografia.

3. Marco d'Eramo. 1978. 'Il disinteresse paga. Introduzione alla sociologia degli intellettuali di Pierre Bourdieu', in Pierre Bourdieu, *Campo del potere e campo intellettuale*, Cosenza, 12–13.

4. Pierre Bourdieu. 1978. 'Tra struttura e libertà. Conversazione con Marco d'Eramo', in ibid., 46–47.

5. Pierre Bourdieu. 1971. 'Champ du pouvoir, champ intellectuel et habitus de classe', *Scolies* 1, 7–26; Italian trans. 'Campo intellettuale, campo del potere e habitus di classe', in ibid., 63.

6. See Giorgio Agamben. 2009. 'What Is an Apparatus?', in *What Is an Apparatus?*, Stanford, CA: Stanford University Press, 1–25. See also Maurizio Ferraris. 2009. *Documentalità. Perché è necessario lasciar tracce*, Rome: Laterza, and the main writings that Régis Debray devoted to mediological transmission.

7. By an 'economy of traces' we mean: 'Chaque religion, idéologie ou doctrine dominante adopte une certaine économie des traces, qui fixe des pratiques et des significations, en ordonnant l'enregistrement, le stockage et la circulation des inscriptions … les traces témoignent ainsi d'une organisation du collectif par l'organisation de la matière'. See Louise Merzeau. 1999. 'Du Monument au document', *Cahiers de médiologie* 7, 47.

8. According to an interesting definition of the heritage apparatus, as constituted between the 1920s and the 1930s, it is composed of 'the sum of three sets of phenomena gradually introduced during the 1920s and 1930s: the exhibition apparatus (film programs, retrospectives, exhibitions) … the archival apparatus (archives and museums) … the publishing apparatus (film history, catalogs, filmographies)'. See Natacha Laurent and Christophe Gauthier. 2007. 'Zoom Arrière: Une tentative pour incarner une idée de cinémathèque', *Journal of Film Preservation* 74/75, 10.

9. See Elena Mosconi. 2006. *L'impressione del film. Contributi per una storia culturale del cinema italiano 1895–1945*. Milan: V&P. Some years later, Chiarini thought of his past activity as an integrated system based on the 'critical method'. See Luigi Chiarini. 1954. *Il film nella battaglia delle idee*, Milan: Fratelli Bocca.

10. For instance, in the preface to his 1941 essay, the author states: 'This book … collects the notes of the lectures I gave at the Centro Sperimentale di Cinematografia'. And commenting on Pasinetti's film history, Chiarini declares: 'Besides cultural needs, his film history responds to pedagogical ones'. See respectively Luigi Chiarini. 1941. *Cinque capitoli sul film*. Rome: Edizioni italiane, 14; Chiarini, *Il film nella battaglia*, 279.

11. Gabriele Turi. 2002. *Lo stato educatore. Politica e intellettuali nell'Italia fascista*. Rome: Laterza, 19.

12. Ibid., 58–59.

13. Alessandra Tarquini. 2011. *Storia della cultura fascista*. Milan: Il mulino, 141.

14. For a detailed description of the role of Giovanni Gentile in fascist culture and his influence, see Alessandra Tarquini. 2009. *Il Gentile dei fascisti. Gentiliani e antigentiliani nel regime fascista*. Bologna: Il mulino.

15. Giovanni Gentile. 1934. 'Idee fondamentali', in Benito Mussolini, *La dottrina del fascismo. Con una storia del movimento fascista di Gioacchino Volpe*, Milan: Hoepli, 1.

16. Giovanni Gentile. 1935. 'Prefazione', in Luigi Chiarini. 1934a. *Cinematografo*, Rome: Cremonese.

17. See for instance Ernesto G. Laura. 1962. 'Luigi Chiarini e il film come assoluta forma', *Bianco e nero* 23/7–8 (July–August), 18–66; Brunetta, *Intellettuali*.

18. A careful and rich depiction of Chiarini's role in Fascist modernity can be found in Ruth Ben-Ghiat. 2001. *Fascist Modernities. Italy 1922–1945*, Berkeley: University of California Press.

19. Luigi Freddi. 1994. 'Rapporto sulla cinematografia' (1933), in Luigi Freddi, *Il cinema. Il governo dell'immagine*, 2nd edn, Rome: Centro sperimentale di cinematografia, 208.

20. Chiarini, *Cinematografo*, 11 [Emphasis added].

21. Some of this heightened attention to cinema was due to the (partial) translation of Béla Balázs into Italian. See Béla Balázs. 1930. 'Lo spirito del film', *L'Italia letteraria* 2(46) (16 November), 5. But see also the rather clumsy attempt to conjugate the philosophy of Benedetto Croce with the technological form of expression, in Alberto Consiglio. 1931. 'Per un'estetica del cinema', *L'Italia letteraria* 3(40) (4 October), 5; Alberto Consiglio. 1931. 'Per un'estetica del cinema (II)', *L'Italia letteraria* 3(41) (11 October), 5; Alberto Consiglio. 1931. 'Per un'estetica del cinema (III)', *L'Italia letteraria* 3(42) (18 October), 5.

22. See for instance Carlo Ludovico Ragghianti. 1933. 'Cinematografo rigoroso', *Cine-convegno* 1(4/5) (25 June), 69–92; Alberto Consiglio. 1933. 'Estetica generale ed estetica del cinema', *Cine-convegno* 1(6) (25 October), 102–13.

23. See, for instance, Eugenio Giovannetti. 1933. 'Il colore come mistero', *Quadrivio* 1(2) (13 August), 11; Leo Longanesi. 1933. 'Il cinema delle intenzioni e dei sentimenti', *Quadrivio* 1(3) (20 August), 7; Umberto Barbaro. 1934. 'Abbasso il cinematografo', *Quadrivio* 2(37) (8 July), 2; Umberto Barbaro. 1933. 'Pende al servizio della supermarionetta', *Quadrivio* 2(40) (29 July), 9.

24. *Quadrivio* 3(10) (6 January 1935).

25. Some interesting reflections on the changes in Chiarini's career that originated in this late approval are to be found in Ernesto G. Laura. 1992. 'Luigi Chiarini: un teorico si fa regista', in Andrea Martini (ed.), *La bella forma. Poggioli, I calligrafici e dintorni*, Venice: Marsilio, 121–34.

26. A claim for cinema artistic autonomy was made quite early by comparing it with theatre. See Luigi Chiarini. 1934b. 'Teatro e Cinematografo (appunti)', *Quadrivio* 2(50) (7 October), 3.

27. Chiarini, *Cinematografo*, 71.

28. Giovanni Gentile, 'Prefazione', in ibid., 4–5. Later on, Chiarini also confirmed this position. See Chiarini, *Cinque capitoli*, 25–26. See also a later article by Chiarini in which he states: 'Cinema's problem does not substantially differ from other arts; therefore, it is mostly a problem of taste, sensibility, culture, even technique, not in a trivial functional sense, but rather where its artistic expressiveness is concerned'. Luigi Chiarini. 1937. 'Didattica del cinema', *Bianco e nero* 1(3) (March), 8.

29. Chiarini, *Cinematografo*, 46–47.

30. Telesio Interlandi. 1935. 'Chi ha paura del cinema politico?', *Quadrivio* 3(36) (7 July), 1.

31. Chiarini, *Cinque capitoli*, 12.

32. Both Balázs and Pudovkin were translated into Italian from the early 1930s onwards, thanks to the mediating role of Chiarini's colleague and friend, Umberto Barbaro. The two film theoreticians constituted a basis for the national discussion, and were of particular relevance in the teaching at the Centro Sperimentale di Cinematografia. Barbaro prepared two anthologies with the writings of the Russian theoretician:

Film e fonofilm, Rome, 1935; and *L'attore nel film*, Rome, 1939. This latter was part of a series published in relation with the activity of the journal *Bianco e nero*, that included also other international contributions, such as Raymond Spottiswoode. 1938. *La grammatica del film*. Rome: Bianco e nero. The Hungarian theoretician was at first partially published in cultural journals such as *L'Italia letteraria*, and then mostly in *Bianco e nero*.

On film acting, Barbaro and Chiarini edited an anthology, in the same series containing the Pudovkin anthology: Umberto Barbaro and Luigi Chiarini (eds). 1938. *L'attore. Saggio di antologia critica*. Rome: Bianco e nero. Later on, they added to this anthology with two special issues of *Bianco e nero*, focused on the theme: *Bianco e nero* 4(7/8) (July/August 1938); *Bianco e nero* 5(1) (January 1941). On the influence of the two theoreticians on Barbaro's thought and the forthcoming neorealism, see Gian Piero Brunetta. 1969. *Umberto Barbaro e l'idea di neorealismo (1930–1943)*, Padova: Liviana.

33. The German theoretician fled Nazi Germany and went to Italy, where he cooperated with the Centro Sperimentale di Cinematografia. His Italian writings have been collected in Rudolf Arnheim. 2009. *I baffi di Charlot. Scritti italiani sul cinema (1932–1938)*, ed. Adriano D'Aloia, Turin: Kaplan.

34. Chiarini, *Cinematografo*, 27–28.

35. Luigi Chiarini and Umberto Barbaro (eds). 1939. *Problemi del film*, Rome: Bianco e nero.

36. Luigi Chiarini. 1938. 'Il film è un'arte, il cinema un'industria', *Bianco e nero* 2(7) (July), 3–8.

37. Ibid., 5.

38. Chiarini, *Cinematografo*, 66.

39. Ibid., 38 and 101–102.

40. Mosconi, *impressione del film*, 225.

41. Luca Mazzei. 2009. 'Luigi Chiarini alla Mostra e il primato morale, civile e cinematografico degli italiani', *Bianco e nero* 70(562) (January–April), 11. See also the links with the exhibition celebrating the tenth anniversary of the Fascist regime (1932), as well as those commemorating the fortieth cinema anniversary in Germany. On the first ones, see Claudio Fogu. 2002. 'Decennale', in Victoria De Grazia and Sergio Luzzatto (eds), *Dizionario del fascismo*, vol. 1, Turin: Einaudi, 397–400; Emilio Gentile. 1993. *Il culto del littorio. La sacralizzazione della politica nell'Italia fascista*. Rome: Laterza.

42. See also the contributions of Massimo Bontempelli, Emilio Cecchi, and Luigi Freddi in *40 anniversario della cinematografia (1895–1935)*, Rome, 1935.

43. For a definition of such activity, see Mazzei, 'Chiarini alla Mostra'. Cf. with Silvio Alovisio and Luca Mazzei. 2011. '"The Star that Never Sets": The Historiographic Canonisation of Silent Italian Cinema', in Pietro Bianchi, Giulio Bursi and Simone Venturini (eds), *Il canone cinematografico/The Film Canon*, Udine: Forum 2011, 393–404; Malte Hagener. 2011. 'Inventing a Past, Imagining a Future: The Discovery and Institutionalisation of Film History in the 1930s', *Cinema & Cie* 16/17 (Spring–Fall), 29–37.

44. See Mosconi, *impressione del film*, 226.

45. A methodological censorship – or at least a removal – banished the first film history ever written in Italian for a long time: Ettore Maria Margadonna. 1932. *Cinema: ieri e oggi*. Milan: Domus. The volume was censored because it gave little space to Italian cinema, it privileged a perspective combining a mediological (and industrial) framework with an aesthetic one; and it stemmed from literary and philosophical circles, such as the already mentioned *Cine-convegno*, that were marginalized

because of their intellectual attitude. There is evidence of the long-lasting influence of Chiarini's institutional activity in the postwar history of film theories from which such intellectual experiences were removed: Guido Aristarco. 1951. *Storia delle teoriche del film*. Turin: Einaudi. Such experiences as those of Antonello Gerbi and Giacomo Debenedetti were reintegrated in the second edition of Aristarco's text, in 1960.

46. See Chiarini, *Cinematografo*, 102. ['Since I could not trace Guazzoni's glorious *Quo vadis?*, I started my selection with *Cabiria*'.]

47. Louise Merzeau. 2006. 'Mémoire', *Médium* 9: 'La mémoire est toujours *des deux côtés*: du côté de la culture (traditions et commémorations) comme de la technique (supports et systèmes d'archivage); du côté de la matière organisée (la trace) comme de l'organisation matérialisée (institutions et politiques mémorielles)'.

48. We are here referring to Ricciotto Canudo's film anthologies. But in particular, see Trond Lundemo. 2010. 'Film Theory as Archive Theory', in Francesco Casetti, Jane Gaines and Valentina Re (eds), *Dall'inizio, alla fine. Teorie del cinema in prospettiva / In the Very Beginning, at the Very End: Film Theories in Perspective*, Udine: Forum, 33–38.

49. Luigi Chiarini. 1939. 'Prefazione', in Francesco Pasinetti, *Storia del cinema dalle origini a oggi*, Rome: Bianco e nero, 5.

50. Ibid., 6.

51. Chiarini. 'Didattica del cinema', 31.

52. See Silvio Celli. 2010. 'Il primo decennio', *Bianco e nero* 71(566), 7–15.

53. Chiarini, *film nella battaglia*, 215–16.

54. Francesco Pitassio. 2010. 'La formazione dell'attore e la discussione teorica', *Bianco e nero* 71(566), 47.

55. Giulio Bursi, 'Inquadrare la materia', *Bianco e nero* 71(566), 53.

56. Cineteca di Bologna, Blasetti Collection, Centro Sperimentale di Cinematografia Folder. Clip from the Director's report (18 Nov. 1940).

57. Antonio Petrucci. 1934. 'Per una Cineteca Nazionale', *Il Tevere* (7 April).

58. See Giorgio Bacchiega. 2006. 'Nascita della Cineteca Italiana', in Orio Caldiron (ed.), *Storia del cinema italiano. 1934–1939*, Venice: Marsilio, 90–91. The contradiction between the two different policies was becoming explosive in postwar Italy, in 1949. A detailed reconstruction of the relationship between the two archives, and the respective policies, and the film-club movement can be found in Virgilio Tosi. 1999. *Quando il cinema era un circolo. La stagione d'oro dei cineclub (1945–1956)*, Venice: Marsilio.

59. See Lundemo, 'Film Theory as Archive Theory', 33–38; Simone Venturini. 2011. 'The Cabinet of Doctor Chiarini: Notes on the Birth of an Academic Canon', in Bianchi, Bursi, Venturini, *The Film Canon*, 451–60.

60. See Vinzenz Hediger. 2011. 'Original, Work, Performance: Film Theory as Archive Theory', in Giulio Bursi and Simone Venturini (eds), *What Burns (Never) Returns/Quel che brucia (non) ritorna*, Udine: Campanotto, 44–56.

61. The CSC archive in Rome preserved a document certifying the films that the German authorities confiscated. For a detailed description of the event, see Alfredo Baldi. 2010. 'I "diari di guerra" e i film requisiti', *Bianco e nero* 71(566), 103–7.

62. ·See Agamben, 'What Is an Apparatus?', 18–19. This sacralization became particularly true in the case of a few Italian films, that disappeared forever, and therefore became myths: SPERDUTI NEL BUIO (1914, Nino Martoglio), SOLE (1929, Alessandro Blasetti), and RAGAZZO (1933, Ivo Perilli).

Chapter 11

A New Art for a New Society? The Emergence and Development of Film Schools in Europe

Duncan Petrie

The interwar period represents a high-water mark in the development of film culture in Europe. On one hand, the aesthetic possibilities of cinematic form were being explored and significantly advanced in innovative ways by filmmakers in France, the Soviet Union and Germany. And while regarded by some as a fundamentally regressive development, the introduction of synchronized sound in the early 1930s provided new creative and technical challenges and proved to be something that further consolidated the popularity of cinema as a true mass medium. At the same time, serious appreciation of film was being promoted by numerous clubs and societies that organized screenings, lectures and discussions of both contemporary and classic works from around the world. This intellectual engagement was reinforced by the publication of what became the first wave of theoretical, critical and even historical studies of the medium, including seminal writings by Hugo Münsterberg, Rudolf Arnheim, Béla Balázs, Sergei Eisenstein, Louis Delluc, Germaine Dulac, Jean Epstein, Siegfried Kracauer, Walter Benjamin, Erwin Panofsky, John Grierson and Paul Rotha. All of this served to confirm and consolidate the cinema as not only a hugely successful popular entertainment and a powerful channel of state propaganda, but also as a progressive social phenomenon and even a bona fide art form – as had been claimed as early as 1911 by the Italian theorist Ricciotto Canudo – worthy of serious study and research.

But during the same period, foundations were also laid for yet another central plank of the development of film that would play a crucial role in bridging the gap between the production and the study and appreciation of the moving image. This was the emergence of the first film schools as centres of film education and training; institutions established as part of a wider process to instigate or rejuvenate specifically national cinemas or film industries at moments of political and social transformation. While the major flourishing of film schools in Europe did not take place until after the Second World War, the model of the national conservatoire was effectively established by pioneering developments in the Soviet Union, Italy and France. The All-Union State Institute of Cinematography (Всесоюзный государственный институт кинематографии) – or VGIK as it came to be known – was founded by the new Bolshevik regime in Moscow in 1919, making it the world's first bona fide national film school and a model for the subsequent emergence of the Centro Sperimentale di Cinematografia, set up by Mussolini's Fascist government in Rome in 1935, and the Institute des hautes etudes cinématographiques (IDHEC), established by a group of committed cinéphiles in Paris in 1943. Significantly, all three schools were created under the auspices of totalitarian governments – or in the case of IDHEC, under military occupation – and so were guided in part by certain political imperatives and constraints. Yet at the same time the circumstances of the genesis of all three schools helped to facilitate a guiding commitment to the integration of the industrial and the cultural aspects of cinema. This was in line with wider developments affecting European filmmaking and its attendant cultures, paving the way for a productive interface between practice and theory that facilitated significant advances in the serious study and understanding of the medium. While the first wave of European film schools were deemed to be necessary for the promotion of economically sustainable and popular national film industries able to resist the threat of Hollywood, the way in which they also engaged with the cultural or intellectual value of cinema suggested that they were equally geared towards the loftier aim of the creation of 'a new art for a new society'.

* * *

'A new art for a new society' was certainly the case with regard to developments in the Soviet Union. In August 1919 Lenin had issued his famous decree that cinema was the most important of the arts and that the fledgling Soviet film industry should be brought under central state control. A key part of the strategy was to be the training of new practitioners and so a film school was established in Moscow by the Soviet State's Peoples Commissariat for Education (NARKOMPROS), the body responsible for the nationalization of cinema. The Moscow school was only one of a number of training establishments for film set up in the major urban centres, being predated by several months by the Petrograd School of Screen Arts, but, as Vance Kepley argues, what set it apart was the degree of 'planning and thought' that went into the creation of an institution of national import that 'would emerge to give direction to Soviet film education and ultimately to the entire Soviet cinema'.[1] Indeed, after an initial period characterized by a chronic shortage of resources and equipment – raw film stock was hard to come by, and for the first four years the school had no cameras and had to rely on visiting filmmakers providing their own – the Moscow school expanded and developed. This was reflected in its official status, which changed in 1930 from the State College of Cinematography (GTK) to the more elevated State Institute of Cinematography (GIK), and then four years later to a the Higher State Institute (VGIK), placing it on a par with universities.

The school's founding director, Vladimir Gardin, was primarily interested in the training of actors and the school began as primarily an actor's studio based on the teaching studio of the Moscow Art Theatre. But as Kepley notes, the curriculum quickly developed into a three-tiered structure that combined general courses in the history of art, literature and culture; courses in cinema technique including cinematography, make-up and costume; and courses on acting and performance.[2] The lack of technical resources in the early days forced a heavy reliance on ingenuity and ideas, beginning with Gardin's promotion of a new anthropology of acting influenced by the ideas of Delsarte and Dalcroze. As Mikhail Yampolsky has demonstrated, this in turn paved the way for the emergence of montage as the central principle in early Soviet film theory and practice, being initially 'understood as a cinematic form of organisation of the actor's behaviour'.[3] Gardin's theatrical background also led him to pioneer the tradition of 'film without film', mounting plays on a special stage using curtains, panels and partitions to fragment the action. This concern with montage was subsequently picked up by Lev Kuleshov, a young teacher at the school, who in 1920 began to experiment with photographic images. Some of these experiments were initially conducted using a still camera, but as Kuleshov started to make his own feature films in the mid-1920s so greater access to cinema production equipment became available. Kuleshov became the most significant figure in the formative phase of the Moscow school and his workshop was attended by the emerging luminaries of Soviet cinema, including Vsevelod Pudovkin and Sergei Eisenstein. Most famous of all was Kuleshov's experiment with the actor Ivan Mozhukhin which demonstrated that cinematic meaning could be created through the juxtaposition of individual shots rather than being intrinsic to the shots themselves, establishing one of the landmarks in the development of montage praxis.

While Kepley argues that the workshop phase of the institute's early years was a consequence of pragmatic necessity as much as pedagogic ideals,[4] Malte Hagener suggests that it encouraged an experimental and avant-garde approach that proved highly conducive to a productive integration within the learning environment:

> The State Film Institute was founded as a *tekhnikum*, a practical school for vocational training organised around workshops and practical work. Within the four-year teaching period, students worked closely with mentors – most of the big names of Soviet cinema at one time or another taught at the school – and were also involved in production work outside the school context. While this scheme grew out of necessity, it also illustrates an approach to cinema that combines intellectual development with practical work.[5]

But from the mid-1920s onwards, the curriculum became more formalized and academic, with the gradual introduction of defined areas of production specialization including directing, acting, animation, set design, camera operating and screenwriting, all with their own separate curricula. This was also a period of major expansion dictated by state policy towards building up capacity within the film industry and widening participation beyond the urban intelligentsia. As Jamie Miller notes, the period of 1928–1932 saw a dramatic rise in the number of students from 400 to 719, with higher quotas drawn from workers and peasants.[6] But while the focus of the school may have become more industry-oriented, this continued to go hand in hand with the commitment to ideas. Much of this impetus was to be driven by the role played by Sergei Eisenstein who had long campaigned for a more overtly academic approach to be adopted and who emerged as the key figure at VGIK during the 1930s. Having participated briefly in Kuleshov's workshop in 1922, Eisenstein had taught a seminar at the school in 1928 before embarking on a three-year international tour. On his return to the Soviet Union he was appointed head of the directing faculty and set about developing a new four-year curriculum. This was to be informed by his characteristically polymathic intellectual ambition:[7]

It is only on the basis of the closest contact with the culture of literature, theatre, painting and music, only in the most serious examination of the newest scientific disclosures in reflexes and psychology and related sciences, that the study of cinema specifics can be coordinated in some constructive and workable system of instruction and perception.[8]

Eisenstein's curriculum still stands as an inspirational landmark in film school education.[9] For Vance Kepley, this is defined by the centrality of the concept of 'expressiveness' which is rooted in Eisenstein's conviction that film could not be separated from other arts. This in turn meant that the central pedagogical problem was to isolate expressive qualities and determine their place in artistic language. Therefore, aspiring film directors should study novels, plays and other expressive forms, and consequently, as Kepley notes, students were to confront the works of Joyce, Zola, Dostoevsky and Dumas while solving problems relating to filmmaking.[10] The activities of teaching, thinking and production were always profoundly interconnected for Eisenstein, and it was during his tenure at VGIK that he was also to write some of his most important and highly influential essays, many of which originated as lectures, which were initially published in the seminal volumes *The Film Form* and *The Film Sense*.[11]

The shift towards a more overtly academic teaching programme within the Moscow State Institute was augmented by a raft of other developments that were designed to promote serious scholarship and study. These included in 1931 the organization of a collection of five hundred films, which in turn provided the basis for the operation of a cinematheque at the institute; this was followed in 1932 by the establishment of an office for the history of Soviet film, comprising an archive and library; then in 1933 postgraduate study was introduced, providing a solid basis on which innovative research into the history and theory of cinema could be conducted; and in 1934 film historian Nikolai Lebedev was appointed as the new director of the institute, the first non filmmaker to hold the position. In addition to Eisenstein, other major thinkers associated with the institute during this period included the Hungarian exile Béla Balázs, who wrote his 1935 book *The Spirit of Film* while working in the film studies section.

Unfortunately, this intellectual flourishing was happening against the backdrop of Stalin's tightening grip on all aspects of Soviet life, including the notorious imposition in 1934 of the proscriptive doctrine of Socialist Realism by Cultural Commissar Andrei Zhdanov. This had profoundly negative consequences for artistic innovation and the international reputation of Soviet cinema. Even Eisenstein, who had been commissioned to direct the film celebrating the tenth anniversary of the revolution, now found himself subject to criticism for his supposed formalist and bourgeois tendencies. Ironically, Eisenstein's most intellectually productive tenure at VGIK coincided with a period in which it became almost impossible for him to make films. This disjuncture was emblematic of the wider situation concerning cultural production within the Soviet Union which, Jamie Miller argues, served to seriously limit the institute's 'relevance to a cinema industry that had moved away from the Formalism of many 1920s films to the "cinema for the millions" of the 1930s, with its simple, comprehensible plots'.[12] Consequently, for Miller, VGIK increasingly 'became an isolated academic community without a clear purpose' which, despite its intellectual and artistic excellence, had little relevance to the needs of the industry, thus 'prolonging a sense of stagnation and undermining the Bolsheviks' political plans for the medium of cinema'.[13] Miller further points out that technical provision at the institute remained poor during the decade, and it was not equipped for sound production until as late as 1935. At the same time, the contraction in Soviet film production was resulting in high levels of unemployment for graduates. Finally, the intellectual vibrancy that had characterized the institute since its inception began to be eroded by Stalin's purges, leading to the arrest and execution of some key staff members during the latter part of the 1930s, including the cinematographer Vladimir Nilsen, a close associate of Eisenstein and an inspiring teacher.

But VGIK was ultimately to survive Stalin's Terror and the Second World War, providing the model for the establishment of a number of similar institutions after 1945, both within the Soviet-controlled communist states of Eastern Europe – such as the famous Polish School in Lodz and FAMU in Prague – and beyond. There was to be a return to greater openness during the Kurschev-inspired thaw of the 1950s, a period which saw inspirational figures such as Mikhail Romm, Alexander Dovzhenko and Sergei Gerasimov (after whom the school was later renamed) teach some of the most important figures to emerge in postwar Soviet cinema, including Andrei Tarkovsky, Elem Klimov, Larisa Shepitko, Sergei Parajanov and Nikita Mikhalkov.

*   *   *

Despite its undoubted impact on the development of Soviet Cinema during the 1920s, it was not until 1935 that a second major film school would be established in Europe. Interestingly, this occurred in Fascist

Italy where Benito Mussolini clearly recognized the importance of film (and other mass media) as a weapon of propaganda. In 1936 he would even declare at a rally that 'cinema is the strongest weapon', directly echoing Lenin's decree of 1919. But the imposition of state control over film in Italy would prove a much slower process compared with the Soviet Union. Mussolini's government had initially become involved in film in 1924 with the establishment of the Instituto LUCE (*L'Unione Cinematografica Educativa*/Educational Film Institute) to facilitate the production of pro-fascist newsreels and educational films. Meanwhile, the Italian cinema – which had briefly flourished in the period just before the First World War – was languishing in the doldrums, and by the 1930s the authorities were keen to rejuvenate the seventh art as a key element in their wider promotion of the glories of imperial Italian culture. And here the Russian example proved influential, as Piero Garofalo argues: 'The Soviet model was instinctively attractive to Fascist hierarchs, both because Russian production conveyed a sense of unity between nation and film that Italian cinema lacked, and because Russian film was politics as well as art'.[14]

In 1932 the president of LUCE, Alessandro Sardi, visited the USSR to learn about the organization of Soviet cinema and returned to Italy with a desire to centralize the entire industry. Two years later the Direzione Generale per la Cinemagrafia (The General Film Office) was set up under the auspices of Mussolini's Press and Propaganda Ministry – subsequently the Ministry of Popular Culture. Under Luigi Freddi, the Direzione set out to bring the Italian film industry under state control and regenerate Italian cinema through boosting production levels and improving the quality of local films, which in turn led to the establishment of a national film school in 1935 and the founding of the Cinecitta Studio in 1937, both of which were located in the Tuscolana district on the south-eastern outskirts of Rome. In addition, Italy could also boast of having inaugurated the world's first film festival in Venice in 1932.

The origins of the Italian film school lay directly in Alessandro Sardi's trip to the Soviet Union where, as Garofalo points out, he had visited the Moscow State Film School. This in turn led to the setting up of the Scuola Nazionale di Cinematografia (National Cinema School) in 1932, out of which three years later emerged a fully fledged film school, the Centro Sperimentale di Cinematografia (Experimental Cinematography Centre), under the directorship of the literary critic Luigi Chiarini. Following the model of VGIK, the curriculum at the Centro Sperimentale combined practical production training with a strong focus on a wider theoretical education, including cinema aesthetics and history, the social function of cinematography, and the history of art. The intellectual dimension was further augmented by the establishment of a library and a film collection to facilitate research and study. In 1937 the Centro also began publishing a journal, *Bianco e Nero* (Black and White), under the editorship of Chiarini. Writing in 1949, Mario Verdone praised the significant contribution made by the journal to the development of Italian film culture, noting that contributors included such international film theorists and historians as Georges Sadoul, Rudolf Arnheim and Béla Balázs, as well as local philosophers like Benedetto Croce and Ugo Spirito.[15] In addition to the journal, the Centro was also responsible for a series of cinematographic publications featuring the theoretical writings of Pudovkin and Eisenstein as well as those of Italian cinéastes such as Chiarini, Umberto Barbaro and Francesco Pasinieti, and the screenplays of the likes of Rene Clair, Jacques Feyder and E.A. Dupont, all of which for Verdone constituted nothing less than 'the nucleus of Italian film culture'.[16] Alongside Chiarini, Barbaro was another key figure both at the Centro and within the development of Italian film culture. A committed Marxist, he had long championed Soviet cinema and had been responsible for translating the writings of Eisenstein, Pudovkin, Arnheim and Balázs into Italian, as well as editing the other major Italian film journal *Cinema*. As Piero Garofalo notes, Barbaro's efforts 'significantly influenced the generation of a new critical conscience in Italian cinema'.[17]

Consequently, despite being a national institution within a Fascist state, the Centro became a site of progressive cultural fermentation. This was in part a reflection of the nature of Italian Fascism itself which, as Jacqueline Reich points out, represented not one political ideology but a synthesis of various positions. Moreover, unlike German National Socialism, Italian Fascism also lacked a clear-cut cultural policy or dominant artistic style but rather was more a manifestation of 'hegemonic pluralism'.[18] Compared with Hitler's Germany, there existed in Italy a remarkably open artistic environment within the film community, with anti-fascist intellectuals and even Jews being able to participate. Moreover, Luigi Freddi's enthusiastic cultivation of an intellectual climate worked against his role as a Fascist bureaucrat, with both the Centro Sperimentale and Cineguf (a network of university film clubs sponsored by the party) becoming effectively anti-fascist breeding grounds. Significantly, both were environments that were not subject to the same strict censorship and so could screen a wide range of international films. Indeed, as Reich notes, the regime was fully aware of the dissent being fostered but chose, as it often did with intellectuals, to look the other way.[19] Many commentators have also noted that the foundations of neorealism were laid during the Fascist period, with the Centro Sperimentale playing its part. Sergio J. Pacifici, for example, argues that the 1930s saw the beginnings of a search for a 'national style' on the part of a diffuse group of artists and intellectuals who were 'disgusted by the emptiness prevailing in the culture of their day and the rhetoric of its form', and part of this spirit of enquiry was the foundation of journals like *Cinema* (1936) and *Bianco e Nero* (1937), both of which 'emphasised the necessity of turning to reality'.[20]

The Centro was forced to close during the latter phase of the war after Mussolini had been deposed and the Germans had assumed control. But by then it had set in motion many of the developments that were to contribute to the postwar flourishing of Italian cinema through its neorealist phase and beyond. Among those who studied at the school during this formative period were the directors Michelangelo Antonioni, Giuseppe De Santis, Luigi Zampa, Stenno and Pietro Germi; the writer Gianni Puccini; the producer Dino De Laurentiis; the cinematographers Pasquilano De Santis and Gianni Di Venanzo; the production designers Mario Chiari and Gianni Polidori; the costume designers Maria De Matteis and Vittorio Nino Novarese; and actors like Gianni Agus, Paolo Carlini, Andrea Checchi, Arnoldo Foa, Alida Valli, Clara Calamai, Leopoldo Trieste and Massimo Serato. The creative legacy of these graduates was to help establish Italian film as a major force in the wider European cinema of the postwar period but also to establish Cinecitta as a major base for Hollywood runaway productions during the 1950s.

Despite the serious damage done to the Centro's archives during the war, it resumed its activities in 1946 under the directorship of Umberto Barbaro. It quickly responded to industry need by regulating particular production specialism, placing an emphasis on the training of actors and actresses in 1948–49, while admitting no new camera or sound specialists during the same period.[21] During this period, former students such as Michelangelo Antonioni and Pietro Germi returned to the school to teach seminars alongside such leading lights of neorealism as Vittorio Di Sica and Luchino Visconti. Then, in 1949, the Centro became the home of the newly established Cineteca Nazionale (National Film Archive), cementing its position at the heart of Italian film culture.

*   *   *

Perhaps unsurprisingly, the third major European film school emerged in France. Paris had been one of the centres of the proliferation of artistic experimentation and intellectual engagement with the cinema during the interwar period. The serious appreciation of film was propagated by the establishment of numerous ciné-clubs, while the integration of filmmaking practice and intellectual analysis by pioneers like Jean Epstein, Germaine Dulac, Marcel L'Herbier and René Clair generated a film culture that came to rival that of the Soviet Union. The cultivation of poetic realism during the Popular Front era of the 1930s by Jean Renoir, Marcel Carné, Jean Vigo and Julien Duvivier also proved influential on the later development of neorealism in Italy. It was inevitable that this environment would also encourage developments in practical film education, and in 1926 L'Ecole technique de photographie et de cinema was set up by leading industry figures such as Louis Lumière and Léon Gaumont. Subsequently know as L'Ecole Louis Lumière or Vaugirard (after the school's location in the rue Vaugirard in Paris) this was effectively an institution concerned with technical training, rather than a fully formed national film school geared towards the formation of key creative personnel such as directors and writers. Such an institution would finally emerge in 1943, with the creation of the Institute des hautes etudes cinématographiques (IDHEC).

The roots of IDHEC lie not only in the legacy of the intellectual activity of the interwar period, but also in the hiatus created by the Second World War and the temporary shift of cultural activity away from occupied Paris to the Vichy-controlled south. In 1940 the Centre des jeunes du cinéma français was formed in Castellaras near Cannes with a mission to propagate film culture, knowledge and skills. In the following year it relocated to Nice and was renamed the Centre artistique et technique des jeunes du cinéma (CATJC) where its members included the cinematographers Henri Alekan, Philipe Agostini, Claude Renoir and Louis Page, the critic/filmmaker Jean Lods and the director René Clement. CATJC operated like the ciné-clubs of the 1920s but was also interested in certain practical aspects of filmmaking and the training of new technicians. Clement, for example, undertook the production of two short films in 1942 and 1943. The CATJC also began to establish a specialized library that later became the basis for the IDHEC library. Activities were transferred to Paris in October 1943 and IDHEC began teaching in January 1944, with the veteran avant-garde filmmaker and theorist Marcel L'Herbier as president. It would be a full six months before the liberation of Paris by the Allies and, as Susan Hayward has noted, 'it took the rationalising and organisational modalities of the Occupation to put in place a fully fledged school of film studies',[22] in addition to the institutional framework that would prove so vital to the survival and subsequent flourishing of French cinema after the war.

L'Herbier had long been campaigning for a film school as a necessary precondition for a reinvigorated national cinema in France. In 1938 he had called for the establishment of an institution to train film personnel as part of a 'University of the New Arts'. Moreover, unlike many of his more radical colleagues, L'Herbier had accepted the reality of occupation and he put his energies into the continuity of French life, including that of filmmaking, making him an acceptable individual to become the founding director of IDHEC. The school was set up in a town house in Rue de Penthièvre in Paris, occupying the cramped offices that were formerly those of a chemical company. Alain Resnais, Stellio Lorenzi, Yannick Bellon, Maurice Cazeneuve, Ghislain Cloquet and René Vautier were among the first intake of students.

L'Herbier retained a strong commitment to cinema as an important artistic and cultural phenomenon, and he attempted to reflect this in the new school which, according to Colin Crisp, was established with three primary aims.[23] The first of these aims was the formation of filmmakers whose work would be endowed with profound human values, and this quickly became the core mission of the institute delivered via its curriculum. The second aim was the fostering of research on a wide range of artistic and technical subjects relevant to the development of the cinema, and this was facilitated primarily by the library of films and printed material that had been initiated in Nice. The third aim was to contribute to the propagation of cinema culture within the society, but this remained more of an aspiration than a reality – although arguably this was achieved by individuals such as Henri Langlois and André Bazin, and by institutions like the Cinémathèque Française, and publications like *Cahiers du cinéma*.

IDHEC enjoyed, almost instantly, an interest in the wider artistic and intellectual community in Paris, and in the early years welcomed important guests such as Maurice Merleau-Ponty, who came to lecture in 1945 on the links between cinema and the 'new psychology'. The presence of significant filmmakers and intellectuals on the teaching staff such as L'Herbier, Jean Lods, the Marxist critic Léon Moussinac, the theorist Jean Mitry and the historian Georges Sadoul also ensured that the institute embodied a profound commitment to ideas. In 1946 the French actor Charles Boyer argued that IDHEC's principal mission was to further 'the French pioneering tradition – a pioneering of the intellect'.[24] While four years later, writing in *Sight and Sound*, John

Francis Lane noted the influence of the general principles laid down by Eisenstein at VGIK:

> We have learned from Eisenstein's writings that the fundamental basis of film study is the absorption of what he terms 'montage creation in all cultures'. For many whose minds are more practical in their approach to the cinema (and this, strangely enough, describes most of the French students), the idea of learning about Stanislavsky or Shakespeare; of delving into the past wonders of prehistoric art; or of investigating the intricacies of musical form and rhythm, may seem somewhat unnecessary to the study of the *craft* of a film director. But although everyone cannot be expected to agree with Eisenstein's conception of cinema as the sublime realisation of all art creation, no one with genuine sympathies for the film will deny that such an education is absolutely essential to the director's *art*.[25]

But at the same time the institute also developed a strong emphasis on craft training and professionalism, and after the war it took a central role in the reinvigoration of the French film industry.[26] IDHEC was funded by the Centre national de la cinématographie (CNC), the renamed Comité d'organisation de l'industrie cinématographique which clearly signified the re-emphasis on a truly national cinema during this period. For Crisp, this role ultimately served to undermine some of L'Herbier's founding ambitions, notably the desire to instigate an ongoing aesthetic revolution in French filmmaking. Consequently, IDHEC became caught in a paradox between the desire to foster creativity that transcended rules and the training of professionals with established skills. And as Crisp opines, 'in the course of these fifteen years then, there seems to have been a slow move away from revolution and radicalism towards system, technique and competence'.[27]

Whether or not this served to place the institute firmly on the side of the cinema of quality that the young Truffaut had infamously excoriated,[28] and which he and the other filmmakers of *la nouvelle vague* – whose formation had been the Cinémathèque Française and *Cahiers du cinéma* rather than film school – had actively opposed in their commitment to raw-edged innovation and playfulness, is beyond the scope of this chapter. But it is hard to deny the significance that graduates of IDHEC – including directors such as Alain Resnais, Louis Malle, Claude Sautet, Claude Miller and Andre Téchiné; the producer Marin Karmitz; and the cinematographer Sacha Vierny – would have within the flourishing of postwar French cinema.

* * *

Collectively, the emergence and early development of the All-Union State Institute of Cinematography, the Centro Sperimentale Di Cinematografia and the Institute des hautes études cinématographiques established the model for subsequent national film schools across Europe and beyond. The primary purpose of these institutions was to ensure a flow of appropriately educated and trained practitioners who possessed the necessary creative and technical skills to ensure the success of thriving national film industries. But this success entailed both an industrial and a cultural component, reflecting the belief that film's value was much more than just being popular mass entertainment and the basis of a highly profitable local industry. It was also central to questions of national specificity and cultural identity, providing a means of constructing and reflecting a nation's sense of itself, its beliefs and values, both to itself and to the rest of the world. The seriousness of this purpose is reflected in the pedagogical missions and curricula of the three institutions examined above, all of which combine advanced skills training to ensure high production values with the cultivation of the intellect and the propagation of ideas to provide ultimate direction and purpose to cinematic production. In this way, these institutions should also be regarded as major facilitators of serious theorizing, analysis and research that would in due course provide the basis for the emergence of university departments of film studies. Indeed, what is striking – some may say regrettable – is the way in which theory and practice would subsequently diverge within film education, a situation true in both single discipline institutions, which have tended to become increasingly practice oriented, and in universities, where the pattern has been the development of separate departments, specializing in either film studies or production.

While the national frame of reference is central to the institutions discussed here, it is important to note that this was not at the exclusion of important international dimensions. The essentially cosmopolitan nature of the interwar European film culture is implied throughout, and this was also to prove instructive in the development of film schools which constituted spaces of transnational exchange and dialogue that further enhanced the status and significance of the medium during a tumultuous period of conflict and transformation in European and world history. Moreover, this process intensified after the Second World War. As Dina Iordanova notes, internationalization was particularly important within the film schools of the Soviet Union and Eastern Europe which began having 'a permanent contingent of international students from "brotherly" countries'.[29] The first foreign student to attend VGIK was the Czech screenwriter Frantisek Daniel, who went on to become a celebrated film teacher in the United States.[30] He was followed by others, including several pioneers of African cinema such as Djidril Diop Mambety, Ousmane Sembene and Souleymane Cissé, all of whom graduated in the 1960s. Internationalism was also important at IDHEC. Colin Crisp notes that during the first fifteen years of its operations more than 44 per cent of IDHEC graduates were from overseas,[31] while by the late 1960s the figure was only in region of 20 per cent. Graduates of the school include European directors like Costa-Gavras, Volker Schlöndorff and Theo Angelopolous, as well as various Columbian, Mexican, Vietnamese and significant numbers of West and North African filmmakers. American academic Robert Rauch recalls his experience as a student in the director's class at the Centro Sperimentale in the early 1950s as one in which half the cohort of twelve comprised foreigners like himself.[32] This cosmopolitanism resonates with the integration of theory and practice to mark out these pioneering institutions as worthy of serious recognition within the historical development of European cinema as an intellectually rich, formally innovative and socially progressive cultural phenomenon.

Notes

1. Vance Kepley Jr. 1987. 'Building a National Cinema: Soviet Film Education 1918–1934', *Wide Angle* 9(3), 9.
2. Ibid.
3. See Mikhail Yampolsky. 1991. 'Kuleshov's Experiments and the New Anthropology of the Actor', in Richard Taylor and Ian Christie (eds), *Inside the Film Factory: New Approaches to Russian and Soviet Cinema*, London: Routledge.
4. Kepley Jr., 'Building a National Cinema'.
5. Malte Hagener. 2007. *Moving Forward, Looking Back: The European Avant-garde and the Invention of Film Culture 1919–1939*, Amsterdam: Amsterdam University Press, 136.
6. Jamie Miller. 2007. 'Educating the Filmmakers: The State Institute of Cinematography in the 1930s', *Slavonic and Eastern European Review* 85(3). This was eventually seen as a failure given the high intellectual level required of the students and there was a high dropout rate, rising to a peak of 52 per cent by 1935. In that year the student population at the institute had fallen to 230.
7. See S.M. Eisenstein. 1996. 'Teaching Programme for the Theory and Practice of Direction', in Richard Taylor (ed.), *Sergei Eisenstein: Selected Works. Vol. III: Writings, 1934–1947*, trans. William Powell, London: BFI. For a commentary on Eisenstein's teaching, see Vance Kepley Jr. 1993. 'Eisenstein as Pedagogue', *Quarterly Review of Film and Video* 14(4).
8. Sergei Eisenstein. 1982. 'GTK-GIK-VGIK Past-Present-Future', in Sergei Eisenstein: *Film Essays and a Lecture*, trans. Jay Leyda, Princeton, NJ: Princeton University Press, 71.

9. See Eisenstein, 'Teaching Programme'.

10. Vance Kepley Jr. 1993. 'Eisenstein as Pedagogue', *Quarterly Review of Film and Video* 14(4).

11. These both appeared in English translation (by Jay Leyda) in the 1940s: Sergei Eisenstein. 1942. *The Film Sense*, New York: Harcourt; Sergei Eisenstein. 1949. *Film Form: Essays in Film Theory*, New York: Harcourt.

12. Miller, 'Educating the Filmmakers', 489.

13. Ibid., 490.

14. Piero Garafalo. 2002. 'Seeing Red: The Soviet Influence on Italian Cinema in the Thirties', in Jacqueline Reich and Piero Garofalo (eds), *Re-Viewing Fascism: Italian Cinema, 1929–1943*, Bloomington: Indiana University Press, 233.

15. Mario Verdone. 1949. 'The Experimental Cinema Center in Italy', in *Hollywood Quaterly* 4(1), 68.

16. Ibid.

17. Garafalo, 'Seeing Red', 233.

18. Jacqueline Reich. 2002. 'Mussolini at the Movies: Fascism, Film and Culture', in Jacqueline Reich and Piero Garofalo (eds), *Re-Viewing Fascism: Italian Cinema, 1929–1943*, Bloomington: Indiana University Press. The phrase is originally attributed to Marla Stone.

19. Ibid., 17.

20. Sergio J. Pacifici. 1956. 'Notes toward a Definition of Neorealism', *Yale French Studies* 17: Art of the Cinema, 48.

21. Verdone, 'Experimental Cinema Center', 65–68.

22. Susan Hayward. 2005. *French National Cinema*, 2nd edition, London: Routledge, 37.

23. C.G. Crisp. 1993. *The Classic French Cinema 1930–1960*, Bloomington: Indiana University Press. Crisp notes that there were suggestions that while not an open anti-Semite, L'Herbier was nevertheless antagonistic towards the arrival in the French film industry of Jewish immigrants from Russia in the early 1930s.

24. Charles Boyer. 1946. 'Advanced Training for Film Workers: France', *Hollywood Quarterly* 1(3), 289.

25. John Francis Lane. 1950. 'Amateur Activities: On Studying the Film', *Sight and Sound* 19(2).

26. Dudley Andrew. 1983. 'IDHEC', *Journal of Film and Video* 35(1).

27. Crisp, *Classic French Cinema*, 211.

28. Francois Truffaut. 1954. 'Une Certaine Tendance du cinema française', *Cahiers du Cinèma*, 31.

29. Dina Iordanova. 2003. *Cinema of the Other Europe: The Industry and Artistry of East Central European Film*, London: Wallflower, 22.

30. Following the crushing of the Prague Spring in 1968, Frank Daniel emigrated to the USA where he became the first Dean of the American Film Institute's film school in Los Angeles. He subsequently worked at Columbia University, the Sundance Institute and USC until retiring in 1990.

31. Crisp, *Classic French Cinema*.

32. Robert J. Rauch. 1957. 'An American in a European Film School', *Journal of the University Film Producers Association* 10(1): 9–11. However, Rauch also suggests that the overseas students were taking the course on a different basis – as auditors – from the local Italians.

Chapter 12

INSTITUTIONS OF FILM CULTURE

Festivals and Archives as Network Nodes

Malte Hagener

What constitutes film culture these days appears to be obvious – film criticism and film theory, festivals and prizes, archives and repertoire cinemas, film schools and museums – all spawn a network that is so familiar that we tend to forget that the shapes and contours of these institutions and networks were far from obvious in the 1920s and 1930s. Film festivals and film archives are both important aspects of this validation of cinema as an art form and as a productive cultural force. By putting forward two case studies I want to examine what the conditions for the existence of these institutions were. How did they come about, what support was necessary for them to find a stable and durable form? Moreover, the 1930s, often seen as a decade of nationalization and protectionism, emerges as an era of international exchange and cooperation.

Film Festivals: The Invention of a Tradition

The history of film festivals (and, implicitly, also its hierarchy) seems obvious when viewed from today: starting with the big three, Venice in 1932, Cannes in 1939/46, Berlin in 1951, the list usually continues to include Karlovy Vary and Locarno (both 1946), San Sebastian (1953) and other spas and holiday destinations in off-season, later joined by de-industrialized hot spots and post-industrial centres eager to reinvent themselves as media locations such as Oberhausen and Rotterdam. Finally, there are the events of 1968 and the worldwide proliferation of festivals, with the emergence of new players such as Pusan and Sundance, the shift to digital and the increased opening up of the festivals towards the art gallery and the internet.[1] While this sketch is certainly not wrong in itself, it begs the question of rupture because it constructs a linear development with a clearly circumscribed point of origin and a telos – a game equally popular and futile.

As much as the beginning of the cinema is still a contested issue, so the emergence of film festivals will never be unequivocally pinned down to one specific time and place. Because the question 'What is a film festival?' is as difficult to answer as the question of what constitutes the cinema or the documentary; any answer has to remain preliminary, contestable and controversial. Today, any series of screenings looking for public attention sells itself as a festival because of the prestige attached to the term. Contrary to the received notion sketched above, I believe that there is no clear-cut parentage to fall back upon. By pointing out some possible genealogies and proto-festivals, I will attempt to open up a historical horizon in order to destabilize the fixed notion and history of the film festival phenomenon and, secondly, to ascertain the reasons for the success of the international festival circuit as we see it today.

The genealogy of film festivals and the story of the avant-garde are overlapping in significant ways in the 1920s, which raises a number of issues. Why were the festivals able to create and sustain an international network that is still alive and kicking today whereas the historical avant-garde is retrospectively often diagnosed as a failure in the face of so much change: technological (the coming of sound), economic (the depression of the 1930s) and social (the growing political polarization in the course of the 1930s)? If the 'first' film festival took place in Venice in 1932, why there and why then? In order to answer this question, it is necessary to return once more to the broad activities of the avant-garde which encompassed all different kinds of screenings, but it is also productive to look at events resembling trade fairs and educational activities, because the strength of film festivals lies in their capacity to be many different things for different people. So, if we want to understand the festival phenomenon in historical terms, we have to look at the various strands feeding into it.

In the 1920s alternative screening institutions mushroomed across Europe; film societies and ciné-clubs proliferated, especially in major West European cities such as Paris, Berlin, London, Prague, Zurich,

Brussels, Amsterdam and Rotterdam.[2] These audience organizations and temporary exhibition venues, in some sense forerunners of today's art houses, constituted the screening wing of the international film avant-garde that was taking shape over the course of the decade. Among the wide-ranging activities of the avant-garde, one finds several instances which could qualify in some senses as prototypes of film festivals. In contrast to commercial cinemas selling films to a paying audience on the strength of a star or a story, the ciné-clubs aimed at developing a discourse expounding the cultural and artistic value of film. In France, lectures, extended introductions to films, presentations by filmmakers and evaluative discussions were a mainstay of the flourishing ciné-club scene that developed, first in Paris and then throughout the country. These potential proto-festivals were more transnational than the film clubs because they tried to attract an audience beyond the local, and their event status motivated many key figures of the film avant-garde to participate. In their effort to compress weekly or monthly events into a few days, they resembled the shape of festivals, yet they did not find a stable form typical of today's festivals as they often encompassed exhibitions and debates.

France with its intellectual and artistic scene was the pacemaker as far as exhibitions and concentrated screening series were concerned. The ciné-club ran by Ricciotto Canudo, Club des amis du septième art (CASA), was frequented by artists and intellectuals who were able to include film programmes and lectures on film in the prestigious Salon d'Automne, a visual art exhibition. For four consecutive years, from 1921 to 1924, the film programme ran back to back with the exhibition, almost a model for later developments because the Venice Film Festival likewise started as an annex to an art exhibition. The increasing convergence of different ciné-clubs and the generally favourable devotion to the cinema in Parisian intellectual circles led to a major exhibition on the cinema (L'art dans le cinéma français) from May through to October 1924 at the Musée Galliera.[3] A first major series of lectures was held in conjunction with this exhibition in May and June of 1924, and a second cycle in October 1924. Talks were given by central figures of the avant-garde scene such as Léon Moussinac, Marcel L'Herbier, Jaque Catelain, Robert Mallet-Stevens, Jean Epstein and others.[4] A year later the new Ciné-club de France organized a lecture cycle at the recently opened Théâtre du Vieux Colombier from 28 November 1925 to 20 February 1926, with a similar cast of speakers: Jean Epstein, Jean Tedesco, Germaine Dulac and Marcel L'Herbier.[5] In contrast to commercial cinemas which in the course of the 1920s framed the film with lush architecture and elaborate stage programmes, selling an extravagant experience, the avant-garde created a discursive system with magazines and lectures as an integral part of a new kind of cinema. Without taking film seriously as an aesthetic object and as a discursive fact, the idea of the film festival is unfathomable; so these series of lectures and screenings – even though they lacked the condensed intensity of festivals as we know them today – nevertheless can be seen as important forerunners because they ascertained the value of the cinema and developed possible formats.

In Germany, a country characterized in the 1920s by the strongest European film industry (and with Ufa a large international player), one regular event was the Funkausstellung (radio communication exhibition) which took place annually in Berlin from 1924 onwards, and included film programmes on a regular basis. The Funkaustellung in general aimed at demonstrating the convergence of radio, television and (sound) film, but being a show of consumer culture it was dominated by the industry.[6] A big event that foreshadowed in some ways later developments was the Kino- und Photoausstellung (Kipho) in Berlin, from 25 September to 5 October 1925. This exhibition mixed technological, economic, social, educational and artistic concerns and proved to be a huge audience success, drawing approximately one hundred thousand spectators. The exhibition itself was a mixture between the Funkausstellung (a consumer show in which the industry had a ready-made showcase for its products) and more artistically minded conferences. The Kipho was characterized by conflicting interests and diverging paths, so the event remained singular as it ultimately lacked a clear focus: it attempted to cater to the industry as well as to a broader public, and was interested in artistic and educational as well as in economic and cultural matters. Even though it attracted many visitors, the exhibition nevertheless had a frame so wide that it was not followed up. Moreover, it lacked a committed sponsor who would be more interested in long-term success than in just direct return-on-investment.

One way to characterize these events would be to understand them as experimental venues for the exploration of how regular, but compressed events could deal with the cinema, to see them as experimental formations or proto-festivals. In a contemporary article in the transnational journal *Close Up*, Andor Kraszna-Krausz criticized these early attempts at exhibiting films for their concentration on the economic side of the cinema: 'the principal mistake of all such attempts was that they had tried to show the commercial side before all and left the nucleus of the craft in the shadows of the background'.[7] From today's

Figure 12.1 Poster for the Kino- und Photoausstellung (Kipho) in Berlin, from 25 September to 5 October 1925. [Deutsche Kinemathek]

vantage point, Kraszna-Krausz' criticism is well taken, as any festival that arouses suspicion of being overly dependent on sponsors and economic interest is in danger of losing its reputation. Balancing financial requirements (the need to acquire funding) with artistic integrity (the publicly stated independence of juries and programmers) is now a requisite for being taken seriously by filmmakers, the press and the public at large. In the 1920s though, the events were either artistically minded (and therefore lacked funding) or run by the industry (and therefore not independent).

With the benefit of hindsight, one can discern at least three models overlapping in these early exhibition formats which were further developed and differentiated over the course of the following decades. First of all, these conferences were harking back to proven and tested formulas from the spectacular nature of the World Fairs which lured a mass audience with modern technological wonders.[8] Here, the novelty of the cinema, its promise of amazement and the fascination of technology were exploited, often by manufacturers of hardware and inventors who had developed new ideas and products. Secondly, these events could be seen as catering to a trade fair audience of insiders, mostly interested in a business platform. In this model, the audience is rather specialized and the general public is not openly addressed – the way film festivals layer and grade admission to screenings is a testament to how these two different concepts can be accommodated within the same event. The third model to keep in mind, the art exhibition, had taken its quintessential modern form from the French salon of the nineteenth century. Film festivals took elements of all these models, but combined them differently when they turned into regular events from the 1930s onwards. By the mid-1920s these formats were not yet clearly differentiated, so in practice they touched and overlapped. It was in 1929 at the mid-point and watershed of the interwar period that two events highlighted the chances and risks of further developments. They are worth discussing in some detail here.

These two key events of the avant-garde took place in the summer of 1929, geographically less than 300 km apart and temporally within three months (one mid-June, the other early September): the exhibition 'Film und Foto' (film and photo, for short 'FiFo') in Stuttgart, south-west Germany; and the 'Congrès International du Cinéma Independent' (international congress of independent cinema, for short 'CICI'), in La Sarraz in the French-speaking part of Switzerland, close to Lausanne. The Werkbund-exhibition Film und Foto in the summer of 1929 in Stuttgart was an epoch-making event. It concentrated on the artistic and cultural side of the medium, as it was not being (co-)organized by the industry.[9] Both events had a decisive advantage of timing: by the end of the 1920s the trend of *Neue Sachlichkeit* (new sobriety) had been established, and the cinema had been widely recognized. The exhibition FiFo had the function of collecting material from Germany and abroad which was seen together for the first time and contextualized, turning the photo exhibition effectively into a provisional appraisal and a retrospective. FiFo garnered huge interest not only in Germany, but more importantly all over Europe.

The photo exhibition at the Neue Städtische Ausstellungshalle opened on 18 May and closed on 7 July 1929. In thirteen rooms, the exhibition aimed at giving an overview of contemporary trends in photography. The film section consisted of fifteen film programmes curated by Hans Richter, shown over a two week period from 13 to 26 June at the Königsbau-cinema in Stuttgart.[10] The films were grouped into three sections: (1) Master works of cinematic production; (2) Advances of the avant-garde; and (3) Soviet features and documentaries.[11] The majority of films shown were not new, but came from the 1920s; the programme consisted of the now classic canon of the avant-garde, but also encompassed what came to be known as the highlights of the European art cinema of the 1920s (films by G.W. Pabst, Jacques Feyder and others). Besides these older films, there were also international premieres such as the films of Dziga Vertov (himself the guest of honour at the event) which were virtually unknown in the West before. The FiFo film programme foreshadows two later models – the film festival and the retrospective, aiming on the one hand at the valorization of film as an art form, and on the other, at beginning the historization of film.

The second major event of the summer of 1929, the meeting in La Sarraz, rightfully occupied a central position for the European avant-garde of the interwar period for a couple of reasons: never before or after have so many protagonists of the movement met in one place at one time.[12] Many of the key figures of these years were present in La Sarraz: Hans Richter, Béla Balázs, Léon Moussinac, Sergei Eisenstein and Alberto Cavalcanti. During the La Sarraz meeting films were shown, lectures were given, discussions were held, and even a film was shot. Just like in Stuttgart it was an event at which the industry was conspicuously absent.[13] Yet, in the long run, this proved to be a problem since the avant-garde was as much in need of the industry as the other way around because a film festival is characterized by its mixture of business, art, glamour, publicity and culture. Even though it seemed to contemporaries as if a transnational avant-garde was on the verge of a breakthrough, La Sarraz marked the peak of the developments of the 1920s that took a very different direction in the 1930s. In fact, one could argue that it was the coming of sound, inevitable by 1929, that helped along the film festivals, because language 're-nationalized' film culture and the nation state proved crucial in providing a steady basis for the regular occurrence of an event.

When looking at FiFo and CICI from a retrospective vantage point, it becomes apparent that what held the avant-garde together in fact showed some cracks and fissures; the later breaking points and fault lines were already apparent to keen observers. FiFo and CICI can be seen as proto-festivals which lacked some factors and therefore stability and longevity. It was not until an art exhibition, a totalitarian state and a will to put a national cinema on the map coincided that the film festival as we know it was born. In this confluence of national interest, aesthetic argument and state sponsorship, the film festival could even be likened to the documentary film, which emerged in a comparable configuration in the U.K. at about the same time. Here, it was not until John Grierson found sponsors, in the form of the Empire Marketing Board and the General Post Office, that were not interested in short-term financial returns on the films themselves but rather in the build-up of a reputation, that the documentary as a film form of its own could emerge.[14]

The avant-garde with their screenings and magazines, their discourses and discussion culture, had made crucial contributions to film culture in the 1920s. Around 1930, three events had unforeseeable consequences, but it was their unexpected and unintended interaction that proved to be decisive: the introduction of sound was not an aesthetic problem in itself, as the interesting early sound films from avant-garde circles and the lively theoretical debates testify. The introduction of sound had different, far-reaching effects – it transformed the economic dynamics of the film industry by introducing new management methods and pushing conglomerization. The effects of the depression – the second major factor in these years – affected the film business in many ways, especially in combination with the introduction of sound which required an enormous financial engagement. And thirdly, the resurgence of nationalism across Europe hampered the pronounced internationalism of the avant-garde. Under these circumstances, the continuation of the established success formulas from the 1920s proved to be difficult; instead activities that connected avant-garde ideas with the self-interest of the film industry and the strategies of self-legitimization of the nation state came to the fore: for example, the founding of film archives (in Germany and England with the support of the state), the emergence of the documentary, and the establishment of the first film festival.

When Venice held its first film festival in 1932, it was part of an art exhibition that had inherited the idea of competition between nation states from such events as the World Exhibitions and the Olympics. Quite contrary to avant-garde convictions which were transnational and never cared much about national background, films were invited according to the country from which they hailed. Moreover, the nation state provided the necessary stability to the Venice festival as the main source of funding, because screening series and exhibitions with a pronounced aesthetic focus always had the problem of achieving stability. In the postwar era, it would often be a combination of national, regional and municipal institutions which funded film festivals, regularly motivated by touristic interests (such as filling hotels and restaurants in the off-season). The idea of the nation state was thus present on at least two levels: as the key partner in funding film festivals and as a means of distinction on the level of programming when, well into the 1960s, national bodies decided which films would be sent to festivals to represent their respective nation states.

What, then, turned the film festivals into such a successful concept when compared to the avant-garde was the ability to tap into many different discourses at many different levels. Whereas the avant-garde attempted to achieve complete autonomy and independence (they would hardly ever accept ready-made audience bases, aesthetic concepts or pre-fabricated discourses), film festivals connected with many existing entities: in terms of economy and organization they cooperated with political, touristic and economic institutions that would support the festivals in organizational and financial terms. Regarding the specialized needs of the film industry, festivals were (and still are) able to provide local showcases for international products (test screenings, so to speak) while also gathering a trade fair audience of potential buyers, which again is important for producers. At the same time, festivals also use existing networks of cultural value: by bringing together filmmakers and critics and by presenting numerous novel works the festival caters also to the artistic-cultural side of filmmaking. On a local level, festivals thrive on the audience's desire to visit and become part of a media event, while internationally they have to sustain themselves as a destination at a specific time. The film festival does not need to produce the discourses that it needs for support, it just has to remember all the different constituencies that it plays towards: not too much

Hollywood because then the quality press snubs, and not too little because then the tabloids and television stations do not report (which, in turn, might endanger the sponsor acquisition); enough tickets for the industry (because they pay high entry fees), but also enough for the international press (you do not want unfavourable results) and for the local audience (or the local politicians might reconsider their financial investment). Of course, this balance is difficult to achieve, but it shows how the discourses, cannibalizing on film festivals while also being cannibalized upon by them, do exist independently. The film festival can thus be seen as a hybrid node in a complex and dynamic network.

Discovering and Institutionalizing Film History in the 1930s

The development of film archives and, more broadly speaking, film history took a decisive turn in the 1930s.[15] Film history, as understood here, refers to the relation between the past as something that has to be imagined, constructed and discursively shaped time and again, and the future as an equally imagined place where these constructs can be put to use. It was this relation that was addressed by the avant-garde as the crucial hinge of an emergent film history.[16] A key moment in the shaping of this configuration is the near-simultaneous emergence in the mid-1930s of four different, yet related institutions for collecting, safeguarding and accessing films. Curiously, they chose different generic names which raises the question of whether there are different functional ideas behind their institutionalization: an archive (Reichsfilmarchiv in Berlin, founded in 1935),[17] a library within a modern art museum (Film Library as part of the Museum of Modern Art, New York, founded in 1935), a library within a film institute (National Film Library [NFL] as part of the British Film Institute, London, founded in 1935), and a ciné-mathèque (Cinémathèque française, 1936).[18] Of course, the history of these institutions is not unknown, but they are usually framed nationally thereby stressing their respective divergences and idiosyncrasies; a transnational look, by contrast, teases out their similarities and their shared ground, but most importantly their interconnectedness and mutual dependency.

An archive cannot be put into existence by a sheer act of will; there need to be reasons for its existence. A nascent institution has to be legitimized in order to rally public and private, political and social support, backing and financing. The organizations under discussion here therefore invented a past in dire need of retrieval, safeguarding, and public access, so that a future for which this material is kept might take shape. As these institutions exist to this day and are among the most influential of their kind (not least because they came first and therefore provided models which later activists in the field adopted, transformed or rejected, but in any case could not ignore), their discourses and strategies still bear strongly on our current conception of history, memory and the (cinematographic) past.

As is well documented, thoughts about film archiving emerged before the mid-1930s. Much has been written about Bolesław Matuszewski's early call for the archival safeguarding of images as early as 1898, aptly titled 'Une nouvelle source de l'histoire'.[19] Apparently these ideas, no matter how visionary they might seem in retrospect, were largely ignored at the time since the cinema as an art form and as a cultural force lacked support from those in a position to actively put such an effort into practice, both in politics and in the industry. In fact, history as a discipline has been rather slow to engage seriously with moving images as a valuable source of knowledge about the past. The First World War, as film historians such as Steven Bottomore and Martin Loiperdinger have demonstrated, proved to be crucial in generating interest in the cinema in political and military circles because it demonstrated the value of film for the modern nation state, its army and the mobilization of public support.[20] It was at this time that official agencies in the military apparatus and in government institutions started to systematically store film (most famously the collection that later became the archive of the Imperial War Museum), but they were neither comprehensive nor consistent at this point in time. In the 1920s, calls for film archives could be heard across Europe, and often the state was addressed as being the only agent that could act as the instigator and sponsor of such an endeavour. Yet again, those efforts undertaken were half-hearted, limited to specific uses or variations of film, so that the cinema in its totality was not sufficiently addressed, something that the avant-garde attempted in the 1920s which would contribute to the emergence of archives in the following decade.[21]

Seen from the vantage point of the late 1920s, it is surprising what happened only a few years later in four of the most important film-producing countries (United States, France, Germany and Great Britain), yet the context had changed and so what came about was not exactly what had been envisioned in the decade before. The period from 1933 to 1938 (more specifically 1935–36) not only saw the foundation and establishment of four major institutions that provided models for all later developments, but it also witnessed the establishment of the Fédérations International des Archives du Film (FIAF),[22] proving that the archives saw themselves from the very start not as a series of isolated entities, but as a transnational network of exchange and communication.

Why did this boom in activity and institution building happen at this particular moment and in this particular form? The standard answer sees the introduction of sound film as being the key trigger that spelt doom to old film and thus alerted activists to the urgent task of saving film. Yet again, there are two facts which make this explanation somewhat unconvincing. First of all, the film industry ever since its beginning in the late nineteenth century was by and large not interested in keeping used film material – old films could not, under normal circumstances, be watched again once they had finished their theatrical career. Long before the introduction of sound, used films were discarded as soon as they appeared worthless to exhibitors, distributors and producers. The massive destruction of the cinematic heritage was a fact long before the introduction of sound, and already in the 1920s one can find many lamentations from the circles of ciné-clubs about the inaccessibility of classic films. The other doubt concerns timing: if sound film really was the trigger for the archive movement, why did it take more than five years to bear fruit, as the introduction of sound was basically over by 1930 in those countries where archives were founded in the mid-1930s. Similar to the mythical rivalry of Langlois and Lindgren which personifies the basic dilemma and dialectical tension between storage and access that every archive is facing, the standard argument seems rather a shorthand that stands in for something else than a real explanation. I believe that the introduction of sound might have played a role in some individuals changing their mind, but much more decisive for the possibility of founding institutions was the attitude of the state and the public at large towards film, as well as the willingness of the film industry to cooperate with nascent institutions. In fact, the different role that film played for the public at large is also visible in large-scale documentary projects in Britain and the United States, in the foundation of film schools and film festivals, and in other film cultural activities elsewhere.

The other question concerns, as mentioned before, the similarity and difference of these early archival initiatives. If we follow Penelope Houston in her history of the film archive movement these were all markedly differently: 'These four archives were founded by very different organisations and people, for very different purposes. They reflect not so much the unity of the archive movement … as its startling diversity'.[23] To reiterate the standard version in somewhat simplistic, but still popular terms: the French archive was a private and amateur effort, in Germany it was the Nazi party, in Britain the initiative came from educators and the state, while in the United States rich philanthropists wanted to spend their money wisely and have their name remembered. Not coincidentally, this version of events sees developments as national and circumscribed, as it ignores the transnational dynamics of exchange and contact. By contrast, I want to argue that there was indeed a lot of shared ground between the archives, both in their genealogy, in their operation and, most importantly, in how they discursively conceived of their project.

The foundation of the Reichsfilmarchiv (imperial film archive) has to be seen in direct connection with the film policy of the Nazis.[24] Under the rule of Goebbels, the newly founded propaganda ministry considered the cinema and the radio as the key media for the control and manipulation of the public at large.[25] The Reichsfilmarchiv can be seen as a symptom of how important film was to the political and social efforts of Fascist Germany. Established in January 1934 on the first anniversary of the 'rise to power', but not officially opened until a year later in February 1935,[26] the archive at first concentrated on documentary and non-fiction film. It also actively worked on gathering those films from abroad that could not be officially screened in Nazi Germany, but that were considered of interest because they could be taken up as potential models, such as Sergei Eisenstein's BRONENOSEZ POTEMKIN [Battleship Potemkin] (1926). Even though a large number of these films were prohibited and could no longer be publicly exhibited, directors and screenwriters as well as academics and researchers had access to those films, making this an institution of research and learning as much as one of propaganda and state control. Thus, the Reichsfilmarchiv, in very limited ways, kept a memory of (foreign) films in Germany alive that was not possible publicly and that very seldom found its way into films.

While one can easily see the Reichsfilmarchiv as being just another cog in the machine of Nazi ideology (and in one way this is exactly how it functioned), a look at the key figure in these early years complicates the history even more. Frank Hensel was an enigmatic character, an equally ardent cinéphile and Nazi, who had already joined the National Socialist Party in 1928; he was a polyglot and a charming man by all accounts, who loved masquerade and whose life would provide material for a veritable spy thriller.[27] Born in 1893 to a British mother and a German father, who was a winemaker and hotel owner on the Rhine (Bingen), he travelled the world and dabbled in photography before he began making films for the Nazis in the late 1920s.[28] Despite his quick rise within the Nazi Party and an undercover stint in the then still free Saar region where he filmed political activists (so they could be identified, and incarcerated, later on), he nevertheless was most keen on international contacts and exchange. Meeting Iris Barry and her husband John Abbott when they travelled in Germany in 1936, showing up at the founding session of FIAF in 1938 and possibly acting as a double agent in occupied Paris when he actively helped Henri Langlois to hide some of his treasures, he is not an easy character to pinpoint. Even a fascist-nationalist project such as the Reichsfilmarchiv had at the helm a film activist that apparently had his cinéphile leanings, even though he was undoubtedly a convinced Nazi.

In the United States, the Museum of Modern Art (MoMA) had introduced a new model of how modern art could be communicated to the public at large. Founded in 1929 only ten days after the stock market crashed, the institution under the directorship of Alfred Barr took the Bauhaus as its model for integrating the arts and crafts, design and theory into a synthesis that resonated with the culture of modernity.[29] The original plans for the museum had encompassed film and photography, and design and radio, but due to the economic crisis which had hit the private patrons hard these plans were indeterminately suspended.[30] Barr kept on lobbying though, and he employed Iris Barry – British émigré, film critic and veteran of the London Film Society – in the library. The formation of the Film Library, supported with a grant by the Rockefeller Foundation, was publicly announced in June 1935 by John Hay Whitney who also became its first president, with Barry as curator and her later husband John Abbott as director. Even though one might argue that MoMA, a private enterprise solely founded by endorsement, was a long way from the state institutions that were being set up in the same year in Germany and Britain, MoMA nevertheless understood itself as a radically public institution, geared not towards small elite circles but towards educating the masses, making it, in Haidee Wasson's words 'a privately endowed institution with an ostensibly public mandate'.[31] One has to keep in mind the fundamental differences between Europe and the United States in order to understand that MoMA was basically geared towards educating the public and making an intervention in ongoing discourses about art, the role of technology and the modern life world.

The film library set about collecting the canon of classics, which had been developed over the course of the 1920s and consolidated in many film programmes of the screening clubs across Europe, as well as a number of books on film history that had been published in the previous ten years, among them: Georges Michel Coissac's *Histoire du cinématographie*, Léon Moussinac's *Naissance du cinéma* (both in 1925), Hans Richter's *Filmgegner von heute – Filmfreunde von morgen* accompanying the Stuttgart exhibition in which Richter curated a programme (1929), Paul Rotha's *The Film Till Now* (1930), and the notorious *Histoire du cinéma* (1935) by Maurice Bardèche and Robert Brasillach (whose fascist leanings later became the material for controversy), translated by Iris Barry into English in 1938. In brief, the emerging archives employed the canon established in the wider avant-garde circles in the 1920s, but in order to stabilize this canon relied on support from the public at large, be it in the form of reformist circles, the fascist state or the civic society of rich East Coast socialites.

In Britain, it was an official government report, *The Film in National Life* written by the 'Commission on Educational and Cultural Films' and published in 1932, which argued for setting up a British Film Institute (BFI) that was to be put in charge of cultural activities in the field of cinema. The BFI, which was officially founded in September 1933, was financed via a special tax on film screenings on Sundays. Thus, the project was supported by and dependent upon the state, but at the same time the institute was not directly a government institution, a fact which sometimes proved difficult for winning official support. Within the institute, a film library was established (on 9 July 1935) which for almost forty years was headed by information officer Ernest Lindgren, legendary nemesis of the equally legendary Henri Langlois.[32] Their personal animosity and rivalry can be seen as the reason why these two personalities and institutions are still so often juxtaposed, because a more sober look reveals that they were quite similar in a lot of respects. Even though the original plans for the film library concentrated on educational film and the connection between schools and producers – the film library was to have three parts concerned with circulation, reference and repository respectively – the early practice (in the 1930s) turned out to be very different.[33] The circulating library rapidly turned into an archive, a place for storage, as more than 80 per cent of the prints held by the institution in the late 1930s were in the storage section, while only 2 per cent were in the circulating library.[34] The library received donations, both in the form of films and money, from a small number of collectors and film enthusiasts, among them

Adrian Brunel who was a vital part of British alternative film culture in the late 1920s.[35] Moreover, the two names that conspicuously show up on a list of donors within a week of the NFL's launch are H.G. Wells and George Bernard Shaw, not coincidentally also founding members of the London Film Society in 1925 (Lindgren himself, being born in October 1910, was too young to have played an active part in that chapter).

Whereas the BFI and the NFL are often portrayed as originating from the circles of educators and schools, the early practice of the library rather seems to be that of an archive that was in its practice much closer to avant-garde film clubs of the 1920s than normally assumed. Already in 1935, Lindgren lamented that classics such as METROPOLIS, CALIGARI and POTEMKIN were not publicly available in Britain, and he attempted to acquire the collection of Will Day which proved to be too expensive for the fledgling institution and was finally bought by the Cinémathèque Française in 1959. Also, in February 1936, seven months after its institution, the first public screening took place commemorating forty years of cinema in Britain with a programme ranging from Lumière to Griffith – the same canon reiterated across these different nation states and institutions. In fact, by '1940, the distribution section had completely abandoned its educational remit to focus exclusively on films based on prints kept in the preservation section and illustrating the history of the cinema'.[36] While the public image of the British archive, possibly due to the juxtaposition of Lindgren and Langlois, sees these institutions as educational providers of film, the actual practice of the NFL in the second half of the 1930s reveals it as quite similar to the other institutions: based on a largely agreed upon catalogue of 'classics', the library collected and screened the same films as MoMA, the Cinémathèque Française and the Reichsfilmarchiv.

Even though France had the most active alternative film scene in the 1920s,[37] no French archive was founded at the time. In the late 1920s, a young Jean Mitry had hoped that Jean Mauclaire would financially back an archive, but he started his own avant-garde cinema instead – 'Studio 28'.[38] It was not until 2 September 1936, when Henri Langlois and Georges Franju (with important help from Mitry) got together with Pierre Auguste Harlé, editor of the trade paper *Cinématographie française* who acted as a liaison with the French film industry, that an archive could be established in France. The French archive is most closely linked to avant-garde institutions, as it emerged from a film society (Cercle du Cinéma), but this was already markedly different in style from earlier models as discussions did not take place in order to be able to show more films (even their film programmes and flyers note 'Sans debate' [no discussion] as a marker of distinction). Whereas in the 1920s the avant-garde had seen film as a means to restructure the relationship of life and art (with the ultimate goal of breaking the distinction down altogether), Langlois and Franju claimed aesthetic autonomy for film and wanted to maximize the number of films being shown because they believed in the intrinsic value of film.

Whereas in traditional histories of the Cinémathèque française and of Langlois the whole becomes a one-man show,[39] the revisionist reconstructions by Patrick Olmeta and Laurent Mannoni paint a different picture:[40] Harlé and Mitry emerge as considerable helpers, especially in channelling Langlois' will and energy towards adequate solutions with their connections both in the film industry and in state institutions. Despite Langlois' efforts, the Cinémathèque française remained a poor institution with little means and few films at their disposal until the war. It is conceivable that under different circumstances the institution would have met the fate of other short-lived institutions which had to discontinue their efforts. Franju goes as far as to claim that it was during the occupation that the number of films held by the Cinémathèque française increased tenfold, from three hundred to three thousand, thanks to Frank Hensel who tipped off Langlois and Franju when films were about to be confiscated. In this perspective, it was less Langlois' personality and more the political and institutional machinations on an international level that was the decisive factor for the long-term success of the archive. True enough, it was Langlois' will and stamina that had carried the project through its first years, but it was only once sufficient official support had been established that the Cinémathèque française could develop into a sustainable institution.

This opens up the international dimension, with the Federation International des Archives du Film (FIAF) as the crucial hub for exchange and collaboration on an international level. Despite huge political differences, the foundation of the FIAF appears to have been a harmonious occasion; John Abbott and Iris Barry had been in close contact with Frank Hensel when they visited Berlin for the Olympic Games in 1936, and international exchange of film material between archives was being put into practice on an informal level, formalized two years later, in June 1938, when FIAF was established in Paris. The inclusion of the Reichsfilmarchiv as well as the fact that this happened only very shortly after the institutions came into existence shows that the archives conceived of themselves as part of an international network (much like the ciné-clubs of the 1920s and early 1930s), but they also considered themselves to be similar enough to communicate and collaborate.

Figure 12.2 Lotte Eisner and Henri Langlois at the opening of the Deutsche Kinemathek in 1963. [Deutsche Kinemathek]

I would argue that the long-term success of these institutions, again, depended on the active involvement of three factors – firstly, avant-garde ideas about the value and the function of the cinema, secondly a broad public support (whether the state as such, governmental agencies or influential social circles), and thirdly, the cooperation of the film industry. Despite all political, social and ideological differences between the U.S., France, the U.K. and Germany, there were influential groups of people in all countries that realized the value and impor-tance of film for the nation state, which was needed as a support mech-anism not only in terms of financing, but also regarding regulatory and legislative issues. The avant-garde on the other hand had run out of steam after 1930 concerning its revolutionary potential, but it had laid the groundwork in respect to the serious and sustainable engagement with film: film theory provided a basis for thinking about the cinema and gave criteria for value judgements; film histories proved that the cinema was a dynamic cultural object worthy of study; and special-ized film theatres, festivals and magazines aimed at gathering a larger public. While the state would provide the framework and the basis for any archival undertaking and the avant-garde had constructed the discursive superstructure, the industry was necessary because, without them, the majority of films would not have been available.

The mid-1930s thus saw a serious engagement with the cinema as an art form and as a cultural force on many different levels. The near-simultaneous emergence of archives in four major film-producing countries, despite all differences, is far from coincidental and illustrates the emergence of film culture on a broad transnational basis. What Haidee Wasson has argued for the Museum of Modern Art, is similarly valid for the archival movement in general:

> Undergirded by archival logics, MoMA established a distinct mode of exhibition, and by extension, of viewing, films. It presupposed that non-commercial and non-theatrical exhibition constituted an essential element of the cinematic and civic infrastructure. As a result, it contributed inestimably to shaping a much wider field of debate about culture, museums, and modern life, securing a stage for film in the ongoing drama of precisely what objects and media matter within the politics of cultural value and visual knowledge.[41]

The archival movement was important since film needed to be available for screening and study if one wanted to engage seriously with the cinema. At the same time, the side effect, and a testament to the similarity of the four projects, was standardization and canonization, as invariably the same films were selected as being worthy of storing, restoring, screening and studying. As much as these institutions then shaped the path towards disciplining the study of film, as much did they also block out those elements of film culture that were not deemed to be important at the time. Yet again, perhaps the most lasting legacy of these institutions is how they engendered important postwar activities such as the French cinéphile culture, which heavily influenced the *Nouvelle Vague* (the new wave), and the important work done by Siegfried Kracauer, Lotte Eisner and Jay Leyda within these institutions, which stretched far into the postwar era.

Into the 1940s and Beyond: Legacy and Further Development

It would be a misunderstanding to see a clear and linear development from the avant-garde ideas of the 1920s to the film culture of the postwar era. Many of the activities withered away or took off into completely unexpected directions. The 1930s saw a number of activities that emulated success formulas from the 1920s, but put them to a different purpose and into a different framework. Such an example would be the 'International Film Congress Berlin' in 1935, which was in fact meant to be a demonstration of the *'völkisch'* character of the German film, a nationalistic display that disguised itself as international.[42] In many respects, film culture is always contradictory, and this seems to be especially true of the 1930s.

In the postwar era, the French cinéphile culture not only gave rise to the *Nouvelle Vague* and the auteur pantheon of the *Cahiers du cinéma*, but also to a broad film culture of teaching and learning, of value building and appreciation.[43] In this way, a lot of the discussion around media pedagogy and education can be traced back to ideas first ventilated within the circles of the avant-garde. As the ground had been prepared with specialized cinemas and little magazines, with festivals and archives, and with theories and histories, these discourses could take off from a different level and they would reach further. Yet again, it would be wrong to draw a direct line from the avant-garde to the new waves. It is a convoluted and complicated history that we can only begin to uncover here.

Notes

1. For more detailed examinations of film festivals, see Marijke de Valck. 2007. *Film Festivals: From European Geopolitics to Global Cinephilia.* Amsterdam: Amsterdam University Press; Dina Iordanova and Ruby Cheung (eds). 2010. *Film Festivals and Imagined Communities,* St Andrews: St Andrews Film Studies; Dina Iordanova and Ragan Rhyne (eds). 2009. *The Festival Circuit,* St Andrews: St Andrews Film Studies.
2. See Malte Hagener. 2007. *Moving Forward, Looking Back: The European Avantgarde and the Invention of Film Culture, 1919–1939.* Amsterdam: Amsterdam University Press, 77–120.
3. See Christophe Gauthier. 1999. *La passion du cinéma. Cinéphiles, Ciné-Clubs et salles specialisées à Paris de 1920 à 1929.* Paris: Association Française de Recherche sur l'Histoire du Cinéma / Ecole des Chartes, 72–74 on the *Salon d'automne,* and 74–76 on *L'art dans le cinéma français.* See also Richard Abel. 1984. *French Cinema: The First Wave, 1915–1929.* Princeton: Princeton University Press, 252f.
4. Gauthier, *La Passion du cinéma,* annexe no. 6: Programme des conférences du Musée Galliera (Mai–Octobre 1924), 356f; Abel, *The First Wave,* 254f.
5. Gauthier: *La Passion du cinéma,* 123 and 136f; Abel, *The First Wave,* 256f.
6. See Wolfgang Mühl-Benninghaus. 1999. *Das Ringen um den Tonfilm. Strategien der Elektro- und Filmindustrie in den 20er und 30er Jahren.* Düsseldorf: Droste, 207f.

7. A. Kraszna-Krausz. 1929. 'Exhibition in Stuttgart, June 1929, and Its Effects', *Close Up* 5/6 (December), 455–64, here 455.

8. See Alexander C.T. Geppert. 2010. *Fleeting Cities: Imperial Expositions in fin-de-Siècle Europe*. Basingstoke: Palgrave Macmillan.

9. A context for this exhibition with a discussion of the status of photography, of previous exhibitions and of the general discourse around photography is provided by Ute Eskildsen. 1979. 'Fotokunst statt Kunstphotographie. Die Durchsetzung des fotografischen Mediums in Deutschland 1920–1933', in Ute Eskildsen and Jan-Christopher Horak (eds), *Film und Foto der Zwanziger Jahre*, Stuttgart: Hatje, 8–25.

10. For the programme, see wh. 1929. 'Die Stuttgarter Sondervorführungen der Werkbundausstellung Film und Photo [*sic*]', *Lichtbildbühne* 22(145) (19 June); and ad. 1929. 'Die Avantgarde im Stuttgarter Programm. Donnerstag – Beginn der Filmschau', *Film-Kurier* 11(139) (13 June).

11. See the annotated reconstruction of the film programme in Helma Schleif (ed.). 1988. *Stationen der Moderne im Film I: FiFo – Film- und Fotoausstellung Stuttgart 1929*. Berlin: Freunde der Deutschen Kinemathek.

12. On accounts and documentation of the La Sarraz meeting, see Freddy Buache. 1979/1980. 'Le cinéma indépendant et d'avant-garde à la fin du muet', *Travelling. Cahiers de la Cinémathèque Suisse* 55 (Summer) and 56/57 (Spring); Roland Cosandey and Thomas Tode. 2000. 'Le 1er congrès international du cinéma indépendant. La Sarraz, Septembre 1929', *Archives, Perpignan* 84 (April), 1–30; and Helma Schleif. 1989. *Stationen der Moderne im Film. II. Texte, Manifeste, Pamphlete*. Berlin: Freunde der Deutschen Kinemathek, 200–19; a detailed bibliography can be found in Thomas Tode. 1999. 'Auswahlbibliographie zu La Sarraz', *Filmblatt* 11 (Autumn), 31–33.

13. For cautious evaluation from the film trade press, see Anon. 1929. 'Filmtagung in der Schweiz. Ein bedeutsames Meeting', *Film-Kurier* 11(206) (30 August); and Paul Medina. 1929. 'Das Fazit der Schweizer Filmtagung', *Film-Kurier* 11(219) (14 September).

14. See Bill Nichols. 2001. 'Documentary Film and the Modernist Avant-Garde', *Critical Inquiry* 27 (Summer), 580–610, for a similar assessment of how the confluence of diverse, even contradictory forces contributed to the emergence of the documentary as a stable film form. For an appraisal of the contradictions inherent in the documentary project, see Scott Anthony. 2011. 'Imperialism and Internationalism: The British Documentary Movement and the Legacy of the Empire Marketing Board', in Lee Grieveson and Colin MacCabe (eds). 2011a. *Empire and Film*, London: British Film Institute, 135–48.

15. This part is a revised version of Malte Hagener. 2011. 'Inventing a Past, Imagining a Future: The Discovery and Institutionalisation of Film History in the 1930s', *Cinema & Cie* 16/17, 29–37.

16. See the contribution by Natalie Ryabchikova in this volume for a detailed examination of how this question played itself out in the Soviet context.

17. See Rolf Aurich's contribution in this volume for a detailed examination of the early history of the Reichsfilmarchiv.

18. Similar activities, albeit on a much smaller level, took place in Sweden; see Mats Björkin and Pelle Snickars. 2003. '1923/1933. Production, Reception and Cultural Significance of Swedish Non-Fiction Film', in Peter Zimmermann and Kay Hoffmann (eds), *Triumph der Bilder. Kultur- und Dokumentarfilme vor 1945 im internationalen Vergleich*, Konstanz: UVK, 272–90.

19. Originally published in *Le figaro* on 25 March 1898, then later as a mimeographed pamphlet; see the English translation in *Screening the Past*, introduced by William D. Ruott, retrieved on 20 July 2011 from http://www.latrobe.edu.au/screeningthepast/classics/clasjul/mat.html

20. See the special issue on 'Cinema during the Great War' of *Film History* 22(4) (2010), edited by Stephen Bottomore; see also Martin Loiperdinger. 2001. 'Die Erfindung des Dokumentarfilms durch die Filmpropaganda im Ersten Weltkrieg', in Kay Hoffmann and Ursula von Keitz (eds), *Die Einübung des dokumentarischen Blicks. Fiction Film und Non Fiction Film zwischen Wahrheitsanspruch und expressiver Sachlichkeit 1895–1945*, Marburg: Schüren, 71–79; and the contributions in Uli Jung and Martin Loiperdinger (eds). 2005. *Geschichte des dokumentarischen Films in Deutschland. Band 1: Kaiserreich 1895–1918*. Stuttgart: Philipp Reclam jun.

21. See Hagener, *Moving Forward, Looking Back*, 113–19.

22. On the (early) history of FIAF, see Penelope Houston. 1994. *Keepers of the Frame: The Film Archives*. London: British Film Institute, 60–77.

23. Houston, *Keepers of the Frame*, 18.

24. For the history of the institution written by a long-term employee, see Hans Barkhausen. 1970. 'Zur Geschichte des ehemaligen Reichsfilmarchivs', in Günter Moltmann and Karl Friedrich Reimers (eds), *Zeitgeschichte im Film- und Tondokument. 17 historische, pädagogische und sozialwissenschaftliche Beiträge*. Göttingen, Zurich and Frankfurt: Musterschmidt, 241–50.

25. On the central role of Goebbels in the propaganda efforts of the Nazis, see Felix Moeller. 2000. *The Film Minister: Goebbels and the Cinema in the 'Third Reich'*. Stuttgart and London: Edition Axel Menges; on the organization of the cinema sector in the years 1933 to 1945, see Jürgen Spiker. 1975. *Film und Kapital. Der Weg der deutschen Filmwirtschaft zum nationalsozialistischen Einheitskonzern*. Berlin: Volker Spiess; and Boguslaw Drewniak. 1987. *Der deutsche Film 1933–1945. Ein Gesamtüberblick*, Düsseldorf: Droste.

26. On the early development of the Reichsfilmarchiv, see Rolf Aurich. 2009a. 'Kurvenreiche Geschichte: vor 75 Jahren wurde das "Reichsfilmarchiv" gegründet', *Film-Dienst* 8, 15–17; and Rolf Aurich. 2009b. 'Film als politischer Zeuge. Zur Geschichte des einstigen deutschen Reichsfilmarchivs', *Neue Zürcher Zeitung* (20 June). For a detailed overview, see Rolf Aurich's contribution in this volume.

27. See Rolf Aurich. 2001. 'Cineast, Sammler, Nationalsozialist. Der Funktionär Frank Hensel und das Reichsfilmarchiv', *Film-Dienst* 15; English translation 2002 in *Journal of Film Preservation* 64(4), 16–21.

28. On the film production of the Fascist Party, see Thomas Hanna-Daoud. 1996. *Die NSDAP und der Film bis zur Machtergreifung*. Cologne: Böhlau.

29. For a general history of the institution, see Sam Hunter. 1984. *The Museum of Modern Art, New York: The History and the Collection*. New York: H.N. Abrams; and Sybil Gordon Kantor. *Alfred H. Barr, jr. and the Intellectual Origins of the Museum of Modern Art*. Cambridge, MA: MIT Press.

30. See the original paper by John E. Abbott and Iris Barry. 1935. 'An Outline of a Project for Founding the Film Library of the Museum of Modern Art'. Reprinted in *Film History* 7(3) (Autumn 1995), 325–35.

31. Haidee Wasson. 2005. *Museum Movies: The Museum of Modern Art and the Birth of Art Cinema*. Berkeley: University of California Press, 88.

32. For the Langlois-Lindgren rivalry, see Houston, *Keepers of the Frame*, 37–59; and Richard Roud. 1983. *A Passion for Film: Henri Langlois and the Cinémathèque Française*, New York: Viking / London: Secker & Warburg.

33. For a detailed look at this practice, see Christopher Dupin. 2007. 'The Origins and Early Development of the National Film Library: 1929–1936', *Journal of Media Practice* 7(3) (March), 199–217.

34. Ibid., 211.

35. Jamie Sexton. 2000. 'Parody on the Fringes: Adrian Brunel, Minority Film Culture and the Art of Deconstruction', in Alan Burton and Laraine Porter (eds), *Pimple, Pranks and Pratfalls: British Film Comedy Before 1930*. Wiltshire: Flicks; and Jamie Sexton. 2008. *Alternative Film Culture in Inter-War Britain*. Exeter: University of Exeter Press.

36. Dupin, 'Origins and Early Development', 215f.

37. Gauthier, *La Passion du cinéma*.

38. Patrick Olmeta. 2000. *La Cinémathèque française de 1936 à nos jours*. Paris: CNRS, 24f.

39. See for example the classic biography, Roud, *A Passion for Film*.

40. Olmeta, *La Cinémathèque française*; and Laurent Mannoni. 2006b. *Histoire de la Cinémathèque française*, Paris: Gallimard.

41. Wasson, *Museum Movies*.

42. See Yong Chan Choy. 2006. *Inszenierungen der völkischen Filmkultur im Nationalsozialismus:, Der internationale Filmkongress Berlin 1935'*. Berlin: Technical University. (Ph.D. thesis; retrieved on 11 Nov. 2011 from http://opus.kobv.de/ tuberlin/volltexte/2006/1214/)

43. Bettina Henzler. 2011. '"Il les conduit ailleurs". Gespräch mit Alain Bergala zu Cinéphilie, Wissenschaft und Pädagogik', in Gudrun Sommer, Vinzenz Hediger and Oliver Fahle (eds), *Orte filmischen Wissens. Filmkultur und Filmvermittlung im Zeitalter digitaler Netzwerke*. Marburg: Schüren, 161–75.

Chapter 13

THE GERMAN REICH FILM ARCHIVE IN AN INTERNATIONAL CONTEXT

Rolf Aurich

For a long time, film copies and negatives were destroyed once they had fulfilled their economic purpose and there was no storage space for them. To stem this loss, enthusiasts, companies, and private and public institutions collected films in Germany and elsewhere that they considered important or useful. German newspapers of the 1920s in particular were full of items reporting how towns and cities had set up agencies of their own to preserve film copies. In Germany in the 1930s, screenings of earlier film productions organized by intermediaries such as Ernst Angel, Alfred Jungermann and Johannes Eckardt, or by collectors such as Walter Jerven and Walter Steinhauer, enjoyed immense popularity. In his childhood the film director Gerhard Lamprecht became involved in collecting not only film copies but also other materials and documents related to film, as well as technical equipment. And day-to-day editing tasks at the Berlin trade paper *Lichtbild-Bühne* gave rise to a highly reputed archive that comprised all manner of collected material, including film copies, which proved of great service especially to the film industry. This archived material was confiscated from its Jewish owner Karl Wolffsohn and withdrawn as early as 1933 by the Ministry of Propaganda. For a long while, no measures were taken by Germany to establish a central authority for collecting films, despite repeated and sustained calls in the press and specialist publications. It was only with the shift from silent to sound films that an awareness of the historicity of the immediate past began to grow, and it gradually found acceptance as art. Concrete changes in terms of media policy were spawned above all by 'the media awareness of the Nazis, whose measures to restructure the film industry in Germany prepared the ground for a centralized German film archive'.[1]

Founded in late January 1934 on the anniversary of the 'National Socialist revolution' and inaugurated the following year in Berlin in the presence of Hitler and Goebbels, the official task of the new Reichsfilmarchiv (Reich Film Archive) was to collect and conserve 'films that in any respect deserve special interest regardless of their commercial distribution'. Whether feature films, documentaries ('*Kulturfilme*', as they were called at the time), newsreels or other genres, productions 'of the past and the present' were supposed to 'be preserved for the future as reference material, especially for study purposes'. Thus, 'by collecting such footage' the Reich Film Archive was entrusted with 'a key cultural and political task in the interest of later generations and the entire film industry'.[2] Prior to the archive's inauguration, the president of the Reichsfilmkammer (Reich Chamber of Film), Fritz Scheuermann, even spoke of the need to set up repertory film theatres 'to ensure the best films would not fade into obscurity after just eighteen months' – in other words after a film's average period of exhibition on the cinema screen.[3] All relevant authorities, private individuals and businesses were publicly called upon to hand in films that were in their possession. As Frank Maraun reports, veritable razzias were visited on the 'warrens of funfair and show booth operators' who sought to make money from old stocks of film from cinema's early years.[4] But individual cases of film copies being confiscated from private collections are also known, as happened to the Munich film producer Franz Steinbacher.[5] Nonetheless, several officially sanctioned, regionally organized film collections continued operating during the Third Reich, such as the educational archive 'Ufa-Lehrschau' with its innovative film archival concept, the research archives of the Ufa and the Bavaria studios.[6]

Given the provenance of the footage, the initial collections of the Reich Film Archive focused on documentary material, among which were the state-controlled propaganda productions of the Bild und Filmamt (BUFA), the Image and Film Authority, from the Potsdam Reich Archive, Ufa's weekly newsreels, party political films made by the NSDAP, documentaries and city films.

The first director of this institution was Leonhard Böttger, who had previously been at the Foreign Office. He was soon replaced, in 1935, by the Nazi Party member Frank Hensel, who in turn was succeeded in

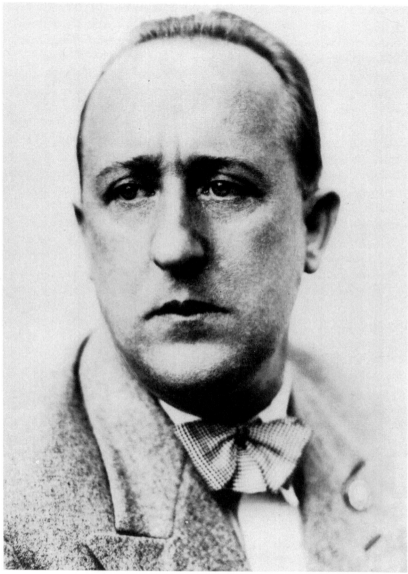

Figure 13.1 Portrait of Frank Hensel (1935). [Deutsche Kinemathek]

1937 by his party colleague Richard Quaas.[7] Both men had joined the Nazi party very early on and had also been responsible for several Nazi propaganda films in the 1930s. The second reshuffle was prompted by Goebbels' dissatisfaction with the stagnating centralization of the collected film material still dispersed among numerous different agencies. The minister wrested the Reich Film Archive from the authority of the Reich Film Chamber and incorporated it into measures for 'conserving contemporary documents' that were channelled into plans for the scheduled umbrella organization of the Reichskulturarchive, the Reich Cultural Archives (but which then more or less petered out). This gave him direct powers of control.[8] In the 1930s the specialist film press frequently reported on international guests visiting the Reich Film Archive, whose existence for people in the film business was gradually taken for granted.

Users and Access

Prior to his military service in November 1943, Hans Barkhausen worked as a consultant at the Reich Film Archive; in the late 1950s he was largely involved in setting up a film department at the Bundesarchiv (Federal Archives) in Coblence and in retrieving German films that had been confiscated by the Western Allies. He published essays about the history of this Nazi institution in several journals. Barkhausen roughly divided the Reich Film Archive's users into three groups: users concerned with academic research, universities and institutes; the film industry; and various administrative authorities of the Reich, party organs and agencies. Even during the war, as Barkhausen recalls, the media scholar Emil Dovifat was a constant visitor to the archive, as too was 'a certain Dr. Schottländer, a professor at the academy of music'.[9] Another user was the Deutsche Filmakademie, which was temporarily housed in Babelsberg (1938–40). Numerous documents have survived bearing witness to the keen interest on the part of political circles and the film industry. For instance, in early 1942 Fritz Hippler, director of the film department in the Propaganda Ministry, requested to see Fritz Lang's first American film FURY (1936) in a supervised screening in the Tobis studios. Two years later, the director Erich Engel was given permission to watch Jean Renoir's film adaptation of Emile Zola's LA BÊTE HUMAINE (1938) as preparation for his own – never to be completed – production WO IST HERR BELLING [Where is Herr Belling].

By contrast, only incidental evidence is available telling us how the still nascent realm of film studies and, occasionally, even restricted sections of the general public were permitted access to the Reich Film Archive's holdings. Eva M.J. Schmid recalls how the department of journalism at Leipzig University set up a film study group for students which, besides the participants' own small gauge footage, was also allowed limited access to parts of the Reich Film Archive.[10] A later member of the archive's staff, her colleague Heinz Küttner, organized for a copy of Fritz Lang's DAS TESTAMENT DES DR. MABUSE (1932/33), which was banned in Germany, to be shown in a cinema in Leipzig. Being on the staff of the Reich Film Archive he had the authority to allow other staff members, soldiers, and also outsiders like Schmid, to see films from the archive's collection at in-house viewings in Berlin.[11] To what degree such concrete opportunities had an influence on film research in the 1930s would need to be examined case by case.[12] For the art historian Thomas Meder, the Reich Film Archive – alongside the Ufa's educational archive and the Deutsche Filmakademie – is unquestionably an important institution but has only modest significance for scholarly research. He bases his view on the fact that the circle of those who, from the late 1930s onwards, published 'the first systematic film "histories"' on an international level includes no German authors. The 'given political premises' imposed too strict a distinction from the so-called Weimar 'System period' and Hollywood as a centre of production, thus prohibiting the emergence of an 'autonomous historiography and theory of film'. According to Meder, a small 'residuum' for this was provided nonetheless by the Munich theatre studies scholar Artur Kutscher, whose milieu spawned more independent and discerning studies.[13] In the 1930s Kutscher also corresponded with the journalism scholar Hans Traub, a man of conservative nationalist views who was director of the Ufa educational archive that had been founded in early 1936, and who several years earlier had been one of the first to call for the introduction of film studies.[14] Thus, as early as 1940, Traub was in a position to claim that 'far more than half of all films are no longer available'.[15]

Laying Hands on Film

The documentary footage in the Reich Film Archive, on the other hand, was of considerable significance. As Barkhausen recalls, 'all the films the political police confiscated from the banned parties from 1933 onwards … were handed over to the Reich Film Archive in 1938', where they were 'carefully indexed, their content registered, sorted into files according to various criteria and assigned serial numbers', and then put in store.[16] A prominent example of an early confiscation is the operation carried out by the SA and auxiliary police in mid-March

1933 to seize copies of the sixteen films belonging to the communist film distributor Film-Kartell Welt-Film. Mostly Soviet films, among them BRONENOSEZ POTEMKIN [Battleship Potemkin] (1925, Sergei Eisenstein), but also several German silent films, such as EISBRECHER KRASSIN (1928), were impounded without receipt, thereby preventing the film company from meeting its obligations towards the photo and film department of the Soviet trade mission in Germany.[17] That such unequivocally left-wing films were considered valuable archival items is indicated by their repeated transfer and the separate storage of film copies and negatives, as well as by the preservation of duplicates and 'lavender prints' in vaults far from Berlin. After the annexation of Austria in 1938, the archive was augmented by footage confiscated from the Rote Bildungszentrale (Red education centre) in Vienna.[18] How much easier it would have been for occupying German forces to impound film stock in Austria had a centralized International Socialist Film Archive already been set up, as had been called for in 1934 by the Austrian film critic and Social Democrat Fritz Rosenfeld.[19] An index of the foreign-made documentary films held in the Reich Film Archive was compiled for internal use, but for German films no such research tool existed.[20] Hans Barkhausen explained the index's purpose: 'The privileged treatment of foreign documentary films stemmed from the desire by state bodies to be kept up to date during the war about the latest reports from enemy countries'.[21] In addition, this overweening interest applied to every genre of film since Goebbels and his staff, as Clemens Zimmermann observes, 'needed constantly to be kept abreast of all foreign and domestic activities related to film so they could steer film production in the right direction, in aesthetic terms too'. Besides, economic interests alone were a good enough reason for staying informed about public tastes.[22]

The FIAF: A Pre-war Foundation

Films, even those from abroad,[23] entered the Reich Film Archive in a variety of ways. Negatives registered by the producer to be destroyed were purchased at the price of their net scrap film value. Films produced in Germany with the highest government rating had to be submitted as a copy, while for all other films 'similar requirements applied eight months following their cinema release in Germany'.[24] In the countries occupied by Germany after 1938, films were confiscated in large quantities and then passed on to the archive. At the International

Figure 13.2 Portrait of Richard Quaas (1946). [Hans-Rainer Quaas, Gröbenzell]

Film Congress held in Berlin in late April 1935, which was recently interpreted as a 'nationalistic (*völkisch*) mise en scène of German film culture',[25] a commission led by Frank Hensel recommended that film archives be set up in all countries and linked together in a collaborative network.[26] A similar path was pursued in the far-reaching proposals by Adolf Hübl for the creation of an international, 'world-embracing' film museum – as a part of the League of Nations' International Institute for Educational Film in Rome.[27] Shortly before the war broke out, just after the fall of the Front Populaire in France and several months preceding the anti-Semitic *Kristallnacht* pogrom in November, and while civil war was still raging in Spain, the Fédération Internationale des Archives du Film (FIAF) was founded – on, it should be mentioned, German initiative.[28] Besides the Reich Film Archive (represented by Frank Hensel and Richard Quaas), the FIAF's founding members were the Cinémathèque Française (represented by Henri Langlois and Paul-Auguste Harlé, former chief editor of *La Cinématographie Française*), the English National Film Library (represented by its chairman Harry Price and secretary Olwen Vaughan) and the Film Library of the Museum of Modern Art in New York (represented by the museum patron John Hay Whitney and John E. Abbott, who became the FIAF's first president). Alfred-Ingemar Berndt, one of Goebbels' department heads and later chief representative for archives and contemporary documents, wrote to his superior about the FIAF in early 1939: 'The advantage of this foundation for us is that the exchange agreement will allow the Reich Film Archive to bring in films we consider important at no foreign currency cost. In deference to America, whose films one could hardly do without, Paris had to be chosen as the seat of the International Film Archive'.[29] Shortly after the Munich Agreement permitting the annexation of Czechoslovakia's Sudetenland territories into the German Reich, the Manchester Guardian lauded the foundation of the FIAF, saying it 'was an excellent idea to preserve the best films and exchange them with our neighbours'.[30] At the outset 'exchange' could be interpreted in a number of ways: as an agreement about temporary loans, as reciprocal sales or as one-to-one swaps – a question that Frank Hensel's letter to John Abbott in late October 1938 indeed left unresolved.[31]

The German Film Archive's Relations to the USA

In the run-up to the FIAF's foundation, the major national film archives were already moving closer together. Films first began to be exchanged between the French, English and American institutions in 1937, and during the war material was occasionally even passed between the United States and the USSR for use in compilation films.[32] In 1936, during their visit to Europe as representatives of the MoMA, John Abbott and his wife Iris Barry also spent some time in Germany immediately prior to the 9th Olympic Games in Berlin. They had made contact with government authorities and people who might be able to supply them archived German and foreign films for the Film Library they had founded in 1935; among their contacts was Frank Hensel, who in early 1937 voiced a firm belief that the archives in England, America and Poland had been set up based on 'his system'.[33] Abbott subsequently informed the American embassy in Berlin that of the films he had been offered 70 per cent were 'clearly propaganda with no other outstanding features', although it was his opinion that Germany was also producing 'some excellent films which are entirely devoid of propaganda'.[34] With great relief it was noted that many films by artists who had now emigrated had not yet been destroyed.[35] Further light is shed on the tastes of the two MoMA representatives in a retrospective essay published by Iris Barry one year after their visit, in which she not only speaks enviously of the 'Lehrschau', Ufa's educational archive in Babelsberg, but also openly expresses her enthusiasm for Leni Riefenstahl's film of the Nazis' Nuremberg Rally, Triumph des Willens [Triumph of the Will] (1935,) as 'one of the most brilliantly assembled and edited films imaginable'. In her view it represents an endeavour to capture exceptional national events with the means available to film, wholly in the tradition of earlier painters and poets commissioned by the state. In particular, the author emphasizes the almost indissoluble fusion of mass choreography and technical staging required both for the 1934 Nuremberg Rally itself and for this film – albeit entirely without critical distance.[36] No wonder, then, that in late 1938 Abbott asked Frank Hensel to supply his archive with Riefenstahl's Olympia films, together with other works they had viewed in Berlin, such as Walter Ruttmann's Berlin. Sinfonie einer Grossstadt (1927) and Frank Wysbar's Fährmann Maria (1936), in addition to Eisenstein's Battleship Potemkin, which he requested in the best possible print quality.[37] Abbott and Barry also held talks with officials in the Soviet Union who, however, voiced serious misgivings about a privately run film collection such as the one at the MoMA. The first centralized film archive in the USSR (Gosfilmofond) was opened – after lengthy preparations – in 1948. Their visit nonetheless gave the two American representatives a chance to meet the American-born, left-wing avant-gardist Jay Leyda, who had followed Eisenstein to the

Figure 13.3 Iris Barry during her Berlin visit in 1936. [Museum of Modern Art]

USSR in 1933 and now agreed to return to New York to take up a position in the Film Library. Not every film that could be procured with relative ease in Europe was welcomed in the USA. This was of course particularly true of films from the Soviet Union and Nazi Germany. Several years before her death in 1969, Iris Barry recalled the underlying mood among the first film archivists: 'The point there, I think, is that those of us in various countries who had really loved the cinema now, with the advent of talkies, realized that probably we should never see again the films that had enchanted us and therefore that an effort was needed to preserve as much as one could of the films of the past'.[38]

Two Cinéphiles, Frank Hensel and Henri Langlois

Surely it can only be considered a mockery when, in a letter to John Abbott in spring 1939, as war was approaching, Frank Hensel asserted that the FIAF had nothing to do with politics, while barely a few lines earlier he had declared that in the event of an armed conflict their collaboration would be terminated, regardless of where those film copies happened to be at the given time – a future war would mean 'a total revolution of all the world'.[39] All the same, after the German occupation of France in summer 1940 this claim was no barrier to the German side continuing its collaboration with the Cinémathèque Française in the form of a 'reduced FIAF', as it were. In August of the previous year Hensel had been elected president at the second FIAF congress in New York, formally retaining his position for several years to come. Due to the war the meeting scheduled for August 1940 never took place, and in July 1946, at the third congress in Paris, Hensel was succeeded by Iris Barry. His career in the SS raised him from the position of *Sturmbannführer* in 1938 (one of his twelve sponsors was Adolf Eichmann) to the grade of *SS-Obersturmbannführer* (promoted on 20 April 1939, Hitler's 50th birthday). As a so-called film ombuds-man (*Film-Vertrauensmann*) he was also involved in intelligence opera-tions by the SD (Sicherheitsdienst) headed by Reinhard Heydrich. The additional tasks he took on in 1936 in the political leadership of the Mitteleuropäisches Reisebüro (MER), the Central European Travel Agency, presumably served the sole purpose of conspiratori-ally procuring secret documents[40] and requisitioning foreign films. Hensel was a spy. A few months prior to the second congress and to the outbreak of the Second World War, he voiced his strong belief to Abbott that the FIAF needed to be given a broader scope 'as the Office, according to my opinion, has not been established only to procure films for Miss Vaughan, Mr Abbott, Mr Hensel and Mr Langlois. This is not the idea of the Federation, and I believe that the funds were chiefly intended for the purpose to promote international coopera-tion between film archives, and this to a far greater extent'.[41] Hensel's intensive contacts with Henri Langlois, a relationship the Frenchman used to protect film stocks now under threat of confiscation by the Germans, have been described by Laurent Mannoni in his history of the Cinémathèque Française.[42] 'Enthusiasts among themselves' was how Hensel and Langlois were described by the writer Georg Stefan Troller in 1964 when in his diary he noted an anecdote about the two men as told to him by Lotte Eisner. The German, she said, 'used his position of power during the Occupation to illegally furnish his friend Langlois with hundreds of films that he personally had confiscated from all over Europe'.[43] Together with Marcel L'Herbier, incumbent president of the Cinémathèque since 1941, Hensel was also respon-sible for ensuring that the institution was able to continue various activities during the Occupation, 'collecting, exchanging films with the Reichsfilmarchiv, and in 1941 creating a Commission for Historical Research'.[44] The author Jerome Charyn summed it up when he said that 'during the Occupation of Paris, Hensel had his own secret life';

and 'he was almost *hollywoodien*, like a benign Fantômas or Scarlet Pimpernel'.[45] If one reads how Hensel was described by Goebbels' personnel department when he turned fifty, this characterization seems all too justified: 'In the ongoing war Hensel's task is to procure foreign films for our organization and for the Wehrmacht of particular propagandistic, military or artistic value. Through the special unit 'Sonderkommando Hensel' he founded he has succeeded in obtaining numerous incendiary propaganda films, entertainment films and newsreels of interest to us from all kinds of foreign countries. And for the Ministry he has also managed to procure technical film devices from abroad when these were not available in the Reich'.[46] He himself boasted to his superiors that, partially aided by the Gestapo, 'only half a year after the return of the Saarland he had fished out tons of films from under the beds of the Communists in the Saar region'.[47] Quite evidently with Frank Hensel, the first generation of archivists, later hailed by Ulrich Gregor as an 'epoch of heroic individual endeavours in the service of film culture',[48] also included a Nazi of relatively international thinking and actions. All of Hensel's pre-war colleagues rose to become more or less legendary figures in their postwar professions. Yet after the war and several years spent in a prison camp, Hensel, who owed his career to his Nazi views, turned his back on the film world and faded into obscurity. For a while he ran a sauna in Bonn, the capital of Germany's new parliamentary democracy, which was popular among politicians.

Film Exile in New York and Paris

On either side of the Atlantic, in France and the United States, two Jewish intellectuals who had been driven out of Germany in 1933 were simultaneously working in their respective FIAF archives. A graduate of art history, Lotte H. Eisner – inasmuch as her daily struggle to earn a living permitted – soon became involved in unpaid volunteer work for the Cinémathèque Française, which had been founded in 1936 on the private initiative of Paul-Auguste Harlé, Henri Langlois, Georges Franju and Jean Mitry, and had started up as a ciné-club called 'Cercle du cinéma'. Having gone into hiding during the German occupation of Paris, in a remote chateau Eisner began viewing and assessing films Langlois sought to conceal from the occupiers – such as KUHLE WAMPE ODER WEM GEHÖRT DIE WELT? (1932, Slatan Dudow), THE GREAT DICTATOR (1941, Charles Chaplin) and various works of

Soviet cinema.[49] 'Now she herself was saved, she set about saving old films', as Karsten Witte characterizes her situation.[50] At this point, she was still unacquainted with expressionist cinema from Germany. She first became familiar with it at the Cinémathèque, these being the kind of silent movies that Langlois eagerly went in search of – and tracked down – in the vaults of old cinemas. Even in its early days the Cinémathèque could already boast of films like DAS CABINET DES DR CALIGARI (1920, Robert Wiene), BIRTH OF A NATION (1915, D.W. Griffith) and other non-French works.[51] It was not until after the war, in 1952, that her study *L'Ecran démoniaque. Influence de Max Reinhardt et de l'Expressionnisme* [The Haunted Screen], later described by Witte as 'rigorous stylistic analysis',[52] was published in Paris.

In late April 1941, at the age of 52, the film critic and journalist Siegfried Kracauer and his wife arrived as last-minute refugees in New York, where, from July onwards, he received a one-year 'grant-in-aid' worth $2,000. The grant was to enable him to compile an analysis of Fascist film and war propaganda at the MoMA's Film Library, which had been set up with private funds of $120,000 from the Rockefeller Foundation. The library's curator, Iris Barry, described Kracauer's study as 'an integrated content-analysis of totalitarian communication in wartime'.[53] Unlike Eisner, who (under a false name) remained active in the film scene in France, Kracauer was 'never part of the New York cinéphilia', as Enno Patalas relates, nor did he play an active role in the work of the Film Library at the MoMA.[54] Nonetheless Kracauer's arguably more passive contribution surely must have left an impression, as is amply evidenced by the diverse contacts he made during his time at the library – on the émigré Erwin Panofsky,[55] for instance, or Hans Richter.[56] He managed to access the Nazi films he required for his work at the MoMA 'really quite quickly', reports Ingrid Belke, the editor of Kracauer's writings.[57] Indeed, according to Iris Barry in early 1941 some twenty thousand feet of official German film footage from the Nazi period between 1934 and 1940 were available in New York – and there were hopes of soon procuring a similar quantity of even more up-to-date material. 'In addition, the Film Library's archives contain most of the outstanding Russian films from 1922 to 1938, including those towards which the attention of German filmmakers was directed as models to study and surpass.'[58]

In 1944, among the films Iris Barry considered worth collecting for the Film Library were not only avant-garde works but also numerous other films, including explicitly 'propaganda films', whether 'pacifist or Nazi'.[59] Yet this inevitably required contacts and an exchange of films and literature on an international level.[60] The Film Library went to considerable effort to ensure the success of Kracauer's research, which was assisted by the sociologist Hans Speier and the art historian and psychoanalyst Ernst Kris, both émigrés. On Barry's instructions, her assistant curator Richard Griffith explored how permission could be gained to obtain footage, located in Canada, of the German film SIEG IM WESTEN [Victory in the West] (1941, Svend Noldan), a production of the German army high command that in early 1941 had been censored in Germany, and for several weeks could be seen in cinemas in New York.[61] This proved a protracted task, and a key role in solving it was played by the National Film Board and its director John Grierson.[62] Yet it is doubtful that Kracauer ever got to see the film BILDDOKUMENTE 1912–1918 [Visual documentation 1912–1918] that Jay Leyda mentions in his 1964 study *Films beget Films*, a compilation of contemporary newsreel footage along Nazi ideological lines made by Frank Hensel in 1936 for the Reich Chamber of Film (in other words, presumably for the Reich Film Archive). According to Leyda, this film material was later used to the opposite effect under the title WHITHER GERMANY? – 'one of the earliest attempts to turn an antagonist's material into an attack on him'.[63]

Among the first people to use the Film Library were film directors like Luis Buñuel and Fernand Léger, documentarists and historians such as Paul Rotha and Jay Leyda, and authors such as Lewis Jacobs and Gilbert Seldes. The significance of the Film Library for applied film history cannot be overstated. In this it fundamentally differs from the Reich Film Archive, which – unlike its American and French equivalents – is not known to have made efforts to show the archived films in any public form, thereby appreciating them as a means to stimulate pluralist debate and untrammelled thinking. On the contrary, in the view of Wolfgang Klaue, former director of the State Film Archive of the GDR, the archive had an altogether different purpose for propaganda minister Goebbels than simply collecting and preserving in the service of art, namely: to 'educate filmmakers in the ways of Nazi ideology, with the aim of creating a "German BATTLESHIP POTEMKIN"'.[64] This international disparity is also echoed on a more general level. The relatively hermetic Berlin institution of the German Film Archive contrasted strongly with the open approach of the Film Library in New York, which was eager to pursue all manner of contacts and forms of use, and was supported by an institution with a pedagogic mission. Films were supposed 'to be studied and enjoyed like the other arts', in the words of Iris Barry, who in every respect placed strong emphasis on the social impact of films.[65] She stated that the eight film programmes titled *The Film in Germany and France* that were shown to American audiences from 1937 onwards had been as a direct result of her trip to Germany in summer 1936.[66] The specialist press passed judgement on the Film Library's first ten years of operation: 'From these archives numerous programs have been made up in series or separately for showing at the Museum and for circulation to other non-commercial institutions throughout the country. In addition to the daily programs at the Museum, 819 other organisations or groups have shown its films'.[67] This newly introduced film loan service had also been reported in Germany's specialist press.[68]

At the MoMA, silent films were generally accompanied by piano – which seems surprising from today's perspective. In mid-March 1945, less than two months before the end of the war, Siegfried Kracauer mentioned in a letter to Fritz Lang, with whom he had made contact two years earlier at the prompting of Hans Richter and Paul Falkenberg, that Lang's film DER MÜDE TOD [Destiny] (1921) was being shown at the MoMA in the afternoons – a work that the Film Library had requested from the Reich Film Archive in late 1938 and received in early 1939.[69] At this time, with films being shown publicly in New York while in Berlin and Babelsberg they had to be sheltered from the Allies' bombs, Kracauer was, as he reported, making good progress with his *Caligari* book, for which he had been granted a Guggenheim Fellowship in 1943.[70] That might have been helped by his contact with Jay Leyda, whom he had approached in summer 1943 asking for a preview of his manuscript on Soviet cinema: 'for I might learn a lot from your techniques in handling the variegated relations between films and simultaneous social, political and cultural currents'.[71] In early 1942 Leyda himself was seeking assistance with quotations and references for his almost completed Eisenstein translation *The Film Sense*, so he turned to the émigré Kurt Pinthus who had just previously been employed as a consultant for the drama collection of the Library of Congress in Washington.[72] German film studies were taking root – in exile.

There was much in the United States indicating that Kracauer's research into the history of German cinema would become a longer-term engagement, as Ingrid Belke confirms. As a critic he had seen almost all the important German films produced in the Weimar period and, as well as having a manifestly good knowledge of politics and history, he had also taken a keen interest in film theory since the 1920s. Yet a crucial criterion for the award of the fellowship was the condition of academic research in North America at that juncture: a coherent history of German cinema had yet to be written.[73] 'This task went on to determine the further development of his work', as Johannes Riedner has observed.[74] To which should be added the protracted controversy surrounding his *Psychological History of the German Film* published in 1947 under the title *From Caligari to Hitler*.

But Siegfried Kracauer too had already gained experience at the Cinémathèque Française before the war broke out. In a brief meeting with Kracauer and his wife in Hamburg in summer 1958, the journalist Ingeborg Brandt mentioned 'unforgettable Paris and its superb Cinémathèque', which had been planned as a leg of a trip to Europe on which Kracauer was hoping to collect material for his study *Theory of Film: The Redemption of Physical Reality*, due to be published two years later.[75] Paris, to where before 1933 Kracauer would love to have moved as a correspondent for the *Frankfurter Zeitung*, was the European city he was most familiar with after Berlin, and his interest in French culture was immense. Yet his first years of exile in France between 1933 and 1941 were clouded by poverty and humiliation. Kracauer was under pressure to publish a lot, which he did in, among others, the *Neue Zürcher Zeitung* and the Basel newspaper *National-Zeitung*. After Max Horkheimer and Meyer Schapiro recommended in 1937 that he turn to the MoMA's Film Library and to Iris Barry, by summer 1938 this support had begun to bear fruit.[76] Although the Cinémathèque's first exhibition was dedicated to the French film pioneer Georges Méliès, who had died in early 1938, the exhibition was held in London. Yet at the same time the MoMA had been invited to stage an exhibition in Paris: Langlois was a great enthusiast and admirer of America and its cinema, besides which he had always been internationalist in his thinking. Kracauer reported on the exhibition in the Jeu de Paume, *Trois siècles d'art aux États-Unis* (Three Centuries of Art in the United States), which was praised by critics in particular for its independently conceived special exhibition about film and the hugely popular programme of anthology films. His report focused on the exhibition of the Film Library, analysing it in affectionate detail, before he reached an astonishing conclusion about the institution: 'If it is true that the interpretation of contemporary life is also linked to the immersive contemplation of films, then in course this institute is due to assume some extraordinary tasks'.[77] While the exhibition was still running he managed to arrange a meeting with John Abbott. As successful as the Paris exhibition was for Abbott's Film Library in gaining international recognition of American film as 'art', nonetheless it was still unable to rid the Film Library of its status as an 'adopted child' within the framework of the MoMA.[78]

Being friends with Langlois and frequently visiting his Cinémathèque for work, Kracauer turned to him in May 1938 to ask for information about the Film Library at the MoMA.[79] It was probably around this time that he was invited to New York 'to write at this institute a study on the History and Sociology of German Moving Pictures'.[80] Towards the end of the year he commented in one of his 'Film letters from Paris' on the founding of the FIAF, thanks to which 'the future collaboration of the French, American, German, English and Italian film libraries has finally been secured'; in clear terms Kracauer speaks of the 'mutual interests' that supposedly would be rationally fostered by this new venture.[81] Leading figures from the four great film archives of England, Germany, France and the United States were guests at the Paris exhibition that provided an atmospherically propitious backdrop to the founding of the FIAF.[82] Thus at this point the French government announced their interest in supporting the new organization. It offered rent-free offices and an annual maintenance subsidy of 25,000 French francs – as John Abbott reported in summer 1938 to John Marshall, assistant director of the Rockefeller Foundation. In his letter he emphasized the interest of European film directors like Pabst, Clair and Hitchcock, as well as the producer Pommer, in the planned preservation of film history.[83] Yet in spring 1939 the scheduled contribution to the FIAF of the initial sum of 12,000 francs from each member archive ran into difficulties – New York complained that Germany had still not paid its due, a rebuke Berlin countered by pointing out that a down payment of 5,000 francs had already been made in Paris, and that further payments would not be forthcoming until the need arose, acknowledging that this indeed was intended as a lever for exercising control. This partisan strategy sprang from the Germans' assessment of their French colleagues: 'You will realize that although the gentlemen in Paris are very nice chaps, they are, on the other hand, still rather young and inexperienced'.[84] A few weeks later, in mid-May 1939, Frank Hensel discovered that as yet not a penny of the French money had been paid. This is why he felt it was his duty as the FIAF vice-president to act in this way.[85]

Kracauer's *Caligari* book from 1946 and its relation to contemporary academic research is discussed by Karsten Witte: 'Eisner had nothing to do with this work. She does not even mention it in her memoirs. Kracauer's approach must have been a thorn in her side'.[86] Indeed, Eisner's relations to other authors, Kracauer included, do not appear to have been entirely free of personal rivalry. In a letter to Kurt Pinthus in late 1953, who that year was making his first return visit to Germany, she remarked that producing a U.S. edition of her *L'Écran démoniaque* will be difficult 'because you also have the Kracauer here, even if this quite interesting book has been written from an entirely different perspective than mine'.[87] And a few years later, writing to Pinthus again, she declared, 'My book has now four editions: French, Italian, German, Spanish but not one in English because of the Kracauer and Wollenberg books on German cinema'.[88] In 1952 the West Berlin critic Friedrich Luft had pointed out that 'the most important and fundamental books on German film' have been published 'outside Germany'.[89] He was referring to Kracauer and Eisner, but fully failed to mention that his surprise lay in the fact that both authors were living in exile. It was not until 1946 that Eisner and Kracauer began exchanging letters.

According to the film historian Bernard Eisenschitz, Lotte Eisner, whose writings have still not been published in an exhaustive edition in Germany, was 'highly regarded as a source, as a contemporary witness and an archivist. But in her role as a historian she received little recognition. Like Kracauer, she actually lived through the period she describes and, in my opinion, historians living in the period they study and historians born later are two different "schools" which are very difficult to reconcile'.[90] For Enno Patalas, both Eisner's book as well as Kracauer's have 'contributed less to the scholarship of film history than to our concrete knowledge of it'.[91]

The founding of the FIAF and the increasing impact made by German intellectuals and specialists in exile precipitated the turning point when film production and film distribution ceased being the only major factors of international importance (in spite of growing protectionist tendencies) and the issue of preserving films and their copies that had dropped out of the economic loop began to be addressed and concretely tackled on an international scale. In short, production, economic exploitation and archiving – a film's entire 'existence' – were now governed by a largely unimpeded and globalized flow of exchange, despite being temporarily interrupted at the outset by the war from autumn 1939 onwards. But it should not be forgotten that the film archives and cinémathèques of the free world in the so important 1930s were still in their infancy. Standards and methodological practices had still to be evolved. Their common purpose was to establish a comprehensive study of film as a living art. That this was not the aim of the Reich Film Archive is utterly self-evident.

Predatory Expansion of the
Reich Film Archive's Holdings

German agencies were constantly able to 'acquire' feature films and newsreels 'from enemy powers' through neutral foreign countries.[92] According to Richard Quaas in a report from 1954, through these channels it remained possible up until March 1945 to get hold of 'every enemy weekly newsreel' and even the 'latest movies from America and elsewhere'. They were classified 'secret'.[93] This was compounded by the filmic 'war loot' amassed in Czechoslovakia, Poland, Denmark and Norway, especially by the Gestapo and the Abwehr (military intelligence).[94] The files are filled with references to such hauls, and in some cases the Reich Film Archive registered veritable wholesale deliveries of film copies – so many that they were almost impossible to process. As the Polish film historian Boguslaw Drewniak has explained, 'some films were impounded en route as so-called "incendiary" films, either by the German customs authorities or by the Wehrmacht. In addition, the German legation in Stockholm had been instructed by the ministry of propaganda to find ways of procuring "enemy incendiary films"'.[95] But there was also interest in anti-Semitic films made abroad. Thus in June 1943 the Reich Film Archive paid from its own budget to have a new copy of the medium-length French film FORCES OCCULTES (1943) made for its collection – considered by Roy Armes to be an 'assault on freemasonry'[96] – just a quarter of a year after its Paris premiere.[97] In March 1943, Alfred Rosenberg, who for barely two years had been 'Reich minister for the occupied eastern territories', lodged a protest with the director of the Reich Chancellery in his self-appointed function as 'the Führer's commissary for the supervision of the entire intellectual and ideological instruction and education of the NSDAP', complaining that he should have to borrow every sequestered film of Soviet origin individually from the Reich Film Archive, as was stipulated in one of the Führer's decrees. He often required his administrative staff to watch such films 'for the purpose of instruction'. This, he argued, was 'absolutely necessary' since the films 'conveyed a knowledge of the industry, culture and history of the countries and inhabitants of the East that could not be gained so clearly and vividly by any other means'.[98] Against this Goebbels voiced 'most emphatic misgivings', saying that the 'propaganda impact' of these 'cunning war propaganda films' with their 'brutal style of depiction' was too powerful. 'I myself invariably watch these films on my own, always employing a carefully chosen projectionist'.[99] Rosenberg and his organization (which also included the 'Archive for Cultural Police') had previously been used to more accommodating treatment by the Reich Film Archive, hence probably their indignation. Up until the Führer's decree, the film archive had always offered Rosenberg's staff an 'orientation in foreign film production', 'in particular concerning the part played in this by the Jews and emigrants after the accession to power', which allowed impressions and experiences to 'be fruitfully assessed' through corresponding memoranda and addenda in the files.[100]

Certainly by the time the war began, the Reich Film Archive had become an important ideological and military pillar within Nazi policies of war and persecution. It is indeed telling that one of the short films made by Frank Hensel many years before, Volksverrat gegen Deutsches Land [Treason against German Territory] (1934), was later used as a tool to assist Nazi persecution. In 1934/35, in the months prior to the 'Saarland Plebiscite' that was accompanied by massive Nazi intimidation, Hensel (working under a false name) had filmed German emigrants – so-called 'notorious individuals' and 'demagogic electioneers' according to the archive's filing card, and thus opponents of the Nazis – who had fled Germany to the presumed safety of Saarland when it was still under a League of Nations mandate; the film was later used to identify them. Under the storage number 1764 the catalogue of the Reich Film Archive contains a brief note describing Hensel's silent film: 'The Jewish struggle before the plebiscite in Saarland'. Today the film, which seemingly also featured the British journalist Sefton Delmer and the Communist writer Erich Weinert, is thought to be lost.

In the Nazis' eyes, film was vital to their war effort. On 12 July 1944, just a few days after the Allies launched their invasion, Goebbels was informed that the day before a Swedish version of the latest Paramount newsreel had arrived from Stockholm, showing shots from the invasion front. 'It is the first original material shown in Sweden that depicts enemy operations at the conquered beachhead. A translation of the Swedish commentary is included.'[101] At the same time, in a parallel action, the American 'enemy' was dispatching an officer of the OWI (United States Office of War Information) to follow its invading troops into Europe and 'impound all available enemy films in the respective areas and immediately replace them with American films', as the centrist Basel newspaper *National-Zeitung* reported at Christmas 1944. Indeed, 'not even for a single day were the liberated territories left without film', because the slogan that had been put out, that 'Hollywood will invade Europe behind the armies', was systematically implemented; postwar planning for the political, economic and cultural meaning of film in the world of tomorrow had long since been set in motion.[102]

   In the period between 1938 and early 1943 the Reich Film Archive considerably expanded its stocks from 2¼ million to 19 million metres of film.[103] They consisted of more than 29,000 feature, educational and documentary films from Germany and abroad. Among them were over 17,500 unedited sequences shot by the so-called 'propaganda companies' (PKs) – material used to compile war newsreels that then had to be submitted to the Reich Film Archive.[104] Besides the films acquired from the PKs, since the beginning of the war the archive had 'processed some 8,000 films from abroad, occupied territories and enemy countries', of which, as one archive work report recorded,[105] 4,000 films were handled in 1942 alone. By doing so, the archive 'was drawing attention to its part in fulfilling so-called war-strategic tasks', as was observed by Botho Brachmann, an archivist and historian who taught in the GDR, in a critical review of Peter Bucher's 1984 catalogue of film held by the German Federal Archive.[106]

Propaganda Company (PK) Footage from the 'Home Front'

The tasks assigned to the Reich Film Archive began to multiply from 1943 onwards, while accompanied – with the exception of the department PK-Archiv – by a reduction in the number of staff.[107] In due course, numerous assignments were classified 'non-essential to the war effort' and hence suspended. After the department for silent film had been scrapped, whole cases of silent film footage were put unseen into storage. In 1941, staff shortages forced work on the archive's comprehensive catalogue of feature films to be abandoned – by that time thirty volumes had already been completed.[108] Expanding its original remit – which included responsibility for a centralized film index, the registration and processing of German film production, and the conservation of important documentary material – the archive also had to take on the task of processing the constant influx of 'enemy films' arriving via Sweden, Spain and Portugal.[109] Additional duties included processing and storage of film footage supplied by the PKs; likewise (as dictated by a ministerial directive of 7 January 1943) the centralized collection of all films from abroad, including 'looted films' (which by then already filled some one hundred rail carriages); controlling so-called 'transit films' that had been transported across the country;

the provision of important documentary material for war-strategic film projects; and film distribution (with the exception of PK films). Lending transactions in 1942 were for 1,756 feature films and 1,180 newsreels.[110] But it was particularly the reports by the 'propaganda companies' – in Nazi terminology divided into 'battle-zone reports', 'front reports' and 'reports from territories behind the lines' – that provided the largest component of war newsreels.[111] As this material was in constant demand for newsreel production it made logistical sense to store it close to a city, although this of course would heighten the risk of exposure to bombardment – the more so as by 1943, with the increased effectiveness of enemy weapons, none of the archive's film depots could be considered bombproof. The status of the work performed by the men of the PKs can be measured not least by the financial privileges enjoyed by their wives: on the instructions of the ministry of propaganda they were paid a 'professional allowance' by the state-run newsreel company Deutsche Wochenschau.[112]

The department for propaganda companies (PK) was subordinate to the Reich Film Archive only in respect to administration and storage logistics. There is an interesting short film titled *Rund um das PK-Filmarchiv* (all about the propaganda companies' film archive), the footage of which now lies in the archive of Gosfilmofond and has still not been returned to Germany. It appears to have been shot by archive staff in 1942/43 as a private record. The film shows a typical day at work against the backdrop of the ongoing war. Some of the men turn up to work in uniform, and Dr Heinz Küttner, drafted in as director of the archive, is seen dealing with administrative tasks. PK-relevant themes are being prepared for filing, secretaries are typing letters and making coffee, someone is feeding ornamental fish, lunch is eaten on the roof terrace of the office building at Berlin's Tempelhofer Ufer, and then it is time for a short afternoon nap, interrupted by the delivery of empty film cans that have to be unloaded from a lorry. In the afternoon a soldier travels by S-Bahn to the Tesch film labs to deliver a film can.[113] The final credits list the 'members of the brotherhood' at the institute; many of the seventy names are marked with a cross – presumably dead. It is a film about a microcosm of a *Volksgemeinschaft*, a people's community, at work on the 'home front'. Their work consists of archiving the filmed war and making this material accessible by means of annotated entries organized in various files. As Richard Quaas recalled in 1954, 'At that time the war placed a curb on purely academic research, bringing other tasks to the fore'. He did not describe this 'academic research' in closer detail, but he did raise the prospect of plans for the future: 'We had set ourselves plenty to do for the period after the war and would have focused these activities on creating probably the biggest film archive in Europe[114] – but without doubt an archive whose size would have been founded largely on conquest and subjugation. Instead it was Kracauer and Eisner who, during and after the war, used archival material compiled partly with the help of the very people who had driven them into exile to write their historical accounts that made history. In this way these two formerly German authors contributed to a greater understanding of the Germans.

Acknowledgements

I wish to offer my warmest thanks to Renate Göthe and Hans-Gunter Voigt (both Potsdam) for their comprehensive help and discussions, as well as to Jeanpaul Goergen (Berlin) and others, too numerous to mention, for conversations, material and all manner of advice and information.

Notes

Translated by Matthew Partridge.
This is an extensively revised version of an essay that first appeared in Wolfgang Beilenhoff and Sabine Hänsgen (eds). 2009. *Der gewöhnliche Faschismus. Ein Werkbuch zum Film von Michail Romm*. Berlin: Vorwerk 8, 310–17.

1. Wolfgang Ernst. 2003. *Im Namen von Geschichte. Sammeln – Speichern – Er/Zählen. Infrastrukturelle Konfigurationen des deutschen Gedächtnisses*. Munich: Fink, 694.
2. Hans Hinkel (Hrsg.). 1937. *Handbuch der Reichskulturkammer*. Berlin: Deutscher Verlag für Politik und Wirtschaft, 280.
3. Hans Barkhausen.n.d. *Zur Geschichte des ehemaligen Reichsfilmarchivs. Gründung – Aufbau – Arbeitsweise*. n.p., (manuscript, 19 pages, owned by the author), 3.
4. Frank Maraun (i.e. Erwin Goelz). 1939. 'Weltgeschichte auf Zelluloid. Besuch im Reichsfilmarchiv', *Der deutsche Film* 10 (April), 291. Material was also acquired from the collector Walter Jerven.
5. Interview, Julie Steinbacher with Gerhard Lamprecht, 17 January 1954, Deutsche Kinemathek, Sammlungen; this and other interviews with Lamprecht is published in Eva Orbanz. 2013. *Miteinander und gegenüber. Gerhard Lamprecht und seine Zeitzeugengespräche*. Munich: edition text + kritik.
6. See Rolf Aurich. 2007. 'Filmvermittlung und Filmausbildung im Nationalsozialismus', *Recherche Film und Fernsehen* 2, 20ff; for contemporary sources see F.J. von Steinaecker. 1943. 'Das Filmauswertungsarchiv der Ufa', *Der deutsche Film* 7, 14–15; and Anon. 1941. 'Bild- und Tonarchiv der Bavaria in Geiselgasteig', *Film-Kurier* 299 (20 December).

7. Karl Friedrich Reimers, a media historian, characterized Quaas, who was also a cameraman and cutter, as one 'of the few among the early/old party comrades of the Hitler movement with a "sense of film"' (letter to Rolf Aurich, Ismaning, 15 June 2008). For Frank Hensel see Rolf Aurich. 2001. 'Cineast, Sammler, Nationalsozialist. Der Funktionär Frank Hensel und das Reichsfilmarchiv', *Film-Dienst* 15 (17 July): 39ff; English translation in *Journal of Film Preservation* 64(4) (April 2002), 16ff.

8. See primarily Barkhausen, *Zur Geschichte*; Hans Barkhausen. 1960. 'Zur Geschichte des ehemaligen Reichsfilmarchivs. Gründung – Aufbau – Arbeitsweise', *Der Archivar* 1 (April); Peter Bucher. 1984. *Wochenschauen und Dokumentarfilme 1895–1950 im Bundesarchiv-Filmarchiv (16 mm-Verleihkopien)*, Coblence: Bundesarchiv, VIff.

9. Hans Barkhausen, 'Betr. Reichsfilmarchiv, Koblenz, 28.5.1980', in *Privatarchiv Quaas*, Gröbenzell; copy held by the author. Contemporary Frank Hensel also stressed the 'scientific purposes' of the archive: Frank Hensel. 1936. 'Die Arbeit des Reichsfilmarchivs. Eine in der Welt einzigartige staatliche Einrichtung', *Volk und Welt. Das deutsche Monatsbuch* (January).

10. On the conditions of film studies in Leipzig, see Clemens Zimmermann. 2001. 'Filmwissenschaft im Nationalsozialismus – Anspruch und Scheitern', in Armin Kohnle and Frank Engehausen (eds), *Zwischen Wissenschaft und Politik. Studien zur deutschen Universitätsgeschichte. Festschrift für Eike Wolgast zum 65. Geburtstag*, Stuttgart: F. Steiner, 212f. According to a press report, the university of Leipzig owned 'the largest film archive of all German universities'. See k. 1938. 'Hochschule und Film. Erfolgreiche Filmforschung an der Leipziger Universität', *Neue Leipziger Zeitung*, 18 June.

11. Interview with Eva M.J. Schmid by the author, Recklinghausen, 12 August 2000.

12. 'A number of dissertations on film topics' arose in this way. Hans Barkhausen. 1970. 'Zur Geschichte des ehemaligen Reichsfilmarchivs', in Günter Moltmann and Karl Friedrich Reimers (eds), *Zeitgeschichte im Film- und Tondokument*, Göttingen: Musterschmidt, 248.

13. Thomas Meder. 2006. *Produzent ist der Zuschauer. Prolegomena zu einer historischen Bildwissenschaft des Films*. Berlin: Bertz und Fischer, 211ff.

14. Oskar Kalbus and Hans Traub. n.d. [1933]. *Wege zum Deutschen Institut für Filmkunde*, Berlin: printed by August Scherl.

15. Hans Traub. 1940. 'Filmzeitschriften', in Walther Heide (ed.), *Handbuch der Zeitungswissenschaft*, Leipzig: Hiersemann, issues 3 and 4, column 1027/28.

16. Hans Barkhausen. 1978. 'Verbleib von Dokumentar- und Propagandafilmen der deutschen Arbeiterbewegung vor 1933', *Der Archivar* 31(2) (May).

17. The embassy of the Soviet Union, in a verbal note to the Ministry of Foreign Affairs on 5 April 1933, protested against the proceedings; the German ministry answered negatively on 10 May. See Bundesarchiv, Reichsministerium des Inneren, R 1501 / 125684; and Hermann Herlinghaus and Lissi Zilinski (eds). 1967. 'Sowjetischer Film in Deutschland 1922–1932. Eine Dokumentation'. Berlin/GDR: Institut für Filmwissenschaft an der Deutschen Hochschule für Filmkunst, 991ff (issue 8, no. 3). A useful 'index of film documents related to the revolutionary German working-class movement 1911–1932' (as known in 1974) contains the filmography Gertraude Kühn, Karl Tümmler and Walter Wimmer (eds), *Film und revolutionäre Arbeiterbewegung in Deutschland 1918–1932*, Berlin/GDR: Henschel 1978.

18. Barkhausen, 'Verbleib von Dokumentar- und Propagandafilmen'. Officially it was called 'Zentralstelle für das Bildungswesen der Sozialdemokratischen

Arbeiterpartei Österreichs' (Central Office of Education of the Austrian Social Democratic Workers Party). The institution had started with the distribution of films, followed by in-house productions and the founding of a small-gauge film archive. A 1931 report lists slightly fewer than 4,800 small-gauge films in distribution, while more than 2,000 35 mm films were distributed (email from Christian Dewald to the author, dated 1 July 2010). See Christian Dewald. 2007. '"Schaffen wir uns unsere Revolutionsfilme!" Notate zur Filmschau Proletarisches Kino in Österreich', *filmarchiv* 47, 10–11, 8ff. In the 1960s the Austrian Social Democratic Party retrieved 'a number of films from Coblence as negative duplicates' (email from Thomas Hlinak, WIFAR-Wiener Filmarchiv der Arbeiterbewegung, to the author, dated 2 September 2009). Only a few weeks after the 'Anschluss' and the establishment of a branch of the Reichsfilmkammer in Vienna (mid-March 1938), the Reich Film Archive had a Viennese address and a contact person, the Dovifat student Robert Kümmerlen (Jg. 1902); to give just one example: the Selenophon Licht- und Tonbildgesellschaft sent their *Kulturfilme* (documentaries) there in mid-May 1938. See Österreichisches Staatsarchiv, Archiv der Republik der Akt AdR / BMHV (Bundesministerium für Handel und Verkehr), 581c (Karton 3766). In the early stages of the Reichsfilmarchiv, Kümmerlen had been employed as an academic advisor before being appointed head of the silent film department. After the war, at the Institute for Journalism at the Free University of Berlin, he presented archival films made by Walter Jerven, who had died in a bombing raid in 1945. Kümmerlen managed the estate of Jerven.

19. See Fritz Rosenfeld. 1934. 'Wege zum sozialistischen Film. Reportage oder Satire? – Charlie Chaplin und René Clair – Wo bleibt das sozialistische Filmarchiv?', *Sozialdemokrat* (Vienna), 12 May, quoted from Brigitte Mayr and Michael Omasta (eds), *Fritz Rosenfeld, Filmkritiker*, Vienna: Filmarchiv Austria, 207.

20. See the index of contemporary sound documents (as of April 1943), with regard to newsreel subjects, sorted by countries and genres. Berlin: Reichsfilmarchiv (1943). The introduction to the substantial work (559 pages) which links every title to a number, states in reference to the state of war: 'Due to topical causes Germany could not be listed in this work'. English newsreels from 1939 showing air-raid training were probably assessed as essential for the war effort. There are also a number of 'personalities' listed, including Ernst Lubitsch and Fritz Hippler, Marlene Dietrich and Charlie Chaplin, as well as archive director Richard Quaas and the French communist Paul Vaillant-Couturier.

21. Barkhausen, 'Zur Geschichte'.

22. Zimmermann, 'Filmwissenschaft im Nationalsozialismus', 203. For a contemporary assessment, see Anon. 1946. 'Nazis sehen sich amerikanische Filme an', *Mein Film* (Vienna), 28 (19 July).

23. In 1943, Goebbels' ministry issued an order to the Reichsfilmarchiv to supplement all films coming from so-called 'enemy nations' with a *Geheimhaltungsvorspann* (secrecy trailer). This regulation was relaxed in summer 1944, when 'normal features and entertainment films by enemy power' no longer needed this trailer. Director of Film / Intendant of Reich Film, Berlin, 24 July 1944, *Bundesarchiv, Ministerium für Volksaufklärung und Propaganda*, R 55/665.

24. Maraun, 'Weltgeschichte auf Zelluloid', 291.

25. Yong Chan Choy. 2006. 'Inszenierungen der völkischen Filmkultur im Nationalsozialismus: "Der Internationale Filmkongress Berlin 1935"' (Ph.D. dissertation, Technical University of Berlin). Retrieved on 20 December 2010 from

http://deposit.ddb.de/cgi-bin/dokserv?idn=978431200&dok_var=d1&dok_ext=pdf
&filename=978431200.pdf.

26. Anon. 1935. 'Einrichtung von Filmarchiven in allen Ländern', *Lichtbild-Bühne* 102
(2 May). Hensel claimed credit for his initiative. Frank Hensel to Staatskommissar
(Hans) Hinkel, Berlin, 3 Dec. 1935, *Bundesarchiv (formerly Berlin Document Center),
Reichskulturkammer, Hensel, Frank, geb. 9.7.1893*.

27. Adolf Hübl. 1935. 'Internationales Filmmuseum', *Intercine. Internationales Institut
für Lehrfilmwesen. Völkerbund* 7(7) (July), 398ff.

28. In spring 1968, Lotte H. Eisner credited Henri Langlois – just reinstated as head
of the Cinémathèque Française – with the idea of connecting the film archives of
various countries 'for joint action to safeguard historical and artistically valuable
films'. This vindication is probably part of the mythification of Langlois' standing. See Lotte H. Eisner. 1968. 'Louvre der Filmkunst. Henri Langlois und seine
Cinémathèque', *Die Welt*, 17 May.

29. Leiter VIII [Schrifttum] to the minister, Berlin, 23 January 1939. Bundesarchiv,
Reichsministerium für Volksaufklärung und Propaganda, R 55/1242.

30. Quoted from Jerzy Toeplitz. 1968. 'Die Filmkunst zu bewahren ... Die FIAF feierte
ihr 30jähriges Bestehen', *Die Tat*, 27 July.

31. Frank Hensel to John Abbott, Berlin, 31 October 1938, and John Abbott's answer to
Frank Hensel, New York, 1 December 1938. Both in Film Study Center/Museum of
Modern Art, MoMA/LoC File 2-F.

32. See Elisabeth Manthey. 1968. 'Der politische Kompilationsfilm – seine
Entwicklung, seine Besonderheiten, seine propagandistische Wirkung und die
Bedeutung der Filmarchive für seine Produktion', thesis, Potsdam-Babelsberg:
German University of Cinema, 15.

33. Frank Hensel to state commissioner (Hans) Hinkel, Berlin, 6 February 1937, in
Bundesarchiv, Hensel, Frank.

34. Memorandum for the files (29 June 1936). Addendum to the letter of the
American ambassador in Berlin, William E. Dodd, to the Secretary of State
in Washington, Berlin, 8 February 1937. Copy owned by the author (thanks to
Markus Spieker).

35. Iris Barry. 1969. 'The Film Library and How It Grew', *Film Quarterly* 22(4) (Summer);
quoted after Haidee Wasson. 1998. *Modern Ideas About Old Films: The Museum of
Modern Art's Film Library and Film Culture, 1935–39*, Montreal: McGill University,
199; retrieved on 19 February 2011 from http://www.collectionscanada.gc.ca/obj/
s4/f2/dsk1/tape10/PQDD_0025/NQ50280.pdf.

36. Iris Barry. 1937. 'Hunting the Film in Germany', *The American-German Review*
(June), 40–45, reprinted in Eva Orbanz (ed.), *East Side – West Side. Schätze aus dem
Filmarchiv des MoMA. Eine Filmreihe im Kino Arsenal*, 9 May–5 June 2004, Berlin:
Stiftung Deutsche Kinemathek, 60–63.

37. John Abbott to Frank Hensel, Hollywood, CA, 30 August 1938, in Film Study
Center/Museum of Modern Art, MoMA/LOC file 2-F.

38. Iris Barry, quoted in Anon. 1970. 'Iris Barry (Obituary)', in *The Silent Picture* 6
(Spring), 16.

39. Frank Hensel to John E. Abbott, Berlin, 13.5.1939, in: Film Study Center/Museum
of Modern Art, MoMA/LOC file 2-F.

40. Thanks to Bernd Sambale for this information, whose research on the history of
MER suggests that the deportation of Jews from France was almost entirely carried
out by the MER; it also took part in the forced transportation of the workers from

the 'Protektorat Böhmen and Mähren' (email to the author from 11 November 2010). In 1947, in a court hearing in Darmstadt, Hensel stated he had arranged the 'emigration of 1,800 Jews overseas', in collaboration with the 'American Zoint Comitee' [sic!]. Reasons given for the sentence against Frank Hensel, born 9 July 1893, in *Hessisches Hauptstaatsarchiv, Spruch der Spruchkammer Darmstadt-Lager (Abt. 520 DLg)*.

41. Hensel to Abbott, 13 May 1939, op.cit. In 1939, bilateral rhetorical statements about international collaboration between the film archives were still being made. In March the director of the BFI, Oliver Bell, and British Government representatives for documentary and educational film were received by FIAF Vice-President Hensel at the 'Kameradschaft der deutschen Künstler'. In their speeches, Hensel and Bell explicitly mention the cultural and amicable collaboration of the two 'peoples'. Anon. 1939. 'Oliver Bell weilt in Berlin', *Film-Kurier* 68 (21 March).

42. Laurent Mannoni. 2006b. *Histoire de la Cinémathèque française.* Paris: Gallimard. See also the description by Pierre Barbin who was briefly successor to Langlois in 1968 during the 'affair': Pierre Barbin. 2005. *La Cinémathèque française. Inventaire et légendes (1936–1986).* Paris: Vuibert; see also Richard Roud. 1983. *A Passion For Films: Henri Langlois and The Cinémathèque Française.* London: Secker & Warburg; Raymond Borde. 1983. *Les Cinémathèques.* Paris: L'Age d'Homme; idem. 1991. 'Die Beziehungen zwischen deutschen und französischen Filmarchiven seit 1938', in Heike Hurst and Heiner Gassen (eds), *Kameradschaft – Querelle. Kino zwischen Deutschland und Frankreich*, Munich: Institut Français de Munich, CICIM, 44ff; Glenn Myrent and Georges P. Langlois. 1995. *Henri Langlois: First Citizen of Cinema.* New York: Twayne; Patrick Olmeta. 2000. *La Cinémathèque Française de 1936 à nos jours.* Paris: CNRS Editions.

43. Georg Stefan Troller. 1990. *Personenbeschreibung. Tagebuch mit Menschen.* Hamburg: Rasch & Röhring, 61f.

44. Laurent Mannoni. 2006a. 'Henri Langlois and the Musée du Cinéma', *Film History* 18(3), 275.

45. Jerome Charyn. 1989. *Movieland: Hollywood and the Great American Dream Culture.* New York: G.P. Putnam's Sons, 149; emphasis in original.

46. Director of Human Resources, Oberregierungsrat Reimer, to the minister, 16 June 1943, in *Bundesarchiv, Reichsministerium für Volksaufklärung und Propaganda, R 55/30221.*

47. Frank Hensel to state commissioner (Hans) Hinkel, Berlin, 6 February 1937, in *Bundesarchiv, Hensel, Frank.*

48. Ulrich Gregor. 1977. 'Ein Visionär und Sammler. Zum Tode des Cinémathèque-Leiters Henri Langlois', *Die Zeit*, 21 January.

49. See Günther Jurczyk. 1982. 'Voll Mut – wenn's auch nicht stimmt. Gespräch mit der Filmhistorikerin Lotte Eisner', *Süddeutsche Zeitung*, 6 September; also idem. 1983. '"Ich hatte immer Entdeckerfreude". Gespräch mit der Filmhistorikerin Lotte Eisner', *Saarbrücker Zeitung*, 6 May.

50. Karsten Witte. 1986. 'Ein oft gemischtes Glück. Die Bewahrerin des alten, die Muse des neuen deutschen Films', *Die Zeit*, 31 October.

51. Henri Langlois. 1936. 'Fondation de la cinémathèque', *La Cinématographie française* 932 (12 September), also idem. 1986. *Trois cents ans de cinéma. Écrits*, ed. Jean Narboni, Paris: Cahiers du Cinéma, 39.

52. Ibid.

53. Iris Barry to John Marshall, New York, 14 May 1941, in David Culbert. 1993. 'Document: The Rockefeller Foundation, the Museum of Modern Art Film Library, and Siegfried Kracauer, 1941', *Historical Journal of Film, Radio and Television* 13(4), 499. In comparison, German attempts to report on 'English film propaganda' from the First World War and stir sentiments are simple-minded and obvious. Robert Kümmerlen and Uhlhorn used material from the Reichsfilmarchiv in their article: 1939.'Filme im Dienst der englischen Kriegspropaganda', *Der deutsche Film* 4 (October), 86–88. Gertraude Uhlhorn (born Bub) was assistant academic consultant at the Reichsarchiv. Her dissertation was entitled 'Der deutsche Film im Weltkrieg und sein publizistischer Einsatz'. Quakenbrück: Trute, 1938.

54. Enno Patalas. 2005. 'Die heilige Madonna der Schlafwagen. Eisner, Kracauer und das Kino von Weimar', *Frankfurter Allgemeine Zeitung*, 6 January.

55. Volker Breidecker. 1994. 'Kracauer und Panofsky. Ein Rencontre im Exil', in *Konstruktionen der Moderne*, Hamburger Kunsthalle (ed.), Hamburg: Christians, 125ff; also Volker Breidecker (ed.). 1996. *Briefwechsel Kracauer – Panofsky 1941–1966*, Berlin: Akademie.

56. Helmut G. Asper. 2004. 'Träume für 25 Dollar. Hans Richter, Siegfried Kracauer und "Dreams That Money Can Buy"', *Film-Dienst* 3 (5 February): 22ff; and Mirjam Wenzel. 2004. 'Der "Neuerer" und sein Kritiker. Siegfried Kracauer und Hans Richter. 1943 bis 1947', *Filmexil* 19, 27ff. For more on Richter, see also Yvonne Zimmermann's contribution in this volume.

57. Letter from Ingrid Belke to Rolf Aurich, 29 November 2006.

58. Iris Barry to John Marshall, New York, 14 May 1941, in David Culbert 'Document: The Rockefeller Foundation', 499.

59. Iris Barry. 1944. 'The Film Library', in *Art in Progress: 15th Anniversary Exhibition*, New York: MoMA; quoted after Wasson, *Modern Ideas*, 196.

60. On Iris Barry and the Film Library see Bruce Henson. 1997. 'Iris Barry: American Film Archive Pioneer', *The Katharine Sharp Review* 4, 1–6, retrieved on 19 February 2011 from http://mirrored.ukoln.ac.uk/lis-journals/review/review/winter1997.

61. David Culbert. 2007. 'German Films in the United States, 1933–45', in Roel Vande Winkel and David Welch (eds), *Cinema and the Swastika: The International Expansion of Third Reich Cinema*, Houndmills and New York: Palgrave Macmillan, 313.

62. See Culbert, 'Document: The Rockefeller Foundation', 500ff.

63. Jay Leyda. 1964. *Films Beget Films*, New York: Hill and Wang, 38f. The provenance of the film material is listed as Reichsfilmarchiv, Bufa and 'Kunde'; the latter refers of the Düsseldorf-based film collector Wilhelm Kunde, pioneer of 'Kulturfilm', about whom nothing more is known except that he was an important patron of the Reichsfilmarchiv.

64. Wolfgang Klaue in the film À LA RECHERCHE DES FILMS PERDUS" (1995, Jacques Meny). The East German *Staatliches Filmarchiv der DDR* absorbed the vast majority of the extensive holdings of the former Reichsfilmarchiv, handed over by the Soviet authorities in 1954/55.

65. Iris Barry. 1939. 'Films for History', *Special Libraries: Official Journal of the Special Libraries Association* 30, 259; and Iris Barry's statement in the survey: 'Symposium. Do you think that the films have a pedagogical mission for the masses? If so, has Hollywood production over the last decade lived up to it?', *Decision* 1(3) (March 1941), 65–66. Directly after the foundation of the Reichsfilmarchiv, film pioneer Max Skladanowsky participated in a radio debate with Richard Ohrtmann – who, though announced as a 'film historian', also happened to be Skladanowsky's

private secretary – and proposed the idea of creating a German 'film museum'. Clearly setting itself apart from the Reichsfilmarchiv, the venture was to be based in Munich and would involve the collaboration of 'film historians' such as Walter Jerven, Eduard Andrés, Walter Steinhauer and Ohrtmann himself, with the aim of 'exemplifying and bringing alive film's historical heritage in a visually conveyable form as a mirror of our time of egregious depth'. Anon. 1934. 'Film-Museum gefordert! Max Skladanowski spricht im Reichssender Frankfurt', *Lichtbild-Bühne* 107 (9 May).

66. Barry, 'Hunting the Film', 63.
67. Irving Browning. 1945. 'The Museum of Modern Art Film Library', *American Cinematographer* 26(7) (July), 226.
68. s. 1939. 'Ein Archiv, das sich selbst erhalten will', *Lichtbild-Bühne* 45 (22 Februar).
69. John Abbott (?) to Frank Hensel, 1 December 1938, in *Film Study Center/Museum of Modern Art, MoMA/LoC File 2-F*. This letter lists a dozen film titles, including Wiene's GENUINE, Pabst's GEHEIMNISSE EINER SEELE and Murnau's NOSFERATU, which had to be purchased before the end of the year since by then allocated financial resources needed to be used up.
70. Siegfried Kracauer to Fritz Lang, New York, 17 March 1945, in *Nachlass Siegfried Kracauer, Deutsches Literaturachiv Marbach, Zugangsnummer 72.1536/4*. As well as Culbert, 'Document: The Rockefeller Foundation', 504.
71. Siegfried Kracauer to Jay Leyda, n.p., 23 October 1943, in *Nachlass Siegfried Kracauer, Deutsches Literaturachiv Marbach, Zugangsnummer 72.1557/1*.
72. Jay Leyda to Kurt Pinthus, New York, 11 January 1942, in *Nachlass Kurt Pinthus, Deutsches Literaturarchiv Marbach, Zugangsnummer 71.2745/1*.
73. See Ingrid Belke (no title, manuscript of lecture), n.d., owned by the author.
74. Johannes Riedner. 2003. 'Die Abgestellten. Heute vor 70 Jahren flüchtete Siegfried Kracauer aus Berlin', *Süddeutsche Zeitung*, 28 February.
75. Ingeborg Brandt. 1958. 'Film ist Kunst des Wirklichen. Wir sprachen mit dem Kulturphilosophen Siegfried Kracauer', *Die Welt*, 28 July.
76. Culbert, 'Document: The Rockefeller Foundation', 495ff.
77. Siegfried Kracauer. 1938. 'Ausstellung der New-Yorker Film Library', *Neue Zürcher Zeitung*, 24 July, here quoted after Kracauer, *Kleine Schriften zum Film. Band 6.3 (1932–1961)*, (ed. Inka Mülder-Bach), Frankfurt/Main: Suhrkamp 2004, 216.
78. See Wasson, *Modern Ideas*, 212f.
79. Siegfried Kracauer to Henri Langlois, Paris, 23 May 1938, in *Nachlass Siegfried Kracauer, Deutsches Literaturarchiv Marbach, Zugangsnummer 72.1537/1*.
80. Siegfried Kracauer to John Marshall, New York, 9 May 1941, supplement: Curriculum Vitae, in Culbert, 'Document: The Rockefeller Foundation', 497.
81. Siegfried Kracauer. 1938. 'Pariser Filmbrief', *Basler "National-Zeitung"*, 15 November, quoted from Kracauer, *Kleine Schriften. Band 6.3 (1932–1961)*, 236. There is no evidence for the definitive inclusion of an Italian institution in early FIAF, but it was expected: Anon. 1938. 'Zusammenarbeit der Weltfilmarchive', *Film-Kurier*, 182 (6 August). It is possible that Kracauer was thinking of the Mario Ferrari Collection in Milan, founded in 1935, which would later become the Cineteca Italiana. Henri Langlois is said to have shown 'a rather conflicting nature … concerning the Italians' in summer of 1939, as Abbott writes to Hensel on 27 June 1939. In *Film Study Center/Museum of Modern Art, MoMA/Loc File 2-F*.
82. This is confirmed by Henri Langlois. 1947. 'The Cinémathèque Française', *Hollywood Quarterly* 2(2) (January), 207.

83. See John E. Abbott to John Marshall, 1 June 1938, in *MoMA, Dept. Of Film, Rockefeller Collection, Box 250, Folder 2986.*

84. John E. Abbott to Frank Hensel, 10 March 1939, and Frank Hensel to John E. Abbott, Berlin, 31 March 1939, both in *Film Study Center/Museum of Modern Art, MoMA/LoC File 2-F.* Frank Hensel was born in 1893, Georges Franju in 1912, and Henri Langlois in 1914.

85. Frank Hensel to John Abbott, Berlin, 13 May 1939, op. cit. The German side referred to Hensel in early 1939 as an 'administrator for foreign affairs' who was expected to supervise FIAF through the Paris office, i.e. coordinate the necessary activities (communications, accounting etc.). Anon. 1939. '"Internationale Vereinigung der Film-Archive" unter deutscher Leitung', *Filmwelt* 1 (6 January), 31.

86. Karsten Witte. 1986. 'Ein oft gemischtes Glück. Die Bewahrerin des alten, die Muse des neuen deutschen Films', *Die Zeit*, 31 October.

87. Lotte H. Eisner-Escoffier to Kurt Pinthus, Paris, 5 November 1953, in *Nachlass Kurt Pinthus, Deutsches Literaturarchiv Marbach, Zugangsnummer 71.1990/3.*

88. Lotte H. Eisner to Kurt Pinthus, Paris, 15 July [1957], in *Nachlass Kurt Pinthus, Deutsches Literaturarchiv Marbach, Zugangsnummer 71.1990/4.* Reference here is to Hans H. Wollenberg. 1948. *Fifty Years of German Film*, London: Falcon Press.

89. –ft. 1952. 'Dämonische Leinwand', *Die Neue Zeitung*, 25 July.

90. Bernard Eisenschitz, editor of the French edition of Eisner's book 'Fritz Lang', in *'Die Eisnerin' - Kritikerin und Kronzeugin der Kinokunst*, Ralph Eue, RBB-Kulturradio, 19 October 2006, transcript owned by the author.

91. Patalas, 'Die heilige Madonna'.

92. Barkhausen, 'Zur Geschichte'.

93. Report by Richard Quaas, in Friedrich Terveen (IWF Göttingen) to Bundesarchiv (Koblenz), Göttingen, 15 November 1954. *Handakten Hans-Gunter Voigt, Bundesarchiv-Filmarchiv, Berlin.*

94. See the memorandum by archivist Wolfgang Kohte, Coblence, 10 December 1954, concerning an explanation given by by Richard Quaas regarding the films stocks from 'enemy countries' which were held 'in trusteeship' by the Reichsfilmarchiv, in Handakten, Hans-Gunter Voigt, Bundesarchiv-Filmarchiv, Berlin. In the capitals of German-occupied countries, Gestapo officers had the task of confiscating films and sending them to the Reichsfilmarchiv for screening and classification. There, a team of linguistically competent assistants on temporary contracts were employed to view the films and register data and content. Statement by Hans Barkhausen in a radio feature by Jeanpaul Goergen: *Geschichte des Reichsfilmarchivs*. Deutschlandradio Berlin, 30 October 1995 (manuscript and copy owned by the author).

95. Bogusław Drewniak. 1987. *Der deutsche Film 1938–1945. Ein Gesamtüberblick*, Düsseldorf: Droste, 28.

96. Roy Armes. 1991. 'Kino der Widersprüche: Französische Filmarbeit unter der Besatzung', in Gerhard Hirschfeld and Patrick Marsh (eds), *Kollaboration in Frankreich. Politik, Wirtschaft und Kultur während der nationalsozialistischen Besatzung 1940–1944*, Frankfurt: Fischer, 162.

97. Brief excerpts from this film which prove its anti-parliamentary and anti-Semitic character can be seen in Claude Chabrol's documentary L'ŒIL DE VICHY (1992).

98. Alfred Rosenberg to Hans Heinrich Lammers, Berlin, 11 March 1943, in *Bundesarchiv, Reichskanzlei, R 43 II/389.*

99. Dr Goebbels to Hans Heinrich Lammers, Berlin, 26 March 1943, in *Bundesarchiv, Reichskanzlei, R 43 II/389.*
100. Amt Kulturpolitisches Archiv Dr. Sa/Lr to Hauptamt Kunstpflege z. Hd. Dienstleiter Dr. Stang im Hause, 12 June 1942, in: *Bundesarchiv, Der Beauftragte des Führers für die Überwachung der gesamten geistigen und weltanschaulichen Schulung und Erziehung der NSDAP, NS 15/131.*
101. Director Film/Reichsfilmintendant to Goebbels, 12 July 1944, in *Bundesarchiv, Reichsministerium für Volksaufklärung und Propaganda, R 55/665.*
102. dlk., 'Hollywood bereitet den Nachkrieg vor', *National-Zeitung*, no. 601, 24 December 1944 (Sunday supplement).
103. Bucher, *Wochenschauen und Dokumentarfilme.*
104. See Ulrike Bartels. 2004. *Die Wochenschau im Dritten Reich. Entwicklung und Funktion eines Massenmediums unter besonderer Berücksichtigung völkisch-nationaler Inhalte.* Frankfurt: Lang, 240ff (also dissertation, Göttingen, 1996).
105. General Division of Archives and Contemporary Documentation to the Reich Minister, Berlin, 24 February 1943, in *Bundesarchiv, Reichsministerium für Volksaufklärung und Propaganda, R 55/1242.* At this time, the Reichsfilmarchiv, besides its director Quaas, comprised five departments: finances, silent film, sound film, PK films and archive administration, and technology. A technical department specifically responsible for film transfer did not exist because one 'relied on the fact that the film negatives were in safe care with the printing laboratory'. Negatives were only kept in rare cases, 'most attention was paid to processing the intake' of films (Anon., 'Vermerk. Betr.: Geschäftsverteilungsplan Reichsfilmarchiv. Bundesarchiv, Koblenz, 9.8.1972', in *Privatarchiv Quaas, Gröbenzell*). Prints of films were also destroyed in no small measure, such as existing duplicates and material held in storage in occupied territories. The old material was intended for use as new raw stock.
106. Botho Brachmann. 1985. 'Rezension von Wochenschauen und Dokumentarfilme 1895–1950 im Bundesarchiv-Filmarchiv (1984)', in *Archivmitteilungen* 5, 182.
107. On 5 November 1942 the ministerial department of finances wrote to Goebbels that more personnel were needed by the 'department for assessing and handling PK films in the Reichsfilmarchiv', since the material is in constant demand. The sixty 'additional staff' required should be recruited from soldiers who 'due to war injuries are in the process of being discharged'; in *Handakten Hans-Gunter Voigt, Bundesarchiv-Filmarchiv, Berlin.*
108. In the summer of 1942, twenty-six catalogues listing 3,500 films, mainly features, were finished. The cataloguing of silent films 'should be reserved for the time after the war'. G.H. [Georg Herzberg]. 1942. 'Aus der Arbeit des Reichsfilmarchivs', *Film-Kurier* 126 (2 June).
109. On this, for instance: K.W. 1947. 'Kleines Kino in der Mauerstrasse. Ein Kapitel NS-Filmpolitik', *Der neue Film* 13 (21 November).
110. Numbers given by the General Division of Archives and Contemporary Documentation to the Reich Minister, Berlin, 24 February 1943, in *Bundesarchiv, Reichsministerium für Volksaufklärung und Propaganda, R 55/1242.*
111. Benno Klapp. 1968. 'Die deutschen Kriegswochenschauen des II. Weltkrieges als publizistische Erscheinung' (diss., Westfälische Wilhelms-Universität Münster), 89. See also Rainer Rother and Judith Prokasky (eds). 2010. *Die Kamera als Waffe. Propagandabilder des Zweiten Weltkrieges*, Munich: edition text + kritik.
112. Memorandum Wolfgang Kohte, Coblence, 26 May 1955, after a conversation on 23 May 1955 with H.O. Doerr, former warfront PK cameraman, about his activities

and views on the legal status of the PK films; in *Handakten Hans-Gunter Voigt*, Bundesarchiv-Filmarchiv, Berlin.

113. 'Paul Tesch was an old Nazi party member': Hans Barkhausen to Richard Quaas, Coblence, 12 January 1989 (copy owned by the author).

114. Report Richard Quaas, in Friedrich Terveen (IWF Göttingen) to Bundesarchiv (Coblence), Göttingen, 15 November 1954, *Handakten Hans-Gunter Voigt*, Bundesarchiv-Filmarchiv, Berlin.

NOTES ON CONTRIBUTORS

Lars Gustaf Andersson is professor in Film Studies at the Centre for Languages and Literature, Lund University. His research focuses on minor cinema and European art-cinema. Together with John Sundholm he has directed several research projects on Swedish minor cinema and transnational cinema. He is the co-author of *A History of Swedish Experimental Film Culture* (John Libbey/Indiana UP, 2010) and *Historical Dictionary of Scandinavian Cinema* (Scarecrow, 2012). He is associate editor of the *Journal of Aesthetics and Culture*.

Rolf Aurich is a lecturer, editor and author at the Stiftung Deutsche Kinemathek (German film archive) in Berlin, for which he edits, together with Wolfgang Jacobsen, the book series *Filit* and *Film & Schrift*. Recent publications are: *Reineckerland* (2010, with Jacobsen and Niels Beckenbach), *Agrarfilmbestände in Deutschland und Österreich* (2010), *Edition Gerhard Lamprecht* (2013, with Jacobsen and Eva Orbanz), and *Kein letztes Wort. Die Filme von Rainer Erler* (2013, with Jacobsen). His research interests include history of film archives, and film education.

Erica Carter is professor of German and Film at King's College London, and a founding member of the U.K. German Screen Studies Network. Her publications on early film theory, German-language cinema and cultural history include *Béla Balázs: Early Film Theory* (2010); *The German Cinema Book* (co-edited with Tim Bergfelder and Deniz Göktürk, 2002); *Dietrich's Ghosts: The Sublime and the Beautiful in Third Reich Film* (2004); and *How German Is She? Postwar West German Reconstruction and the Consuming Woman* (1997). Journal editorial affiliations include *Screen; Cinema et Cie;* and *Women: A Cultural Review*.

Ian Christie is professor of Film and Media History at Birkbeck, University of London, having previously taught in Oxford and Canterbury. He has co-curated many exhibitions, especially on Russian art and film, and written on historical and contemporary avant-garde film. A regular critic and commentator on film in both academia and the popular media, his work is increasingly concerned with audiences and contexts of reception. Recent publications include: *Stories We Tell Ourselves: The Cultural Impact of UK Film* (co-author, BFI/UKFC, 2009) and *Audiences: Defining and Researching Screen Entertainment Reception* (ed. AUP, 2012). www.ianchristie.org

Greg de Cuir, Jr. is the managing editor of *NECSUS – European Journal of Media Studies* (www.necsus-ejms.org). His book *Yugoslav Black Wave* was published by Film Center Serbia in 2011. De Cuir also works as the selector/programmer for Alternative Film/Video Belgrade.

Tom Gunning is distinguished service professor in the Department of Cinema and Media at the University of Chicago, and author of *D.W. Griffith and the Origins of American Narrative Film* (University of Illinois Press), *The Films of Fritz Lang: Allegories of Vision and Modernity* (British Film Institute), and over a hundred articles.

Malte Hagener is professor for the History, Aesthetics and Theory of Film at Philipps-Universität Marburg. A founding member of *NECS* (*European Network for Cinema and Media Studies*), editor of *NECSUS – European Journal of Media Studies*, and chairman of the German association for media studies (*GfM – Gesellschaft für Medienwissenschaft*), he has written many articles on film and media history, and on German film and avant-garde. Recent book publications include *Moving Forward, Looking Back: The European Avant-garde and the Invention of Film Culture* (2007), and *Film Theory: An Introduction through the Senses* (with Thomas Elsaesser, 2010; translations into German, Italian, French, Korean and Spanish).

Tobias Nagl is associate professor of Film Studies at the University of Western Ontario, and he also teaches at the interdisciplinary Center for the Study of Theory and Criticism. He is a member of CineGraph, the author of *Die unheimliche Maschine – Rasse und Repräsentation im Weimarer Kino* [The Uncanny Machine – Race and Representation in Weimar Cinema], and winner of the international Willy Haas Award in 2009. He has published articles on German film history, film theory, race and colonial culture, Afro-German history and politics, abstract painting and the Black diaspora, the Holocaust and cinematic testimony, Rainer Werner Fassbinder, Michael Haneke and Veit Helmer.

Duncan Petrie is professor of Film at the University of York. He is the author of *Creativity and Constraint in the British Film Industry* (Macmillan, 1991); *The British Cinematographer* (BFI, 1996); *Screening Scotland* (BFI, 2000); *Contemporary Scottish Fictions* (EUP, 2004); and *Shot in New Zealand: The Art and Craft of the Kiwi Cinematographer* (Random House, 2007). His most recent research on the history of film schools has generated several publications, including *Educating Film-Makers: Past, Present and Future* (Intellect, 2014; with Rod Stoneman). He is co-principal editor of *The Journal of British Cinema and Television*, and a member of the editorial board of *The Journal of Media Practice*.

Francesco Pitassio is associate professor of Film Studies at the Università degli Studi di Udine. Since 1997 he has been a member of the scientific committee of the Udine International Film Studies Conference, and since 2002 he has also been a member of the scientific board of MAGIS – Gradisca Film Studies Spring School. He is one of the editors of *NECSUS – European Journal of Media Studies*, and he coordinates the editorial staff of *Cinéma & Cie*. His research interests focus on stardom and screen acting, Italian and Czech cinema, and film theory. His books include *Ombre silenziose. Teoria dell'attore cinematografico negli anni Venti* (Udine, 2002); *Maschere e marionette. Il cinema ceco e dintorni* (Udine, 2002); *Attore/Divo* (Milan, 2003); and *Il neorealismo cinematografico* (Bologna, 2010; with Paolo Noto).

Natalie Ryabchikova is a Ph.D. student in the Film Studies Program at the University of Pittsburgh (with a concentration in Slavic). She received her BA in Film Studies from the Russian State University of Cinematography (VGIK), and her MA in Slavic Languages and Literatures from the University of Pittsburgh. She has contributed to *Directory of World Cinema: Russia* (Bristol: Intellect, 2010) and has written Hyperkino commentary for Sergei Eisenstein's STRIKE, released as part of Ruscico DVD series Kino Academia. Her articles on early Russian and Soviet film history have appeared in *Kinovedcheskie zapiski* and *Studies in Russian and Soviet Cinema*.

Masha Salazkina is research chair in Transnational Media Arts and Culture, and is associate professor of Film Studies at Concordia University, Montreal. Her work incorporates transnational approaches to film theory and cultural history. She is the author of *In Excess: Sergei Eisenstein's Mexico* (University of Chicago Press, 2009) and co-editor (with Lilya Kaganovsky) of *Sound, Speech, Music in Soviet and*

Post-Soviet Cinema (Indiana University Press, forthcoming 2014). Her new book project traces a trajectory of materialist film theory through the discourses of early Soviet cinema, institutional film cultures of 1930s–1950s Italy, and critical debates surrounding the emergence of New Cinemas in Brazil, Argentina and Cuba. She has published essays in *October*; *Cinema Journal*; *Screen*; *KinoKultura* and in several edited collections. She is the coordinator of the global film theory translation project for the Permanent Seminar on Histories of Film Theories, and of the new collaborative project on the history of the Tashkent Festival of Asian, African and Latin American Cinemas.

Simone Venturini is assistant professor at the University of Udine. Since 2003 he has been a member of the scientific committee of the Udine International Film Studies Conference and a member of the scientific board of MAGIS – Gradisca Film Studies Spring School. His research interests focus on film preservation and presentation; media archaeology and archival theory; and the economic and cultural history of Italian cinema. His publications include *Il restauro cinematografico. Principi, teorie, metodi* (2006); and *Revisiting the Archive* (2011).

Yvonne Zimmermann is professor of Media Studies at Philipps-Universität Marburg. As a visiting scholar at New York University, she researched Hans Richter's exile in Switzerland (1937–1941) and the transatlantic exchange of film culture. She holds a Ph.D. from the University of Zurich, and was a guest professor at the University Sorbonne Nouvelle Paris 3. She is the author of *Bergführer Lorenz: Karriere eines missglückten Films* (2005), and editor and co-author of *Schaufenster Schweiz: Dokumentarische Gebrauchsfilme 1896–1964* (2011). She has published widely on documentary and non-theatrical exhibition.

SELECT BIBLIOGRAPHY

Abbott, John E., and Iris Barry. 1935. 'An Outline of a Project for Founding the Film Library of the Museum of Modern Art'. Reprinted in *Film History* 7(3) (Autumn 1995), 325–35.

Abel, Richard. 1984. *French Cinema: The First Wave, 1915–1929*. Princeton: Princeton University Press.

———. 1988. *French Film Theory and Criticism, 1907–1939. A History/Anthology. I: 1907–1929. II: 1929–1939* (2 vols), Princeton, NJ: Princeton University Press.

Acland, Charles R., and Haidee Wasson (eds). 2011. *Useful Cinema*, Durham, NC and London: Duke University Press.

Adamson, Walter. 2007. *Embattled Avant-Gardes: Modernism's Resistance to Commodity Culture in Europe*, Berkeley: University of California Press.

Agamben, Giorgio. 2009. 'What Is an Apparatus?', in *What Is an Apparatus?*, Stanford, CA: Stanford University Press, 1–25.

Albera, François. *Albatros: des russes à Paris 1919–1929*, Paris: Cinémathèque française.

Allberg, Ragnar. 1947. 'Gösta Hellström i vännernas krets. Några personliga minnen', *Biografbladet* 4, 224–27.

Almqvist, Stig. 1947. 'Gösta Hellström – en ung filmentusiast. Till 15-årsminnet av hans bortgång', *Biografbladet* 4, 215–23.

Alovisio, Silvio, and Luca Mazzei. 2011. '"The Star that Never Sets": The Historiographic Canonisation of Silent Italian Cinema', in Pietro Bianchi, Giulio Bursi and Simone Venturini (eds), *Il canone cinematografico/The Film Canon*, Udine: Forum, 393–404.

Alpers, Svetlana. 1983. *The Art of Describing: Dutch Art in the Seventeenth Century*, Chicago: University of Chicago Press.

Altenloh, Emilie. 1914. *Zur Soziologie des Kino. Die Kino-Unternehmung und die sozialen Schichten ihrer Besucher*, Jena: Diederichs; English version: *Screen* 42(3) (2001), 249–93.

Andersson, Lars Gustaf, John Sundholm and Astrid Söderbergh Widding. 2010. *A History of Swedish Experimental Film Culture: From Early Animation to Video Art*, Stockholm: National Library of Sweden.

Andrew, Dudley. 1983. 'IDHEC', *Journal of Film and Video* 35(1).

———. 2010. 'Time Zones and Jetlag: The Flows and Phases of World Cinema', in Nataša Ďurovičová and Kathleen Newman (eds), *World Cinemas, Transnational Perspectives*, New York and London: Routledge, 59–89.

Anon. 1944. 'Tio år – en cavalcade', in Ragnar Allberg, Arne Bornebusch and Bengt Idestam-Almquist (eds), *Filmboken. Svenska Filmsamfundets årsskrift 1944*, Stockholm, 17–38.

Anon. 1982. 'Tweede voorstelling. Programma', in *Filmliga 1927–1931. Met een inleiding door Jan Heijs* (Reprint), Nijmegen: SUN.

Anthony, Scott. 2011. 'Imperialism and Internationalism: The British Documentary Movement and the Legacy of the Empire Marketing Board', in Lee Grieveson and Colin MacCabe (eds), *Empire and Film*, London: British Film Institute, 135–48.

Aristarco, Guido. 1951. *Storia delle teoriche del film*. Turin: Einaudi.

Armes, Roy. 1991. 'Kino der Widersprüche: Französische Filmarbeit unter der Besatzung', in Gerhard Hirschfeld and Patrick Marsh (eds), *Kollaboration in Frankreich. Politik, Wirtschaft und Kultur während der nationalsozialistischen Besatzung 1940–1944*, Frankfurt: Fischer.

Arnheim, Rudolf. 2009. *I baffi di Charlot. Scritti italiani sul cinema (1932–1938)*, ed. Adriano D'Aloia. Turin: Kaplan.

Asper, Helmut G. 2004. 'Träume für 25 Dollar. Hans Richter, Siegfried Kracauer und "Dreams That Money Can Buy"', *Film-Dienst* 3 (5 February).

Askander, Mikael. 2001. 'Gamla stan. Reflektioner kring ett modernistiskt filmförsök', *HumaNetten* (2001), 8. Retrieved on 29 August 2013 from http://lnu.se/polopoly_fs/1.26003!HumaNetten,%20Nr%208,%20v%C3%A5ren%202001.pdf

———. 2003. *Modernitet och intermedialitet i Erik Asklunds tidiga romankonst*, Växjö: Växjö University Press.

Aurich, Rolf. 2001. 'Cineast, Sammler, Nationalsozialist. Der Funktionär Frank Hensel und das Reichsfilmarchiv', *Film-Dienst* 15, 39ff.

———. 2007. 'Filmvermittlung und Filmausbildung im Nationalsozialismus', *Recherche Film und Fernsehen*, 20ff.

———. 2009a. 'Kurvenreiche Geschichte: vor 75 Jahren wurde das "Reichsfilmarchiv" gegründet', *Film-Dienst* 8, 15–17.

———. 2009b. 'Film als politischer Zeuge. Zur Geschichte des einstigen deutschen Reichsfilmarchivs', *Neue Zürcher Zeitung* (20 June).

Babac, Marko. 2001. *Kino-klub 'Beograd'* [Belgrade Ciné-club], Belgrade: Jugoslovenska kinoteka.

Bacchiega, Giorgio. 2006. 'Nascita della Cineteca Italiana', in Orio Caldiron (ed.), *Storia del cinema italiano. 1934–1939*, Venice: Marsilio.

Backstrom, Per, and Hubert van den Berg (eds). 2013. *Decentering the Avant-Garde: Towards a New Topography of the International Avant-Garde*, Amsterdam: Rodopi.

Balázs, Béla. 1982. *Napló 1914–1922*, Budapest: Magvető.

———. 1922. *Der Mantel der Träume*, Munich: Verlagsanstalt D. & R. Bischoff, available in English translation in Balázs, *The Cloak of Dreams: Chinese Fairy Tales*.

———. 1924. *Der sichtbare Mensch oder die Kultur des Films*, Vienna and Leipzig: Deutsch-Österreichischer Verlag (Reprint Frankfurt: Suhrkamp 2001).

———. 1930. *Der Geist des Films*, Halle: W. Knapp (Reprint Frankfurt: Suhrkamp 2001).

————. 1953. *Theory of the Film: Character and Growth of a New Art*, trans. Edith Bone, London: Dobson.

————. 2001. *Die Jugend eines Träumers. Autobiografischer Roman*, Berlin: Das Arsenal.

————. 2010. *Béla Balázs: Early Film Theory. Visible Man and The Spirit of Film*, ed. Erica Carter, trans. Rodney Livingstone, Oxford: Berghahn Books.

Baldi, Alfredo. 2010. 'I "diari di guerra" e i film requisiti', *Bianco e nero* 71(566), 103–7.

Barbin, Pierre. 2005. *La Cinémathèque française. Inventaire et légendes (1936–1986)*, Paris: Vuiber.

Barkhausen, Hans. 1970. 'Zur Geschichte des ehemaligen Reichsfilmarchivs', in Günter Moltmann and Karl Friedrich Reimers (eds), *Zeitgeschichte im Film- und Tondokument. 17 historische, pädagogische und sozialwissenschaftliche Beiträge*, Göttingen, Zurich, Frankfurt: Musterschmidt, 241–50.

————. 1978. 'Verbleib von Dokumentar- und Propagandafilmen der deutschen Arbeiterbewegung vor 1933', *Der Archivar* 31(2) (May).

Barry, Iris. 1937. 'Hunting the Film in Germany', *The American-German Review* (June), 40–45, reprinted in Eva Orbanz (ed.), *East Side – West Side. Schätze aus dem Filmarchiv des MoMA. Eine Filmreihe im Kino Arsenal*, 9 May – 5 June 2004, Berlin: Stiftung Deutsche Kinemathek, 60–63.

————. 1939. 'Films for History', *Special Libraries: Official Journal of the Special Libraries Association* 30.

————. 1969. 'The Film Library and How It Grew', *Film Quarterly* 22(4) (Summer).

Bartels, Ulrike. 2004. *Die Wochenschau im Dritten Reich. Entwicklung und Funktion eines Massenmediums unter besonderer Berücksichtigung völkisch-nationaler Inhalte*. Frankfurt: Lang.

Beilenhoff, Wolfgang. 2011. 'Montage 1929 / Montage 1939', *Montage/av* 20(1), 213–22.

Beilenhoff, Wolfgang, and Sabine Hänsgen (eds). 2009. *Der gewöhnliche Faschismus. Ein Werkbuch zum Film von Michail Romm*. Berlin: Vorwerk 8.

Ben-Ghiat, Ruth. 2001. *Fascist Modernities. Italy 1922–1945*, Berkeley: University of California Press.

Bengtsson, Bengt. 2007. 'Vad suckar gästboken? Uppsala Studenters Filmstudio som arena för konstfilmsinstitution och filmdebatt', in Per Vesterlund (ed.), *Mediala hierarkier*, Gävle: Högskolan i Gävle, 13–48.

————. 2008. 'Filmstudion och drömmen om den stora uppsalafilmen: Uppsala Studenters Filmstudio som filmproducent och plantskola', in Erik Hedling and Mats Jönsson (eds), *Välfärdsbilder. Svensk film utanför biografen*, Stockholm: Statens Ljud- och Bildarkiv, 205–27.

Benjamin, Walter. (1936) 2008. *The Work of Art in the Age of Its Technological Reproducibility, and Other Writings on Media*, Cambridge, MA: Harvard University Press.

Bennett, Tony. 1992. 'Useful Culture', *Cultural Studies* 6(3), 395–408.

Berghaus, Gunter. 1998. *Italian Futurist Theater, 1909–1944*, Oxford: Clarendon.

Berglund, Kurt. 1993. *Stockholms alla biografer*, Stockholm: Svenska Turistföreningen, 321–22.

Beusekom, Ansje van. 1998. *Film als kunst. Reacties op een nieuw medium in Nederland, 1895–1940*, Amsterdam: Unpublished Ph.D.

———. 2007a. 'Theo van Doesburg and Writings on Film in *De Stijl*', in Klaus Beekman and Jan de Vries (eds), *Avant-Garde and Criticism*, Amsterdam: Rodopi, 55–66.

———. 2007b. '"Avant-guerre" and the International Avant-Garde: Circulation and Programming of Early Films in the European Avant-garde Programs in the 1920s and 1930s', in Frank Kessler and Nanna Verhoeff (eds), *Networks of Entertainment: Early Film Distribution 1895–1915*, Eastleigh: J. Libbey, 285–94.

Bhabha, Homi. 1994. *The Location of Culture*, London: Routledge.

Birkhäuser, Kaspar. 1981. 'Fünfzig Jahre im Dienste der Filmbesucher und des guten Films', in Le Bon Film (ed.), *50 Jahre Le Bon Film*, Basel: Le Bon Film, 5–46.

Bjärlund, Eva. 1970. '30-talsdebatten om den svenska filmen', *Filmrutan* 4, 166–74.

Björkin, Mats, and Pelle Snickars. 2003. '1923/1933. Production, Reception and Cultural Significance of Swedish Non-Fiction Film', in Peter Zimmermann and Kay Hoffmann (eds), *Triumph der Bilder. Kultur- und Dokumentarfilme vor 1945 im internationalen Vergleich*, Konstanz: UVK, 272–90.

Blankenship, Janelle. 2006. 'Leuchte der Kultur: Imperialism, Imaginary Travel, and the Skladanowsky Welt-Theater', in Martin Loiperdinger (ed.), *KINtop: Jahrbuch zur Erforschung des frühen Films: Sources and Perspectives on Early Cinema*, 14–15, 150–70.

Bloom, Peter. 2008. *French Colonial Cinema: Mythologies of Humanitarianism*, Minneapolis: University of Minnesota Press.

Bolas, Terry. 2009. *Screen Education: From Film Appreciation to Media Studies*, Bristol: Intellect.

Bol'shakov, Ivan. 1944. *25 let sovetskogo kino*, Moscow, 3.

Boltianskii, Grigorii. 1925. *Lenin i kino*, Moscow and Leningrad: Gos. izd-vo.

Bone, Edith. 1957. *Seven Years Solitary*, London: H. Hamilton.

Borde, Raymond. 1983. *Les Cinémathèques*, Paris: L'Age d'Homme.

———. 1991. 'Die Beziehungen zwischen deutschen und französischen Filmarchiven seit 1938', in Heike Hurst and Heiner Gassen (eds), *Kameradschaft – Querelle. Kino zwischen Deutschland und Frankreich*, Munich: Institut Français de Munich, CICIM.

Bordwell, David, and Kristin Thompson. 1994. *Film History: An Introduction*, New York: McGraw-Hill.

Bordwell, David, Janet Staiger and Kristin Thompson. 1986. *The Classical Hollywood Cinema: Film Style and Mode of Production to 1960*, London: Routledge & Kegan Paul.

Bornebusch, Arne. 1935. *De lever ett rikt liv. Filmdiktare*, Stockholm: Bonniers.

Bourdieu, Pierre. 1971. 'Champ du pouvoir, champ intellectuel et habitus de classe', *Scolies* 1, 7–26.

Boyer, Charles. 1946. 'Advanced Training for Film Workers: France', *Hollywood Quarterly* 1(3).

Brederoo, N.J. (ed.). 1979. *Film en beeldende kunst, 1900–1930*, Utrecht: Centraal Museum.

Breidecker, Volker. 1994. 'Kracauer und Panofsky. Ein Rencontre im Exil', in *Konstruktionen der Moderne*, Hamburger Kunsthalle (ed.), Hamburg: Christians.

———— (ed.). 1996. *Briefwechsel Kracauer – Panofsky 1941–1966*, Berlin: Akademie.

Brinck-E:son, Birger. 1923. 'Linjemusik på vita duken. "Konstruktiv film", ett intressant experiment av en svensk konstnär', *Filmjournalen* 4; 50.

Browning, Irving. 1945. 'The Museum of Modern Art Film Library', *American Cinematographer* 26(7) (July).

Brunetta, Gian Piero. 1969. *Umberto Barbaro e l'idea di neorealismo (1930–1943)*, Padova: Liviana.

————. 1972. *Intellettuali, cinema e propaganda tra le due guerre*, Bologna: Patron.

————. 1993. *Storia del cinema italiano, vol. 2, Il cinema del regime 1929–1945*, Rome: Riuniti.

Buache, Freddy. 1979/1980. 'Le cinéma indépendant et d'avant-garde à la fin du muet', *Travelling. Cahiers de la Cinémathèque Suisse* 55 (Summer) and 56/57 (Spring).

Buchanan, Tom. 2007. *The Impact of the Spanish Civil War on Britain: War, Loss And Memory*, Eastbourne: Sussex Academy Press.

Bucher, Peter. 1984. *Wochenschauen und Dokumentarfilme 1895–1950 im Bundesarchiv-Filmarchiv (16 mm-Verleihkopien)*, Coblence: Bundesarchiv, Viff.

Bulgakowa, Oksana. 2001. *Sergei Eisenstein: A Biography*, Berlin: Potemkin Press.

Burlyuk et al. 1912. 'A Slap in the Face of Public Taste', in Christie and Gillett, *Futurism*; retrieved on 20 Oct. 2012 from http://www.unknown.nu/futurism/slap.html

Bursi, Giulio. 2010. 'Inquadrare la materia', *Bianco e nero* 71(566).

Caldiron, Orio (ed.). 2011. *Luigi Chiarini, 1900–1975. 'Il film è un'arte, il cinema un'industria'*, Rome: Centro Sperimentali di Cinematografia.

Campbell, Jan. 2005. *Film and Cinema Spectatorship: Melodrama and Mimesis*, Cambridge: Polity.

Carlstoft Bramell, Anna-Karin. 2007. *Vilhelm Moberg tar ställning. En studie av hans journalistik och tidsaktuella diktning*, Stockholm: Carlssons.

Carpi, Umberto. 1981. *Bolscevico immaginista. Comunismo e avanguardie artistiche nell'Italia degli anni venti*, Naples: Liguori.

Carroll, Noël. 1988. *Philosophical Problems of Classical Film Theory*, Princeton, NJ: Princeton University Press.

Casetti, Francesco. 2008. *Eye of the Century: Film, Experience, Modernity*, New York: Columbia University Press.

Castello, Guilio Caseare, and Claudio Bertieri (eds). 1959. *Venezia 1932–1939. Filmografia critica*, Rome: Bianco e nero, 243–55.

Celli, Silvio. 2010. 'Il primo decennio', *Bianco e nero* 71(566), 7–15.

Charyn, Jerome. 1989. *Movieland: Hollywood and the Great American Dream Culture*. New York: G.P. Putnam's Sons.

Cheeke, Stephen. 2008. *Writing for Art: The Aesthetics of Ekphrasis*, Manchester and New York: Manchester University Press.

Chiarini, Luigi. 1934a. *Cinematografo*, Rome: Cremonese.

————. 1934b. 'Teatro e Cinematografo (appunti)', *Quadrivio* 2(50) (7 October).

————. 1937. 'Didattica del cinema', *Bianco e nero* 1(3) (March).

————. 1938. 'Il film è un'arte, il cinema un'industria', *Bianco e nero* 2(7) (July), 3–8.

————. 1939. 'Prefazione', in Francesco Pasinetti, *Storia del cinema dalle origini a oggi*, Rome: Bianco e nero.

————. 1941. *Cinque capitoli sul film*, Rome: Edizioni italiane.

————. 1954. *Il film nella battaglia delle idee*, Milan: Fratelli Bocca.

————. 1969. *Un Leone e altri animali*, Milan: Sugar.

Chiarini, Luigi, and Umberto Barbaro (eds). 1939. *Problemi del film*, Rome: Bianco e nero.

Choy, Yong Chan. 2006. 'Inszenierungen der völkischen Filmkultur im Nationalsozialismus: "Der Internationale Filmkongress Berlin 1935"'. Berlin: Technical University. (Ph.D. thesis, retrieved on 11 Nov. 2011 from http://opus.kobv.de/tuberlin/volltexte/2006/1214/).

Christie, Ian. 1979. 'French Avant-garde Film in the Twenties: From Specificity to Surrealism', in Philip Drummond et al. (eds). *Film as Film: Formal Experiment in Film, 1910–1975*, London: Arts Council of Great Britain, 37–46.

————. 1999. 'Censorship, Culture and Codpieces: Eisenstein's Influence in Britain during the 1930s and 40s', in Albert J. LaValley and Barry P. Scherr (eds), *Eisenstein at 100: A Reconsideration*, New Brunswick, NJ: Rutgers University Press.

————. 2001. 'Before the Avant-Gardes: Artists and Film, 1910–1914', in Leonardo Quaresima and Laura Vichi (eds), *The Tenth Muse*, Udine: Film Forum, 369–70.

————. 2006. 'Film as a Modernist Art', in Christopher Wilk (ed.). *Modernism: Designing a New World, 1914–1939*, London: Victoria and Albert Museum.

————. 2008. 'Histories of the Future: Mapping the Avant-garde', *Film History* 20(1), 6–13.

Christie, Ian, and John Gillett (eds). 1978. *Futurism/Formalism/FEKS: Eccentrism and Soviet Cinema, 1918–1936*, London: British Film Institute.

Clark, Katerina. 2011. *Moscow, the Fourth Rome: Stalinism, Cosmopolitanism, and the Evolution of Soviet Culture, 1931–1941*. Cambridge, MA: Harvard University Press.

Close Up (1927–1933). Territet (CH). Complete reprint in 10 volumes Nendeln (Liechtenstein): Kraus Reprint 1969; and James Donald, Anne Friedberg and Laura Marcus (eds). 1998. *Close Up, 1927–1933: Cinema and Modernism*, London: Cassell.

Corney, Frederick C. 2004. *Telling October: Memory and the Making of the Bolshevik Revolution*, Ithaca, NY: Cornell University Press.

Cosandey, Roland. 2000a. 'De l'Exposition nationale Berne 1913 au CSPS 1921. Charade pour un cinema vernaculaire', in Maria Tortajada and François Albera (eds), *Cinéma Suisse. Nouvelle approaches. Histoire – Esthétique – Critique – Thèmes – Matériaux*, Lausanne: Payot, 91–109.

————. 2000b. 'Expo 64. Un cinéma au service du "scénario"', in *Mémoire vive. Pages d'histoire lausannoise* 9, 18–23.

Cosandey, Roland, and Thomas Tode. 2000. 'Quand l'avant-garde projetait son avenir. Le 1er Congrès international du cinéma indépendant, La Sarraz,

Septembre 1929', in *Archives, Perpignan* 84 (April); retrieved 25 Nov. 2011 from http://www.cinematheque.ch/f/documents-de-cinema/cinema-et-avant-garde/archives-n-84.html.

Crisp, C.G. 1993. *The Classic French Cinema 1930–1960*, Bloomington: Indiana University Press.

Culbert, David. 1993. 'Document: The Rockefeller Foundation, the Museum of Modern Art Film Library, and Siegfried Kracauer, 1941', *Historical Journal of Film, Radio and Television*, 13(4).

————. 2007. 'German Films in the United States, 1933–45', in Roel Vande Winkel and David Welch (eds), *Cinema and the Swastika: The International Expansion of Third Reich Cinema*, Houndmills and New York: Palgrave Macmillan.

Curtis, Scott. 1994. 'The Taste of a Nation: Training the Senses and Sensibility of Cinema Audiences in Imperial Germany', in *Film History* 6(4), 445–69.

David-Fox, Michael. 2011. *Showcasing the Great Experiment: Cultural Diplomacy and Western Visitors to the Soviet Union, 1921–1941*. Oxford: Oxford University Press.

Decherney, Peter. 2005. *Hollywood and the Cultural Elite: How the Movies Became American*, New York: Columbia University Press.

De Cuir, Greg, Jr. 2011. *Yugoslav Black Wave: Polemical Cinema from 1963–72 in the Socialist Federal Republic of Yugoslavia*, Belgrade: Film Center Serbia.

————. 2012. 'The Nocturnal Affairs of Mr Miletić: Oktavijan's Career, Genre Hybridity, and Ciné-amateurism in Yugoslavia', in *Small-gauge Storytelling: Discovering the Amateur Fiction Film*, ed. by Ryan Shand and Ian Craven, Edinburgh: Edinburgh University Press.

Degenhard, Armin. 2001. *'Bedenken, die zu überwinden sind … ' Das neue Medium Film im Spannungsfeld reformpädagogischer Erziehungsziele, von der Kinoreformbewegung bis zur handlungsorientierten Filmarbeit Adolf Reichweins*, Munich: KoPäd.

Deleuze, Gilles. 1986. *Cinema 1: The Image Movement*, London: Athlone.

Della Casa, Stefano. 2002. 'La contestazione a Venezia', in Gianni Canova (ed.), *Storia del cinema italiano. 1965–1969*, Venice: Marsilio, 356–57.

d'Eramo, Marco. 1978. 'Il disinteresse paga. Introduzione alla sociologia degli intellettuali di Pierre Bourdieu', in Pierre Bourdieu, *Campo del potere e campo intellettuale*, Cosenza, 12–13.

Dewald, Christian. 2007. '"Schaffen wir uns unsere Revolutionsfilme!" Notate zur Filmschau Proletarisches Kino in Österreich', *filmarchiv* 47, 10–11, 8ff.

Dickinson, Thorold, and Catherine de la Roche. 1948. *Soviet Cinema*, London: Falcon Press.

Drewniak, Bogusław. 1987. *Der deutsche Film 1938–1945. Ein Gesamtüberblick*, Düsseldorf: Droste.

Druick, Zoë. 2007. 'The International Educational Cinematograph Institute, Reactionary Modernism, and the Formation of Film Studies', in *Canadian Journal of Film Studies / Revue canadienne d'études cinématographiques* 16(1), 80–97 (retrieved 25 Nov. 2011 from http://www.filmstudies.ca/journal/pdf/cj-film-studies161_Druick_studies.pdf).

Dumont, Hervé. 1987. *Geschichte des Schweizer Films. Spielfilme 1896–1965,* Lausanne: Schweizer Filmarchiv.

Dupin, Christopher. 2007. 'The Origins and Early Development of the National Film Library: 1929–1936', *Journal of Media Practice* 7(3) (March), 199–217.

Dusinberre, Deke. 1996. 'The Avant-Garde Attitude in the Thirties', in Michael O'Pray (ed.), *The British Avant-Garde Film 1926–1995,* Luton: University of Luton, 65–83.

Dymling, Carl Anders, et al. (eds). 1944. *Svensk Filmindustri. Tjugufem år.* Stockholm: AB Svensk Filmindustri.

Ede, Laurie N. 2010. *British Film Design: A History,* London: I.B. Tauris.

Eggeling, Viking. 1921. 'Elvi fejtegetések a mozgómüvészetröl', *MA* 6(8), 105–6.

Eisenstein, Sergei. 1934. 'Sredniaia iz trekh', in *Sovetskoe kino* 11/12, 54–83.

————. 1942. *The Film Sense,* New York: Harcourt.

————. 1949. *Film Form: Essays in Film Theory,* New York: Harcourt.

————. 1982. *Film Essays and a Lecture,* trans. Jay Leyda, Princeton, NJ: Princeton University Press.

————. 1996. *Selected Works. Vol. III: Writings, 1934–1947,* ed. Richard Taylor, trans. William Powell, London: BFI.

————. 2010. *Selected Works. Volume III. Writings, 1934–47,* edited by Richard Taylor. London: I.B. Tauris, 16–41.

Elder, R. Bruce. 2007. 'Hans Richter and Viking Eggeling: The Dream of Universal Language and the Birth of The Absolute Film', in Alexander Graf and Dietrich Scheunemann (eds), *Avant-Garde Film,* Amsterdam: Rodopi, 3–53.

Ernst, Wolfgang. 2003. *Im Namen von Geschichte. Sammeln – Speichern – Er/Zählen. Infrastrukturelle Konfigurationen des deutschen Gedächtnisses,* Munich: Fink.

Eskildsen, Ute. 1979. 'Fotokunst statt Kunstphotographie. Die Durchsetzung des fotografischen Mediums in Deutschland 1920–1933', in Ute Eskildsen and Jan-Christopher Horak (eds), *Film und Foto der Zwanziger Jahre,* Stuttgart: Hatje, 8–25.

Essed, Philomena. 1991. *Understanding Everyday Racism: An Interdisciplinary Theory,* London: Sage.

Fábián, Katalin. 2007. 'Making an Appearance: The Formation of Women's Groups in Hungary', *Aspasia* 1, 110–13.

Felski, Rita. 1995. *The Gender of Modernity,* Cambridge, MA: Harvard University Press.

Ferraris, Maurizio. 2009. *Documentalità. Perché è necessario lasciar tracce,* Rome: Laterza.

Florin, Bo. 1997. *Den nationella stilen. Studier i den svenska filmens guldålder,* Stockholm: Aura.

Fogu, Claudio. 2002. Decennale', in Victoria De Grazia and Sergio Luzzatto (eds), *Dizionario del fascismo,* vol. 1, Turin: Einaudi, 397–400.

Fomin, Viktor, and Aleksandr Deriabin (eds). 2004. *Letopis' rossiiskogo kino: 1863–1929,* Moscow: Materik.

Fore, Devin. 2006. 'The Operative Word in Soviet Factography', *October* 118 (Fall), 95–131.

Forslund, Bengt. 1998. *Vilhelm Moberg. Filmen och televisionen*, Stockholm: Carlssons.

Frank, Tibor. 2007. 'The Social Construction of Hungarian Genius (1867–1930)', Von Neumann Memorial Lecture, Princeton.

Freddi, Luigi. (1933) 1994. 'Rapporto sulla cinematografia', in Luigi Freddi, *Il cinema. Il governo dell'immagine*, 2nd edition, Rome: Centro sperimentale di cinematografia.

Freeman, Judi. 1996. 'Bridging Purism and Surrealism: The Origins and Production of Fernand Léger's Ballet Mécanique', in Rudolf E. Kuenzli (ed.), *Dada and Surrealist Film*, Cambridge, MA and London: MIT Press, 28–45.

Frey, Mattias, 'Cultural Problems of Classical Film Theory: Béla Balázs, '"Universal Language" and the Birth of National Cinema', *Screen* 51(4), 324–40.

Fuhrmann, Wolfgang. 2003. 'Propaganda, Science, and Entertainment. German Colonial Cinematography: A Case Study in the History of Early Nonfiction Cinema'. Unpublished dissertation, Utrecht University.

Furberg, Kjell. 2000. *Svenska biografer*, Stockholm: Prisma.

Furhammar, Leif. 1991. *Filmen i Sverige. En historia i tio kapitel*, Höganäs: Wiken.

Füzi, Izabella. 2009. 'Arc, hang, tekintet: szemiotikai, esztétikai és politikai összefüggések Balázs Béla filmesztétikájában' [Face, Sound, Gaze: Semiotic, Aesthetic and Political Relations of Béla Balázs' Film Aesthetics], *apertúra. Film-Vizualitás-Elmélet*. Retrieved 21 October 2012 from http://apertura.hu/2009/osz/fuzi

Garafalo, Piero. 2002. 'Seeing Red: The Soviet Influence on Italian Cinema in the Thirties', in Jacqueline Reich and Piero Garofalo (eds), *Re-Viewing Fascism: Italian Cinema, 1929–1943*, Bloomington: Indiana University Press.

Gauthier, Christophe. 1999. *La Passion du cinéma. Cinéphiles, ciné-clubs et salles spécialisées à Paris de 1920 à 1929*, Paris: Association Française de Recherche sur l'Histoire du Cinéma / Ecole des Chartes.

Geldern, James von. 1993. *Bolshevik Festivals, 1917–1920*, Berkeley: University of California Press.

Gelmis, Joseph. 1970. *The Film Director as Superstar*, Garden City, NY: Doubleday. Retrieved on 20 Oct. 2012 from http://www.visual-memory.co.uk/amk/doc/0069.html

Gentile, Emilio. 1993. *Il culto del littorio. La sacralizzazione della politica nell'Italia fascista*, Rome: Laterza.

Geppert, Alexander C.T. 2010. *Fleeting Cities: Imperial Expositions in fin-de-Siècle Europe*, Basingstoke: Palgrave Macmillan.

Gertiser, Anita. 2011. 'Schul- und Lehrfilme', in Yvonne Zimmermann (ed.), *Schaufenster Schweiz. Dokumentarische Gebrauchsfilme 1896–1964*, Zurich: Limmat, 431–47.

Ghali, Noureddine et al. (eds). 1995. *L'Avant-garde cinématographique en France dans les années vingt: idées, conceptions, théories*, Paris: Paris expérimental.

Giedion, Siegfried. 1995. *Building in France, Building in Iron, Building in Ferro-concrete*, Santa Monica, CA: Getty Center for the History of Art and the Humanities.

Goldberg, David Theo. 1993. *Racist Culture: Philosophy and the Politics of Meaning*, Chichester: Wiley-Blackwell.

————. 1997. *Racial Subjects: Writing on Race in America*, New York: Routledge.

Gorky, Maksim. 1946. *Literature and Life: A Selection from the Writings of Maxim Gorki*, intr. V.V. Mikhailovski, trans. Edith Bone, London and New York: Hutchinson International Authors Ltd.

Goulding, Daniel J. 1985. *Liberated Cinema: The Yugoslav Experience*, Bloomington: Indiana University Press.

Graf, Alexander. 2007. 'Paris – Berlin – Moscow: On the Montage Aesthetic in the City Symphony Films of the 1920s', in Alexander Graf and Dietrich Scheunemann (eds), *Avant-Garde Film*, 77–91.

Grierson, John. 1966. 'The Russian Example', in Forsyth Hardy (ed.), *Grierson on Documentary*, London: Faber.

Grieveson, Lee. 2004. *Policing Cinema: Movies and Censorship in Early-Twentieth-Century America*, Berkeley and Los Angeles: University of California Press.

Grieveson, Lee, and Colin MacCabe (eds). 2011a. *Empire and Film*, London: Palgrave Macmillan and British Film Institute.

———— (eds). 2011b. *Film and the End of Empire*, London: Palgrave Macmillan and British Film Institute.

Grieveson, Lee, and Haidee Wasson (eds). 2008. *Inventing Film Studies: Towards a History of a Discipline*, Durham, NC: Duke University Press.

Gunning, Tom. 1997. 'Before Documentary: Early Nonfiction Films and the "View" Aesthetic', in Daan Hertogs and Nico de Klerk (eds), *Uncharted Territory: Essays on Early Nonfiction Film*, Amsterdam: Nederlands Filmmuseum.

————. 2003. 'A Quarter of a Century Later: Is Early Cinema Still Early?', *KINtop* 12, 17–31.

Gurevich, Stella. 1998. *Leningradskoe kinovedenie (Zubovskii osobniak, 1925–1936)*, Saint Petersburg: Rossiĭskiĭ in-t istorii iskusstv.

Gustafsson, Tommy. 2007. *En fiende till civilisationen. Manlighet, genusrelationer, sexualitet och rasstereotyper i svensk filmkultur under 1920-talet*, Lund: Sekel.

Haan, Franziska de, Krasimira Daskalova, and Anna Loutfi (eds). 2006. *Biographical Dictionary of Women's Movements and Feminisms in Central, Eastern, and South Eastern Europe*, Budapest: CEU Press.

Hagener, Malte. 2006. 'Programming Attractions: Avant-Garde Exhibition Practice in the 1920s and 1930s', in Wanda Strauven (ed.), *The Cinema of Attractions Reloaded*, Amsterdam: Amsterdam University Press, 265–79.

————. 2007. *Moving Forward, Looking Back: The European Avantgarde and the Invention of Film Culture*, Amsterdam: Amsterdam University Press.

————. 2011. 'Inventing a Past, Imagining a Future: The Discovery and Institutionalisation of Film History in the 1930s', *Cinema & Cie* 16/17 (Spring–Fall), 29–37.

Häger, Bengt. 1989. *Ballets suédois*, Stockholm: Streiffert.

Hake, Sabine. 1992. *Passions and Deceptions: The Early Films of Ernst Lubitsch*, Princeton, NJ: Princeton University Press.

————. 1993. *The Cinema's Third Machine: Writing on Film in Germany 1907–1933*, Lincoln: University of Nebraska Press

Haller, Andrea. 2012. 'Diagnosis: "Flimmeritis". Female Cinemagoing in Imperial Germany, 1911–18', in Daniel Biltereyst, Richard Maltby and Philippe

Meers, (eds), *Cinema, Audiences and Modernity: New Perspectives on European Cinema History*, London and New York: Routledge, 130–41.

Hammond, Paul (ed.). 1978. *The Shadow and Its Shadow: Surrealist Writings on the Cinema*, London: British Film Institute.

Hanna-Daoud, Thomas. 1996. *Die NSDAP und der Film bis zur Machtergreifung*, Cologne: Böhlau.

Hayward, Susan. 2005. *French National Cinema*, 2nd edition, London: Routledge.

Hediger, Vinzenz. 2011. 'Original, Work, Performance: Film Theory as Archive Theory', in Giulio Bursi and Simone Venturini (eds), *What Burns (Never) Returns/Quel che brucia (non) ritorna*, Udine: Campanotto, 44–56.

Hediger, Vinzenz, and Patrick Vonderau (eds). 2007. *Filmische Mittel, industrielle Zwecke. Das Werk des Industriefilms*, Berlin: Vorwerk 8.

Hein, Birgit, and Wulf Herzogenrath. 1978. *Film als Film. 1910 bis heute*, Stuttgart: Gerd Hatje.

Heinemann, Franz. 1924. *Der Film in der Schweiz. Privatwirtschaft. Zeitgemässe Anregungen*, Zurich: Orell Füssli.

———. 1941. 'Ein Viertel-Jahrhundert schweizerische Kinematographie: 1915–1940. Frühe schweizer. Mittelpunkte internationalen Filmschaffens', in *Jahrbuch der Schweizer Filmindustrie / Annuaire de la cinématographie suisse*, 3–34.

Hellström, Gösta. 1931. 'En natt – banbrytande?', *Filmjournalen* 11.

Hensel, Frank. 1936. 'Die Arbeit des Reichsfilmarchivs. Eine in der Welt einzigartige staatliche Einrichtung', *Volk und Welt. Das deutsche Monatsbuch* (January).

Henson, Bruce. 1997. 'Iris Barry: American Film Archive Pioneer', *The Katharine Sharp Review* 4, 1–6, retrieved on 19 February 2011 from http://mirrored.ukoln.ac.uk/lis-journals/review/review/winter1997.

Henzler, Bettina. 2011. '"Il les conduit ailleurs". Gespräch mit Alain Bergala zu Cinéphilie, Wissenschaft und Pädagogik', in Gudrun Sommer, Vinzenz Hediger and Oliver Fahle (eds), *Orte filmischen Wissens. Filmkultur und Filmvermittlung im Zeitalter digitaler Netzwerke*, Marburg: Schüren, 161–75.

Herlinghaus, Hermann, and Lissi Zilinski (eds). 1967. 'Sowjetischer Film in Deutschland 1922–1932. Eine Dokumentation'. Berlin/GDR: Institut für Filmwissenschaft an der Deutschen Hochschule für Filmkunst, 991ff (issue 8, no. 3).

Higson, Andrew, and Richard Maltby (eds). 1999. *'Film Europe' and 'Film America': Cinema, Commerce and Cultural Exchange, 1920–1939*, Exeter: Exeter University Press.

Hinkel, Hans (Hrsg.). 1937. *Handbuch der Reichskulturkammer*, Berlin: Deutscher Verlag für Politik und Wirtschaft.

Hjort, Mette, and Scott McKenzie (eds). 2000. *Cinema and Nation*, London and New York: Routledge.

Hoijer, Harry. 1947. 'Our Swedish Contemporary', *Hollywood Quarterly* 3(1), 100–101.

Houston, Penelope. 1994. *Keepers of the Frame: The Film Archives*. London: British Film Institute.

Hübl, Adolf. 1935. 'Internationales Filmmuseum', *Intercine. Internationales Institut für Lehrfilmwesen. Völkerbund* 7(7) (July), 398ff.

Hunter, Sam. 1984. *The Museum of Modern Art, New York: The History and the Collection*. New York: H.N. Abrams.

Iezuitov, Nikolai. 1934. *Puti sovetskogo fil'ma*, Moscow.

Interlandi, Telesio. 1935. 'Chi ha paura del cinema politico?', *Quadrivio* 3(36) (7 July).

Iordanova, Dina. 2003. *Cinema of the Other Europe: The Industry and Artistry of East Central European Film*, London: Wallflower.

Iordanova, Dina, and Ruby Cheung (eds). 2010. *Film Festivals and Imagined Communities*, St Andrews: St Andrews Film Studies.

Iordanova, Dina, and Ragan Rhyne (eds). 2009. *The Festival Circuit*, St Andrews: St Andres Film Studies.

Iurenev, Rostislav. 1977. *Sovetskoe kinovedenie*, Moscow: Vsesoiuz. gos. in-t kinematografii.

Ivens, Joris. 1969. *The Camera and I*, Berlin: Seven Seas.

James, David. 2005. *The Most Typical Avant-Garde: History and Geography of Minor Cinemas in Los Angeles*. Berkeley: University of California Press.

Janser, Andres. 2001. 'Es kommt der gute Film. Zu den Anfängen der Filmclubs in Zürich', in Vinzenz Hediger, Jan Sahli, Alexandra Schneider and Margrit Tröhler (eds), *Home Stories: Neue Studien zu Film und Kino in der Schweiz / Nouvelles approaches du cinéma et du film en Suisse*, Marburg: Schüren, 55–69.

Jaques, Pierre-Emmanuel. 2005. 'L'Ovomaltine et un cinéaste d'avant-garde. Hans Richter et le film de commande en Suisse', *Décadrages. Cinéma, à travers champs* 4(5), 154–66.

———. 2007. 'La propaganda nationale par le film. Albert Masnata et l'Office suisse du d'expansion commerciale', *Revue historique vaudoise* 115, 65–78.

Jaques, Pierre-Emmanuel, and Gianni Haver. 2004. 'Le cinema à la Landi. Le documentaire au service de la Défense nationale spirituelle', in Gianni Haver (ed.), *Le cinéma au pas. Les productions des pays autoritaires et leur impact en Suisse*, Lausanne: Antipodes, 97–110.

Jay, Martin. 1993. *Downcast Eyes: The Denigration of Vision in Twentieth-Century French Thought*, Berkeley: University of California Press.

Johnson, Eyvind. 2002. 'En film om Gamla stan. Förslag I. (stumfilm)', *Pequod* 31/32, 9–12.

Jung, Uli, and Martin Loiperdinger (eds). 2005. *Geschichte des dokumentarischen Films in Deutschland. Band 1: Kaiserreich 1895–1918*, Stuttgart: Philipp Reclam jun.

Junod, Barbara. 2009. 'From a Focus on Products to a Focus on Customers: The Advertising Policies and Practices at the Basel Headquarters', in Andres Janser and Barbara Junod (eds), *Corporate Diversity: Swiss Graphic Design and Advertising by Geigy 1940–1970*, Baden: Lars Müller.

Kaijser, Eva. 2008. 'Gerda Marcus – "den stora tiggerskan" på Svenska Dagbladet', in Ami Lönnroth (ed.), *Empati och engagemang. En kvinnolinje i svensk journalistik*, Enhörna: Tusculum, 39–51.

Kalbus, Oskar. 1922. *Der Deutsche Lehrfilm in Wissenschaft und Unterricht*, Berlin: Heymann.

Kantor, Sybil Gordon. *Alfred H. Barr, jr. and the Intellectual Origins of the Museum of Modern Art*, Cambridge, MA: MIT Press.

Keitz, Ursula von. 2000. 'Films before the Court: The Theory and Practice of Film Assessment in Germany from 1920 to 1938', in Leonardo Quaresima, Alessandra Raengo and Laura Vichi (eds), *I limiti della rappresentazione. Censura, visibile, modi di rappresentazione nel cinema* [The Bounds of Representation: Censorship, the Visible, Modes of Representation in Film], Udine: Forum, 381–402.

Kepley Jr., Vance. 1987. 'Building a National Cinema: Soviet Film Education 1918–1934', *Wide Angle* 9(3).

———. 1993. 'Eisenstein as Pedagogue', *Quarterly Review of Film and Video* 14(4).

Kessler, Frank. 2006. 'The Cinema of Attractions as *Dispositif*', Strauven, *Attractions Reloaded*, 57–69.

———. 2011. 'Programming and Performing Early Cinema Today: Strategies and *Dispositifs*', in Martin Loiperdinger (ed.), *Early Cinema Today: The Art of Programming and Live Performance*, New Barnet: John Libbey.

Klapp, Benno. 1968. 'Die deutschen Kriegswochenschauen des II. Weltkrieges als publizistische Erscheinung' (diss., Westfälische Wilhelms-Universität Münster).

Kleiman, Naum, and Antonio Somaini (eds). Forthcoming. *Sergei M. Eisenstein: Notes for a General History of Cinema*, Amsterdam: Amsterdam University Press.

Koch, Gertrud. 1987. 'Béla Balázs: The Physiognomy of Things', *New German Critique* 40, Special Issue on Weimar Film Theory, 167–77.

Kosanović, Dejan. 2011. *Kinematografija i film u Kraljevini SHS/Kraljevini Jugoslaviji 1918–1941* [Cinematography and Film in the Kingdom of Yugoslavia 1918–1941], Belgrade: Filmski centar Srbije.

Koszarski, Richard. 1990. *An Evening's Entertainment: The Age of the Silent Feature Picture, 1915–1928*, New York: Scribner.

Kracauer, Siegfried. 1947. *From Caligari to Hitler: A Psychological History of the German Film*, Princeton, NJ: Princeton University Press.

———. 2004. *Kleine Schriften zum Film. Band 6.3 (1932–1961)*, (ed. Inka Mülder-Bach), Frankfurt/Main: Suhrkamp.

Krarup, Helge, and Carl Nørrested. 1986. *Eksperimentalfilm i Danmark*, København: Borgen.

Kubelka, Peter. 1990. 'La theorie du cinéma métrique', in Christian Lebrat (ed.), *Peter Kubelka*, Paris: Expérimental.

Kuhn, Annette. 1988. *Cinema, Censorship, and Sexuality, 1909–25*, New York: Routledge.

Kühn, Gertraude, Karl Tümmler and Walter Wimmer (eds). 1978. *Film und revolutionäre Arbeiterbewegung in Deutschland 1918–1932*, Berlin/GDR: Henschel.

Lane, John Francis. 1950. 'Amateur Activities: On Studying the Film', *Sight and Sound* 19(2).

Langlois, Henri. 1936. 'Fondation de la cinémathèque', *La Cinématographie française* 932 (12 September).

———. 1947. 'The Cinémathèque Française', *Hollywood Quarterly* 2(2) (January).

Länzlinger, Stefan, and Thomas Schärer. 2009. *'Stellen wir diese Waffe in unseren Dienst'. Film und Arbeiterbewegung in der Schweiz*, Zurich: Chronos.

Laura, Ernesto G. 1962. 'Luigi Chiarini e il film come assoluta forma', *Bianco e nero* 23/7–8 (July–August): 18–66.

———. 1976. 'CSC dal fascismo allo stato democratico', *Bianco e Nero* 5/6: 4–29.

———. 1992. 'Luigi Chiarini: un teorico si fa regista', in Andrea Martini (ed.), *La bella forma. Poggioli, I calligrafici e dintorni*, Venice: Marsilio, 121–34.

Laurent, Natacha, and Christophe Gauthier. 2007. 'Zoom Arrière: Une tentative pour incarner une idée de cinématheque', *Journal of Film Preservation* 74/75.

Lebedev, Nikolai. 1924. *Kino: ego kratkaia istoriia, ego vozmozhnosti, ego stroitel'stvo v sovetskom gosudarstve*, Moscow.

———. 1934. 'O nauchno-issledovatel'skoi rabote v oblasti kino'. *Sovetskoe kino* 10, 43.

———. 2002. 'Kul'turfil'ma na Zapade i u nas. Glavy iz neizdannoi knigi'. *Kinovedcheskie zapiski* 58.

LeGrice, Malcolm. 1982. *Abstract Film and Beyond*, Cambridge, MA: MIT Press.

Lesznai, Anna. 1918. 'Babonásészrevételek a meseés a tragédialélektanához' [Superstitious Remarks on the Psychology of the Fairy Tale and of Tragedy], *Nyugat* 13. Retrieved 16 October 2012 from http://epa.oszk.hu/00000/00022/nyugat.htm

———. 1965. *Spätherbst in Eden*, Karlsruhe: Stahlberg.

———. 2008. *Wahre Märchen aus den Garten Eden*, ed. György Fehéri, trans. András Hecker and Ilka Russy, Berlin: Das Arsenal.

Levi, Pavle. 2012. *Cinema by Other Means*, Oxford: Oxford University Press.

Leyda, Jay. 1964. *Films Beget Films*, New York: Hill and Wang.

Leyda, Jay, and Zina Voynow. 1982. *Eisenstein at Work*, New York: Pantheon.

Ligensa, Annemone. 2013. 'Asta Nielsen in Germany: A Reception-oriented Approach', in Martin Loiperdinger and Uli Jung (eds), *Importing Asta Nielsen: The International Film Star in the Making (1910–1914)*, New Barnet: John Libbey, 343–52.

Liljedahl, Elisabeth. 1975. *Stumfilmen i Sverige – kritik och debatt. Hur samtiden värderade den nya konstarten*, Stockholm: Proprius.

Lindström, Jan-Gunnar. 1938. 'Svensk filmstudiorörelse', in Bengt Idestam-Almquist and Ragnar Allberg (eds), *Om film. Svenska Filmsamfundets årsbok 1937–38*, Stockholm, 103–10.

Linssen, Céline, Hans Schoots and Tom Gunning (eds). 1999. *Het gaat om de film! Een nieuwe geschiedenis van de Nederlandsche Filmliga 1927–1933*, Amsterdam: Bas Lubberhuizen.

Lista, Giovanni. 1988. *Dal futurismo all'immaginismo: Vinicio Paladini*, Bologna: Il cavaliere azzurro.

Listov, Viktor. 1992. 'Kino: iskusstvo ili promyshlennost?', in *Teoreticheskie chteniia pamiati S.I.Iutkevicha*, Moscow.

———. 1995. *Rossiia. Revoliutsiia. Kinematograf*, Moscow: Materik.

———. 2007. 'Ostorozhno, arkhivy …', in Viktor Listov, *I dol'she veka dlitsia cinema*, Moscow.

Loewy, Hanno. 2003. *Béla Balázs. Märchen, Ritual, Film*, Berlin: Vorwerk 8.

Loiperdinger, Martin. 2001. 'Die Erfindung des Dokumentarfilms durch die Filmpropaganda im Ersten Weltkrieg', in Kay Hoffmann and Ursula von Keitz (eds), *Die Einübung des dokumentarischen Blicks. Fiction Film und Non Fiction Film zwischen Wahrheitsanspruch und expressiver Sachlichkeit 1895–1945*, Marburg: Schüren, 71–79.

————. 2012. 'Afgrunden in Germany: Monopolfilm, Cinemagoing and the Emergence of the Female Star Asta Nielsen, 1910–11', in Daniel Biltereyst, Richard Maltby and Philippe Meers (eds), *Cinema, Audiences and Modernity: New Perspectives on European Cinema History*, London and New York: Routledge, 142–53.

Low, Rachael. 1971 *The History of the British Film 1918–1929*, London: Allen & Unwin.

Lukić, Vladeta. 1952. 'Amaterski film kod nas i u svetu/Amateur Film at Home and in the World', *Film* 24: 4.

Lundemo, Trond. 2010. 'Film Theory as Archive Theory', in Francesco Casetti, Jane Gaines and Valentina Re (eds), *Dall'inizio, alla fine. Teorie del cinema in prospettiva / In the Very Beginning, at the Very End: Film Theories in Perspective*, Udine: Forum, 33–38.

Lundkvist, Artur. 1966. *Självporträtt av en drömmare med öppna ögon*, Stockholm: Bonnier.

Luthersson, Peter. 2002. *Svensk litterär modernism: en stridsstudie*, Stockholm: Atlantis.

McCabe, Susan. 2005. *Cinematic Modernism: Modernist Poetry and Film*, Cambridge and New York: Cambridge University Press.

Macpherson, Don, and Paul Willemen (eds). 1980. *Traditions of Independence: British Cinema in the Thirties*, London: British Film Institute.

Maillart, Claude. 2010. *L'homme Visible et l'Esprit du Cinéma*, Belval: Circé.

Majcen, Vjekoslav. 2003. 'Hrvatski neprofesijski film: 70 godina kinoamaterizma u Hrvatskoj (1928–1998)' [Croatian Non-Professional Film: 70 Years of Ciné-Amateurism in Croatia (1928–1998)], *Hrvatski filmski ljetopis* 29.

Malitsky, Joshua S. 'Ideologies in Fact: Still and Moving-Image Documentary in the Soviet Union, 1927–1932', *Journal of Linguistic Anthropology* 20(2) (Fall), 352–71.

Mannoni, Laurent. 2006a. 'Henri Langlois and the Musée du Cinéma', *Film History* 18(3).

————. 2006b. *Histoire de la Cinémathèque française*, Paris: Gallimard.

Manthey, Elisabeth. 1968. 'Der politische Kompilationsfilm – seine Entwicklung, seine Besonderheiten, seine propagandistische Wirkung und die Bedeutung der Filmarchive für seine Produktion', thesis, Potsdam-Babelsberg: German University of Cinema.

Manzoli, Giacomo. 2009. 'Il carnevale di Venezia', *Bianco e nero* 70(563), 40–49.

Maraun, Frank (i.e. Goelz, Erwin). 1939. 'Weltgeschichte auf Zelluloid. Besuch im Reichsfilmarchiv', *Der deutsche Film* 10 (April).

Margadonna, Ettore Maria. 1932. *Cinema: ieri e oggi*, Milan: Domus.

Martov, Boris. 1936. 'Otzyv o rabote V.S. Rosolovskoi *Kinematografiia v 1917 godu*', in Vanda Rosolovskaia. *Kinematografiia nakanune Velikoi Proletarskoi Revoliutsii. TS. 16881. Laboratoriia otechestvennogo kino*, Moscow: VGIK.

Mazzei, Luca. 2009. 'Luigi Chiarini alla Mostra e il primato morale, civile e cinematografico degli italiani', *Bianco e nero* 70(562) (January–April).

Meder, Thomas. 2006. *Produzent ist der Zuschauer. Prolegomena zu einer historischen Bildwissenschaft des Films*, Berlin: Bertz und Fischer.

Mekas, Jonas, et al. (eds). 1991. *Swedish Avantgarde Film 1924–1990*, New York: Anthology Film Archives.

Merzeau, Louise. 1999. 'Du Monument au document', *Cahiers de médiologie*, 7.

Metz, Christian. 1986. *The Imaginary Signifier: Psychoanalysis and the Cinema*, trans. Celia Britton and Annwyl Williams, Bloomington: Indiana University Press.

Miller, Henry K. 2012. *Where We Came In: The Origins of a Minority Film Culture in Britain, 1917–1940*. London: Unpublished thesis.

Miller, Jamie. 2007. 'Educating the Filmmakers: The State Institute of Cinematography in the 1930s', *Slavonic and Eastern European Review* 85(3).

Mitchell, W.J.T. 2005. *What do Pictures Want? The Lives and Loves of Images*, Chicago: University of Chicago Press.

Moderna Museet. 1969. *Svenska Baletten/Les Ballets Suédois 1920–1925. Ur Dansmuséets samlingar*, Stockholm: Moderna Museet.

Moeller, Felix. 2000. *The Film Minister: Goebbels and the Cinema in the 'Third Reich'*, Stuttgart and London: Edition Axel Menges.

Mosconi, Elena. 2006. *L'impressione del film. Contributi per una storia culturale del cinema italiano 1895–1945*, Milan: V&P.

Mühl-Benninghaus, Wolfgang. 1999. *Das Ringen um den Tonfilm. Strategien der Elektro- und Filmindustrie in den 20er und 30er Jahren*, Düsseldorf: Droste.

Murray, Bruce. 1990. *Film and the German Left in the Weimar Republic: From Caligari to Kuhle Wampe*, Austin: University of Texas Press.

Mussolini, Benito. 1934. *La dottrina del fascismo. Con una storia del movimento fascista di Gioacchino Volpe*, Milano: Hoepli.

Myl'nikova, V. 1990. 'Istoriia izdaniia odnoi knigi. (Perepiska A.A. Khanzhonkova s V.E.Vishnevskim)', in *Minuvshee: Istoricheskii al'manakh 10*, Paris: Atheneum, 415–64.

Myrent, Glenn, and George P. Langlois. 1995. *Henri Langlois: First Citizen of Cinema*, New York: Twayne.

Nagl, Tobias. 2009a. *Die unheimliche Maschine. Rasse und Repräsentation im Weimarer Kino*, Munich: edition text + kritik.

———. 2009b. 'The Aesthetics of Race in European Film Theory', in Trifonova Temenuga (ed.), *European Film Theory*, London and New York: Routledge, 17–31.

Näslund, Erik. 2008. *Rolf de Maré. Konstsamlare, balettledare, museiskapare*, Stockholm: Langenskjöld.

Näslund, Erik, et al. 1995. *Svenska Baletten i Paris 1920–1925. Ballet Suédois*, Stockholm: Dansmuseet.

Nichols, Bill. 2001. 'Documentary Film and the Modernist Avant-Garde', *Critical Inquiry* 27 (Summer), 580–610.

Nikulin, Lev. 1934. 'Vzgliad nazad'. *Sovetskoe kino* 11/12, 124–25.

Oever, Annie van den (ed.). 2010. *Ostrannenie: On 'Strangeness' and the Moving Image. The History, Reception and Relevance of a Concept*, Amsterdam: Amsterdam University Press.

O'Konor, Louise. 1971. *Viking Eggeling 1880–1925: Artist and Film-Maker. Life and Work*, Stockholm: Almqvist & Wiksell.

Oksiloff, Assenka. 2001. *Picturing the Primitive: Visual Culture, Ethnography, and Early German Cinema*, New York: Palgrave.

Olmeta. Patrick. 2000. *La Cinémathèque Française de 1936 à nos jours*, Paris: CNRS Editions.

Olsson, Jan. 1991. 'I offentlighetens ljus – några notiser om filmstoff i dagspressen', in Jan Olsson (ed.), *I offentlighetens ljus. Stumfilmens affischer, kritiker, stjärnor och musik*, Stockholm: Symposion, 211–74.

Pacifici, Sergio J. 1956. 'Notes toward a Definition of Neorealism', *Yale French Studies* 17: Art of the Cinema, 44–53.

Paladini, Vinicio. 1925. *Arte nella Russia dei Soviets: il padiglione dell'U.R.S.S. a Venezia*, Roma: La Bilancia.

Pansini, Mihovil. 2003. 'Pet razdoblja Kinokluba Zagreb' [Five Eras of Zagreb Ciné-club], in *Kinoklub Zagreb 1928./2003./ Zagreb ciné-club 1928/2003*, edited by Duško Popović, Zagreb: Hrvatski filmski savez/Kino klub Zagreb.

Pehla, Karen. 1991. 'Joe May und seine Detektive', in Hans-Michael Bock and Claudia Lenssen (eds), *Joe May: Regisseur und Produzent*, Munich: edition text + kritik.

Petrić, Vladimir, Alojz Ujes and Dragan Anđelković. 1971. *Almanah: dvadeset godina akademije za pozorište film radio i televiziju* [Almanac: Twenty Years of the Academy of Theatre, Film, Radio and Television], Belgrade: Umetnička akademija u Beogradu.

Petrović, Miroslav Bata (ed.). 2008. *Alternativni film u Beogradu od 1950. do 1990. godine* [Alternative Film in Belgrade from the Years 1950 to 1990], Belgrade: Dom kulture studentski grad.

Petrucci, Antonio. 1934. 'Per una Cineteca Nazionale', *Il Tevere* (7 April).

Pisu, Stefano. 2010. 'L'Urss e l'Occidente: L'Unione Sovietica alla Mostra del cinema di Venezia negli anni Trenta', *Bianco e nero* 567 (May–August), 93–109.

Pitassio, Francesco. 2010. 'La formazione dell'attore e la discussione teorica', *Bianco e nero* 71(566).

Pöch, Rudolf. 1907. 'Reisen in Neu-Guinea in den Jahren 1905–1906', in *Zeitschrift für Ethnologie* 39, 383–400.

Polan, Dana. 2007. *Scenes of Instruction: The Beginning of the US Study of Film*, Berkeley: University of California Press.

Popović, Duško (ed.). 2003. *Kinoklub Zagreb 1928./2003./ Zagreb ciné-club 1928/2003*, Zagreb: Hrvatski filmski savez/Kino klub Zagreb.

Prawer, S.S. 2005. *Between Two Worlds: The Jewish Presence in German and Austrian Film, 1910–1933*, New York and Oxford: Berghahn Books.

Pudovkin, Vsevolod. 1974. 'Kollektivizm – baza kinoraboty', in V. Pudovkin, *Sobranie sochinenii v trekh tomakh*, Volume 1, Moscow: Iskusstvo.

Quaresima, Leonardo. 2008. *L'uomo visibile*, Turin: Lindau.

Qvist, Per Olov. 1995. *Folkhemmets bilder: Modernisering, motstånd och mentalitet i den svenska 30-talsfilmen*. Lund: Arkiv, 30–36.

Rauch, Robert J. 1957. 'An American in a European Film School', *Journal of the University Film Producers Association* 10(1): 9–11.

Regis, Julius. 1920. *Filmens roman. En världserövrares historia, berättad i korta kapitel*, Stockholm: Hugo Gebers.

Reich, Jacqueline. 2002. 'Mussolini at the Movies: Fascism, Film and Culture', in Jacqueline Reich and Piero Garofalo (eds), *Re-Viewing Fascism: Italian Cinema, 1929–1943*, Bloomington: Indiana University Press.

Richter, Hans. 1940. 'Der Filmessay. Eine neue Form des Dokumentarfilms', in Christa Blümlinger and Constantin Wulff (eds). 1992. *Schreiben Bilder Sprechen. Texte zum essayistischen Film*, Vienna: Sonderzahl, 195–98.

———. 1947. 'A History of the Avantgarde', in Frank Stauffacher (ed.), *Art in Cinema: A Symposium on the Avantgarde Film together with Program Notes and References for Series One of Art in Cinema*, San Francisco: Museum of Art, 6–21.

———. 1949. 'Avant-Garde Film in Germany' in Roger Manvell (ed.), *Experiment in the Film*, London: Grey Walls.

———. 1955. 'The Film as an Original Art Form', *Film Culture* 1(1), reprint in P. Adams Sitney (ed.). 1970. *Film Culture Reader*, New York: Praeger, 15–20.

———. 1976. *Der Kampf um den Film. Für einen gesellschaftlich verantwortlichen Film*. (edited by Jürgen Römhild), Munich: Hanser; English translation: Hans Richter. 1986. *The Struggle for the Film: Towards a Socially Responsible Cinema*, New York: St Martin's Press.

Rony, Fatimah Tobing. 1996. *The Third Eye: Race, Cinema, and Ethnographic Spectacle*, Durham, NC: Duke University Press.

Rosaldo, Renato. 1989. 'Imperialist Nostalgia', in *Representations* 26 (Special Issue: Memory and Counter-Memory), Spring, 107–22.

Rother, Rainer, and Judith Prokasky (eds). 2010. *Die Kamera als Waffe. Propagandabilder des Zweiten Weltkrieges*, Munich: edition text + kritik.

Roud, Richard. 1983. *A Passion for Films: Henri Langlois and the Cinémathèque Française*, New York: Viking / London: Secker & Warburg.

Said, Edward. 2003. *Orientalism*, London: Penguin.

Salazkina, Masha. 2011. 'Moscow–Rome–Havana: A Film-Theory Roadmap', *October* 139 (Winter), 97–116.

Schleif, Helma (ed.). 1988. *Stationen der Moderne im Film I: FiFo – Film- und Fotoausstellung Stuttgart 1929*, Berlin: Freunde der Deutschen Kinemathek.

———. 1989. *Stationen der Moderne im Film. II. Texte, Manifeste, Pamphlete*, Berlin: Freunde der Deutschen Kinemathek, 200–19.

Schlüpmann, Heide. 2010. *The Uncanny Gaze: The Drama of Early German Cinema*, transl. Inga Pollmann, Urbana and Chicago: University of Illinois Press.

Schoots, Hans. 1995. *Gevaarlijk leven. Een biografie van Joris Ivens*, Amsterdam: Mets.

Schüen, Heinrich. 1927. *Geographischer Lehrfilm und moderne Geographie: eine methodisch-kritische Untersuchung*, Greifswald: Hartmann.

Seton, Marie. 1960. *Sergei M. Eisenstein: A Biography*, New York: A.A. Wyn.

Sexton, Jamie. 2000. 'Parody on the Fringes: Adrian Brunel, Minority Film Culture and the Art of Deconstruction', in Alan Burton and Laraine Porter (eds), *Pimple, Pranks and Pratfalls: British Film Comedy Before 1930*, Wiltshire: Flicks.

———. 2008. *Alternative Film Culture in Inter-War Britain*, Exeter: University of Exeter Press.

Shand, Ryan. 2008. 'Theorizing Amateur Cinema', *The Moving Image* 8(2): 36–60.

Shumiatskii, Boris. 1934. 'K chemu obiazyvaet nas iubilei', *Sovetskoe kino* 11/12, 12–13.

Sjöholm, Carina. 2003. *Gå på bio. Rum för drömmar i folkhemmets Sverige*, Stockholm and Stehag: Brutus Östling.

Soila, Tytti, Astrid Söderbergh Widding and Gunnar Iversen. 1998. *Nordic National Cinemas*, London and New York: Routledge.

Sörenson, Margareta. 2007. 'Sverige och Svenska baletten', in Tomas Forser and Sven Åke Heed (eds), *Ny svensk teaterhistoria*, vol. 3, Hedemora: Gidlund, 46–56.

Spiker, Jürgen. 1975. *Film und Kapital. Der Weg der deutschen Filmwirtschaft zum nationalsozialistischen Einheitskonzern*, Berlin: Volker Spiess.

Staiger, Janet. 1992. *Interpreting Films: Studies in the Historical Reception of American Cinema*, Princeton, NJ: Princeton University Press.

Steinaecker, F.J. von. 1943. 'Das Filmauswertungsarchiv der Ufa', *Der deutsche Film* 7, 14–15.

Stewart, Fiona. 2011. *In the Beginning was the Garden: Anna Lesznai and Hungarian Modernism 1906–1919*, Ph.D. Dissertation, York University. Retrieved 16 October 2012 from http://udini.proquest.com/view/in-the-beginning-was-the-garden-pqid:2409600781/

Streible, Dan. 2008. *Fight Pictures: A History of Boxing and Early Cinema*, Berkeley: University of California Press.

Strukov, Nikolai. 1929. 'Alla ricerca del meteorite nella taiga', *RICE* (July): 69–72.

Svenstedt, Carl Henrik. 2007. 'Halva historien', in *Film & TV* 1, 36–41.

Szapor, Judith. 2004. 'Sisters or Foes: The Shifting Front Lines of the Hungarian Women's Movements, 1896–1918', in Sylvia Palatschek and Bianka Pietrow-Ennker (eds), *Women's Emancipation Movements in the Nineteenth Century: A European Perspective*, Stanford, CA: Stanford University Press.

Taillibert, Christel. 1999. *L'Institut international du cinématographe éducatif. Regards sur le rôle du cinéma éducatif dans la politique internatonale du fascisme italien*, Paris: L'Harmattan.

Tarquini, Alessandra. 2009. *Il Gentile dei fascisti. Gentiliani e antigentiliani nel regime fascista*. Bologna: Il mulino.

———. 2011. *Storia della cultura fascista*, Milan: Il mulino.

Taylor, Richard. 1979. *The Politics of the Soviet Cinema, 1917–1929*, Cambridge and New York: Cambridge University Press.

——— (ed.). 1982. *The Poetics of Cinema*, Oxford: RPT.

Taylor, Richard, and Ian Christie (eds). 1988. *The Film Factory: Russian and Soviet Cinema in Documents, 1896–1939*, London and New York: Routlege.

Terkessidis, Mark. 2004. *Banalität des Rassismus. Migranten zweiter Generation entwickeln eine neue Perspektive*, Bielefeld: transcript.

Thompson, Kristin. 1992. 'Government Policies and Practical Necessities in the Soviet Cinema of the 1920s', in Anna Lawton (ed.), *Red Screen: Politics, Society, Art in Soviet Cinema*, London and New York: Routledge, 19–41.

Tode, Thomas. 1999. 'Auswahlbibliographie zu La Sarraz', *Filmblatt* 11 (Autumn), 31–33.

Tolstoy, Alexei. 1935. *Darkness and Dawn*, trans. Edith Bone and Emile Burns, London: Victor Gollancz.

Tosi, Virgilio. 1999. *Quando il cinema era un circolo. La stagione d'oro dei cineclub (1945–1956)*, Venice: Marsilio.

Traub, Hans. 1940. 'Filmzeitschriften', in Walther Heide (ed.), *Handbuch der Zeitungswissenschaft*, Leipzig: Hiersemann, issues 3 and 4, column 1027/28.

Tret'iakov, Sergei. 1931. *Feld–Herren: der Kampf um eine Kollektiv–Wirtschaft*, Berlin: Malik.

Troller, Georg Stefan. 1990. *Personenbeschreibung. Tagebuch mit Menschen*, Hamburg: Rasch & Röhring.

Truffaut, Francois. 1954. 'Une Certaine Tendance du cinema française', *Cahiers du Cinèma*.

Tsivian, Yuri. 1996. 'Two "Stylists" of the Teens: Franz Hofer and Yevgenii Bauer', in Thomas Elsaesser and Michael Wedel (eds), *A Second Life: German Cinema's First Decades*, Amsterdam: Amsterdam University Press, 264–77.

Turi, Gabriele. 2002. *Lo stato educatore. Politica e intellettuali nell'Italia fascista*, Rome: Laterza.

Turković, Hrvoje. 2003. 'Kinoklub Zagreb: Filmsko sadište i rasadište' [Zagreb Ciné-club: The Seeds and Development of Film], in Duško Popović, *Kinoklub Zagreb 1928./2003./ Zagreb ciné-club 1928/2003*, Zagreb: Hrvatski filmski savez/Kino klub Zagreb.

———. 2009. 'Paralelni, alternativni i subkulturni opstanak – neprofesijski dokumentarizam u Hrvatskoj' [Parallel, Alternative and Sub-Cultural Survival – Non-Professional Documentary Filmmaking in Croatia], in *ZagrebDox – International Documentary Film Festival/Međunarodni festival dokumentarnog filma 2009*, Zagreb: Factum.

Valck, Marijke de. 2007. *Film Festivals: From European Geopolitics to Global Cinephilia*, Amsterdam: Amsterdam University Press.

Vasey, Ruth. 1997. *The World According to Hollywood, 1918–1939*, Madison: University of Wisconsin Press.

Venturini, Simone. 2011. 'The Cabinet of Doctor Chiarini: Notes on the Birth of an Academic Canon', in Pietro Bianchi, Giulio Bursi and Simone Venturini, *Il canone cinematografico/The Film Canon*, Udine: Forum, 451–60.

Verdone, Mario. 1949. 'The Experimental Cinema Center in Italy', in *Hollywood Quaterly* 4(1).

Vertov, Dziga. 1959. 'Tvorcheskaia deiatel'nost' G.M.Boltianskogo', in *Iz istorii kino: Materialy i dokumenty* 2, Moscow, 66–69.

———. 1984. *Kino-Eye*, Berkeley: University of California Press.

Vishnevskii, Veniamin. 2000. 'Istoriia gosudarstvennogo instituta kinematografii v khronologicheskikh datakh', in Marat Vlasov (ed.), *K istorii VGIKa. Kniga I (1919–1934)*, Moscow: VGIK, 8–20.

Vlasov, Marat (ed.). 2000. *K istorii VGIKa. Kniga I (1919–1934)*, Moscow: VGIK.

——— (ed.). 2004. *K istorii VGIKa. Kniga II (1935–1945)*, Moscow: VGIK.

Volk, Petar. 1986. *Istorija jugoslovenskog filma* [The History of Yugoslav Cinema], Belgrade: Institut za film/Partizanska knjiga.

Volkmann, Barbara, et al. (eds). 1982. *Hans Richter 1888–1976. Dadaist, Filmpionier, Maler, Theoretiker*, Berlin: Frölich and Kaufmann.

Vučićević, Branko. 1998. *Paper Movies*, Belgrade-Zagreb: Arkzin & B 92.

Wahlgren, Anders. 2007. 'Otto G. Carlsund – ett konstnärsliv', in Anders Wahlgren, Niclas Östlind and Helena Persson (eds), *Otto G. Carlsund 11.12.1897–25.7.1948. Konstnär, kritiker och utställningsarrangör*, Stockholm: Arena.

Waldekranz, Rune. 1982. 'Filmstudier och filmforskning. En orientering i internationell och svensk filmlitteratur', in Gösta Werner (ed.), *Svensk filmforskning*, Stockholm: Norstedt, 28–31.

Walther, Alexandra. 2007. *La suisse s'interroge ou l'exercice de l'audace*. University of Lausanne: unpublished master's thesis.

Wasilewska, Wanda. 1945. *Just Love*, trans. Edith Bone, London: Hutchinson International Authors Ltd.

Wasson, Haidee. 1998. *Modern Ideas about Old Films: The Museum of Modern Art's Film Library and Film Culture, 1935–39*, Montreal: McGill University; retrieved on 19 February 2011 from http://www.collectionscanada.gc.ca/obj/s4/f2/dsk1/tape10/PQDD_0025/NQ50280.pdf

———. 2005. *Museum Movies: The Museum of Modern Art and the Birth of Art Cinema*, Berkeley: University of California Press.

Weinbaum, A.E. 2008. *The Modern Girl around the World: Consumption, Modernity and Globalization*, Durham, NC and London: Duke University Press.

Wengström, Jon. 2008. 'Föreningen Film och Fonogram. The Forgotten Archive', *Journal of Film Preservation* 77/78, 77–81.

Wenzel, Mirjam. 2004. 'Der "Neuerer" und sein Kritiker. Siegfried Kracauer und Hans Richter. 1943 bis 1947', *Filmexil* 19.

Werner, Gösta. 1935. *Förteckning over Lunds studenters filmstudios bibliotek*, Lund.

———. 1952. 'Kortfilm, experimentfilm, dokumentärfilm', in *Filmboken*.

———. 1979. 'En natt', in Lars Åhlander (ed.), *Svensk Filmografi 1930–1939*, Stockholm: Svenska Filminstitute, 93–95.

———. 1981. 'Svenska Bios produktionspolitik fram till 1920', in Leif Furhammer (ed.), *Rörande bilder. Festskrift till Rune Waldekranz*, Stockholm: Norstedt, 160–86.

———. 1999. 'Spearhead in a Blind Alley: Viking Eggeling's DIAGONAL SYMPHONY', in John Fullerton and Jan Olsson (eds), *Nordic Explorations: Film Before 1930*, London: J. Libbey, 232–35.

Werner, Gösta, and Per Olof Wredlund. 1952. 'Den svenska filmstudiorörelsen. Från pionjärår till studiecirkelsrutin', in Hugo Wortzelius and Nils Larsson, *Filmboken: En bok om film och filmskapare*, Uppsala: Orbis, 600–10.

Werner, Michael, and Bénédicte Zimmermann. 2006. 'Beyond Comparison: *Histoire croisée* and the Challenge of Reflexivity', *History and Theory* 45 (February), 30–50.

Wilke, Jürgen. 1991. 'Cinematography as a Medium of Communication: The Promotion of Research by the League of Nations and the Role of Rudolf Arnheim', *European Journal of Communication* 6(3), 337–53.

Williams, Alan (ed.). 2002. *Film and Nationalism*, New Brunswick, NJ: Rutgers University Press.

Wollen, Peter. 1975. 'The Two Avant-Gardes', *Studio International* 190(978), 171–75.

———. 2002. *Paris Hollywood: Writings on Film*, London and New York: Verso, 39–54.

Wollenberg, Hans H. 1948. *Fifty Years of German Film*, London: Falcon Press.
Yamplosky, Mikhail. 1991. 'Kuleshov's Experiments and the New Anthropology of the Actor', in Richard Taylor and Ian Christie (eds), *Inside the Film Factory: New Approaches to Russian and Soviet Cinema*, London: Routledge.
Zagarrio, Vito. 2004. *Cinema e fascismo: Filmi, modeli, immaginarii*. Venice: Marsilio.
Zimmermann, Clemens. 2001. 'Filmwissenschaft im Nationalsozialismus – Anspruch und Scheitern', in Armin Kohnle and Frank Engehausen (eds), *Zwischen Wissenschaft und Politik. Studien zur deutschen Universitätsgeschichte. Festschrift für Eike Wolgast zum 65. Geburtstag*, Stuttgart: F. Steiner.
Zimmermann, Patricia. 1995. *Reel Families: A Social History of Amateur Film*, Bloomington: Indiana University Press.
Zimmermann, Yvonne. 2006. 'Maggis Wandervortragspraxis mit Lichtbildern. Ein Schulmädchenreport aus der Schweiz', *KINtop* 14/15, 53–65.
———. 2007. 'Heimatpflege zwecks Suppenpromotion. Zum Einsatz von Lichtbildern und Filmen in der Schweizer Lebensmittelbranche am Beispiel von Maggi', *Zeitschrift für Unternehmensgeschichte* 52(2), 203–26.
———. 2008. 'Training and Entertaining Consumers: Travelling Corporate Film Shows in Switzerland', in Martin Loiperdinger (ed.), *Travelling Cinema in Europe: Sources and Perspectives*, Frankfurt am Main: Stroemfeld/Roter Stern, 168–79.
———. 2009. 'Target Group Oriented Corporate Film Communication: Geigy Films', in Andres Janser and Barbara Junod, *Corporate Diversity: Swiss Graphic Design and Advertising by Geigy 1940–1970*, Baden: Lars Müller, 48–57.
———. 2010. 'Nestlé's Fip-Fop Club: The Making of Child Audiences in Non-Commercial Film Shows in Switzerland (1936–1959)', in Irmbert Schenk, Margrit Tröhler and Yvonne Zimmermann (eds), *Film – Kino – Zuschauer. Filmrezeption / Film – Cinema – Spectator. Film Reception*, Marburg: Schüren, 281–303.
Zipes, Jack. 2010. 'Béla Balázs, the Homeless Wanderer, or, The Man who Sought to Become One with the World', in Béla Balázs, *The Cloak of Dreams: Chinese Fairy Tales*, trans. and intr. Jack Zipes, Princeton, NJ: Princeton University Press.
Zsuffa, Joseph. 1987. *Béla Balázs, the Man and the Artist*, Berkeley: University of California Press.

INDEX